REAL WORLD

MACRO

TWENTY-SEVENTH EDITION

EDITED BY AMY GLUCKMAN, JOHN MILLER, BRYAN SNYDER,

AND THE *DOLLARS & SENSE* COLLECTIVE

REAL WORLD MACRO

ISBN: 978-1-878585-99-8

Published by:
Economic Affairs Bureau, Inc. d/b/a *Dollars & Sense*
29 Winter Street, Boston, MA 02108
617-447-2177; dollars@dollarsandsense.org.
For order information, contact Economic Affairs Bureau or visit: www.dollarsandsense.org.

Real World Macro is edited by the *Dollars & Sense* Collective, which also publishes *Dollars & Sense* magazine and the classroom books *Real World Micro, The Economic Crisis Reader, Current Economic Issues, Real World Globalization, Real World Latin America, Real World Labor, Real World Banking and Finance, The Wealth Inequality Reader, The Environment in Crisis, Introduction to Political Economy, Unlevel Playing Fields: Understanding Wage Inequality and Discrimination, Striking a Balance: Work, Family, Life*, and *Grassroots Journalism*.

The 2010 *Dollars & Sense* Collective:
Arpita Banerjee, Ben Collins, Amy Gluckman, Ben Greenberg, Mary Jirmanus, James McBride, James Miehls, John Miller, Larry Peterson, Linda Pinkow, Paul Piwko, Smriti Rao, Alejandro Reuss, Dave Ryan, Bryan Snyder, Chris Sturr, Ramaa Vasudevan, and Jeanne Winner.

Co-editors of this volume: Amy Gluckman, John Miller, and Bryan Snyder
Editorial assistant: Jill Mazzetta
Production assistant: Katharine Davies
Design and layout: Chris Sturr

Printed in U.S.A.

CONTENTS

III

CHAPTER 6 • UNEMPLOYMENT AND INFLATION

CHAPTER 7 • PERSPECTIVES ON MACROECONOMIC POLICY

CHAPTER 8 • INTERNATIONAL TRADE AND FINANCE

INTRODUCTION

THE TWO ECONOMIES

It sometimes seems that the United States has not one, but two economies. The first economy exists in economics textbooks and in the minds of many elected officials. It is an economy in which no one is unemployed for long, families are rewarded with an ever-improving standard of living, and anyone who works hard can live the American Dream. In this economy, people are free and roughly equal, and each individual carefully looks after him- or herself, making voluntary choices to advance their own economic interests. Government has some limited roles in this world, but it is increasingly marginal, since the macroeconomy is a self-regulating system of wealth generation.

The second economy is described in the writings of progressives, environmentalists, union supporters, and consumer advocates—as well as honest business writers who recognize that the real world does not always conform to textbook models. This second economy features vast disparities of income, wealth, and power. It is an economy where economic instability and downward mobility are facts of life. Jobs disappear, workers suffer long spells of unemployment, and new jobs seldom afford the same standard of living as those lost. And, periodically, market economies unravel, much like today. As for the government, it sometimes adopts policies that ameliorate the abuses of capitalism, and other times does just the opposite, but it is always an active and essential participant in economic life.

If you are reading this introduction, you are probably a student in an introductory college course in macroeconomics. Your textbook will introduce you to the first economy, the harmonious world of self-regulating stability. *Real World Macro* will introduce you to the second.

Why "Real World" Macro?

A standard economics textbook is full of powerful concepts. It is also, by its nature, a limited window on the economy. What is taught in most introductory macroeconomics courses today is a relatively narrow set of concepts. Inspired by classical economic theory, most textbooks depict an inherently stable economy in little need of government intervention. But fifty years ago, textbooks were very different. Keynesian economic theory, which holds that government action can and must stabilize modern monetized economies, occupied a central place in introductory textbooks. Even Marxist economics, with its piercing analysis of class structure and instability in capitalism, appeared regularly on the pages of those textbooks. The contraction of economics education has turned some introductory courses into little more than celebrations of today's economy as "the best of all possible worlds."

Real World Macro, designed as a supplement to a standard macroeconomics textbook, is dedicated to widening the scope of economic inquiry. Its articles rub mainstream theory up against reality by providing vivid, real-world illustrations of economic concepts. And where most texts uncritically present the key assumptions and propositions of traditional macroeconomic theory, *Real World Macro* asks provocative questions: What are alternative propositions about how the economy operates and who it serves? What difference do such propositions make? What might *actually* constitute the best of all possible macroeconomic worlds?

For instance, *Real World Macro* questions the conventional wisdom that economic growth lifts all boats or benefits all of us. While mainstream textbooks readily allow that economic growth has not benefited us all to the same degree, we go further and ask, "Who benefits from economic growth and by how much?" "Who has been left behind by the economic growth of the last two decades?" The answers are quite disturbing. Today, economic growth, when it occurs, benefits far fewer of us than it did just a few decades ago. The most recent recovery did more to boost profits and less to lift wages than any economic upswing since World War II. The truth is that spreading the benefits of economic growth more widely, through public policy intended to improve the lot of most people in the work-a-day world, would not only make our economy more equitable, but would start to resolve today's economic crisis.

Today's economy is emerging from what is widely recognized to be the worst crisis since the Great Depression. But you might not know that the day-to-day operation of the market economy, left to its own devices, brought on that crisis. Unregulated financial markets, the concentration of political and social power in the hands of powerful business interests, and gaping inequality pushed most people into debt at the same time that it fueled speculative excesses sparking the crisis. Explaining how and why that happened and what to do about it is every responsible economist's job.

Today, with unemployment still at its highest levels in seven decades, government needs to step up and become the economy's employer of last resort. Similarly, with the financial system having been shaken to the core, the government needs to step in and properly regulate financial markets and institutions. Those two steps will go a long way toward improving the lot of those who have fallen on hard times and will reduce the likelihood of future crises. Finally, genuine and sustained full employment, with unemployment rates as low as 2%, will lead to "a major reduction in the incidence of poverty, homelessness, sickness, and crime," as William Vickery, the Nobel-prize winning economist, once argued. We think that policies like this, and the alternative propositions that lie behind them, are worth debating—and that requires hearing a range of views.

What's in This Book

Real World Macro is organized to follow the outline of a standard economics text. Each chapter leads off with a brief introduction, including study questions for the chapter, and then provides several short articles from *Dollars & Sense* magazine that illustrate the chapter's key concepts—76 articles in all. In many cases, the articles have been updated or otherwise edited to heighten their relevance.

Here is a quick walk through the chapters.

Chapter 1, **Measuring Economic Performance**, starts off the volume by taking a critical look at the standard measures of economic activity. What do those measures actually tell us about the quality of life in today's economy, and what crucial aspects of economic life do they leave uncounted? This chapter also asks why the latest ups and downs of the business cycle, the current crisis and the anemic economic expansion that preceded it, left so many in dire straits.

Chapter 2, **Wealth, Inequality, and Poverty**, examines these three end products of economic growth. *Dollars & Sense* authors show who is accumulating wealth and who isn't, and argue that inequality is not a prerequisite to economic growth, but rather a major contributor to today's economic crisis.

Chapter 3, **Savings and Investment**, peers inside the pump house of economic growth and comes up with some probing questions. How are stock prices determined? Who owns them; who doesn't? What caused the mortgage crisis and what can be done about it? Finally, what public policies have proven track records of encouraging investment and promoting stable and functional housing and financial markets.

Chapter 4, **Fiscal Policy, Deficits, and Debt**, assesses current government spending and tax policy. The chapter's authors examine the Obama stimulus package, arguing that more needs to be done and that unprecedented "peacetime" deficits should not be an impediment to government action. But pro-rich tax cuts, the military buildup, and failed health care policy that helped get us into this fiscal and economic mess will not get us out of it. Nor will privatizing Social Security. Rather what is needed, according to our authors, are stronger social programs, expanded and greener infrastructure investment, and the government's commitment to be the economy's employer of last resort.

Chapter 5, **Monetary Policy and Financial Markets**, explains how the Federal Reserve Board (aka "the Fed") conducts monetary policy and how its actions contributed to today's financial crisis. It details the Fed's efforts to bail out investment banks and other financial institutions brought down in the crisis. The chapter asks whose interests the Fed serves: those who hold financial assets, or the rest of us? The authors also address how the Fed and financial institutions can be transformed to better serve our needs.

Chapter 6, **Unemployment and Inflation**, reveals how macroeconomic policy that prioritizes price stability over full employment puts the interests of business owners and bondholders ahead of the interests of workers. The chapter begins with a critique of the "natural rate" of unemployment. It then looks at the effects of unemployment, inflation, and productivity growth on workers' bargaining power and living standards. In addition, it discusses how stock-market fundamentals and the spread of offshore outsourcing stand in the way of most workers getting ahead.

Chapter 7, **Perspectives on Macroeconomic Policy**, introduces alternatives to classical-inspired macroeconomic theory. It begins with a critical analysis of the New Classical economists' claim that the macroeconomy is inherently stable, and then discusses what Keynes *actually* said about the practice of fiscal policy in an economic crisis. The chapter also develops Marxist and feminist perspectives on macroeconomic theory and policy, and on neoliberal economic policymaking. Finally, the chapter explains in everyday language how the economy fell into crisis during 2008 and 2009, uncovering the causes of the crisis and its roots in the inequalities of the real economy and the unregulated excesses of the housing and financial markets.

Chapter 8, **International Trade and Finance**, critically assesses the prevailing neoliberal policy prescriptions for the global economy. The articles criticize globalization based on "free trade" and financial liberalization, looking closely at its effects on economic growth, global inequality and poverty, and "economic freedom." They also look at the role of China in the world economy, the global oil market, and the U.S. economy's dependence on foreign capital. Finally, the articles look critically at the effects of remittances and global trade agreements on workers in the developing world and assess proposals to improve international labor standards and to eliminate sweatshop conditions.

Chapter 1

MEASURING ECONOMIC PERFORMANCE

INTRODUCTION

Most macroeconomics textbooks begin with a snapshot of today's economy as seen through the lens of the standard measures of economic performance. This chapter provides a different view of today's economy, one far more critical of current economic policy and performance, one that asks what the standard measures of economic performance really tell us.

In "When is a Recession Over?" economist John Miller explains how the National Bureau of Economic Research identifies the waves of business activity that constitute the business cycle. Miller traces the course of this decade's business cycle from a feeble expansion, which did little to improve the standard of living of most people, to the Great Recession, which has left millions of people in dire straits. He asks when the disastrous downturn will be officially declared over—and when it will end in the real world (Article 1.1). Not for quite a while, according to economist Fred Moseley. He points out that high unemployment is likely to be with us for quite a while, if job creation in the recovery from the Great Recession mirrors that in the two most recent recoveries, following the 1991 and 2001 recessions (Article 1.3). In "Thirty-Five Years of Economic Indicators," *Dollars & Sense* intern Katherine Faherty and economist Alejandro Reuss provide four measures—unemployment, inflation, income inequality, and the activity and strength of organized labor—to assess where today's economy stands compared to the performance of the U.S. economy over the last three and a half decades (Article 1.2).

Miller's next article shows how the official unemployment rate understates the extent of unemployment. Correcting the official rate for underemployed workers and discouraged job-seekers, the unemployment rate reaches a *68-year high* (Article 1.4). Job losses in this downturn have hit male-dominated jobs especially hard, as economist Heather Boushey documents. She calls for more support for female workers who increasingly find themselves in the role of family breadwinners (Article 1.5).

Economists' measures of inflation also suffer from serious deficiencies. Joshua Holland documents how recent changes in the Consumer Price Index, the best-known inflation measure, dramatically reduced the "official" rate of inflation. Those changes spruced up reported economic performance and reduced the cost-of-living adjustments received by seniors on Social Security and others (Article 1.6).

Real GDP, or Gross Domestic Product adjusted for inflation, is the economist's measure of the value of economic output. Increases in real GDP define economic growth, and for economists, rising real GDP per capita shows that a nation's standard of living is improving. Our authors are not convinced. Jonathan Rowe argues that GDP actually counts environmental destruction, worsening health, and ruinous overconsumption as contributions to economic growth and national well-being (Article 1.7). While Rowe worries that GDP includes the wrong things, Lena Graber and John Miller discuss what it excludes: work in the home that is essential to economic well-being. They report that counting home-based work—from cleaning to child care—would add 33% to 112% to the GDP of industrialized economies and even more to the GDP of developing economies (Article 1.8).

Of course, macroeconomics textbooks examine not only the ups and downs of the business cycle, but also trade-offs in economies whose resources are fully employed. Many present the famed trade-off between "guns" and "butter." Economists use a production possibilities curve to demonstrate the opportunity cost of devoting economic resources to certain kinds of production. For example, the opportunity cost of producing arms ("guns") is the set of social goods ("butter") that society must forego. That trade-off is being made today in the United States, and *Dollars & Sense* co-editor Amy Gluckman illustrates its staggering cost in terms of environmental protection (Article 1.9).

Discussion Questions

1. (Article 1.1, 1.3) How does the National Bureau of Economic Research determine when a recession has begun and when it is over? Under what conditions would you declare the Great Recession over?

2. (Article 1.1, 1.2) How does the expansion of this decade's business cycle compare to the typical postwar expansion? How does the recent contraction compare to the typical postwar recession?

3. (Article 1.4) What are the shortcomings of the official (U-3) unemployment rate? Using the data in Table 2, calculate the more comprehensive U-6 unemployment rate for February 2010. Be sure to show each step of the conversion from the U-3 unemployment rate to the U-6 rate.

4. (Article 1.6) How did the changes in the Consumer Price Index in the 1990s lower the reported rate of inflation? In your opinion, which of those changes, if any, were justified? Why?

5. (Article 1.7) How is GDP measured, and what does it represent? What are Rowe's criticisms of GDP? Do you find them convincing?

6. (Article 1.7) Rowe discusses the Genuine Progress Indicator (GPI) as an alternative measure of economic progress. What are the differences between GDP per capita and the GPI? Which do you think provides a better measure of economic progress and why?

7. (Article 1.5) Why did men's unemployment increase more quickly than women's unemployment in the recent economic contraction? What are some possible policy responses that could address this gender disparity in unemployment levels? Is it important or desirable to do so?

8. (Article 1.8) Wages for housework might sound outlandish, but there are several economic justifications for valuing work in the home. What are they? In your opinion, should this work be paid? If so, by whom?

9. (Article 1.8) Suppose we decided that home-based work should be included in macroeconomic measures. How should it be counted?

10. (Article 1.9) Describe the opportunity cost of today's military buildup with respect to addressing the environmental threat of climate change. Then identify where the U.S. economy is today on a production possibilities curve.

Article 1.1

WHEN IS A RECESSION OVER?

BY JOHN MILLER
April 2010

Yogi Berra, the Yankee great, once said about a baseball game, "It ain't over until it's over." If Yogi had been talking about the Great Recession, he would have said, "It ain't over even when it's over."

As far back as September 2009, when the economy was first showing signs of a return to economic growth, Federal Reserve Board chair Ben Bernanke called the Great Recession of 2008 and 2009 "likely over" and declared that the U.S. economy had begun a recovery. He quickly added that the economy would continue to lose jobs. And it did—with the unemployment rate climbing to double digits later in the fall.

When economists at the National Bureau of Economic Research (NBER), a private research organization designated by the Commerce Department as the nation's arbiter of the business cycle, officially declare the Great Recession over, they will likely identify September 2009 as its end date and the beginning of the economic recovery. But people surely will not believe the recession is over, despite the NBER's pronouncement, until jobs return and their economic well-being improves. And that could be quite a while.

Let's look at what economists mean when they declare that a recession is over and a recovery is underway, and why that announcement is unlikely to mean that happy days are here again for most people in the work-a-day economy, let alone those looking for work.

A Date with a Business Cycle

The NBER tracks the ebb and flow of economic activity , from the trough of a recession to the peak of an expansion and back down into a trough. In the first phase of the cycle—the expansion—the economy grows as companies produce more goods and services and hire more workers. In the second phase, companies produce fewer goods and throw workers out of their jobs, and the economy contracts. The NBER has identified nine complete business cycles in the U.S. economy since World War II (see table).

The NBER's Dating Committee, currently a group of seven economists, admits that the dating process is "fuzzy." The committee has no rigid rules for determining the start or end of a business cycle. The members reach a consensus after studying a broad array of macroeconomic indicators. In short, they eyeball the data. The committee's founders worked with 46 indicators. Today the NBER's Business Conditions Digest lists around 1,000 measures. Members study the GDP, industrial production, employment, real income, trade, several interest rates, and personal income, as well as several composite indices, including the index of coincident indicators, which measures employment, income, output, and sales.

The Great Recession shows how hard it is to date business cycles. Economists define a recession as two consecutive quarters of negative real growth, or declining output, as measured by GDP. But applying even this shorthand definition is not easy. It takes time for the federal government to publish official GDP figures. And the committee looks for several indicators to show that a decline in activity has spread across the economy before it feels comfortable declaring a recession.

In December 2008, the economy had not yet suffered two consecutive quarters of negative economic growth. Nonetheless, mounting monthly job losses convinced the NBER to declare that a recession had begun a whole year earlier, in December 2007. The economy had lost jobs every month from December 2007 on—the longest period of job-loss since the Great Depression.

If dating the onset of a recession is difficult, dating its end is even harder. Economists agree even less on how to determine when a recession finishes and an expansion begins. They generally divide expansions into two phases. In the first phase, the economy recovers the ground it lost—in terms of jobs, output, and other measures—during the recession. When the economy grows beyond its pre-recession levels, the expansion enters its second phase. Economists declare a recession over only when they know a recovery has reached this second phase. They then date the expansion back to when the economy began recouping the lost output. Should the

U.S. BUSINESS CYCLES, 1949-2010

Trough	Peak	Trough	Expansion (months)	Contraction (months)	Full Cycle (months)
Oct 1949	July 1953	Aug 1954	45	13	58
Aug 1954	July 1957	Apr 1958	35	9	44
Apr 1958	May 1960	Feb 1961	25	9	34
Feb 1961	Nov 1969	Nov 1970	105	11	117
Nov 1970	Dec 1973	Mar 1975	37	16	53
Mar 1975	Jan 1980	July 1980	57	6	63
July 1980	July 1981	Nov 1982	12	16	28
Nov 1982	July 1990	Mar 1991	93	8	101
Mar 1991	Mar 2001	Nov 2001	120	8	128
Nov 2001	Dec 2007	??	73	?	?

Source: Economic Cycle Research Institute, National Bureau of Economic Research.

recovery falter and the economy start to contract again before it reaches that second phase, economists consider the recession to have continued.

As of April 2010, the NBER had yet to declare the Great Recession officially over. At this point, economic growth had already returned to the U.S. economy. Beginning in the third quarter of 2009, the economy stopped contracting and then grew substantially in the last three months of 2009, boosted by businesses restocking their depleted inventories. By that measure the Great Recession seemed to have ended. But job losses continued until March 2010, when a surge of temporary hiring, mostly of government census workers, along with the stanching of job losses across the private sector and modest job growth in some sectors, produced the first non-trivial monthly net job gains since November 2007. The official unemployment rate still hovered near double-digit levels. If the NBER, in the name of consistency, uses employment to date the end of the recession as it did to date its onset, then the recession surely continued into 2010.

The Business Cycle and the Zero Decade

Beyond that, the NBER measures the ups and downs of a business cycle, not how the economy affects people's economic well-being. Over the last decade, a lengthy economic expansion did less to improve the economic well-being of most people and the ensuing contraction did more to decimate the economic well-being of most people than any business cycle since the Great Depression of the 1930s.

Economic expansions are supposed to improve our life-chances, not just swell the economy. But not this decade's.

Beginning in November 2001, the economy grew for 73 months or just over six years, reaching a peak in December 2007. That is longer than the 57-month average duration of other postwar expansions. But GDP grew at an anemic annual rate of 2.5% in the 2001-07 expansion, far below the 4.3% average for post-World War II expansions.

Job creation was even more dismal than output growth during the expansion. From 2001 to the end of 2007 the economy added jobs more slowly than during any other postwar expansion—only at about one-third the rate posted by the average postwar expansion. With sluggish economic growth and few new jobs, economic expansion did little to lift incomes, alleviate poverty, or improve the economic well-being of all but the best-off.

- For the first time in the postwar period, median household income (corrected for inflation) at the peak of this expansion was still below its level at the previous peak in 2000.

- For the first time in a postwar expansion, the poverty rate failed to decline.

- After correcting for inflation, wages and salaries grew at just half the rate of the average postwar expansion.

As these figures make clear, the combination of sluggish economic growth, few new jobs, and stagnant wages and incomes had left many people behind long before the economy collapsed in 2008 and intensified their hardship.

And the Great Recession did make things worse, far worse. A frightening financial panic, a virulent housing bust, and plummeting economic output left export-driven economies and financial centers across the globe in crisis. Japan and Eurozone major exporters suffered steep declines in output, as did Asian tigers such as Singapore. Even the red-hot Chinese economy hit the pause button in the first half of 2009. U.S. autoworkers, European and U.S. finance workers, Japanese electronics workers, Chinese garment workers, and Indian software workers lost their jobs as world export markets dried up.

In the United States, by March 2010, the recession had wiped out 8.4 million jobs. Construction, manufacturing of all sorts, and the financial industry, all male-dominated sectors, were especially hard hit. Retail sales, typically more recession-proof, were decimated as well. Electronics giant Circuit City closed its doors, and the venerable Filene's Basement laid off scores of workers.

After reviewing the feeble expansion and devastating recession that followed, economist and *New York Times* columnist Paul Krugman suggested that we call the first decade of this century "the zero decade." Job creation for the decade was basically zero. Zero economic gains for the typical family. Zero gains for homeowners. And zero gains on the stock market, even before taking inflation into account.

Dim Prospects for a Genuine Recovery

Even though the economy has begun growing again, the prospects of lower unemployment rates anytime soon remain bleak. Following the last downturn, in 2001, the U.S. economy took more than three years to replace the jobs lost in the recession. If the current sluggish recovery creates jobs at the same pace as the last one, it would take 86 months, or until December 2016, to replace all of the jobs lost in this downturn.

In that case, many people will endure great economic suffering long after the date the NBER declares the official end of the recession.

Sources: "Determination of the December 2007 Peak in Economic Activity," National Bureau of Economic Research, Dec. 11, 2008, www.nber.org/cycles/dec2008.html; Sara Murray and Ann Zimmerman, "Bernanke: Recession Likely Over—Fed Chief Doesn't Expect Many New Jobs to Appear Soon: Retail Sales Climb 2.7%," *Wall Street Journal*, Sept. 16, 2009; Paul Krugman, "The Big Zero," *New York Times*, Dec. 28, 2009; Josh Bivens and John Irons, "A Feeble Recovery," Economic Policy Institute Briefing Paper #214; Aviva Aron-Dine, Chad Stone, and Richard Kogan, "How Robust Is the Current Economic Expansion?," Center on Budget and Policy Priorities, Jan. 14, 2008.

Article 1.2

THIRTY-FIVE YEARS OF ECONOMIC INDICATORS

BY KATHERINE FAHERTY AND ALEJANDRO REUSS
November/December 2009

For many years, the "Economy in Numbers" department of *Dollars & Sense* provided current data on standard economic indicators: unemployment, wages, interest rates, and so on. Once that data became available in real time online, the department switched gears. The Economy in Numbers for this, our 35th anniversary issue, returns to its roots—but with data showing the trends over the past 35 years in some key indicators.

UNEMPLOYMENT
UNEMPLOYMENT RATE, AGE 16-PLUS; AFRICAN AMERICANS AND ALL WORKERS

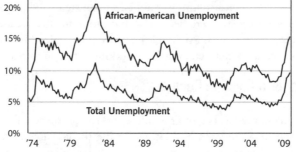

Two deep recessions in the 1970s and 1980s sent the official unemployment rate soaring over 10%, a height it did not approach again until this year. African-American unemployment has been higher, in both "good" times and bad.

ORGANIZED LABOR
UNIONIZED SHARE OF WAGE & SALARY WORKERS; WORK STOPPAGES ≥1,000 WORKERS

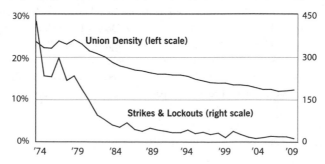

Union density has been falling since the 1950s, but increased employer attacks and anti-labor government policies have sped the decline since the 1980s. Employers' use of permanent replacements has made strikes difficult to win, and large strikes have become rare.

INFLATION
CONSUMER PRICE INDEX (CPI-U): MONTHLY YEAR-OVER-YEAR CHANGE

The inflation rate spiked over 10% during the 1970s and early 1980s but has been much lower since. In the current recession, the rate has actually been negative ("deflation"), belying fears of renewed inflation.

INCOME INEQUALITY
MEAN HOUSEHOLD INCOME: TOP 20% AND BOTTOM 20%

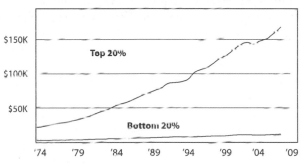

Income inequality has increased dramatically over the last three decades. As the average incomes of lower- and middle-income people have stagnated, the incomes of those at the top have soared.

Article 1.3

UNEMPLOYMENT: HOW BAD FOR HOW LONG?

The outlook is grim unless there is serious government intervention.

BY FRED MOSELEY
March/April 2010

How bad will unemployment be in the months and years ahead? One way to answer that question is to look at how long it took the U.S. economy to regain jobs in previous post-war recessions. By this measure, the employment outlook is quite grim.

Since the recession began in December 2007, the U.S. economy has lost 8.4 million jobs, or 6.2% of employment, over 25 months. This is the biggest decline in the postwar period, and the recession is not yet over.

In none of the other recessions since World War II has the economy lost such a large percentage of its employment base. None of the other recessions in the figure below show such a high cumulative percent decline of employment. (The vertical axis shows the percentage cumulative decline from the beginning of the recession, i.e., the month employment peaks; the horizontal axis shows the number of months from the peak of employment.)

The 1981-82 recession gives us some hint of what would happen if the U.S. economy falls into "double-dip" recession in the years ahead, which many economists consider a distinct possibility. The total decline of employment in the recession of 1981-82 was only 3% and the jobs lost in recession were recovered in just 11 months. Nonetheless, the rate of unemployment reached a peak of 10.8%, the highest of the postwar period. That was because the 1981-82 recession followed close on the heels of a recession in 1980. In this "double-dip" recession, the two declines of employment were smaller than the current decline and yet the combined effect was a rate of unemployment of almost 11%.

The two most recent recessions, 1990 and 2001, look distinctly different from the 1981-82 recession. These were mild recessions and the declines of employment were only 1.5% and 2% respectively. But for both of these recessions, the recoveries were disturbingly slow and it took much longer to replace the jobs lost in the recession than after previous recessions. It took 30 months in the early 1990s and 47 months in the early 2000s to return to the previous peak in employment. In these "jobless recoveries," the rate of unemployment continued to increase for months after the recovery of employment began.

The main causes of the slow growth of employment in these recent jobless recoveries were the slow growth of output, or Gross Domestic Product (GDP), and business emphasis on cost-cutting, especially labor costs. The latter factor led companies to force existing employees to work harder and produce more output rather than hire more workers as demand picked up. The emphasis on cost-cutting also led companies to outsource operations to low-wage areas of the world.

These factors are still very much present in the U.S. economy today. It is widely forecast that GDP growth in the years ahead will be very slow by historical comparisons (perhaps even slower than in the previous two jobless recoveries) and business seems as eager as ever to cut labor costs. In addition, as demand picks up, companies will first increase the hours of the large number of existing part-time workers before they start hiring new workers. So this is shaping up to be the mother of all jobless recoveries, which will result in high rates of unemployment for years to come.

How long will it take for employment in the U.S. economy to return to its previous peak? The graph suggests that it will take at least 48 months. Of course, returning to the previous peak would not guarantee that the rate of unemployment would decline because of the growth of the labor force. But increasing employment at least makes it possible that the rate of unemployment might start to decline.

How many months will it take to recover the 8.4 million jobs that have been lost? That depends on the average monthly increase of employment in the months and years ahead. If the average monthly increase of employment turns out to be 200,000 per month—which would be more than twice as fast as in the last recovery—then it would take 42 more months to return to the previous peak employment.

Even if the average monthly increase turns out to be 300,000—and this is surely over-optimistic—it would take 28 more months, or until mid-2012, to return to the previous peak employment. In this scenario, what would the rate of unemployment likely be in mid-2012? Employment would be the same as in December 2007. At that time, the official rate of unemployment was 5%. Assuming that the labor force increases 1% per year, it will have increased at least 4% between December 2007 and mid-2012. So the rate of unemployment in mid-2012 would be about 4% higher than in December 2007, or around 9%.

And this is the optimistic scenario. If there is a "double-dip" recession, then the official rate of unemployment will still be over 10% for years to come. This means that the true rate of unemployment—including involuntary part-time workers and marginally attached or discouraged workers who have stopped looking for jobs—would likely top 15%.

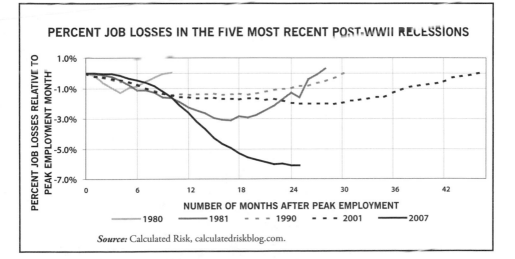

Source: Calculated Risk, calculatedriskblog.com.

In other words, U.S. workers will be facing a long period of very high unemployment. Already, 40% of the officially unemployed have been unemployed for six months or more—the highest since records have been kept starting in 1948—and the percentage of total unemployed (including "discouraged workers") is much higher. And these percentages will go even higher in the months ahead.

Long-term unemployment like this has very serious negative effects on workers—it makes it much harder to return to employment and it has hidden costs on families, children, and communities.

To avoid this economic disaster for working people, we should demand that Congress pass a Full Employment Law, committing the federal government to provide jobs for all workers willing and able to work any time there are not enough private sector jobs. Such a law would be based on the principle that a job with a decent income is a basic economic right.

Could we afford a full-employment law? Contrary to what the deficit hawks claim, the answer is yes. A full-employment jobs program could be paid for by higher taxes on the rich and by a significant reduction in military spending. It's not about a lack of funds—it's about priorities. If the government abandoned its current priorities of keeping tax rates on the rich low and giving the military a blank check for foreign wars, it could instead help workers cope with the long-term after-effects of recession.

Thanks to the website Calculated Risk (calculatedriskblog.com) for the idea for the graph accompanying this article and for sharing the data.

Article 1.4

THE *REAL* UNEMPLOYMENT RATE HITS A 68-YEAR HIGH

BY JOHN MILLER
July/August 2009; updated April 2010

Although you have to dig into the statistics to know it, unemployment in the United States over the last year has been worse than at any time since the end of the Great Depression.

From December 2007, when the recession began, to February 2010, 8.4 million U.S. workers lost their jobs. The big three U.S. automakers closed plants and let white-collar workers go too. Heavy equipment manufacturer Caterpillar and giant banking conglomerate Citigroup both laid off thousands of workers. Alcoa, the aluminum maker, let workers go. Computer maker Dell and express shipper DHL both canned many of their workers. Circuit City, the leading electronics retailer, went out of business, costing its 40,000 workers their jobs. Lawyers in large national firms got the ax. Even on Sesame Street, workers lost their jobs.

The official unemployment rate peaked at 10.1% in October 2009—higher than in all but the 1982 recession, the worst since World War II. The current downturn pushed up unemployment rates more than any other postwar recession, even including the double dip recessions of the early 1980s (see figure, next page).

Some groups of workers faced even higher official unemployment rates. As of February 2010, unemployment rates for black, Hispanic, and teenage workers were 15.8%, 12.4% and 25.0% respectively. Workers without a high-school diploma confronted a 15.6% unemployment rate, while the unemployment rate for workers with just a high-school diploma was 10.5%. More than one in four (26.5%) construction workers were unemployed. In Michigan, the hardest hit state, unemployment was at 14.1% in February 2010. Unemployment rates in fifteen other states and the District of Columbia were at double-digit levels as well.

As bad as they are, these figures dramatically understate the true extent of unemployment. First, they exclude anyone without a job who is ready to work but has not actively looked for a job in the previous four weeks. The Bureau of Labor Statistics classifies such workers as "marginally at-

THE FEBRUARY 2010 UNEMPLOYMENT PICTURE (DATA IN THOUSANDS, NOT SEASONALLY ADJUSTED)	
Civilian Labor Force	153,194
Employed	137,203
Unemployed	15,991
Marginally Attached Workers	2,527
Discouraged workers	1,204
Reasons other than discouragement	1,323
Part-time for Economic Reasons	9,282
Slack work or business conditions	6,708
Could only find part-time work	2,252

Sources: Bureau of Labor Statistics, Tables A-1, A-8. A-15, A-16. Data are not seasonally adjusted because seasonally adjusted data for marginally attached workers are not available.

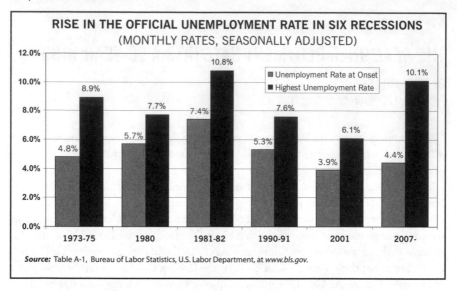

RISE IN THE OFFICIAL UNEMPLOYMENT RATE IN SIX RECESSIONS
(MONTHLY RATES, SEASONALLY ADJUSTED)

Source: Table A-1, Bureau of Labor Statistics, U.S. Labor Department, at *www.bls.gov.*

tached to the labor force" so long as they have looked for work within the last year. Marginally attached workers include so-called discouraged workers who have given up looking for job-related reasons, plus others who have given up for reasons such as school and family responsibilities, ill health, or transportation problems.

Second, the official unemployment rate leaves out part-time workers looking for full-time work: part-time workers are "employed" even if they work as little as one hour a week. The vast majority of people working part-time involuntarily have had their hours cut due to slack or unfavorable business conditions. The rest could only find part-time work.

To its credit, the BLS has developed alternative unemployment measures that go a long way toward correcting the shortcomings of the official rate. The broadest alternative measure, called U-6, counts as unemployed "marginally attached workers" as well as those employed "part time for economic reasons."

When those adjustments are taken into account for February 2010, the unemployment rate soars to 16.8%. While below its peak of 17.4% back in October 2009, the February 2010 adjusted unemployment rate still represents a historic high. Leaving aside the current downturn, it is higher than at any time back to 1994, when the BLS introduced the U-6 measure. It is also higher than the BLS's earlier and yet broader adjusted unemployment rate, the U-7, ever was. The BLS began calculating the U-7 rate in 1976 but discontinued it in 1994 in favor of the U-6 rate. In the 1982 recession the U-7 reached 15.3%, its highest level. In fact, no bout of unemployment since the last year of the Great Depression in 1941 would have produced an adjusted unemployment rate as high as what workers in the United States have suffered over the last year.

Why is the real unemployment rate so much higher than the official, or U-3, rate? First, forced part-time work in the last year reached higher levels than any all the way back to 1956 and including the 1982 recession. In February 2010, 8.8 million workers were forced to work part time for economic reasons. Forced part-timers are concentrated in retail, food services, and construction; about a quarter of them

Calculating the Real Unemployment Rate

The BLS calculates the official unemployment rate, U-3, as the number of unemployed as a percentage of the civilian labor force. The civilian labor force consists of employed workers plus the officially unemployed, those without jobs who are available to work and have looked for a job in the last four weeks. Applying the data found in the table yields an official unemployment rate of 10.4%, or a seasonally adjusted rate of 9.7%, for February 2010.

The comprehensive U-6 unemployment rate adjusts the official rate by adding marginally attached workers and workers forced to work part time for economic reasons to the officially unemployed. To find the U-6 rate the BLS takes that higher unemployment count and divides it by the official civilian labor force plus the number of marginally attached workers. (No adjustment is necessary for forced part-time workers since they are already counted in the official labor force as employed workers.)

Accounting for the large number of marginally attached workers and those working part-time for economic reasons raises the count of unemployed to 27.8 million workers for February 2010. Those numbers push up the U-6 unemployment rate to 17.9%, or a seasonally adjusted rate of 16.8%.

are young workers between 16 and 24. The number of discouraged workers is high today as well. In February 2010, the BLS counted 2.5 million "marginally attached" workers. That is the highest number since 1994, when the agency introduced this measure (although it was matched by the January 2010 number).

While the economy may be escaping the throes of a catastrophic downturn, unemployment, no matter how it's measured, will continue to impose devastating costs on society and on those without a job or unable to find full-time work.

Sources: U.S. Dept. of Labor, "The Unemployment Rate and Beyond: Alternative Measures of Labor Underutilization," *Issues in Labor Statistics,* June 2008; John E. Bregger and Steven E. Haugen, "BLS introduces new range of alternative unemployment measures," *Monthly Labor Review*, October 1995.

Article 1.5

WOMEN BREADWINNERS, MEN UNEMPLOYED

BY HEATHER BOUSHEY
July 2009

The employment situation over the past 19 months has dramatically changed for millions of American families. Since the Great Recession began in December 2007, there has been a sharp rise in the number of married couples where a woman is left to bring home the bacon because her husband is unemployed. What is striking is not only how many more families are experiencing unemployment among husbands, but also how this loss of the traditional breadwinner has occurred across a variety of demographic groups.

The reason that more married couples now boast women as the primary breadwinners is because men have experienced greater job losses than women over the course of this recession, losing three out of every four jobs lost. This puts a real strain on family budgets since women typically earn only 78 cents for every dollar men earn. In the typical married-couple family where both spouses work, the wife brings home just over a third—35.6%—of the family's income.

What's equally worrisome is that most families receive health insurance through the employers of their husbands. So when husbands lose their jobs, families are left struggling to find ways to pay for health insurance at the same time they are living on just a third of their prior income. These new health insurance costs can be crushing if families have to turn to the individual insurance market, where coverage is limited and expensive, or pay for continued coverage through their husbands' old insurance policies, which is possible because of federal law but is also expensive— though the American Recovery and Reinvestment Act subsidized that cost for many workers. Still, many families with an unemployed worker simply have to go without health insurance.

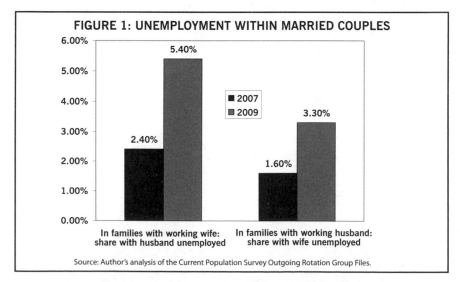

FIGURE 1: UNEMPLOYMENT WITHIN MARRIED COUPLES

■ 2007
■ 2009

5.40%

2.40%

In families with working wife: share with husband unemployed

1.60%

3.30%

In families with working husband: share with wife unemployed

Source: Author's analysis of the Current Population Survey Outgoing Rotation Group Files.

FIGURE 1: NON-EMPLOYMENT WITHIN MARRIED COUPLES

Source: Author's analysis of the Current Population Survey Outgoing Rotation Group Files.

The job losses mounting among husbands are acute this year. Figure 1 shows that the share of families where women hold down a job while men are unemployed jumped sharply in 2009 compared to 2007 at the peak of the last economic cycle. In the first five months of 2009, 5.4% of working wives had an unemployed husband at home— that is, a husband who was actively searching for work, but could not find a job—compared to an average of 2.4% over the first five months of 2007. This means that there are about 2 million working wives today with an unemployed husband.

In contrast, working husbands continue to be less likely to have an unemployed wife. In the first five months of 2009, an average of only 3.3% of husbands had an unemployed wife at home, up from 1.6%. Importantly, the difference in the shares of unemployed husbands and wives is not due to women telling the surveyor that they are "out of the labor force" rather than report they are out of a job, willing to work, and actively seeking employment. Figure 2 examines non-working spouses and shows not only a sharp rise in the share of working wives who have a non-working husband but also the share of both husbands and wives who are either unavailable to work or are not looking for a job.

So far this year, 15.6% of working wives have a husband who is not working, up a stunning 3.5 percentage points from early 2007, when 12.1% of working wives had a husband who did not work. But working husbands did not see a similarly large increase in their chances of having a non-working wife. In 2007, 29.4% of husbands had a non-working wife, up only 0.8 percentage points to 30.2% in 2009.

Families with children have been hit especially hard hit by unemployment. Among working wives in families with a small child—under age six—at home, 5.9% have an unemployed husband. This is higher than among families with a working wife but with no child under age six at home, where 5.3% have an unemployed husband.

Among families with a working wife and a child under age 18, the share with an unemployed husband is 5.7%, compared to 5.0% among those with no children. This means that there are 1 million working wives with children at home, but an unemployed husband. The numbers are smaller for families with a working husband and an unemployed wife. The share with a child under age 18 is 3.2%—compared to 3.4% among those with no children.

The share of workers with an unemployed spouse is lower than the overall unemployment rate of 9.5%. Typically, married workers have lower unemployed rates compared to single workers and they stay unemployed for shorter periods of time. There are many reasons why this is the case, but one is that married workers may have more of an incentive to find work as quickly as possible—if possible—because there are more people relying on their earnings, compared to single workers—at least single workers without children. Of course, single mothers, who typically have higher unemployment than other workers, do have children relying on their earnings and are under similar pressures to find employment.

Especially striking in the recently released data is the sharp increase in breadwinner wives and unemployed husbands across demographic groups. Table 1 shows, for example, that among young (ages 18 to 24) working, one –in ten married women (9.9%) has an unemployed husband, up 5.5 percentage points from early 2007. Among working women without a high school degree, slightly less than one –in ten

TABLE 1. UNEMPLOYMENT AMONG FAMILIES WITH A WORKING SPOUSE

	In families with working wife: Share with husband unemployed			In families with working husband: Share with wife unemployed		
	January - May 2007	January - May 2009	Percentage point change	January - May 2007	January - May 2009	Percentage point change
All families	2.4	5.4	3	1.6	3.3	1.7
Ages 18 to 24	4.4	9.9	5.5	4.8	6	1.2
Ages 25 to 54	2.4	5.5	3.1	1.6	3.3	1.7
Ages 55 to 64	1.9	4.1	2.2	1.4	3	1.6
Less than highschool	4.3	8.3	4	2.7	5.8	3.1
High school	2.7	6.8	4.1	2	3.9	1.9
Some college	2.6	5.5	2.9	1.4	2.8	1.4
College	1.7	3.9	2.2	1.2	2.4	1.2
White, non-Hispanic	2.1	4.7	2.6	1.4	2.8	1.4
Black, non-Hispanic	4.1	7.8	3.7	2.9	3.9	1
Hispanic, any race	3.4	7.7	4.3	2.2	5.1	2.9
Other race, non-Hispanic	2.5	6.3	3.8	1.9	3.2	1.3
No children under age 18	2.3	5	2.7	1.6	3.4	1.8
Children under age 18	2.4	5.7	3.3	1.7	3.2	1.5
No children under age six	2.3	5.3	3	1.6	3.4	1.8
Children under age six	2.5	5.9	3.4	1.7	3	1.3

Source: Author's analysis of the Current Population Survey Outgoing Rotation Group Files.

(8.3%) have an unemployed husband, up four percentage points since 2007. This share of women with unemployed husbands has increased 2.2 percentage points among wives with a college degree.

There has also been a sharp rise in the share of families where both the husband and wife are unemployed. Between the first five months of 2007 and of 2009, the share of married-couple families with both spouses unemployed rose to 0.5% from 0.1%, meaning that one –in 500 families is struggling with dual unemployment. The share of families with a child under age 18 with both parents unemployed is 0.6%, meaning that one in 165 families with children have both parents looking for work.

Among some demographic groups dual unemployment rises to one in –100: young couples (with a spouse between 18 and 24), less-educated couples (where either spouse has no more than a high-school degree), and African-American families (0.9% of African-American wives in the labor force are unemployed and have an unemployed husband, while 0.8% of African-American husbands in the labor force are unemployed with an unemployed wife).

The Great Recession that began in December 2007 has now lasted 19 months. The unemployment picture remains tough: Unemployment rose to 9.5% in June and 29.0% of unemployed workers have been out of work for at least six months—a shocking fact given that 3.4 million of the 6.5 million people to have lost their job since the recession began were laid off only within the past six months. There are now more than five unemployed workers available for every job opening and the employment prospects for men seem especially challenging given the continued lay-offs in manufacturing and construction. Families will continue to rely on the earnings of a working woman for a long time to come.

As families need the earnings of wives more than ever, policymakers should focus their attention on ensuring that women—including mothers—have access to good jobs with benefits that will support their families. There could not be a more important moment to pass legislation ensuring pay equity for all workers. Nor could there be a more important time to ensure that caregivers are not discriminated against by employers.

The Paycheck Fairness Act, which passed the House in January, would go a long way toward eradicating pay inequalities, but it is languishing in the Senate. The Equal Employment Opportunity Commission issued new guidelines in 2007 to help employers avoid caregiver discrimination, but more could be done to use develop this guidance to ensure that every caregiver has the same access to good jobs as other workers. These and other policy solutions to the crisis facing women breadwinners need to be acted upon swiftly.

Source: Bureau of Labor Statistics, "Women in the Labor Force: A Databook," (Washington, DC: U.S. Department of Labor, 2008), Table 24.

The data analysis for this report was conducted by Jeff Chapman. The analysis compares the experiences of married couples from the first five months of 2007 to the first five months of 2009. Note that data are only for married heterosexual couples and do not include cohabitating heterosexual couples or lesbian or gay couples, married or otherwise.

Article 1.6

CPI BLUES

Changes to the Consumer Price Index dramatically reduced the "official" rate of inflation.

BY JOSHUA HOLLAND
November/December 2008

Think about economic conditions in the 1970s, and you're likely to have visions of gas lines snaking around corners, a weary Jimmy Carter looking droopy and forlorn in the Oval Office, and the general sense of "malaise" (Carter's word) that Ronald Reagan exploited so adroitly to give rise to the new conservative movement. You're also likely to think of high rates of inflation.

Over the last few years, even as the prices of food, energy, and other goods have soared, the mainstream media have maintained that today's inflation does not compare to those unhappy years. This past July [2008], *Newsweek* reassuringly noted that "the Consumer Price Index is rising at a 3% annual rate, compared with 13% in 1979." (More recently, in the wake of the global economic turmoil, some commentators are even talking about the danger of *de*flation.) But talk of inflation rarely mentions that the measures of inflation commonly discussed today bear little resemblance to the stats used in the 1970s.

In large part, that's because the Consumer Price Index (CPI)—the measure most frequently cited in media reports—is used to determine government benefits like Social Security, federal and state pensions, and Medicare payments. Recalculating inflation downward was a back-door way of keeping the growth of these entitlements in check without pissing off veterans' groups or the AARP.

The CPI was historically based on a relatively simple formula. Officials took a theoretical "basket of goods" that "typical" consumers required and averaged their current prices. Beginning in the early 1990s, however, conservative economists were unhappy that increases in the CPI kept increasing entitlement payments to government employees, vets, and the elderly—whiners and greedy gray-hairs. Through some impressive intellectual contortions, they came up with a number of proposals for adjusting how inflation is measured.

They began by weighting items in the basket differently. Federal Reserve Chair Alan Greenspan argued that it was wrong to compare the price of a pound of steak one year to the price of a pound of steak the next because when steak gets too expensive, people start eating hamburger—they lead more frugal lives when prices rise, and the measure of inflation should reflect their decisions. But as economist John Williams, author of the *Shadow Government Statistics* newsletter, notes:

> Replacing hamburger for steak in the calculations would reduce the inflation rate, but it represented the rate of inflation in terms of *maintaining a declining standard of living*. Cost of living was being replaced by the cost of survival. The old system told you how much you had to increase your income in order to keep

buying steak. The new system promised you hamburger, and then dog food, perhaps, after that. [emphasis mine]

In the same vein, conservative economists argued that the CPI wasn't taking into account the increased enjoyment people got from buying shiny new consumer goods. That new toaster may have cost you 60% more than the one you bought just five years ago, but the new one has a computer chip that monitors the internal temperature, and that makes it harder to burn the toast. Therefore, they argued, your happiness at having perfect toast every morning should be factored into the CPI.

In 1995, under Bill Clinton, the Boskin Commission—led by a former economic adviser to the first President Bush—was formed to "fix" the way we measure the CPI by applying these economists' views. Changes were quietly made, with little Congressional oversight. Ostensibly designed to improve accuracy, their net result was a dramatic reduction of the official rate of inflation.

While the mainstream media tout our 3% annual rate of inflation (5% since this spring), the reality is that inflation, using the CPI as it was calculated before the Clinton-era changes went into effect, was more than 8% in July. And that's not including a whole other set of methodological changes made in 1983.

Until 1983, the CPI included the cost of owning a house—it factored in home prices, mortgage rates, and real estate taxes. But then the Bureau of Labor Statistics—the agency that crunches all these numbers—decided to replace the cost of home ownership with rents (actually, a rental equivalent) as the key housing component in the CPI. But while home prices increased dramatically between 1995 and 2005, the "owners' equivalent rent" used to calculate inflation actually declined by a few points. As a result, the rising housing costs many U.S. families have faced over the past decade have not been reflected in the CPI. (That rents did not rise along with home prices, argued economists like Dean Baker, was evidence that the housing boom was in fact a "bubble," untethered from the basic laws of supply and demand.)

The average rate of inflation during the 1970s was just over 7% (and 9.75% during the Carter years). Williams estimates that today's CPI understates the inflation rate as it was calculated before the Reagan era by about seven percentage points. The figure above shows the CPI from 1980 to August 2008 as it is measured today compared with Williams' calculation of the inflation rate using the earlier methodologies.

It's a controversial claim, but if Williams is right, inflation in the first eight years of the 21st century has averaged around 9.5%—or two percentage points *higher* than it averaged during the 1970s. Compare that with the official inflation rate, which averaged 2.4% over that period.

Even more misleading is the "core" inflation rate, used by the Federal Reserve. The "core" rate simply excludes certain "volatile" goods from the basket —little things like energy and food. In recent years it's become increasingly popular among pundits to cite the core rate, but with energy and food costs making up about a quarter of most household expenses (and significantly more for low-income households), it's a poor measure of the economic pain most Americans have been feeling.

In just the last year (ending in June), food prices increased by more than 5%, and energy costs skyrocketed by almost 25%.

To gauge what most of us are really experiencing on a day-to-day basis, one might imagine economic reporters relying on a monthly "pizza index" instead of the Consumer Price Index. According to a February report by Al Olson of MSNBC, "Pizza makers have seen their cheese costs soar this year from $1.30 a pound to $1.76 a pound. Even worse, the flour used to make the dough has gone from $3 to $7 a bushel to $25 a bushel in less than a year." Between the second quarters of 2007 and 2008, even the cost of the paperboard used to make pizza boxes increased by 8%. (Several years of rising tomato prices—for the sauce—were blunted by the salmonella scare.)

The same is true for a host of items that working America buys every day. According to Olson, "If you're looking for a sure sign the U.S. economy is headed in the wrong direction, all you need to do is look at the skyrocketing price of 'recession-proof' foods: pizza, hot dogs, bagels and beer." But those items, and other costs that have a significant impact on ordinary people, are under-counted in the Consumer Price Index.

Sources: Daniel Gross, "Why Its Worse Than You Think," *Newsweek.* June 16, 2008; John Williams, "Consumer Price Index," *Government Economic Reports: Things You've Suspected But Were Afraid To Ask,* October 1, 2006; Al Olson, "Pizza and Beer Now Cost an Arm and a Leg," *MSNB,* Feb 29, 2008; Bureau of Labor Statistics, "Consumer Price Index Summary," July 2008 (www.bls.gov); Dean Baker, "Bush's House of Cards," *The Nation,* August 9, 2004.

Article 1.7

THE GROWTH CONSENSUS UNRAVELS

BY JONATHAN ROWE
September/October 2002

Economics has been called the dismal science, but beneath its gray exterior is a system of belief worthy of Pollyanna.

Yes, economists manage to see a dark cloud in every silver lining. Downturn follows uptick, and inflation rears its ugly head. But there's a story within that story—a gauzy romance, a lyric ode to Stuff. It's built into the language. A thing produced is called a "good," for example, no questions asked. The word is more than just a term of art. It suggests the automatic benediction which economics bestows upon commodities of any kind.

By the same token, an activity for sale is called a "service." In conventional economics there are no "dis-services," no actions that might be better left undone. The bank that gouges you with ATM fees, the lawyer who runs up the bill—such things are "services" so long as someone pays. If a friend or neighbor fixes your plumbing for free, it's not a "service" and so it doesn't count.

The sum total of these products and activities is called the Gross Domestic Product, or GDP. If the GDP is greater this year than last, then the result is called "growth." There is no bad GDP and no bad growth; economics does not even have a word for such a thing. It does have a word for less growth. In such a case, economists say growth is "sluggish" and the economy is in "recession." No matter what is growing—more payments to doctors because of worsening health, more toxic cleanup—so long as there is more of it, then the economic mind declares it "good."

This purports to be "objective science." In reality it is a rhetorical construct with the value judgments built in, and this rhetoric has been the basis of economic debate in the United States for the last half century at least. True, people have disagreed over how best to promote a rising GDP. Liberals generally wanted to use government more, conservatives less. But regarding the beneficence of a rising GDP, there has been little debate at all.

If anything, the Left traditionally has believed in growth with even greater fervor than the Right. It was John Maynard Keynes, after all, who devised the growth-boosting mechanisms of macroeconomic policy to combat the Depression of the 1930s; it was Keynesians who embraced these strategies after the War and turned the GDP into a totem. There's no point in seeking a bigger pie to redistribute to the poor, if you don't believe the expanding pie is desirable in the first place.

Today, however, the growth consensus is starting to unravel across the political spectrum and in ways that are both obvious and subtle. The issue is no longer just the impact of growth upon the environment—the toxic impacts of industry and the like. It now goes deeper, to what growth actually consists of and what it means in people's lives. The things economists call "goods" and "services" increasingly don't strike people as such. There is a growing disconnect between the way people experience growth and the way the policy establishment talks about it, and this gap is becoming an unspoken subtext to much of American political life.

The group most commonly associated with an antigrowth stance is environmentalists, of course. To be sure, one faction, the environmental economists, is trying to put green new wine into the old bottles of economic thought. If we would just make people pay the "true" cost of, say, the gasoline they burn, through the tax system for example, then the market would do the rest. We'd have benign, less-polluting growth, they say, perhaps even more than now. But the core of the environmental movement remains deeply suspicious of the growth ethos, and probably would be even if the environmental impacts somehow could be lessened.

In the middle are suburbanites who applaud growth in the abstract, but oppose the particular manifestations they see around them—the traffic, sprawl and crowded schools. On the Right, meanwhile, an anti-growth politics is arising practically unnoticed. When social conservatives denounce gambling, pornography, or sex and violence in the media, they are talking about specific instances of the growth that their political leaders rhapsodize on other days.

Environmentalists have been like social conservatives in one key respect. They have been moralistic regarding growth, often scolding people for enjoying themselves at the expense of future generations and the earth. Their concern is valid, up to a point—the consumer culture does promote the time horizon of a five year old. But politically it is not the most promising line of attack, and conceptually it concedes too much ground. To moralize about consumption as they do is to accept the conventional premise that it really is something chosen—an enjoyable form of self-indulgence that has unfortunate consequences for the earth.

That's "consumption" in the common parlance—the sport utility vehicle loading up at Wal-Mart, the stuff piling up in the basement and garage. But increasingly that's not what people actually experience, nor is it what the term really means. In economics, consumption means everything people spend money on, pleasurable or not. Wal-Mart is just one dimension of a much larger and increasingly unpleasant whole. The lawyers' fees for the house settlement or divorce; the repair work on the car after it was rear-ended; the cancer treatments for the uncle who was a three-pack-a-day smoker; the stress medications and weight loss regimens—all these and more are "consumption." They all go into the GDP.

Cancer treatments and lawyer's fees are not what come to mind when environmentalists lament the nation's excess consumption, or for that matter when economists applaud America's "consumers" for keeping the world economy afloat. Yet increasingly such things are what consumption actually consists of in the economy today. More and more, it consists not of pleasurable things that people choose, but rather of things that most people would gladly do without.

Much consumption today is addictive, for example. Millions of Americans are engaged in a grim daily struggle with themselves to do less of it. They want to eat less, drink less, smoke less, gamble less, talk less on the telephone—do less buying, period. Yet economic reasoning declares as growth and progress, that which people themselves regard as a tyrannical affliction.

Economists resist this reality of a divided self, because it would complicate their models beyond repair. They cling instead to an 18th century model of human psychology—the "rational" and self-interested man—which assumes those complexities away. As David McClelland, the Harvard psychologist, once put it, economists "haven't even discovered Freud, let alone Abraham Maslow." (They also haven't discovered the Apostle Paul, who lamented that "the good that I would I do not, but the evil that I would not, that I do.")

Then too there's the mounting expenditure that sellers foist upon people through machination and deceit. People don't choose to pay for the corrupt campaign finance system or for bloated executive pay packages. The cost of these is hidden in the prices that we pay at the store. As I write this, the *Washington Post* is reporting that Microsoft has hired Ralph Reed, former head of the Christian Coalition, and Grover Norquist, a right-wing polemicist, as lobbyists in Washington. When I bought this computer with Windows 95, Bill Gates never asked me whether I wanted to help support a bunch of Beltway operators like these.

This is compulsory consumption, not choice, and the economy is rife with it today. People don't choose to pay some $40 billion a year in telemarketing fraud. They don't choose to pay 32% more for prescription drugs than do people in Canada. ("Free trade" means that corporations are free to buy their labor and materials in other countries, but ordinary Americans aren't equally free to do their shopping there.) For that matter, people don't choose to spend $25 and up for inkjet printer cartridges. The manufacturers design the printers to make money on the cartridges because, as the *Wall Street Journal* put it, that's "where the big profit margins are."

Yet another category of consumption that most people would gladly do without arises from the need to deal with the offshoots and implications of growth. Bottled water has become a multibillion dollar business in the United States because people don't trust what comes from the tap. There's a growing market for sound insulation and double-pane windows because the economy produces so much noise. A wide array of physical and social stresses arise from the activities that get lumped into the euphemistic term "growth."

The economy in such cases doesn't solve problems so much as create new problems that require more expenditure to solve. Food is supposed to sustain people, for example. But today the dis-economies of eating sustain the GDP instead. The food industry spends some $21 billion a year on advertising to entice people to eat food they don't need. Not coincidentally there's now a $32 billion diet and weight loss industry to help people take off the pounds that inevitably result. When that doesn't work, which is often, there is always the vacuum pump or knife. There were some 110,000 liposuctions in the United States last year; at five pounds each that's some 275 tons of flab up the tube.

It is a grueling cycle of indulgence and repentance, binge and purge. Yet each stage of this miserable experience, viewed through the pollyanic lens of economics, becomes growth and therefore good. The problem here goes far beyond the old critique of how the consumer culture cultivates feelings of inadequacy, lack and need so people will buy and buy again. Now this culture actually makes life worse, in order to sell solutions that purport to make it better.

Traffic shows this syndrome in a finely developed form. First we build sprawling suburbs so people need a car to go almost anywhere. The resulting long commutes are daily torture but help build up the GDP. Americans spend some $5 billion a year in gasoline alone while they sit in traffic and go nowhere. As the price of gas increases this growth sector will expand.

Commerce deplores a vacuum, and the exasperating hours in the car have spawned a booming subeconomy of relaxation tapes, cell phones, even special bibs. Billboards have 1-800 numbers so commuters can shop while they stew. Talk radio thrives on traffic-bound commuters, which accounts for some of the contentious, get-out-of-my-face tone. The traffic also helps sustain a $130 billion a year car wreck industry; and if Gates succeeds in getting computers into cars, that sector should get a major boost.

The health implications also are good for growth. Los Angeles, which has the worst traffic in the nation, also leads—if that's the word—in hospital admissions due to respiratory ailments. The resulting medical bills go into the GDP. And while Americans sit in traffic they aren't walking or getting exercise. More likely they are entertaining themselves orally with a glazed donut or a Big Mac, which helps explain why the portion of middle-aged Americans who are clinically obese has doubled since the 1960s.

C. Everett Koop, the former Surgeon General, estimates that some 70% of the nation's medical expenses are lifestyle induced. Yet the same lifestyle that promotes disease also produces a rising GDP. (Keynes observed that traditional virtues like thrift are bad for growth; now it appears that health is bad for growth too.) We literally are growing ourselves sick, and this puts a grim new twist on the economic doctrine of "complementary goods," which describes the way new products tend to spawn a host of others. The automobile gave rise to car wash franchises, drive-in restaurants, fuzz busters, tire dumps, and so forth. Television produced an antenna industry, VCRs, soap magazines, ad infinitum. The texts present this phenomenon as the wondrous perpetual motion machine of the market—goods beget more goods. But now the machine is producing complementary ills and collateral damages instead.

Suggestive of this new dynamic is a pesticide plant in Richmond, California, which is owned by a transnational corporation that also makes the breast cancer drug tamoxifen. Many researchers believe that pesticides, and the toxins created in the production of them, play a role in breast cancer. "It's a pretty good deal," a local physician told the *East Bay Express*, a Bay Area weekly. "First you cause the cancer, then you profit from curing it." Both the alleged cause and cure make the GDP go up, and this syndrome has become a central dynamic of growth in the U.S. today.

Mainstream economists would argue that this is all beside the point. If people didn't have to spend money on such things as commuting or medical costs, they'd simply spend it on something else, they say. Growth would be the same or even greater, so the actual content of growth should be of little concern to those who promote it. That view holds sway in the nation's policy councils; as a result we try continually to grow our way out of problems, when increasingly we are growing our way in.

To the extent conventional economics has raised an eyebrow at growth, it has done so mainly through the concept of "externalities". These are negative side effects suffered by those not party to a transaction between a buyer and a seller. Man buys car, car pollutes air, others suffer that "externality." As the language implies, anything outside the original transaction is deemed secondary, a subordinate reality, and therefore easily overlooked. More, the effects upon buyer and seller—the "internalities" one might say—are assumed to be good.

Today, however, that mental schema is collapsing. Externalities are starting to overwhelm internalities. A single jet ski can cause more misery for the people who reside by a lake, than it gives pleasure to the person riding it.

More importantly, and as just discussed, internalities themselves are coming into question, and with them the assumption of choice, which is the moral linchpin of market thought.

If people choose what they buy, as market theory posits, then—externalities aside—the sum total of all their buying must be the greatest good of all. That's the ideology behind the GDP. But if people don't always choose, then the model starts to fall apart, which is what is happening today. The practical implications are obvious. If growth consists increasingly of problems rather than solutions, then scolding people for consuming too much is barking up the wrong tree. It is possible to talk instead about ridding our lives of what we don't want as well as forsaking what we do want—or think we want.

Politically this is a more promising path. But to where? The economy may be turning into a kind of round robin of difficulty and affliction, but we are all tied to the game. The sickness industry employs a lot of people, as do ad agencies and trash haulers. The fastest-growing occupations in the country include debt collectors and prison guards. What would we do without our problems and dysfunctions?

The problem is especially acute for those at the bottom of the income scale who have not shared much in the apparent prosperity. For them, a bigger piece of a bad pie might be better than none.

This is the economic conundrum of our age. No one has more than pieces of an answer, but it helps to see that much growth today is really an optical illusion created by accounting tricks. The official tally ignores totally the cost side of the growth ledger—the toll of traffic upon our time and health for example. In fact, it actually counts such costs as growth and gain. By the same token, the official tally ignores the economic contributions of the natural environment and the social structure; so that the more the economy destroys these, and puts commoditized substitutes in their places, the more the experts say the economy has "grown." Pollute the lakes and oceans so that people have to join private swim clubs and the economy grows. Erode the social infrastructure of community so people have to buy services from the market instead of getting help from their neighbors, and it grows some more. The real economy—the one that sustains us—has diminished. All that has grown is the need to buy commoditized substitutes for things we used to have for free.

So one might rephrase the question thus: how do we achieve real growth, as opposed to the statistical illusion that passes for growth today? Four decades ago, John Kenneth Galbraith argued in *The Affluent Society* that conventional economic reasoning is rapidly becoming obsolete. An economics based upon scarcity simply doesn't work in an economy of hyper-abundance, he said. If it takes a $200 billion (today) advertising industry to maintain what economists quaintly call "demand," then perhaps that demand isn't as urgent as conventional theory posits. Perhaps it's not even demand in any sane meaning of the word.

Galbraith argued that genuine economy called for shifting some resources from consumption that needs to be prodded, to needs which are indisputably great: schools, parks, older people, the inner cities and the like. For this he was skewered as a proto-socialist. Yet today the case is even stronger, as advertisers worm into virtually every waking moment in a desperate effort to keep the growth machine on track.

Galbraith was arguing for a larger public sector. But that brings dysfunctions of its own, such as bureaucracy; and it depends upon an enlarging private sector as a fiscal base to begin with. Today we need to go further, and establish new ground rules for the economy, so that it produces more genuine growth on its own. We also need to find ways to revive the nonmarket economy of informal community exchange, so that people do not need money to meet every single life need.

In the first category, environmental fiscal policy can help. While the corporate world has flogged workers to be more productive, resources such as petroleum have been in effect loafing on the job. If we used these more efficiently the result could be jobs and growth, even in conventional terms, with less environmental pollution. If we used land more efficiently—that is, reduced urban sprawl—the social and environmental gains would be great.

Another ground rule is the corporate charter laws. We need to restore these to their original purpose: to keep large business organizations within the compass of the common good. But such shifts can do only so much. More efficient cars might simply encourage more traffic, for example. Cheap renewable power for electronic devices could encourage more noise. In other words, the answer won't just be a more efficient version of what we do now. Sooner or later we'll need different ways of thinking about work and growth and how we allocate the means of life.

This is where the social economy comes in, the informal exchange between neighbors and friends. There are some promising trends. One is the return to the traditional village model in housing. Structure does affect content. When houses are close together, and people can walk to stores and work, it encourages the spontaneous social interaction that nurtures real community. New local currencies, such as Time Dollars, provide a kind of lattice work upon which informal nonmarket exchange can take root and grow.

Changes like these are off the grid of economics as conventionally defined. It took centuries for the market to emerge from the stagnation of feudalism. The next organizing principle, whatever it is, most likely will emerge slowly as well. This much we can say with certainty. As the market hurdles towards multiple implosions, social and environmental as well as financial, it is just possible that the economics profession is going to have to do what it constantly lectures the rest of us to do: adjust to new realities and show a willingness to change.

Article 1.8

WAGES FOR HOUSEWORK: THE MOVEMENT & THE NUMBERS

BY LENA GRABER AND JOHN MILLER
July/August 2002

The International Wages for Housework Campaign (WFH), a network of women in Third World and industrialized countries, began organizing in the early 1970s. WFH's demands are ambitious—"for the unwaged work that women do to be recognized as work in official government statistics, and for this work to be paid."

Housewives paid wages? By the government? That may seem outlandish to some, but consider the staggering amount of unpaid work carried out by women. In 1990, the International Labor Organization (ILO) estimated that women do two-thirds of the world's work for 5% of the income. In 1995, the UN Development Programme's (UNDP) Human Development Report announced that women's unpaid and underpaid labor was worth $11 trillion worldwide, and $1.4 trillion in the United States alone. Paying women the wages they "are owed" for unwaged work, as WFN puts it, would go a long way toward undoing these inequities and reducing women's economic dependence on men.

Publicizing information like this, WFH—whose International Women Count Network now includes more than 2,000 non-governmental organizations (NGOs) from the North and South—and other groups have been remarkably successful in persuading governments to count unwaged work. In 1995, the UN Fourth World Conference on Women, held in Beijing, developed a Platform for Action that called on governments to calculate the value of women's unpaid work and include it in conventional measures of national output, such as Gross Domestic Product (GDP).

So far, only Trinidad & Tobago and Spain have passed legislation mandating the new accounting, but other countries—including numerous European countries, Australia, Canada, Japan, and New Zealand in the industrialized world, and Bangladesh, the Dominican Republic, India, Nepal, Tanzania, and Venezuela in the developing world—have undertaken extensive surveys to determine how much time is spent on unpaid household work.

The Value of Housework

Producing credible numbers for the value of women's work in the home is no easy task. Calculating how many hours women spend performing housework—from cleaning to childcare to cooking to shopping—is just the first step. The hours are considerable in both developing and industrialized economies. (See Table 1.)

What value to place on that work, and what would constitute fair remuneration—or wages for housework—is even more difficult to assess. Feminist economists dedicated to making the value of housework visible have taken different approaches to answering the question. One approach, favored by the UN's International Research and Training Institute for the Advancement of Women (INSTRAW), bases the market value of work done at home on the price of market goods and services that are similar to those produced in the home (such as meals served in restaurants or cleaning done by professional firms). These output-based evaluations estimate that counting unpaid household production would add 30-60% to the GDP of industrialized countries, and far more for developing countries. (See Table 2.)

A second approach evaluates the inputs of household production—principally the labor that goes into cooking, cleaning, childcare, and other services performed in the home, overwhelmingly by women. Advocates of this approach use one of three methods. Some base their calculations on what economists call opportunity cost—the wages women might have earned if they had worked a similar number of hours in the market economy. Others ask what it would cost to hire someone to do the work—either a general laborer such as a domestic servant (the generalist-replacement method) or a specialist such as a chef (the specialist-replacement method)—and then assign those wages to household labor. Ann Chadeau, a researcher with the Organization for Economic Cooperation and Development, has found the specialist-replacement method to be "the most plausible and at the same time feasible approach" for valuing unpaid household labor.

These techniques produce quite different results, all of which are substantial in relation to GDP. With that in mind, let's look at how some countries calculated the monetary value of unpaid work.

Unpaid Work in Canada, Great Britain, and Japan

In Canada, a government survey documented the time men and women spent on unpaid work in 1992. Canadian women performed 65% of all unpaid work, shouldering an especially large share of household labor devoted to preparing meals, maintaining clothing, and caring for children. (Men's unpaid hours exceeded women's only for outdoor cleaning.)

TABLE 1
WOMEN'S TIME SPENT PER DAY PERFORMING HOUSEHOLD LABOR, BY ACTIVITY, IN HOURS:MINUTES

	Childcare Time	Cleaning Time	Food Prep Time	Shopping Time	Water/Fuel Collection	Total Time[a]
Australia (1997[b])	2:27	1:17	1:29	0:58	n.a.	3:39
Japan (1999)	0:24	2:37	n.a.	0:33	n.a.	3:34
Norway (2000)	0:42	1:16	0:49	0:26	0:01	3:56
U.K. (2000)	1:26	1:35	1:08	0:33	n.a.	4:55
Nepal (1996)	1:28	2:00	5:30	0:13	1:10	11:58

Note: Some activities, especially child care, may overlap with other tasks
[a] Totals may include activities other than those listed.
[b] Only some percentage of the population recorded doing these activities. Averages are for that portion of the population. Generally, figures represent a greater number of women than men involved. *Sources:* Australia: <www.abs.gov.au/ausstats>; Japan: <www.unescap.org/stat>; Norway: <www.ssb.no/tidsbruk_en>; United Kingdom: <www.statistics.gov.uk/themes/social_finances/TimeUseSurvey>; Nepal: INSTRAW, *Valuation of Household Production and the Satellite Accounts* (Santo Domingo: 1996), 34-35; <www.cbs.nl/isi/iass>.

The value of unpaid labor varied substantially, depending on the method used to estimate its appropriate wage. (See Table 3.) The opportunity-cost method, which uses the average market wage (weighted for the greater proportion of unpaid work done by women), assigned the highest value to unpaid labor, 54.2% of Canadian GDP. The two replacement methods produced lower estimates, because the wages they assigned fell below those of other jobs. The specialist-replacement method, which paired unpaid activities with the average wages of corresponding occupations—such as cooking with junior chefs, and childcare with kindergarten teachers—put the value of Canadian unpaid labor at 43% of GDP. The generalist-replacement method, by assigning the wages of household servants to unpaid labor, produced the lowest estimate of the value of unpaid work: 34% of Canadian GDP. INSTRAW's output-based measure, which matched hours of unpaid labor to a household's average expenditures on the same activities, calculated the value of Canada's unpaid work as 47.4% of GDP.

In Great Britain, where unpaid labor hours are high for an industrialized country (see Table 1), the value of unpaid labor was far greater relative to GDP. The British Office for National Statistics found that, when valued using the opportunity cost method, unpaid work was 112% of Britain's GDP in 1995! With the specialist-replacement method, British unpaid labor was still 56% of GDP—greater than the output of the United Kingdom's entire manufacturing sector for the year.

In Japan —where unpaid labor hours are more limited (see Table 1), paid workers put in longer hours, and women perform over 80% of unpaid work—the value of unpaid labor is significantly smaller relative to GDP. The Japanese Economic

TABLE 2
VALUE OF UNPAID HOUSEHOLD LABOR AS % OF GDP, USING OUTPUT-BASED EVALUATION METHOD

Country	% of GDP
Canada (1992)	47.4%
Finland (1990)	49.1%
Nepal (1991)	170.7%

Source: INSTRAW, *Valuation of Household Production and the Satellite Accounts* (Santo Domingo, 1996), 62, 229.

TABLE 3
VALUE OF UNPAID HOUSEHOLD LABOR IN CANADA AS % OF GDP, 1992

Evaluation Method	% of GDP
Opportunity Cost (before taxes)	54.2 %
Specialist-Replacement	43.0%
Generalist-Replacement	34.0%
Output-Based	47.4%

Source: INSTRAW, *Valuation of Household Production and the Satellite Accounts* (Santo Domingo: 1996), 229.

Planning Agency calculated that counting unpaid work in 1996 would add be-tween 15.2% (generalist-replacement method) and 23% (opportunity-cost method) to GDP. Even at those levels, the value of unpaid labor still equaled at least half of Japanese women's market wages.

Housework Not Bombs

While estimates vary by country and evaluation method, all of these cal-culations make clear that recognizing the value of unpaid household labor profoundly alters our perception of economic activity and women's contri-butions to production. "Had household production been included in the system of macro-economic accounts," notes Ann Chadeau, "governments may well have implemented quite different economic and social policies."

For example, according to the UNDP, "The inescapable implication [of rec-ognizing women's unpaid labor] is that the fruits of society's total labor should be shared more equally." For the UNDP, this would mean radically altering property and inheritance rights; access to credit; entitlement to social security benefits, tax incentives, and child care; and terms of divorce settlements.

For WFH advocates, the implications are inescapable as well: women's unpaid labor should be paid—and "the money," WFH insists, "must come first of all from military spending."

Here in the United States, an unneeded and dangerous military buildup begun [in 2002] has already pushed up military spending from 3% to 4% of GDP. Devoting just the additional 1% of GDP gobbled up by the military budget to wages for house-work—far from being outlandish—would be an important first step toward fairly re-munerating women who perform necessary and life-sustaining household work.

Sources: Ann Chadeau, "What is Households' Non-Market Production Worth?" *OECD Economic Studies* No. 18 (Spring 1992); Economic Planning Unit, Department of National Accounts, Japan, "Monetary Valuation of Unpaid Work in 1996" <unstats.un.org/unsd/methods/timeuse/ tusresource_papers/japanunpaid.htm>; INSTRAW, *Measurement and Valuation of Unpaid Contribution: Accounting Through Time and Output* (Santo Domingo: 1995); INSTRAW, *Valuation of Household Production and the Satellite Accounts* (Santo Domingo: 1996); Office of National Statistics, United Kingdom, "A Household Satellite Account for the UK," by Linda Murgatroyd and Henry Neuberger, *Economic Trends* (October 1997) <www.statistics.gov.uk/hhsa/hhsa/Index. html>; Hilkka Pietilä, "The Triangle of the Human Ecology: Household-Cultivation-Industrial Production," *Ecological Economics Journal* 20 (1997); UN Development Programme, Human Development Report (New York: Oxford University Press, 1995).

Article 1.9

A GREATER THREAT?

Federal spending on the military vs. climate change.

BY AMY GLUCKMAN
September/October 2009

It's not surprising that it took some time for the world's largest single consumer of oil to start taking climate change seriously. But the U.S. military has finally begun to do so. Intelligence agencies and the Defense Department "for the first time are taking a serious look at the national security implications of climate change," the *New York Times* reported in August, noting that the Pentagon's next Quadrennial Defense Review, due in 2010, will include a section on climate change for the first time.

The discovery of a grave new threat to national security usually means more money for the Defense Department. But the Pentagon is not the locus of U.S. government climate-change policy. Passing legislation to cut greenhouse-gas emissions via a cap-and-trade program or a carbon tax is widely viewed as the most important step the federal government must take—a politically difficult step, but not one requiring large government expenditures.

Federal spending also forms an important component of climate change policy, however. For one thing, the government is itself a major greenhouse-gas emitter and must make clean-energy and energy-efficiency investments for its own facilities and vehicle fleets. Government-funded research and development can facilitate and speed

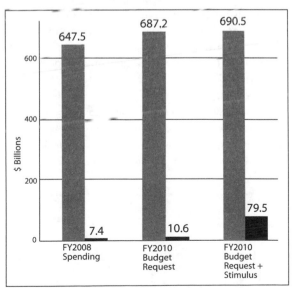

FEDERAL SPENDING ON MILITARY VS. CLIMATE SECURITY

Source: Pemberton, "Military vs. Climate Security," August 2009, data from the Office of Management and Budget and the State Dept.

up the larger transition to a low-carbon economy. U.S. foreign aid dollars can help poorer countries to make that transition and to prepare for climate-change damages that are on the way. And tax expenditures—revenue the government forgoes when it creates special tax incentives—can channel personal and business spending in low-carbon directions.

So how does federal spending on climate change compare to spending on traditional military force? Is climate-change spending rising in line with its new status as a serious security threat?

Military vs. Climate Change Spending in U.S. Foreign Aid ($ billions)

	FY 2008	FY 2010
Climate Change	0.21	0.72
Military	10.17	11.89

Source: Pemberton, "Military vs. Climate Security," August 2009, data from the Office of Management and Budget and the State Dept.

A new Institute for Policy Studies/Foreign Policy in Focus report by Miriam Pemberton tackles this question. Pemberton combed carefully through the FY 2008 budget, the Obama administration's FY 2010 budget request, and the stimulus package passed last February. Her analysis shows that spending to address climate change will be dramatically higher in FY 2010 compared to FY 2008—but that most of that improvement comes from the stimulus package, a one-time shot in the arm. And federal spending on climate change is still just a drop compared to the barrels of money going to reinforce U.S. military power.

In FY 2008, military spending exceeded climate-change spending by a ratio of 88 to1. In FY 2010, that ratio will be down to around 9 to 1, mostly thanks to the stimulus package. Excluding the stimulus money leaves the military-to-climate-change spending ratio at 65 to 1 for FY 2010. (The actual budget figures are shown in the figure.)

The Obama administration plans to hike spending on helping foreign countries tackle climate change more than three-fold in FY 2010 compared to FY 2008. With that increase, the U.S. government will be spending about $20 on foreign military assistance for every $1 on foreign climate-change assistance, down from $50 for every $1 in FY 2008 (see table above).

Sources: Miriam Pemberton, "Military vs. Climate Security: Mapping the Shift from the Bush Years to the Obama Era," Institute for Policy Studies/Foreign Policy in Focus, August 2009; John Broder, "Climate Change Seen as Threat to U.S. Security," *New York Times*, August 9, 2009; Jeff Brady, "Military's Oil Needs Not Deterred by Price Spike," NPR, Nov. 14, 2007.

Chapter 2

WEALTH, INEQUALITY, AND POVERTY

INTRODUCTION

Wealth and inequality are both end products of today's economic growth. But while all macroeconomics textbooks investigate wealth *accumulation*, most give less attention to wealth *disparities*. The authors in this chapter fill in the gap by looking at who makes out, and who doesn't, with the accumulation of wealth.

"Slicing Up at the Long Barbeque" (Article 2.1) starts the discussion by providing hard numbers on today's income and wealth gaps. Economist Jim Cypher documents the alarming increase in U.S. inequality, which has reached levels not seen since the Great Depression. This holds for both income (how much you or your family makes in a year) and wealth (the assets you or your family owns minus your debts). Today, the top 1% of households own nearly two-fifths of the nation's wealth and the richest 20% get nearly three-fifths of our national income. Median household income (after adjusting for inflation) is declining. For Cypher, these numbers define who gorged, who served, and who got roasted during the last thirty years.

All told, greater wealth hasn't made for greater equality or social mobility. As Paul Krugman reports, it is not just left wing critics who say so, but the business press as well. The number of people who go from rags to riches—while always so few as to be near-mythical —has decreased since 1980 (Article 2.4). In addition, low-wage workers are five times less likely to have sick days at their job than workers at the top of the wage scale (Article 2.3). On top of that, poverty rates, which according to most experts badly underestimate the extent of poverty in the U.S. economy, continued to rise during the 2001-2007 economic expansion (Article 2.2).

It doesn't have to be this way. Chris Tilly debunks the myth that inequality is necessary for economic growth, showing that among both developing and industrial economies and across regions within countries, there is no correlation between higher inequality and faster economic growth. He argues that greater equality actually supports economic growth by bolstering spending, promoting agricultural and industrial productivity, and reducing social conflict (Article 2.5). William Greider provides a blueprint for how the engines of inequality of today's economy can be transformed through workplace democracy, strategic investment of public and union-managed pension funds, and shareholder activism (Article 2.6).

What has happened to world income inequality is a matter of intense debate. Many analysts claim that world incomes have converged, leading to a sharp reduction in world inequality in the second half of the twentieth century. Many others report that the gaps between the poorest and the richest people and between countries have continued to widen over the last two decades. In a *Dollars & Sense* interview, economist Bob Sutcliffe reports that "the wide range of different results of respected studies of world inequality in the last two decades casts doubt on the idea that world inequality has sharply and unambiguously declined or increased during the epoch of neoliberalism" (Article 2.7). In the final article of the chapter, economist John Miller takes on the *Wall Street Journal* editors' claim that policies that promote equality stand in the way of rapid economic growth. Miller argues that, on the contrary, the experience of the East Asian economies shows that poverty reduction depends on both raising a nation's income and reducing its inequality (Article 2.8).

Discussion Questions

1. (General) The authors in this chapter believe that the distribution of wealth is as important as wealth itself, and consider greater economic equality an important macroeconomic goal. What are some arguments for and against this position? Where do you come down in the debate?

2. (Articles 2.1, 2.3, 2.4) Who benefited from the wealth accumulation of the last two decades? How did stockholders fare versus wage earners? How did the distribution of wealth by income group and by race change during the decade?

3. (Articles 2.1, 2.2, 2.3, 2.4) "A rising tide lifts all boats," proclaimed John F. Kennedy as he lobbied for pro-business tax cuts in the early 1960s. Did the 1990s boom and the current economic recovery lift all boats? What do the changes in income, wealth, and poverty suggest?

4. (Article 2.2) What are the shortcomings of the federal poverty threshold? How should the United States change the way it calculates the poverty threshold to get a more accurate measure of the incidence of poverty?

5. (Article 2.4) The myth of the "New Economy" bolstered the illusion that anyone can get rich quick in this country, but Paul Krugman says it just ain't so. What evidence does he present to argue that social mobility is declining? Do you find his evidence compelling?

6. (Article 2.5) Why do conservatives argue that inequality is good for economic growth? What counterarguments does Tilly use to challenge this traditional view of the tradeoff between inequality and growth? What evidence convinces Tilly that equality is good for economic growth? Does that evidence convince you?

7. (Article 2.6) Why, in Greider's opinion, is transforming the workplace the key to making the U.S. economy more egalitarian and democratic?

8. (Article 2.7) If Sutcliffe is correct and world inequality has neither declined nor increased sharply during the epoch of neoliberalism, what does his reading of the world inequality data suggest about the convergence hypothesis—the hypothesis that per capita income in countries with similar institutional structures will converge to the higher level?

9. (Article 2.8) What does the experience of the East Asian economies suggest about the relationship between equity, economic growth, and poverty alleviation? Give specific examples from the 22 developing countries studied by the Asian Development Bank.

Article 2.1

SLICING UP AT THE LONG BARBEQUE
Who gorges, who serves, and who gets roasted?

BY JAMES M. CYPHER
January/February 2007

Economic inequality has been on the rise in the United States for 30-odd years. Not since the Gilded Age of the late 19th century—during what Mark Twain referred to as "the Great Barbeque"—has the country witnessed such a rapid shift in the distribution of economic resources.

Still, most mainstream economists do not pay too much attention to the distribution of income and wealth—that is, how the value of current production (income) and past accumulated assets (wealth) is divided up among U.S. households. Some economists focus their attention on theory for theory's sake and do not work much with empirical data of any kind. Others who *are* interested in these on-the-ground data simply assume that each   individual or group gets what it deserves from a capitalist economy. In their view, if the share of income going to wage earners goes up, that must mean that wage earners are more pro-ductive and thus deserve a larger slice of the nation's total income—and vice versa if that share goes down.

Heterodox economists, however, frequently look upon the distribution of income and wealth as among the most important shorthand guides to the overall state of a   society and its economy. Some are interested in economic justice; others may or may not be, but nonetheless are convinced that changes in income distribution signal underlying societal trends and perhaps important points of political tension. And the general public appears to be paying increasing attention to income and wealth inequality. Consider the strong support voters have given to recent ballot questions raising state minimum wages and the ex-tensive coverage of economic inequality that has suddenly begun to appear in mainstream news outlets like the *New York Times*, the *Los Angeles Times*, and the *Wall Street Journal*, all of which published lengthy article series on the topic in the past few years. Just last month, news outlets around the country spotlighted the extravagant bonuses paid out by investment firm Goldman Sachs, including a $53.4 million bonus to the firm's CEO.

By now, economists and others who do pay attention to the issue are aware that income and wealth inequality in the United States rose steadily during the last three decades of the 20th century. But now that we are several years into the 21st, what do we know about income and wealth distribution today? Has the trend toward inequality continued, or are there signs of a reversal? And what can an understanding of the entire post-World War II era tell us about how to move again toward greater economic equality?

The short answers are: (1) Income distribution is even more unequal that we thought; (2) The newest data suggest the trend toward greater inequality continues, with no signs of a reversal; (3) We all do better when we all do better. During the 30 or so years after World War II the economy boomed and every stratum of society did better—pretty much at the same rate. When the era of shared growth ended, so too did much of the growth: the U.S. economy slowed down and recessions were deeper, more frequent, and harder to overcome. Growth spurts that did occur left most people out: the bottom 60% of U.S. households earned only 95 cents in 2004 for every dollar they made in 1979. A quarter century of falling incomes for the vast majority, even though average household income rose by 27% in real terms. Whew!

The Classless Society?

Throughout the 1950s, 1960s, and 1970s, sociologists preached that the United States was an essentially "classless" society in which everyone belonged to the middle class. A new "mass market" society with an essentially affluent, economically homogeneous population, they claimed, had emerged. Exaggerated as these claims were in the 1950s, there was some reason for their popular acceptance. Union membership reached its peak share of the private-sector labor force in the early 1950s; unions were able to force corporations of the day to share the benefits of strong economic growth. The union wage created a target for non-union workers as well, pulling up all but the lowest of wages as workers sought to match the union wage and employers often granted it as a tactic for keeping unions out. Under these circumstances, millions of families entered the lower middle class and saw their standard of living rise markedly. All of this made the distribution of income more equal for decades until the late 1970s. Of course there were outliers—some millions of poor, disproportionately blacks, and the rich family here and there.

Something serious must have happened in the 1970s as the trend toward

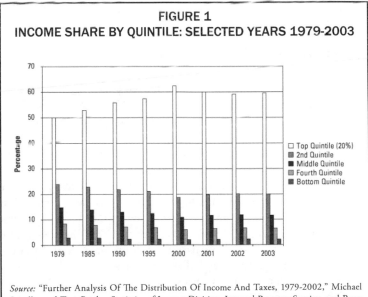

FIGURE 1
INCOME SHARE BY QUINTILE: SELECTED YEARS 1979-2003

Source: "Further Analysis Of The Distribution Of Income And Taxes, 1979-2002," Michael Strudler and Tom Petska, Statistics of Income Division, Internal Revenue Service, and Ryan Petska, Quantitative Economics and Statistics, Ernst and Young LLP. Accompanying Excel files include data to 2003. Available at www.irs.gov/taxstats/article/0,,Id=131260,00.ht

greater economic equality rapidly reversed. Here are the numbers. The share of in-come re-ceived by the bottom 90% of the population was a modest 67% in 1970, but by 2000 this had shrunk to a mere 52%, according to a detailed study of U.S. income distribution conducted by Thomas Piketty and Emmanuel Saez, published by the prestigious National Bureau of Econ-omic Research in 2002. Put another way, the top 10% in-creased their overall share of the nation's total income by 15 percentage points from 1970 to 2000. This is a rather astonishing jump—the *gain* of the top 10% in these years was equivalent to more than the *total income received annually* by the bottom 40% of households.

To get on the bottom rung of the top 10% of households in 2000, it would have been necessary to have an adjusted gross income of $104,000 a year. The real money, though, starts on the 99th rung of the income ladder—the top 1% received an unbelievable 21.7% of all income in 2000. To get a handhold on the very bottom of this top rung took more than $384,000.

The Piketty-Saez study (and subsequent updates), which included in its mea-sure of annual household income some data, such as income from capital gains, that generally are not factored in, verified a rising *trend* in income inequality which had been widely noted by others, and a *degree* of inequality which was far beyond most current estimates.

The Internal Revenue Service has essentially duplicated the Piketty-Saez study. They find that in 2003, the share of total income going to the "bottom" four-fifths of house-holds (that's 80% of the population!) was only slightly above 40%. (See Figure 1.) Both of these studies show much higher levels of inequality than were previously thought to exist based on widely referenced Census Bureau studies. The Census studies still attribute 50% of total income to the top fifth for 2003, but this number appears to understate what the top fifth now receives—nearly 60%, accord-ing to the IRS.

A Brave New (Globalized) World For Workers

Why the big change from 1970 to 2000? That is too long a story to tell here in full. But briefly, we can say that beginning in the early 1970s, U.S. corporations and the wealthy individuals who largely own them had the means, the motive, and the op-portunity to garner a larger share of the nation's income—and they did so.

Let's start with the motive. The 1970s saw a significant slowdown in U.S. eco-nomic growth, which made corporations and stockholders anxious to stop sharing the benefits of growth to the degree they had in the im-mediate postwar era.

Opportunity appeared in the form of an accelerating globalization of economic activity. Beginning in the 1970s, more and more U.S.-based cor-porations began to set up production operations overseas. The trend has only ac-celerated since, in part because international communication and transportation costs have fallen dramatically. Until the 1970s, it was very difficult—essential-ly unprofitable—for giants like General Electric or General Motors to oper-ate plants offshore and then import their foreign-made products into the United States. So from the 1940s to the 1970s, U.S. workers had a geographic lever, one they have now almost entirely lost. This erosion in workers' bargaining power has undermined the middle class and decimated the unions that once managed to assure the working class a generally comfortable economic existence. And today, of course, the tendency to send jobs offshore is affecting many highly trained professionals such as engineers. So this process of gutting the middle class has not run its course.

Given the opportunity presented by globalization, companies took a two-pronged approach to strengthening their hand vis-à-vis workers: (1) a frontal assault on unions, with decertification elections and get-tough tactics during unionization attempts, and (2) a debilitating war of nerves whereby corporations threatened to move offshore unless workers scaled back their demands or agreed to givebacks of prior gains in wage and benefit levels or working conditions.

A succession of U.S. governments that pursued conservative—or pro-corporate—economic policies provided the means. Since the 1970s, both Republican and Democratic administrations have tailored their eco-nomic policies to benefit corporations and shareholders over workers. The laundry list of such policies includes

- new trade agreements, such as NAFTA, that allow companies to cement favorable deals to move offshore to host nations such as Mexico;
- tax cuts for corporations and for the wealthiest house-holds, along with hikes in the payroll taxes that represent the largest share of the tax burden on the working and middle classes;
- lax enforcement of labor laws that are supposed to protect the right to organize unions and bargain collectively.

Exploding Millionairism

Given these shifts in the political economy of the United States, it is not surprising that economic inequality in 2000 was higher than in 1970. But at this point, careful readers may well ask whether it is misleading to use data for the year 2000, as the studies reported above do, to demonstrate rising inequality. After all, wasn't 2000 the year the NASDAQ peaked, the year the dot-com bubble reached its maximum volume? So if the wealthiest households received an especially large slice of the nation's total income that year, doesn't that just reflect a bubble about to burst rather than an underlying trend?

To begin to answer this question, we need to look at the trends in income and wealth distribution *since* 2000. And it turns out that after a slight pause in 2000-2001, inequality has continued to rise. Look at household income, for example. According to the standard indicators, the U.S. economy saw a brief recession in 2000-2001 and has been in a recovery ever since. But the median household income has failed to recover. In 2000 the median household had an annual income of $49,133; by 2005, after adjusting for inflation, the figure stood at $46,242. This 6% drop in median household income occurred while the inflation-adjusted Gross Domestic Product *expanded* by 14.4%.

When the Census Bureau released these data, it noted that median household income had gone up slightly between 2004 and 2005. This point was seized upon by Bush administration officials to bolster their claim that times are good for American workers. A closer look at the data, however, revealed a rather astounding fact:

Only 23 million households moved ahead in 2005, most headed by someone aged 65 or above. In other words, subtracting out the cost-of-living increase in Social Security benefits and increases in investment income (such as profits, dividends, interest, capital gains, and rents) to the over-65 group, workers again suffered a *decline* in income in 2005.

Another bit of evidence is the number of millionaire households—those with net worth of $1 million or more excluding the value of a primary residence and any IRAs. In 1999, just before the bubbles burst, there were 7.1 million millionaire households in the United States. In 2005, there were 8.9 million, a record number. Ordinary workers may not have recovered from the 2000–2001 rough patch yet, but evidently the wealthiest households have!

Many economists pay scant attention to income distribution patterns on the assumption that those shifts merely reflect trends in the productivity of labor or the return to risk-taking. But worker productivity *rose* in the 2000-2005 period, by 27.1% (see Figure 2). At the same time, from 2003 to 2005 average hourly pay *fell* by 1.2%. (Total com-pensation, including all forms of benefits, rose by 7.2% between 2000 and 2005. Most of the higher compensation spending merely reflects rapid increases in the health insurance premiums that employers have to pay just to maintain the same levels of coverage. But even if benefits are counted as part of workers' pay—a common and questionable practice—productivity growth out-

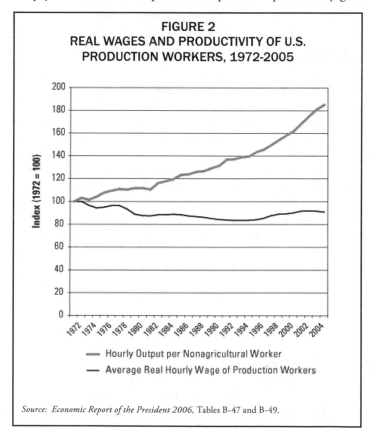

FIGURE 2
REAL WAGES AND PRODUCTIVITY OF U.S.
PRODUCTION WORKERS, 1972-2005

— Hourly Output per Nonagricultural Worker
— Average Real Hourly Wage of Production Workers

Source: Economic Report of the President 2006, Tables B-47 and B-49.

paced this elastic definition of "pay" by 50% between 1972 and 2005.)

And at the macro level, recent data released by the Commerce Department demonstrate that the share of the country's GDP going to wages and salaries sank to its lowest postwar level, 45.4%, in the third quarter of 2006 (see Figure 3). And this figure actually overstates how well ordinary workers are doing. The "Wage & Salary" share includes *all* income of this type, not just production workers' pay. Corporate executives' increasingly munificent salaries are included as well. Workers got roughly 65% of total wage and salary income in 2005, according to survey data from the U.S. Department of Labor; the other 35% went to salaried professionals—medical doctors and technicians, managers, and lawyers—who comprised only 15.6% of the sample.

Moreover, the "Wage & Salary" share shown in the National Income and Product Accounts includes bonuses, overtime, and other forms of payment not included in the Labor Department survey. If this income were factored in, the share going to nonprofessional, nonmanagerial workers would be even smaller. Bonuses and other forms of income to top employees can be many times base pay in important areas such as law and banking. Goldman Sachs's notorious 2006 bonuses are a case in point; the typical managing director on Wall Street garnered a bonus ranging between $1 and $3 million.

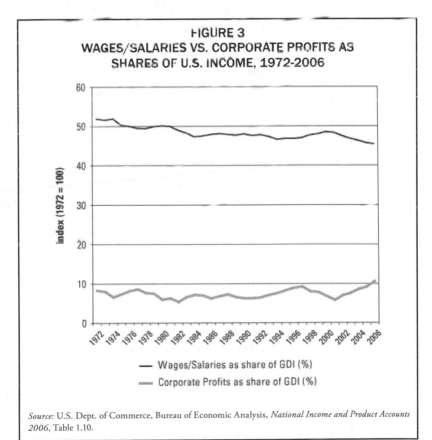

FIGURE 3
WAGES/SALARIES VS. CORPORATE PROFITS AS
SHARES OF U.S. INCOME, 1972-2006

— Wages/Salaries as share of GDI (%)
— Corporate Profits as share of GDI (%)

Source: U.S. Dept. of Commerce, Bureau of Economic Analysis, *National Income and Product Accounts 2006*, Table 1.10.

So, labor's share of the nation's income is falling, as Figure 3 shows, but it is actually falling much faster than these data suggest. Profits, meanwhile, are at their highest level as a share of GDP since the booming 1960s.

These numbers should come as no surprise to anyone who reads the paper: story after story illustrates how cor-porations are continuing to squeeze workers. For instance, workers at the giant auto parts manufacturer Delphi have been told to prepare for a drop in wages from $27.50 an hour in 2006 to $16.50 an hour in 2007. In order to keep some of Caterpillar's manufacturing work in the United States, the union was cornered into accepting a contract in 2006 that limits new workers to a maximum salary of $27,000 a year—no matter how long they work there—compared to the $38,000 or more that long-time Caterpillar workers make today. More generally, for young women with a high school diploma, average entry-level pay fell to only $9.08 an hour in 2005, down by 4.9% just since 2001. For male college graduates, starter-job pay fell by 7.3% over the same period.

Aiding and Abetting

And the federal government is continuing to play its part, facilitating the transfer of an ever-larger share of the nation's income to its wealthiest households. George W. Bush once joked that his constituency was "the haves and the have-mores"—this may have been one of the few instances in which he was actually leveling with his audience. Consider aspects of the four tax cuts for individuals that Bush has implemented since taking office. The first two cut the top *nominal* tax rate from 39.6% to 35%. Then, in 2003, the third cut benefited solely those who hold wealth, reducing taxes on dividends from 39.6% to 15% and on capital gains from 20% to 15%. (Bush's fourth tax cut—in 2006—is expected to drop taxes by 4.8% percent for the top one tenth of one percent of all households, while the median household will luxuriate with an extra nickel per day.)

So, if you make your money by the sweat of your brow and you earned $200,000 in 2003, you paid an *effective* tax rate of 21%. If you earned a bit more, say another $60,500, you paid an effective tax rate of 35% on the additional income. But if, with a flick of the wrist on your laptop, you flipped some stock you had held for six months and cleared $60,500 on the transaction, you paid the IRS an effective tax rate of only 15%. What difference does it make? Well, in 2003 the 6,126 households with incomes over $10 million saw their taxes go down by an average of $521,905 from this one tax cut alone.

These tax cuts represent only one of the many Bush administration policies that have abetted the ongoing shift of income away from most households and toward the wealthiest ones. And what do these top-tier households do with all this newfound money? For one thing, they save. This is in sharp contrast to most households. While the top fifth of households by income has a savings rate of 23%, the bottom 80% as a group dissave—in other words, they go into debt, spending more than they earn. Households headed by a person under 35 currently show a negative savings rate of 16% of income. Today *overall* savings—the savings of the top fifth minus the dis-savings of the bottom four-fifths—are slightly negative, for the first time since the Great Depression.

Here we find the crucial link between income and wealth accumulation. Able to save nearly a quarter of their income, the rich search out financial assets (and sometimes real assets such as houses and businesses) to pour their vast funds into. In many instances, sometimes with inside information, they are able to generate considerable future income from their invested savings. Like a snowball rolling downhill, savings for the rich can have a turbo effect—more savings generates more income, which then accumulates as wealth.

Lifestyles of the Rich

Make the rich even richer and the creative forces of market capitalism will be unleashed, resulting in more savings and consequently more capital investment, raising productivity and creating abundance for all. At any rate, that's the supply-side/neoliberal theory. However—and reminiscent of the false boom that defined the Japanese economy in the late 1980s—the big money has not gone into pro-ductive investments in the United States. Stripping out the money pumped into the residential real estate bubble, inflation-adjusted investment in machinery, equipment, technology, and structures increased only 1.4% from 1999 through 2005—an average of 0.23% per year. Essentially, productive investment has stagnated since the close of the dot-com boom.

Instead, the money has poured into high-risk hedge funds. These are vast pools of unregulated funds that are now generating 40% to 50% of the trades in the New York Stock Exchange and account for very large portions of trad-ing in many U.S. and foreign credit and debt markets.

And where is the income from these investments going? Last fall media mogul David Geffen sold two paintings at record prices, a Jasper Johns ($80 million) and a Willem de Kooning ($63.5 million), to two of "today's crop of hedge-fund billionaires" whose cash is making the art market "red-hot," according to the *New York Times*.

Other forms of conspicuous consumption have their allure as well. Boeing and Lufthansa are expecting brisk business for the newly introduced 787 airplane. The commercial version of the new Boeing jet will seat 330, but the VIP version offered by Lufthansa Technik (for a mere $240 million) will have seating for 35 or fewer, leav-ing room for master bedrooms, a bar, and the transport of racehorses or Rolls Royces. And if you lose your auto as-sembly job? It should be easy to find work as a dog walker: High-end pet care services are booming, with sales more than doubling between 2000 and 2004. Opened in 2001, Just Dogs Gourmet expects to have 45 franchises in place by the end of 2006 selling hand-decorated doggie treats. And then there is Camp Bow Wow, which offers piped-in classical music for the dogs (oops, "guests") and a live Cam-per Cam for their owners. Started only three years ago, the company already has 140 franchises up and running.

According to David Butler, the manager of a premiere auto dealership outside of Detroit, sales of Bentleys, at $180,000 a pop, are brisk. But not many $300,000 Rolls Royces are selling. "It's not that they can't afford it," Butler told the *New York Times*, "it's because of the image it would give." Just what is the image problem in Detroit? Well, maybe it has something to do with those Delphi workers facing a 40% pay cut. Michigan's economy is one of the hardest-hit in the nation. GM, long a symbol of U.S. manufacturing prowess, is staggering, with rumors of possible bankruptcy rife. The best union in terms of delivering the goods for the U.S. working class, the United Auto Workers, is facing an implosion. Thousands of Michigan workers at Delphi, GM, and Ford will be out on the streets very soon. (The top three domestic car makers are determined to permanently lay off three-quar-ters of their U.S. assembly-line workers—nearly 200,000 hourly employees. If they do, then the number of auto-workers employed by the Big Three—Ford, Chrysler, and GM—will have shrunk by a staggering 900,000 since 1978.) So, this might not be the time to buy a Rolls. But a mere $180,000 Bentley—why not?

Had Enough of the "Haves"?

In the era Twain decried as the "great barbeque," the outrageous concentration of income and wealth eventually sparked a reaction and a vast reform movement. But it was not until the onset of the Great Depression, decades later, that massive labor/social unrest and economic collapse forced the country's political elite to check the growing concentration of income and wealth.

Today, it does not appear that there are, as yet, any viable forces at work to put the brakes on the current runaway process of rising inequality. Nor does it appear that this era's power elite is ready to accept any new social compact. In a recent report on the "new king of Wall Street" (a co-founder of the hedge fund/private-equity buyout corporation Blackstone Group) that seemed to typify elite perspectives on today's inequality, the New York Times gushed that "a crashing wave of capital is minting new billionaires each year." Naturally, the Times was too discreet to mention is that those same "crashing waves" have flattened the middle class. And their backwash has turned the working class every-which-way while pulling it down, down, down.

But perhaps those who decry the trend can find at least symbolic hope in the new boom in yet another luxury good. Private mausoleums, in vogue during that earlier Gilded Age, are back. For $650,000, one was recently constructed at Daytona Memorial Park in Florida—with matching $4,000 Medjool date palms for shade. Another, complete with granite patio, meditation room, and doors of hand cast bronze, went up in the same cemetery. Business is booming, apparently, with 2,000 private mausoleums sold in 2005, up from a single-year peak of 65 in the 1980s. Some cost "well into the millions," according to one the nation's largest makers of cemetery monuments. Who knows: maybe the mausoleum boom portends the ultimate (dead) end for the neo-Gilded Age.

Sources: Jenny Anderson, "As Lenders, Hedge Funds Draw Insider Scrutiny," *NY Times* 10/16/06; Steven Greenhouse, "Many Entry-Level Workers Feel Pinch of Rough Market," *NY Times* 9/4/06; Greenhouse and David Leonhardt, "Real Wages Fail to Match a Rise in Productivity," *NY Times* 8/28/06; Paul Krugman, "Feeling No Pain," *NY Times* 3/6/06; Krugman, "Graduates vs. Oligarchs," *NY Times* 2/27/06; David Cay Johnston, *Perfectly Legal* (Penguin Books, 2003); Johnston, "Big Gain for Rich Seen in Tax Cuts for Investments," *NY Times* 4/5/06; Johnston, "New Rise in Number of Millionaire Families," *NY Times* 3/28/06; Johnston, "'04 Income in US was Below 2000 Level," *NY Times* 11/28/06; Leonhardt, "The Economics of Henry Ford May Be

Passé," *NY Times* 4/5/06; Rick Lyman, "Census Reports Slight Increase in '05 Incomes," *NY Times* 8/30/06; Micheline Maynard and Nick Bunkley, "Ford is Offering 75,000 Employees Buyout Packages," *NY Times* 9/15/06; Jeremy W. Peters, "Delphi Is Said to Offer Union a One-Time Sweetener," *NY Times* 3/28/06; Joe Sharky, "For the Super-Rich, It's Time to Upgrade the Old Jumbo Jet," *NY Times* 10/17/06; Guy Trebay, "For a Price, Final Resting Place that Tut Would Find Pleasant" *NY Times* 4/17/06.

Article 2.2

MEASURES OF POVERTY

BY ELLEN FRANK
January/February 2006, updated May 2009

> Dear Dr. Dollar:
> *Can you explain how poverty is defined in government statistics? Is this a realistic definition?*
> —Susan Balok, Savannah, Ga.

Each February, the Census Bureau publishes the federal poverty thresholds—the income levels for different sized households below which a household is defined as living "in poverty." Each August, the bureau reports how many families, children, adults, and senior citizens fell below the poverty threshold in the prior year. As of 2008, the federal poverty thresholds were as follows:

Using these income levels, the Census Bureau reported that 12.5% percent of U.S. residents and 18.0% of U.S. children lived in poverty in 2007. Black Americans experience poverty at nearly double these rates: 24.5% of all Blacks and 34.5% of Black children live in households with incomes below the poverty line.

The poverty threshold concept was originally devised by Social Security analyst Mollie Orshansky in 1963. Orshansky estimated the cost of an "economy food plan" designed by the Department of Agriculture for "emergency use when funds are low." Working from 1955 data showing that families of three or more spent one-third of their income on food, Orshansky multiplied the food budget by three to calculate the poverty line. Since the early 1960s, the Census Bureau has simply re-calculated Orshansky's original figures to account for inflation.

The poverty line is widely regarded as far too low for a household to survive on in most parts of the United States. For one thing, as antipoverty advocates point out, since 1955 the proportion of family budgets devoted to food has fallen from one-third to one-fifth. Families ex-pend far more on non-food necessities such as child care, health care, transportation, and utilities today than they did 50 years ago, for obvious reasons: mothers entering the work force, suburbanization and greater dependence on

Household Size	Federal Poverty Threshold
1 person	$11,201
2 people	14,417
3 people	17,330
4 people	21,834
5 people	25,694

the auto, and soaring health care costs, for example. Were Orshansky formulating a poverty threshold more recently, then, she would likely have multiplied a basic food budget by five rather than by three.

Furthermore, costs—particularly for housing and energy—vary widely across the country, so that an income that might be barely adequate in Mississippi is wholly inadequate in Massachusetts. Yet federal poverty figures make no adjustment for regional differences in costs.

A number of state-level organizations now publish their own estimates of what it takes to support a family in their area, in conjunction with the national training and advocacy group Wider Opportunities for Women. Using local data on housing costs, health care premiums, taxes, and child care costs as well as food, transportation and other necessities, these "self-sufficiency standards" estimate that a two-parent two-child family needs between $40,000 and $70,000 a year, depending on the region, to cover basic needs.

State and federal officials often implicitly recognize that official poverty thresholds are unrealistically low by setting income eligibility criteria for antipoverty programs higher than the poverty level. Households with incomes of 125%, 150%, or even 185% of the federal poverty line are eligible for a number of federal and state programs. In addition, the Census Bureau publishes figures on the number of households with incomes below 200% of the federal poverty line—a level many social scientists call "near poor" or "working poor."

Poverty calculations also have critics on the right. Conservative critics contend that the official poverty rate overstates poverty in the United States. While the Census Bureau's poverty-rate calculations include Social Security benefits, public assistance, unemployment and workers' compensation, SSI (disability) payments, and other forms of cash income, they exclude noncash benefits from state and federal antipoverty programs like Food Stamps, Medicaid, and housing subsidies. If the market value of these benefits were counted in family income, fewer families would count as "poor." On the other hand, by not counting such benefits, policy makers have a better grasp of the numbers of Americans in need of such transfer programs.

Resources: For background information on poverty thresholds and poverty rate calculations, see aspe.hhs.gov/poverty/papers/hptgssiv.htm. Self-sufficiency standards for different states can be found at www.sixstrategies.org/states/states.cfm. In addition, the Economic Policy Institute has calculated family budgets for the 435 metropolitan areas: www.epi.org/content/budget_calculator.

Article 2.3

ACCESS TO PAID SICK DAYS VASTLY UNEQUAL

BY ELISE GOULD
September/October 2007

Just 57% of private-industry workers in the United States have access to paid sick leave; 43% have no paid sick days. When these workers get sick, they are forced either to stay home, without pay and, in many cases, with some risk of losing their job, or else to go to work.

What this number masks, however, is how vastly unequal access to paid sick leave is for workers at different wage levels. Workers at the bottom of the wage scale, those making less than $7.38 an hour, are five times less likely to have sick days than workers at the top of the scale, those making greater than $29.47 an hour. As the figure reveals, only 16% of low-wage workers have access to paid sick days, versus 79% of high-wage workers.

In recent months, legislation has been introduced that would level the playing field and provide much needed paid leave for all workers who are sick. Such legislation—as exists in other advanced economies—would not only give workers an important benefit. Universal paid sick leave could increase productivity by strengthening worker loyalty, decreasing turnover, and cutting down on the number of sick employees who show up to work and infect others.

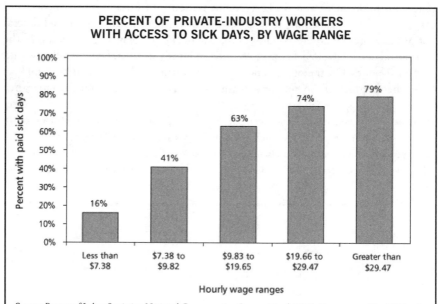

PERCENT OF PRIVATE-INDUSTRY WORKERS WITH ACCESS TO SICK DAYS, BY WAGE RANGE

Source: Bureau of Labor Statistics, National Compensation Survey, March 2006. Data prepared by EPI for the Center for American Progress Task Force on Poverty.

Article 2.4

THE DEATH OF HORATIO ALGER

BY PAUL KRUGMAN
January 2004

The other day I found myself reading a leftist rag that made outrageous claims about America. It said that we are becoming a society in which the poor tend to stay poor, no matter how hard they work; in which sons are much more likely to inherit the socioeconomic status of their fathers than they were a generation ago.

The name of the leftist rag? *Business Week*, which published an article titled "Waking Up From the American Dream." The article summarizes recent research showing that social mobility in the United States (which was never as high as legend had it) has declined considerably over the past few decades. If you put that research together with other research that shows a drastic increase in income and wealth inequality, you reach an uncomfortable conclusion: America looks more and more like a class-ridden society.

And guess what? Our political leaders are doing everything they can to fortify class inequality, while denouncing anyone who complains—or even points out what is happening—as a practitioner of "class warfare."

Let's talk first about the facts on income distribution. Thirty years ago we were a relatively middle-class nation. It had not always been thus: Gilded Age America was a highly unequal society, and it stayed that way through the 1920s. During the 1930s and '40s, however, America experienced what the economic historians Claudia Goldin and Robert Margo have dubbed the Great Compression: a drastic narrowing of income gaps, probably as a result of New Deal policies. And the new economic order persisted for more than a generation. Strong unions, taxes on inherited wealth, corporate profits and high incomes, and close public scrutiny of corporate management all helped to keep income gaps relatively small. The economy was hardly egalitarian, but a generation ago the gross inequalities of the 1920s seemed very distant.

Now they're back. According to estimates by the economists Thomas Piketty and Emmanuel Saez—confirmed by data from the Congressional Budget Office—between 1973 and 2000 the average real income of the bottom 90% of American taxpayers actually fell by 7%. Meanwhile, the income of the top 1% rose by 148%, the income of the top 0.1% rose by 343% and the income of the top 0.01% rose 599%. (Those numbers exclude capital gains, so they're not an artifact of the stock-market bubble.) The distribution of income in the United States has gone right back to Gilded Age levels of inequality.

Never mind, say the apologists, who churn out papers with titles like that of a 2001 Heritage Foundation piece, "Income Mobility and the Fallacy of Class-Warfare Arguments." America, they say, isn't a caste society—people with high incomes this year may have low incomes next year and vice versa, and the route to wealth is open to all. That's where those commies at *Business Week* come in. As they point out (and as economists and sociologists have been pointing out for some time), America actually is more of a caste society than we like to think. And the caste lines have lately become a lot more rigid.

The myth of income mobility has always exceeded the reality. As a general rule, once they've reached their 30s, people don't move up and down the income ladder very much. Conservatives often cite studies like a 1992 report by Glenn Hubbard, a Treasury official under the elder Bush who later became chief economic adviser to the younger Bush, that purport to show large numbers of Americans moving from low-wage to high-wage jobs during their working lives. But what these studies measure, as the economist Kevin Murphy put it, is mainly "the guy who works in the college bookstore and has a real job by his early 30s." Serious studies that exclude this sort of pseudo-mobility show that inequality in average incomes over long periods isn't much smaller than inequality in annual incomes.

It is true, however, that America was once a place of substantial intergenerational mobility—sons often did much better than their fathers. A classic 1978 survey found that among adult men whose fathers were in the bottom 25% of the population as ranked by social and economic status, 23% had made it into the top 25%. In other words, during the first thirty years or so after World War II, the American dream of upward mobility was a real experience for many people.

Now for the shocker: The *Business Week* piece cites a new survey of today's adult men, which finds that this number has dropped to only 10%. That is, over the past generation upward mobility has fallen drastically. Very few children of the lower class are making their way to even moderate affluence. This goes along with other studies indicating that rags-to-riches stories have become vanishingly rare, and that the correlation between fathers' and sons' incomes has risen in recent decades. In modern America, it seems, you're quite likely to stay in the social and economic class into which you were born.

Business Week attributes this to the "Wal-Martization" of the economy, the proliferation of dead-end, low-wage jobs and the disappearance of jobs that provide entry to the middle class. That's surely part of the explanation. But public policy plays a role—and will, if present trends continue, play an even bigger role in the future.

Put it this way: Suppose that you actually liked a caste society, and you were seeking ways to use your control of the government to further entrench the advantages of the haves against the have-nots. What would you do?

One thing you would definitely do is get rid of the estate tax, so that large fortunes can be passed on to the next generation. More broadly, you would seek to reduce tax rates both on corporate profits and on unearned income such as dividends and capital gains, so that those with large accumulated or inherited wealth could more easily accumulate even more. You'd also try to create tax shelters mainly useful for the rich. And more broadly still, you'd try to reduce tax rates on people with high incomes, shifting the burden to the payroll tax and other revenue sources that bear most heavily on people with lower incomes.

Meanwhile, on the spending side, you'd cut back on healthcare for the poor, on the quality of public education and on state aid for higher education. This would make it more difficult for people with low incomes to climb out of their difficulties and acquire the education essential to upward mobility in the modern economy.

And just to close off as many routes to upward mobility as possible, you'd do everything possible to break the power of unions, and you'd privatize government functions so that well-paid civil servants could be replaced with poorly paid private employees.

It all sounds sort of familiar, doesn't it?

Where is this taking us? Thomas Piketty, whose work with Saez has transformed our understanding of income distribution, warns that current policies will eventually create "a class of rentiers in the U.S., whereby a small group of wealthy but untalented children controls vast segments of the US economy and penniless, talented children simply can't compete." If he's right—and I fear that he is—we will end up suffering not only from injustice, but from a vast waste of human potential.

Goodbye, Horatio Alger. And goodbye, American Dream.

Reprinted with permission from the January 5, 2004 issue of *The Nation*. For subscription information call 1-800-333-8536. Portions of each week's Nation Magazine can be accessed at www.thenation.com

Article 2.5

GEESE, GOLDEN EGGS, AND TRAPS
Why inequality is bad for the economy.

BY CHRIS TILLY
July/August 2004

Whenever progressives propose ways to redistribute wealth from the rich to those with low and moderate incomes, conservative politicians and economists accuse them of trying to kill the goose that lays the golden egg. The advocates of unfettered capitalism proclaim that inequality is good for the economy because it promotes economic growth. Unequal incomes, they say, provide the incentives necessary to guide productive economic decisions by businesses and individuals. Try to reduce inequality, and you'll sap growth. Furthermore, the conservatives argue, growth actually promotes equality by boosting the have-nots more than the haves. So instead of fiddling with who gets how much, the best way to help those at the bottom is to pump up growth.

But these conservative prescriptions are absolutely, dangerously wrong. Instead of the goose-killer, equality turns out to be the goose. Inequality stifles growth; equality gooses it up. Moreover, economic expansion does not necessarily promote equality—instead, it is the types of jobs and the rules of the economic game that matter most.

Inequality: Goose or Goose-Killer?

The conservative argument may be wrong, but it's straightforward. Inequality is good for the economy, conservatives say, because it provides the right incentives for innovation and economic growth. First of all, people will only have the motivation to work hard, innovate, and invest wisely if the economic system rewards them for good economic choices and penalizes bad ones. Robin Hood-style policies that collect from the wealthy and help those who are worse off violate this principle. They reduce the payoff to smart decisions and lessen the sting of dumb ones. The result: people and companies are bound to make less efficient decisions. "We must allow [individuals] to fail, as well as succeed, and we must replace the nanny state with a regime of self-reliance and self-respect," writes conservative lawyer Stephen Kinsella in *The Freeman: Ideas on Liberty* (not clear how the free woman fits in). To prove their point, conservatives point to the former state socialist countries, whose economies had become stagnant and inefficient by the time they fell at the end of the 1980s.

If you don't buy this incentive story, there's always the well-worn trickle-down theory. To grow, the economy needs productive investments: new offices, factories, computers, and machines. To finance such investments takes a pool of savings. The rich save a larger fraction of their incomes than those less well-off. So to spur growth, give more to the well-heeled (or at least take less away from them in the form of taxes), and give less to the down-and-out. The rich will save their money and then invest it, promoting growth that's good for everyone.

Unfortunately for trickle-down, the brilliant economist John Maynard Keynes debunked the theory in his *General Theory of Employment, Interest, and Money* in 1936. Keynes, whose precepts guided liberal U.S. economic policy from the 1940s through the 1970s, agreed that investments must be financed out of savings. But he showed that most often it's changes in investment that drive savings, rather than the other way around. When businesses are optimistic about the future and invest in building and retooling, the economy booms, all of us make more money, and we put some of it in banks, 401(k)s, stocks, and so on. That is, saving grows to match investment. When companies are glum, the process runs in reverse, and savings shrink to equal investment. This leads to the "paradox of thrift": if people try to save too much, busi-nesses will see less consumer spending, will invest less, and total savings will end up diminishing rather than growing as the economy spirals downward. A number of Keynes's followers added the next logical step: shifting money from the high-saving rich to the high-spending rest of us, and not the other way around, will spur investment and growth.

Of the two conservative arguments in favor of in-equality, the incentive argument is a little weightier. Keynes himself agreed that people needed financial consequences to steer their actions, but questioned whether the differences in payoffs needed to be so huge. Certainly state socialist countries' attempts to replace material incentives with moral exhortation have often fallen short. In 1970, the Cuban government launched the Gran Zafra (Great Harvest), an attempt to reap 10 million tons of sugar cane with (strongly encouraged) volunteer labor. Originally inspired by Che Guevara's Ideal of the New Socialist Man (not clear how the New Socialist Woman fit in), the effort ended with Fidel Castro tearfully apologizing to the Cuban people in a nationally broadcast speech for letting wishful thinking guide economic policy.

But before conceding this point to the conservatives, let's look at the evidence about the connection between equality and growth. Economists William Easterly of New York University and Gary Fields of Cornell University have recently summarized this evidence:

- Countries, and regions within countries, with more equal incomes grow faster. (These growth figures do not include environmental destruction or improvement. If they knocked off points for environmental destruction and added points for environmental improvement, the correlation between equality and growth would be even stronger, since desperation drives poor people to adopt environmentally destructive practices such as rapid deforestation.)
- Countries with more equally distributed land grow faster.
- Somewhat disturbingly, more ethnically homogeneous countries and regions grow faster—presumably because there are fewer ethnically based inequalities.
- In addition, more worker rights are associated with higher rates of economic growth, according to Josh Bivens and Christian Weller, economists at two Washington think tanks, the Economic Policy Institute and the Center for American Progress.

These patterns recommend a second look at the incentive question. In fact, more equality can actually strengthen incentives and opportunities to produce.

Equality as the Goose

Equality can boost growth in several ways. Perhaps the simplest is that study after study has shown that farmland is more productive when cultivated in small plots. So organizations promoting more equal distribution of land, like Brazil's Landless Workers' Movement, are not just helping the landless poor—they're contributing to agricultural productivity!

Another reason for the link between equality and growth is what Easterly calls "match effects," which have been highlighted in research by Stanford's Paul Roemer and others in recent years. One example of a match effect is the fact that well-educated people are most productive when working with others who have lots of schooling. Likewise, people working with computers are more productive when many others have computers (so that, for example, e-mail communication is widespread, and know-how about computer repair and software is easy to come by). In very unequal societies, highly educated, computer-using elites are surrounded by majorities with little education and no computer access, dragging down their productivity. This decreases young people's incentive to get more education and businesses' incentive to invest in computers, since the payoff will be smaller.

Match effects can even matter at the level of a metropolitan area. Urban economist Larry Ledebur looked at income and employment growth in 85 U.S. cities and their neighboring suburbs. He found that where the income gap between those in the suburbs and those in the city was largest, income and job growth was slower for everyone.

"Pressure effects" also help explain why equality sparks growth. Policies that close off the low-road strategy of exploiting poor and working people create pressure effects, driving economic elites to search for investment opportunities that pay off by boosting productivity rather than squeezing the have-nots harder. For example, where workers have more rights, they will place greater demands on businesses. Business owners will respond by trying to increase productivity, both to remain profitable even after paying higher wages, and to find ways to produce with fewer workers. The CIO union drives in U.S. mass production industries in the 1930s and 1940s provide much of the explanation for the superb productivity growth of the 1950s and 1960s. (The absence of pressure effects may help explain why many past and present state socialist countries have seen slow growth, since they tend to offer numerous protections for workers but no right to organize independent unions.) Similarly, if a government buys out large land-holdings in order to break them up, wealthy families who simply kept their fortunes tied up in land for generations will look for new, productive investments. Industrialization in Asian "tigers" South Korea and Taiwan took off in the 1950s on the wings of funds freed up in exactly this way.

Inequality, Conflict, and Growth

Inequality hinders growth in another important way: it fuels social conflict. Stark inequality in countries such as Bolivia and Haiti has led to chronic conflict that hobbles economic growth. Moreover, inequality ties up resources in unproductive uses such as paying for large numbers of police and security guards—attempts to prevent individuals from redistributing resources through theft.

Ethnic variety is connected to slower growth because,on the average, more ethnically diverse countries are also more likely to be ethnically divided. In other words, the problem isn't ethnic variety itself, but racism and ethnic conflict that can exist among diverse populations. In nations like Guatemala, Congo, and Nigeria, ethnic strife has crippled growth—a problem alien to ethnically uniform Japan and South Korea. The reasons are similar to some of the reasons that large class divides hurt growth. Where ethnic divisions (which can take tribal, language, religious, racial, or regional forms) loom large, dominant ethnic groups seek to use government power to better themselves at the expense of other groups, rather than making broad-based investments in education and infrastructure. This can involve keeping down the underdogs—slower growth in the U.S. South for much of the country's history was linked to the Southern system of white supremacy. Or it can involve seizing the surplus of ethnic groups perceived as better off—in the extreme, Nazi Germany's expropriation and genocide of the Jews, who often held professional and commercial jobs.

Of course, the solution to such divisions is not "ethnic cleansing" so that each country has only one ethnic group—in addition to being morally abhorrent, this is simply impossible in a world with 191 countries and 5,000 ethnic groups. Rather, the solution is to diminish ethnic inequalities. Once the 1964 Civil Rights Act forced the South to drop racist laws, the New South's economic growth spurt began. Easterly reports that in countries with strong rule of law, professional bureaucracies, protection of contracts, and freedom from expropriation—all rules that make it harder for one ethnic group to economically oppress another—ethnic diversity has no negative impact on growth.

If more equality leads to faster growth so everybody benefits, why do the rich typically resist redistribution? Looking at the ways that equity seeds growth helps us understand why. The importance of pressure effects tells us that the wealthy often don't think about more productive ways to invest or reorganize their businesses until they are forced to. But also, if a country becomes very unequal, it can get stuck in an "inequality trap." Any redistribution involves a tradeoff for the rich. They lose by giving up part of their wealth, but they gain a share in increased economic growth. The bigger the disparity between the rich and the rest, the more the rich have to lose, and the less likely that the equal share of boosted growth they'll get will make up for their loss. Once the gap goes beyond a certain point, the wealthy have a strong incentive to restrict democracy, and to block spending on education which might lead the poor to challenge economic injustice—making reform that much harder.

Does Economic Growth Reduce Inequality?

If inequality isn't actually good for the economy, what about the second part of the conservatives' argument—that growth itself promotes equality? According to the conservatives, those who care about equality should simply pursue growth and wait for equality to follow.

"A rising tide lifts all boats," President John F. Kennedy famously declared. But he said nothing about which boats will rise fastest when the economic tide comes in.

Growth does typically reduce poverty, according to studies reviewed by economist Gary Fields, though some "boats"—especially families with strong barriers to participating in the labor force—stay "stuck in the mud." But inequality can increase at the same time that poverty falls, if the rich gain even faster than the poor do. True, sustained periods of low unemployment, like that in the late 1990s United States, do tend to raise wages at the bottom even faster than salaries at the top. But growth after the recessions of 1991 and 2001 began with years of "jobless recoveries"—growth with inequality.

For decades the prevailing view about growth and inequality within countries was that expressed by Simon Kuznets in his 1955 presidential address to the American Economic Association. Kuznets argued that as countries grew, inequality would first increase, then decrease. The reason is that people will gradually move from the low-income agricultural sector to higher-income industrial jobs—with inequality peaking when the workforce is equally divided between low- and high-income sectors. For mature industrial economies, Kuznets's proposition counsels focusing on growth, assuming that it will bring equity. In developing countries, it calls for enduring current inequality for the sake of future equity and prosperity.

But economic growth doesn't automatically fuel equality. In 1998, economists Klaus Deininger and Lyn Squire traced inequality and growth over time in 48 countries. Five followed the Kuznets pattern, four followed the reverse pattern (decreasing inequality followed by an increase), and the rest showed no systematic pattern. In the United States, for example:

- incomes became more equal during the 1930s through 1940s New Deal period (a time that included economic decline followed by growth);
- from the 1950s through the 1970s, income gaps lessened during booms and expanded during slumps;
- from the late 1970s forward, income inequality worsened fairly consistently, whether the economy was stagnating or growing.

The reasons are not hard to guess. The New Deal intro-duced widespread unionization, a minimum wage, social security, unemployment insurance, and welfare. Since the late 1970s, unions have declined, the inflation-adjusted value of the minimum wage has fallen, and the social safety net has been shredded. In the United States, as elsewhere, growth only promotes equality if policies and institutions to support equity are in place.

Trapped?

Let's revisit the idea of an inequality trap. The notion is that as the gap between the rich and everybody else grows wider, the wealthy become more willing to give up overall growth in return for the larger share they're getting for themselves. The "haves" back policies to control the "have-nots," instead of devoting social resources to educating the poor so they'll be more productive.

Sound familiar? It should. After two decades of widening inequality, the last few years have brought us massive tax cuts that primarily benefit the wealthiest, at the expense of investment in infrastructure and the education, child care, and income supports that would help raise less well-off kids to be productive adults. Federal and state governments have cranked up expenditures on prisons, police, and "homeland security," and Republican campaign organizations have devoted major resources to keeping blacks and the poor away from the polls. If the economic patterns of the past are any indication, we're going to pay for these policies in slower growth and stagnation unless we can find our way out of this inequality trap.

Article 2.6

TRANSFORMING THE ENGINES OF INEQUALITY

BY WILLIAM GREIDER
September 2003

American politics has always involved a struggle between "organized money" and "organized people." It's a neglected truth that has resurfaced with ironic vengeance in our own time—ironic because the 20th century produced so much progress toward political equality among citizens, and because the emergence of a prosperous and well-educated middle class was expected to neutralize the overbearing political power of concentrated wealth. Instead, Americans are reminded, almost any time they read a newspaper, that the rich do indeed get richer and that our political system is, as Greg Palast put it, "the best democracy money can buy."

What should we make of this retrogressive turn—a nation of considerable abundance still ruled by gilded-age privilege? A cynic would say it was ever thus, end of story. Political commentators argue it's a sign of the country's maturation that its citizens now accept what they once resisted—gross and growing inequalities of wealth. And many economists simply avert their gaze from the troubling consequences of maldistribution for economic progress and the well-being of society.

I stake out a contrary claim: The United States remains an unfinished nation— stunted in its proclaimed values—so long as it fails to confront the enduring contradictions between wealth and democracy. That is not a utopian lament for radical change, but simply an observation of what our own era has taught us.

Inequality retains its crippling force over society and politics and the lives of citizens, despite the broader distribution of material comforts. We are not the nation of 80 or 100 years ago, when most Americans struggled in very modest circumstances, often severe deprivation. Yet, despite the nation's wealth (perhaps also because of it), the influence of concentrated economic power has grown stronger and more intimate in our lives. Today the social contract is determined more by the needs and demands of corporations and finance than by government or the consensual will of the people.

The federal government and several generations of liberal and labor reformers did achieve great, life-improving gains during the last century. But those reforms and redistributive programs did not succeed in altering the root sources of economic inequality, much less taming them. On the contrary, the U.S. economic system recreates and even expands the maldistribution of incomes and wealth in each new generation.

The root sources of inequality are located within the institutions of advanced capitalism—in the corporation and financial system—with their narrow operating values and the peculiar arrangements that consign enormous decision-making power to a remarkably small number of people. The problem of inequality is essentially a problem of malformed power relationships: Advanced capitalism deprives most people of voice and influence, while it concentrates top-down authority among the insiders of finance and business. Ameliorative interventions by government (for example, through regulation, taxation, and reform) have never succeeded in overcoming the tendency within capitalism toward increased concentrations of economic power.

The drive for greater equality must involve governmental actions, of course, but it cannot succeed unless it also confronts the engines of inequality within the private realm and forces deep changes in how American capitalism functions. The challenge is nothing less than to rearrange power relationships within the corporation and finance capital.

Who has the power to restructure capitalist institutions? In my view, ordinary people do—at least potentially—acting collectively as workers, investors, consumers, managers or owners and, above all, as citizens, to force change. Many are, in small and different ways, already at work on the task of reinventing capitalism.

Transforming the Workplace

The workplace is perhaps the most effective engine of inequality, since it teaches citizens resignation and subservience, while it also maldistributes the returns of enterprise. For most Americans, the employment system functions on the archaic terms of the master-servant relationship inherited from feudalism. The feudal lord commanded the lives and livelihoods of serfs on his land and expelled those who disobeyed. The corporate employer has remarkably similar powers, restrained only by the limited prohibitions in law or perhaps by the terms of a union contract. Elaine Bernard, director of Harvard's trade union studies program, described the blunt reality:

> As power is presently distributed, workplaces are factories of authoritarianism polluting our democracy. Citizens cannot spend eight hours a day obeying orders and being shut out of important decisions affecting them, and then be expected to engage in a robust, critical dialogue about the structure of our society.

Where did people learn to accept their powerlessness? They learned it at work. Nor is this stunted condition confined to assembly lines and working-class occupations. The degradation of work now extends very far up the job ladder, including even well-educated professionals whose expert judgments have been usurped by distant management systems.

In most firms, only the insiders at the top of a very steep command-and-control pyramid will determine how the economic returns are distributed among the participants. Not surprisingly, the executives value their own work quite generously while regarding most of the employees below as mere commodities or easily interchangeable parts. More importantly, these insiders will harvest the new wealth generated by an enterprise, while most workers will not. In the long run, this arrangement of power guarantees the permanence of wealth inequalities.

Joseph Cabral, CEO of Chatsworth Products Inc., a successful employee-owned computer systems manufacturer in California, is an accountant, not a political philosopher, but he understands the wealth effects of closely held control in private businesses. "The wealth that's created ends up in too few hands," he said. "The entrepreneur who's fortunate enough to be there at the start ends up really receiving a disproportionate amount of wealth. And the working folks who enabled that success to take place share in little of that wealth. At some point, capitalism is going to burst because we haven't done right for the folks who have actually created that wealth."

But there are other, more democratic, ways to structure the work environment. At Chatsworth, where the workers collectively purchased the enterprise, "Everyone is sharing in the wealth they're creating. ... We're not just doing this for some outside shareholder. We're doing it because we are the shareholders."

Employee ownership, worker-management, and other systems of worker self-organization provide a plausible route toward reforming workplace power relations and spreading financial wealth among the many instead of the few.

Transforming Finance Capital

The top-down structure of how Wall Street manages "other people's money" ensures the maldistribution of financial returns. As wealthy people know, those who bring major money to the table are given direct influence over their investments and a greater return on their risk-taking. The rank-and-file investors—because their savings are modest and they lack trustworthy intermediaries to speak for them—are regarded as passive and uninformed, treated more or less like "widows and orphans," and blocked from exerting any influence over how their wealth is invested. To put the point more crudely, the stock market is a casino, and the herd of hapless investors is always the "mark."

Nevertheless, finance capital is, I predict, the realm of capitalism most vulnerable to reform pressures. That's mainly because it operates with other people's money, and most of that money belongs not to the wealthiest families but to the broad ranks of ordinary working people. A historic shift in the center of gravity has occurred in U.S. finance over the past decade: Fiduciary institutions like pension funds and mutual funds have eclipsed individual wealth as the largest owner of financial assets. Their collectivized assets now include 60% of the largest 1,000 corporations. Because these funds invest across the broad stock market, they literally own the economy.

Public pension funds, union-managed pension funds, and shareholder activists are already working to forge an engaged voice for the individuals whose wealth is in play, and to force the fiduciary institutions to take responsibility for the social and environmental effects of how these trillions in savings are invested. The collapse of the stock-market bubble and subsequent corporate scandals have accelerated these reform efforts.

Some of the largest public-employee pension funds including the California Public Employees' Retirement System and the New York State public employees fund, joined by state officials who sit on supervisory boards, are aggressively leading the fight for corporate-governance reform and for stricter social accountability on urgent matters like workers' rights and global warming. The labor movement is organizing proxy battles to press for corporate reforms at individual companies including the Disney Corporation and Royal Dutch Shell, while the AFL's Office of Investment won a victory for mutual-fund investors in early 2003 when it persuaded the Securities and Exchange Commission to require mutual funds to disclose their proxy votes in corporate-governance shareholder fights. (The mutual fund industry is working to resist the measure, and for good reason. Investment firms regularly vote against the interests of their own rank-and-file investors in order to curry favor with the corporations that hire them to manage corporate-run pension funds and 401(k) plans.)

The major banks and brokerages cannot brush aside these new critics as easily as corporate directors often do. Wall Street will respond to fiduciary concerns because it must. It needs the rank-and-file's capital to operate. When six or seven major funds, collectively holding nearly $1 trillion, speak to Wall Street, things do change. Their unspoken threat to scorn companies or financial firms that ignore larger social obligations and shift their money elsewhere sends broad shockwaves across both financial markets and corporate boardrooms.

The more profound tasks are to challenge fraudulent economic valuations (think Enron) and to account for (and internalize) the true costs of products and production processes. Both steps would refocus capital investing toward creating real, long-term value and away from the transient thrill of quarterly returns. The fiduciary funds have the potential power to enforce this new economic perspective, though it is not yet widely understood or accepted by them. As universal owners of the economy, their own portfolios are the losers when individual corporations throw off externalities in order to boost their bottom lines. The costs will be borne by every other firm, by the economy as a whole, or by taxpayers who have to clean up the mess. The compelling logic of this new economic argument is this: what is bad for society cannot be good for future retirees or for their communities and their families.

Citizens, in other words, have more power than they imagine. If they assert influence over these intermediaries, they have the power to punish rogue corporations for anti-social behavior and block the low-road practices that have become so popular in business circles. In coalition with organized labor, environmentalists, and other engaged citizens, they have the capacity to design—and enforce—a new social contract that encourages, among other things, participatory management systems and worker ownership, loyalty to community, and respect for our deeper social values.

While none of this promises a utopian outcome of perfect equality, the redistribution of power within capitalism is certainly a predicate for the creation of a more equitable society.

My conviction is that we are on the brink of a broad new reform era, in which reorganizing capitalism becomes the principal objective. What I foresee is a long, steady mobilization of people attempting to do things differently, often in small and local settings, trying out new arrangements, sometimes failing, then trying again. As these inventive departures succeed, others will emulate them. In time, an alternative social reality will emerge with different values, alongside the archaic and destructive system that now exists. When that begins to happen and gains sufficient visibility, the politics is sure to follow. If all this sounds too remote to the present facts, too patient for our frenetic age, remember that this is how deep change has always occurred across American history.

This article is adapted from The Soul of Capitalism *(Simon & Schuster, 2003).*

Article 2.7

RICH AND POOR IN THE GLOBAL ECONOMY
Interview with Bob Sutcliffe

March/April 2005

Whether economic inequality is rising or falling globally is a matter of intense debate, a key question in the larger dispute over how three decades of intensified economic global-ization have affected the world's poor. Bob Sutcliffe is an economist at the University of the Basque Country in Bilbao, Spain, and the author of 100 Ways of Seeing an Un-equal World. *He has been analyzing both the statistical details and the broader politi-cal-economic import of the debate and shared some of his insights in a recent interview with* Dollars & Sense.

DOLLARS & SENSE: If someone asked you whether global inequality has grown over the past 25 years, I assume you'd say, "It depends—on how inequality is defined, on what data is used, on how that data is analyzed." Is that fair?

BOB SUTCLIFFE: Yes, it's fair, but it's not enough. First, the most basic fact about world inequality is that it is monstrously large; that result is inescapable, whatever the method or definition. As to its direction of change in the last 25 years, to some extent there are different answers. But also there are different questions. Inequality is not a simple one-dimensional concept that can be reduced to a single number. Single overall measures of world inequality (where all incomes are taken into ac-count) give a different result from measures of the relation of the extremes (the rich-est compared with the poorest). Over the last 25 years, you find that the bottom half of world income earners seems to have gained something in relation to the top half (so, in this sense, there is less inequality), but the bottom 10% have lost seriously in comparison with the top 10% (thus, more inequality), and the bottom 1% have lost enormously in relation to the top 1% (much more inequality). None of these mea-sures is a single true measure of inequality; they are all part of a complex structure of inequalities, some of which can lessen as part of the same overall process in which others increase.

We do have to be clear about one data-related question that has caused huge confusion. To look at the distribution of income in the world, you have to reduce incomes of different countries to one standard. Traditionally it has been done by using exchange rates; this makes inequality appear to change when exchange rates change, which is misleading. But now we have data based on "purchasing power par-ity" (the comparative buying power, or real equivalence, of currencies). Using PPP values achieves for comparisons over space what inflation-adjusted index numbers have achieved for comparisons over time. Although many problems remain with PPP values, they are the only way to make coherent comparisons of incomes between countries. But they produce estimates that are astonishingly different from exchange rate-based calculations. For instance, U.S. income per head is 34 times Chinese in-come per head using exchange rates, but only 8 times as great using PPP values.

(And, incidentally, on PPP estimates the total size of the U.S. economy is now only 1.7 times that of China, and is likely to be overtaken by it by 2011.) So when you make this apparently technical choice between two methods of converting one currency to another, you come up not only with different figures on income distribution but also with two totally different world economic, and thus political, perspectives.

D&S: So even if some consensus were reached on the choices of definition, data, and method, you're urging a complex, nuanced portrait of what is happening to global inequality, rather than a yes or no answer. Could you give a brief outline of what you think that portrait looks like?

BS: Most integral measures—integral meaning including the entire population rather than comparing the extremes—that use PPP figures suggest that overall income distribution at the global level during the last 25 years has shown a slight decline in inequality, though there is some dissent on this. In any event this conclusion is tremendously affected by China, a country with a fifth of world population which has been growing economically at an unprecedented rate. Second, there seems to me little room for debate over the fact that the relative difference between the very rich and the very poor has gotten worse. And the smaller the extreme proportions you compare, the greater the gap. So the immensely rich have done especially well in the last 25 years, while the extremely poor have done very badly. The top one-tenth of U.S. citizens now receive a total income equal to that of the poorest 2.2 billion people in the rest of the world.

There have also been clear trends within some countries. Some of the fastest growing countries have become considerably more unequal. China is an example, along with some other industrializing countries like Thailand. The most economically liberal of the developed countries have also become much more unequal—for instance, the United States, the United Kingdom, and Australia—and so have the post-communist countries. The most extreme figures for inequality are found in a group of poor countries including Namibia and Botswana in southern Africa and Paraguay and Panama in Latin America.

Finally, the overall index of world inequality (measured by the Gini coefficient, a measure of income distribution) is about the same as that for two infamously unequal countries, South Africa and Brazil. And in the last few years it has shown no signs of improvement whatsoever.

D&S: People use the terms "unimodal" and "bimodal" to describe the global distribution of income. Can you explain what these mean? Also, you have referred elsewhere to a possible trimodal distribution—what does that refer to?

BS: The mode of a distribution is its most common value. In many countries there is one level of income around which a large proportion of the population clusters; at higher or lower levels of income there are progressively fewer people, so the distribution curve rises to a peak and then falls off. That is a unimodal distribution. But in South Africa, for example, due to the continued existence of entrenched ethnic division and economic inequality, the curve of distribution has two peaks—a low one, the most common income received by black citizens, and another, higher one, the the most common received by whites. This is a bimodal distribution because there are two values that are relatively more common than those above or below them. Because of its origins you could call it the "Apartheid distribution." The world distribution is in many respects uncannily like that of South Africa. It could be becoming trimodal in the sense that the frequency distribution of income has three peaks— one including those in very poor countries which have not been growing economically (e.g., parts of Africa), one in those developing countries which really have been developing (e.g., in South and East Asia), and one in the high-income industrialized countries. It's a kind of "apartheid plus" form of distribution.

D&S: In 2002, you wrote that many institutions, like the United Nations and the World Bank, were not being exactly honest in this debate—for example, emphasizing results based on data or methods that they elsewhere acknowledged to be poor. Has this changed over the past few years? Has the quality of the debate over trends in global income inequality improved?

BS: The most egregious pieces of statistical opportunism have declined. But I think there is a strong tendency in general for institutions to seize on optimistic conclusions regarding distribution in order to placate critics of the present world order. This increasingly takes the form of putting too much weight on measures of welfare other than income, for instance, life expectancy, for which there has been more international convergence than in the case of income. But there has been very little discussion of the philosophical basis for using life expectancy instead of or combined with income to measure inequality. If poor people live longer but in income terms remain as relatively poor as ever, has the world become less unequal?

The problem of statistical opportunism is not confined to those who are defending the world economic order; it also exists on the left. So, on the question of inequality, there is a tendency to accept whatever numerical estimate shows greatest inequality on the false assumption that this confirms the wickedness of capitalism. But capitalist inequality is so great that the willful exaggeration of it is not needed as the basis of anti-capitalist propaganda. It is more important for the left to look at the best indicators of the changing state of capitalism, including indicators of inequality, in order to intervene more effectively.

Finally, the quality of the debate, regardless of the intentions of the participants, is still greatly restricted by the shortage of available statistics about inequalities. That has improved somewhat in recent years although there are many things about past and present inequalities which we shall probably never know.

D&S: Do you see any contexts in which it's more important to focus on absolute poverty levels and trends in those levels rather than on inequality?

BS: The short answer is no, I do not. Plans for minimum income guarantees or for reducing the number of people lacking basic necessities can be important. But poverty always has a relative as well as an absolute component. It is a major weakness of the Millenium Development Goals, for example, that they talk about halving the number of people in absolute extreme poverty without a single mention of inequality. [The Millenium Development Goals is a U.N. program aimed at eliminating extreme poverty and achieving certain other development goals worldwide by 2015. —*Eds*.] And there is now a very active campaign on the part of anti-egalitarian, pro-capitalist ideologues in favor of the complete separation of the two. That is wrong not only because inequality is what partly defines poverty but more importantly because inequality and poverty reduction are inseparable. To separate them is to say that redistribution should not form part of the solution to poverty. Everyone is prepared in some sense to regard poverty as undesirable. But egalitarians see riches as pathological too. The objective of reducing poverty is integrally linked to the objective of greater equality and social justice.

D&S: Can you explain the paradox that China's economic liberalization since the late 1970s has increased inequality within China and at the same time reduced global inequality? Some researchers and policymakers interpret China's experience over this period as teaching us that it may be necessary for poor countries to sacrifice some equality in order to fight poverty. Do you agree with this—if not, how would you respond?

BS: When you measure *global* inequality, you are not just totalling the levels of inequality in individual countries. In theory all individual countries could become more unequal and yet the world as a whole become more equal, or vice versa. In China, a very poor country in 1980, average incomes have risen much faster than the world average and this has reduced world inequality. But different sections of the population have done much better than others so that inequality within China has grown. If and when China becomes on average a richer country than it is now, further unequal growth there may contribute to increasing rather than decreasing world inequality.

China's growth has been very inegalitarian, but it has been very fast. And the proportion of the population in poverty seems to have been reduced. But it is possible to envisage a more egalitarian growth path which would have been slower in aggregate but which would have reduced the number of poor people at least as much if not more than China's actual record. So I do not think it is right to say that higher inequality is the cause of reduced poverty, though it may for a time be a feature of the rapid growth which in turn creates employment and reduces poverty.

This does not mean that all increases in inequality are necessarily pathological. The famous Kuznets curve sees inequality first rising and then falling during economic growth as an initially poor population moves by stages from low-income, low-productivity work into high-income, high-productivity work, until at the end of the process 100% of the population is in the second group. If you measure inequality during such a process, it does in fact rise and then fall again to its original level—in this example at the start everyone is equally poor, at the end everyone is equally richer. That might be called transitional inequality; many growth processes may include an element of it. In that case equality is not really being "sacrificed" to reduce poverty—poverty is reduced by a process which increases inequality and then eliminates it again. But at the same time inequality may be growing for many other reasons which are not, like the Kuznets effect, self-eliminating, but rather cumulative. When inequality grows, this malign variety tends to be more important than the self-eliminating variety. But many economists are far too ready to see growing inequality as the more benign, self-eliminating variety.

D&S: Where do you think the question of what is happening to global income inequality fits into the broader debate over neoliberalism and globalization?

BS: Many people say that since some measures of inequality started to improve in about 1980 and that is also when neoliberalism and globalization accelerated, it is those processes which have produced greater equality. There are many problems with this argument, among them the fact that at least on some measures global inequality has grown since 1980. In any case, measures which show global inequality falling in this period are, as we have seen, very strongly influenced by China. China's extraordinary growth has, of course, in part been expressed in and permitted by greater globalization (its internationalization has grown faster than its production), and it is also clear that liberalization of economic policy has played a role, though China hardly has a neoliberal economy. But to permit is not to cause. The real cause is surely to be found not so much in economic policy as in a profound social movement in which a new and highly dynamic capitalist class (combined with a supportive authoritarian state) has once again become an agent of massive capitalist accumulation, as seen before in Japan, the United States, and Western Europe. So, an important part of what we are observing in figures which show declining world inequality is not any growth of egalitarianism, but the dynamic ascent of Chinese and other Asian capitalisms.

This interview also appears on the website of the Political Economy Research Institute at the University of Massachusetts-Amherst, along with Bob Sutcliffe's working paper "A More or Less Unequal World? World Income Distribution in the 20th Century." See <www.umass. edu/peri>.

Article 2.8

INEQUALITY WORSENS ACROSS ASIA, *WALL STREET JOURNAL* CHEERS

BY JOHN MILLER
November/December 2007

> A report from the Asian Development Bank, comparing more than a decade's worth of data from 22 developing countries, found significant increases in inequality across the region [Asia].
>
> But, as the ADB notes, this doesn't mean the rich are taking food from the mouths of the poor. Rather, the rich are getting richer faster than the poor are. In all but one developing country, per capita incomes for the bottom fifth of the work force increased at least slightly; Pakistan was the only exception. Poverty remains a serious problem throughout Asia—the ADB estimates 600 million people still live below the $1-a-day line, to use one popular measure. But "fixing" inequality won't fix poverty. As even the ADB recognizes, inequality can be a symptom of economic growth.
>
> While inequality of outcome can be a good thing, inequality of opportunity is another matter.
>
> The ADB worries that too much of the good inequality can lead to the bad variety by entrenching a new set of self-interested elites.
>
> The danger is that all this talk of "inequality" will lead to policies that, in the name of redistributing income, reduce economic growth and thus make it harder for Asia's poor to join the middle class. The Asian "pie" is growing for everyone. The challenge is to keep it that way, instead of quarreling over the relative size of the pieces.
>
> —*Wall Street Journal* editorial, 8/21/07

When ideologues of global capitalism step out of line, who better to let them know about it than the editors of the *Wall Street Journal*, the keepers of the free-market flame?

Just ask the economists and policy wonks at the Asian Development Bank (ADB), financial capital's Manila-based outpost in East Asia, who had the temerity to report in August that increasing inequality was a serious problem for Asia's economies. The *Journal's* editors let them hear about it. "The danger," scolded the editors, "is that all this talk of 'inequality' will lead to policies that, in the name of redistributing income, reduce economic growth and thus make it harder for Asia's poor to join the middle class."

But the warning issued by the *Journal* editors is not just misleading, it is wrong. The evidence shows that countries that enjoy rapid economic growth are not more unequal than countries that grow slowly. In fact, a more equal distribution of income is not merely compatible with rapid growth; there are a number of avenues by which greater equality can actually promote growth. Finally, and most important for millions of people across Asia: poverty reduction depends on both raising a nation's income and reducing its inequality.

It is not that the ADB's bean counters got the numbers wrong. Of the 22 developing Asian economies in the ADB study, 15 saw inequality worsen since the early 1990s. That includes economic powerhouse China, where inequality worsened more rapidly and to higher levels than in any other country in the study other than Nepal. Even South Korea and Taiwan, once paragons of rapid and equitable growth, have seen inequality rise since 1993 .

Economists at the ADB tracked changes in the levels of inequality using Gini coefficients, economists' standard measure of economic inequality, in the 22 developing Asian countries for which there are sufficient data. The Gini coefficient ranges from zero to one: zero corresponds to perfect equality (every household has the same income), and one corresponds to maximal inequality (one household gets the entire national income). In the real world, Gini coefficients range from around 0.25 (Sweden, Denmark, Hungary) to nearly 0.60 (South Africa, Brazil, Haiti).

The ADB report found Gini coefficients rising across Asia. China's, for instance, rose from 0.41 in 1993 to 0.47 in 2004; it is now higher than that of the United States, 0.46 in 2004. (See Figure 1, which shows inequality levels by country, and Figure 2, which reports on changes in inequality levels.)

The trend toward a widening gap between the rich and poor in Asia is actually more alarming than even the ADB tables suggest. For one thing, the Asian financial crisis of the late 1990s sucked millions of dollars out of the caches of the continent's economic elites. Had it not been for this hit, Malaysia, Indonesia, and probably Thailand as well would have joined the worsening inequality column of the ADB report. Plus, the ADB tables rely on household expenditure data as opposed to the more difficult-to-obtain income data used in some countries to measure inequality. Inequality levels calculated from expenditure data are normally lower than those calculated from income data for the same population. In the Philippines, for example, where inequality data are available on both measures, the expenditure-based Gini coefficient is 0.40 for 2003, while the income-based figure is about 20% higher at 0.48.

The East Asian Miracle Under the Gun

While inequality can be a symptom of economic growth in capitalist economies, as the editors argue, what is remarkable about many East Asian economies is that prior to the 1990s they grew rapidly with far lower levels of inequality than elsewhere in the developing world. In some cases they saw inequality decline rather than worsen. For instance, in South Korea inequality declined from 1976 to 1993 even as the country's economy grew rapidly, posting average growth rates of 7.5% a year. Compared to Brazil, Latin America's fastest growing economy of the period, South Korea grew twice as quickly—with about half of Brazil's level of inequality.

The World Bank's famous 1993 "East Asian Miracle" study celebrated East Asia's "remarkable record of high growth and declining inequality." (Emphasis in the original.) From 1965 to 1990 the 23 economies of East Asia grew faster than all other regions of the world, three times as fast as the economies of Latin America and the Caribbean. Rapid growth in the region was spearheaded by the miraculous growth of eight high-performance economies—Japan; the "Four Tigers," Hong Kong, South Korea, Singapore, and Taiwan; and the three newly industrializing economies of southeast Asia, Indonesia, Malaysia, and Thailand—in which inequality remained low or improved over the same period. Because they were "unusually success- ful at sharing the fruits of growth," as the World Bank report put it, poverty declined rapidly and living conditions, from life expectancy to access to clean water and adequate shelter, improved dramatically in these high performance economies. A 1997 World Bank report went so far as to call rapid growth in East Asia "Everyone's Miracle."

"Everyone's" was surely an exaggeration even then. The editors of the *Wall Street Journal* nonetheless contend that today's much more unequal eco- nomic growth in Asia should still be considered everyone's miracle. As they read the ADB report, despite widening inequality, at least some of the ben- efits of the economic growth have trickled down to the poorest 20% of households in these economies. Since 1993 the expenditures of the bottom quintile increased in all of these 22 Asian economies with the exception of Pakistan, albeit by far less than the expenditures of the richest 20%. (See Figure 3.) "These increases in inequality are not a story of the 'rich getting richer and the poor getting poorer'," confirms the ADB report. "Rather it is the rich getting richer faster than the poor."

That is enough to qualify as "pro-poor growth," according to the editors' abso- lute definition of the term: economic growth that does anything at all to alleviate pov- erty, no matter how lopsidedly it benefits the well-to-do.

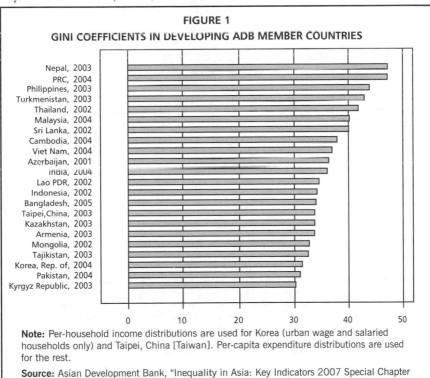

FIGURE 1
GINI COEFFICIENTS IN DEVELOPING ADB MEMBER COUNTRIES

Nepal, 2003
PRC, 2004
Philippines, 2003
Turkmenistan, 2003
Thailand, 2002
Malaysia, 2004
Sri Lanka, 2002
Cambodia, 2004
Viet Nam, 2004
Azerbaijan, 2001
India, 2004
Lao PDR, 2002
Indonesia, 2002
Bangladesh, 2005
Taipei,China, 2003
Kazakhstan, 2003
Armenia, 2003
Mongolia, 2002
Tajikistan, 2003
Korea, Rep. of, 2004
Pakistan, 2004
Kyrgyz Republic, 2003

0   10   20   30   40   50

Note: Per-household income distributions are used for Korea (urban wage and salaried households only) and Taipei, China [Taiwan]. Per-capita expenditure distributions are used for the rest.

Source: Asian Development Bank, "Inequality in Asia: Key Indicators 2007 Special Chapter Highlights," August 2007.

What Is Pro-Poor Growth?

It is true that rapid economic growth usually does more to alleviate poverty than slower economic growth. But if inequality grows at the same time, then much of the poverty-fighting potential of rapid economic growth is being lost. In some sense it may be accurate to say that the rich are not taking food from the mouths of the poor—but it's just as accurate to say that the benefits of economic growth that might otherwise have ended up on the tables of the poor have instead gone to the rich.

The evidence is clear. Had levels of inequality only remained unchanged over the last decade in the 15 countries that suffered worsening inequality, they would have seen a dramatic difference in the numbers of their citizens lifted from poverty. The ADB report documents the large reductions in the percentage of the population living on less than $1 a day (a standard U.N. measure of poverty) that would have occurred had economic inequality not worsened. In China, the number would have been just about halved. (See Figure 4.)

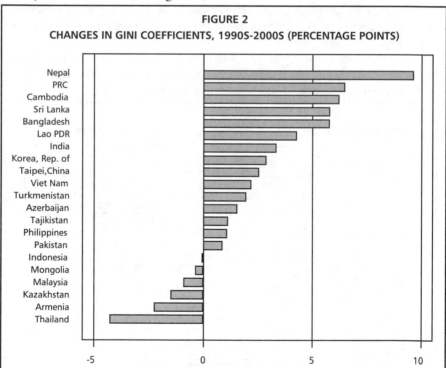

FIGURE 2

CHANGES IN GINI COEFFICIENTS, 1990S-2000S (PERCENTAGE POINTS)

Note: Years over which changes are computed are as follows: Armenia (1998-2003); Azerbaijan (1995-2001); Bangladesh (1991-2005); Cambodia (1993-2004); People's Republic of China (1993-2004); India (1993-2004); Indonesia (1993-2002); Kazakhstan (1996-2003); Republic of Korea (1993-2004); Lao PDR (1992-2002); Malaysia (1993-2004); Mongolia (1995-2002); Nepal (1995-2003); Pakistan (1992-2004); Philippines (1994-2003); Sri Lanka (1995-2002); Taipei,China (1993-2003); Tajikistan (1999-2003); Thailand (1992-2002); Turkmenistan (1998-2003); and Viet Nam (1993-2004). Gini calculated on income distribution for Republic of Korea and Taipei,China; expenditure distribution for all other countries.

Source: Asian Development Bank, "Inequality in Asia: Key Indicators 2007 Special Chapter Highlights," August 2007.

By that standard, economic growth in most of these countries can hardly be considered pro-poor. Each percentage point of economic growth now does less to alleviate poverty than in the past. For instance, economists Hafiz Pasha and T. Palanivel found that national poverty in China fell 9.8% during both the 1980s and 1990s. But the economy needed a 9.0% per capita growth rate in the later decade, as opposed to a 7.8% rate in the earlier one, to effect the same reduction in poverty rates.

And contrary to the claims of the *Journal* editors, a widening difference between rich and poor can be, and at times has been, so great as to bring poverty alleviation to a halt altogether. In Thailand, for instance, the same 1993 World Bank study found that despite growth rates averaging 6.4% a year from 1975 to 1986, poverty rates increased over the same period. Rural Thais were hard hit by the falling prices of farm products, and economic differences between urban and rural dwellers widened. Similarly, between 1984 and 1991, rural Chinese suffered worsening poverty as prices for farm products fell and rural output stagnated—even as the national economy was growing at double-digit rates.

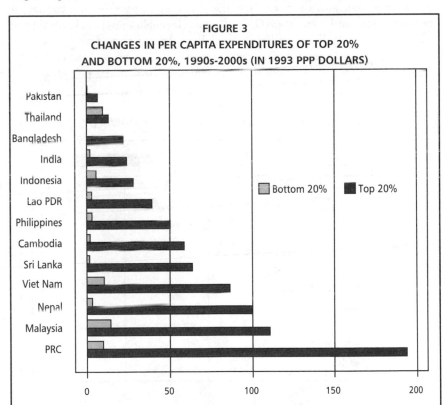

FIGURE 3
**CHANGES IN PER CAPITA EXPENDITURES OF TOP 20%
AND BOTTOM 20%, 1990s-2000s (IN 1993 PPP DOLLARS)**

Notes: PPP, or purchasing power parity, refers to the adjustment made to currency comparisons across countries according to the price of a "basket" of goods in each country; in other words, PPP values control for the different prices of goods in different countries.

Years over which changes are computed are as follows: Bangladesh (1991-2005); Cambodia (1993-2004); People's Republic of China (1993-2004); India (1993-2004); Indonesia (1993-2002); Lao PDR (1992-2002); Malaysia (1993-2004); Nepal (1995-2003); Pakistan (1992-2004); Philippines (1994-2003); Sri Lanka (1995-2002); Thailand (1992-2002); and Viet Nam (1993-2004).

Source: Asian Development Bank, "Inequality in Asia: Key Indicators 2007 Special Chapter Highlights," August 2007.

While China's agricultural output subsequently picked up and poverty alleviation resumed, the widening gap between the economic standing of rural and urban Chinese continues to sap Chinese growth of its potential to ease poverty. Neglect of agriculture and of rural areas is a common feature that has contributed to rising inequality in many Asian economies; to improve the lot of the poor, the ADB recommends switching some public expenditures from urban to rural areas and from post-secondary education, which favors urban dwellers, to basic education, which is still not available to all, particularly in rural areas.

Tackling Poverty and Inequality

Neglecting to address inequality surely can compromise even the most dynamic economy's ability to fix poverty. That is not to say that fixing inequality alone will fix poverty. But there is now plenty of reason to believe that fixing inequality can enhance economic growth at the same time that it fights poverty. And contrary to the editors' admonishment, the ADB's talk about inequality might help lift the 600 million Asians who still live on less than a dollar a day out of poverty.

Today, even some mainstream economists are moving beyond the notion that rising inequality is necessary during developing countries' initial periods of rapid

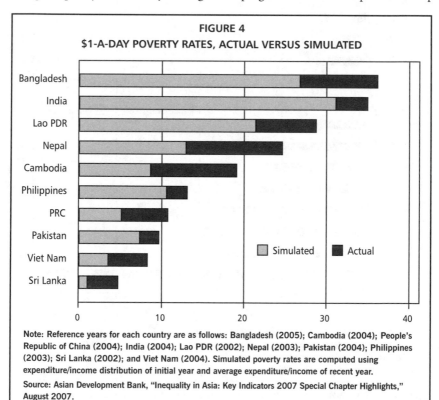

FIGURE 4
$1-A-DAY POVERTY RATES, ACTUAL VERSUS SIMULATED

Note: Reference years for each country are as follows: Bangladesh (2005); Cambodia (2004); People's Republic of China (2004); India (2004); Lao PDR (2002); Nepal (2003); Pakistan (2004); Philippines (2003); Sri Lanka (2002); and Viet Nam (2004). Simulated poverty rates are computed using expenditure/income distribution of initial year and average expenditure/income of recent year.

Source: Asian Development Bank, "Inequality in Asia: Key Indicators 2007 Special Chapter Highlights," August 2007.

growth to establish the incentives to work, save, and invest. The record of the East Asian miracle economies provided an important exemplar of simultaneous rapid growth and low or declining inequality.

In recent years, economists and other social scientists have developed several explanations of how greater equality can in fact promote economic growth. More equal economies have more political stability, grant greater access to credit, spend more on education, and have more widespread land ownership than economies racked by inequality—each a factor that contributes to economic growth. Relative equality eases the social discontents and political conflicts that would otherwise discourage foreign investment and hamper economic growth. A more equal distribution of income allows the poor, who pay much higher interest rates than the rich in many developing countries, greater access to credit, adding to their personal investments and promoting economic growth. In relatively equal societies, more families have the savings necessary to send their children to school—obviously a spur to growth. And land reform, a key policy for reducing inequality in South Korea and Taiwan, raises agricultural productivity because small farmers cultivate their land more intensively than large landholders.

The ADB acknowledges several of these arguments. For instance, in the Beijing news conference launching the report, Ifzal Ali, the ADB's chief economist, called the rise in inequality in Asia today "a clear and present danger to the sustained growth," and warned that growing inequality could in some countries lead to "greater social conflict, from street demonstrations to violent civil wars."

Nonetheless, the ADB was not about to embrace massive redistribution policies that would dull market incentives. They do, however, endorse redistributive policies targeted at promoting "equality of opportunity" and "funded through mechanisms that do not detract from economic growth." Chief among their recommended polices are putting more public moneys into rural infrastructure including irrigation, electricity, transportation, and agricultural extension services, as well as expanding access to basic health care and primary education.

These measures are generally uncontroversial—although that does not mean they will be adopted any time soon. They would surely help. But they would be unlikely to arrest the widening inequality of the current period. To do that, public policy must also address the big picture; the decline in labor's share of the economic pie that corporate-led globalization has brought about.

Greater openness to trade, as economist Dani Rodrik has argued, erodes the bargaining power of labor by exposing workers, especially unskilled workers, to the competition of having their services replaced by imports from abroad.

Beyond that, export-led growth in many developing economies has failed to bring on the expected boom in manufacturing employment. As manufacturing exports from these countries increased with greater openness, so too did the quantity of manufactured goods imported into their domestic markets. So while export expansion was adding jobs, other jobs were being lost because of import penetration. Moreover, the new export industries are typically less labor-intensive than the older industries they replace. In China, for instance, relatively labor-saving joint ventures and foreign-owned firms in the country's new export zones have taken the place of relatively more labor-intensive state-owned manufacturing firms.

As a result, export promotion has done little to tighten labor markets and thereby improve labor's bargaining power. In the most detailed study to date, economists J. Felipe and G. Sipin found that in the Philippines, labor's share of national income fell by six percentage points from 1980 to 2002 as its economy globalized.

The case of China is also instructive, as economic sociologists Peter Evans and Sarah Staveteig point out. According to official statistics, manufacturing employment in China, the world's workshop, increased steadily from 1978 to 1995, nearly doubling from 53 million to 98 million jobs. But since then Chinese employment in manufacturing has fallen off. Manufacturing's share of Chinese employment has actually declined for nearly two decades now, even as China's share of world manufactured exports has increased more than fivefold.

With the manufacturing share of Chinese employment stagnant, hundreds of millions of people currently dependent on agricultural production for their incomes must either stay in that sector or move to the service sector. Both options suggest increased inequality and a more precarious quality of life for the vast majority of the Chinese population, argue Evans and Staveteig. If they stay in agriculture, the Chinese peasantry are likely to face stagnating incomes. A move into the service sector would allow a few new entrants to gain access to the more lucrative service jobs, but the vast majority will find poorly remunerated, insecure jobs offering personal services as the nannies, maids, drivers, and gardeners that their luckier compatriots will be able to hire.

While this widening inequality in the very countries that not long ago served as exemplars of growth with equality might not present a problem to the editors of the *Wall Street Journal*, it surely is a serious problem, as even the ADB acknowledges. But genuinely pro-poor economic growth will only come about when public policy confronts the current rules of the global economy—rules that the editors are so dedicated to defending, and that the ADB itself is reluctant to challenge.

Sources: Asian Development Bank, Key Indicators 2007, Part 1: Inequality in Asia, August 2007; "Inequality Check," *Wall Street Journal* editorial, August 21, 2007; Richard McGregor, "ADB warns on rising inequality in China," *Financial Times*, August 8, 2007; Alan Wheatley, "Rising inequality danger for Asia, says ADB," Reuters, August 8, 2007; "For whosoever hath, to him shall be given, and he shall have more: Income inequality in emerging Asia is heading towards Latin American levels," *The Economist*, August 9, 2007; World Bank, "The East Asian Miracle: Economic Growth and Public Policy," 1993; Vinod Ahuja et al., "Everyone's Miracle," World Bank, 1997; Peter Evans and Sarah Staveteig, "Late 20th Century Industrialization and Changing Employment Structures in the Global South," Univ. of Calif. Berkeley, August 22, 2007; Hafiz A. Pasha and T. Palanivel, "Pro-Poor Growth and Policies: The Asian Experience," U.N. Development Programme, 2004; Judith Banister, "Manufacturing Employment in China," *Monthly Labor Review*, July 2005.

Chapter 3

SAVINGS AND INVESTMENT

INTRODUCTION

Never a slip from the savings cup to the investment lip. That is the orderly world of classical macroeconomics, where every cent of household savings is neatly transferred to corporate investment. In the classical world, savings markets—governed by all-powerful interest rates—work seamlessly to assure that savings are matched by investments, fueling growth in the private economy, which in turn guarantees full employment. Should the flow of savings exceed the uptake of corporate investment, falling interest rates automatically solve the problem.

In the real world, macroeconomies are far messier than classical macroeconomists suggest—a proposition no one doubts today. Keynes argued that there is no neat connection, or nexus, between savings and investment in a modern financial economy. Savings often sit, hoarded and uninvested. And interest rates, no matter how low, seldom coax balky investors to lay out their money in a weak economy. In the Keynesian world, economies regularly suffer from investment shortfalls that lead to recessions and cost workers their jobs.

In this chapter, Gretchen McClain and Randy Albelda report on one critical test of the classical and Keynesian visions, conducted by economist Steven Fazzari. In a massive study of 5,000 manufacturing firms, Fazzari rated the influence of interest rates, business cycle conditions, and firms' financial conditions on their investment in plant and equipment. He concluded that the influence of interest rates is overrated, putting him squarely in the Keynesian camp (Article 3.1).

According to conventional wisdom, the stock market boom of the last decade should have benefited most people in the United States who own corporate stock either directly or indirectly through mutual funds or retirement accounts. But, as Sylvia Allegretto shows, the share of households that own stock has been *falling* in recent years, and the wealthiest Americans own the great bulk of stock by value (Article 3.2). Also, as economist Ellen Frank explains, there is no logical connection between rising stock prices and rising investment. Stock prices are based on traders' guesses about which stocks are likely to catch the eye of other traders—guesses that can have little to do with actual economic conditions (Article 3.3).

But it was residential investment, a housing boom followed by a mortgage crisis and housing bust, that triggered the instability and uncertainty of today's economic crisis. The housing crisis hit the subprime mortgage market and low-income homeowners first. *Dollars & Sense* co-editor Amy Gluckman reports on the confusing and risky mortgage options used to get low-income borrowers into trouble (Article 3.7).

The housing crisis then spread to engulf the entire mortgage market and the new financial instruments derived from mortgages, eventually threatening the entire financial system. Economist Gerald Friedman provides a succinct history of financial bubbles in the U.S. economy that demonstrates why financial markets need to be regulated (Article 3.5).

Just where do the trillions of dollars lost in the stock market crash and the bursting of the housing bubble go? Economist Arthur MacEwan explains how they are lost (Article 3.6). Management consultant Orlando Segura, Jr. gives readers a peak into the notoriously secretive private equity industry. Segura describes how these firms realize huge profits, "uber-profit" in his words, from leveraged buyouts, and how their buying and selling of private corporations neither fosters innovation nor creates output and jobs (Article 3.4).

Finally, economist Ramaa Vasudevan provides a primer on the increased importance of financial markets, financial institutions, and financial elites in today's economy and its governing institutions. That failed financial corporations have received massive bailouts, for Vasudevan, only underlines the power they wield in the era of financialization (Article 3.8).

Discussion Questions

1. (Article 3.1) Keynes argued that savings and investment were not balanced by the interest rate but by changes in the level of aggregate output. How does the essay by McClain and Albelda support this claim?

2. (Article 3.1) According to McClain and Albelda, how did Fazzari rate the influence of interest rates, business cycle conditions, and firms' financial conditions on corporate investment? What do his findings suggest about Keynesian and classical theories of investment? Based on his findings, what stabilization policies might be appropriate to promote investment?

3. (Article 3.2) If nearly half of U.S. households own stock either directly or indirectly, why would a rise in the Dow index be inconsequential for most of them?

4. (Article 3.3) During the 1930s, Keynes compared the stock market to a newspaper beauty contest that asked readers to pick the photo of the contestant that other readers would pick as the prettiest. Frank suggests that Keynes' analogy still holds for today's stock market. How does Frank's explanation of stock prices compare with those in your textbook? Do you find it convincing?

5. (Article 3.4) How do corporations that buy and sell corporations make their mega profits and how does their activity affect the economy?

6. (Article 3.5) What aspects of financial assets make them subject to speculative manias and panics? And what does this pattern suggest about the proper public policy for overseeing financial markets?

7. (Article 3.6) If the increased value of stocks and houses accrue to their owners during booms, explain what happens to the value of those assets in a crash and where it ends up.

8. (Article 3.8) What is financialization? How does it manifest itself in today's economy? How did it contribute to the recent financial crisis?

Article 3.1

BOOSTING INVESTMENT
The overrated influence of interest rates

BY GRETCHEN McCLAIN AND RANDY ALBELDA
July 1993, revised April 2001

Few economists or politicians would disagree that an economy's prospects for long-term growth depend on the productive capacity of its people and its physical equipment. But what to invest in—and how to get the appropriate economic actors to invest—is a matter of much debate.

All economies face a choice between using their productive resources to produce goods and services to be consumed now, and forsaking today's consumption to produce more goods for the future. While catering to consumption today may be more satisfying for wealthier countries and absolutely vital for poor countries, it fails to provide for future growth.

Investing in new plant and equipment can stimulate growth over time, as it provides the physical capacity for new production. Moreover, new plant and equipment tend to be better designed than the existing capital stock, and the improvement usually helps to boost output per worker. If this new productivity translates into higher wages, investment can also increase a country's standard of living and improve employment possibilities. In turn, improving human productive capacity—through training and education—can lead to growth and increased productivity in the long run.

Investment, and the consequent increase in productivity, is critical for international economic success. The more efficiently a country can produce a product, the more competitive that country will be in the world market. Since international markets provide an avenue of demand for our goods, the more domestically produced products and services we can sell abroad, the more jobs we can support here.

Investment can also help stimulate the economy in the short run. During an economic downturn, increased investment will yield more jobs and income for workers who would otherwise be unemployed. They will then return their income to the market when they purchase goods and services, which will boost demand for those products. Economists call this the "multiplier effect." The increase in demand in turn encourages firms to invest more so that they can meet that demand—known to economists as the "accelerator effect." All in all, such a cycle creates more jobs, income, and spending.

While few economists dispute the importance of investment, many disagree on what type is needed, which sectors of the economy are best able to provide it, and what are the best ways to encourage investment. Typically, these debates have revolved around the government's role in encouraging private investment in new plant and equipment. But the role that public investment in infrastructure and education plays in promoting not only our economic well-being and growth, but also in encouraging private investment, could and should widen the terms of the debate.

The Backdrop

The traditional economic argument about investment—and the prevailing conservative line espoused by elected officials at the federal and state levels—has been that the most important fiscal policies to encourage privately owned firms to invest are those which boost profits. If the government helps provide the conditions for profitability, the argument goes, firms will be encouraged to make the right types of investment.

Government tax-and-spend policies during the 1980s and 1990s have often tried to promote investment by reducing corporate taxes, in order to boost profits and stimulate savings. Such measures were supposed to leave firms with a bigger bottom line, in the hope that they would turn profits into new plant and equipment. Cuts in personal income tax rates—especially for the wealthiest—were intended to leave people with more after-tax income that they could save. Higher savings, according to this logic, translates into lower interest rates which in turn lead to more investment. While such policies have been very effective in redistributing money from the poor to the wealthy, they did not do much for investment. For example, the amount of new fixed investment (i.e., new plant and equipment) relative to the total amount of plant and equipment actually sank to its lowest post-World War II mark between 1989 and 1991.

Merely providing the conditions for profit-making does not mean that private firms will plow those profits back into new plant and equipment. Speculation on real estate markets, the value of foreign currencies, or the price of silver and gold could easily eat up new profits. Much of the money generated for investment in the 1980s financed mergers and acquisitions, which generally resulted in less employment and little new physical productive capacity. And, perhaps even more important, new investment by U.S. firms may not take place in the United States. Investing abroad has been the trend since the 1970s. Finally, even if there is domestic investment and it increases productivity, unless workers share in those gains it may not promote robust growth or increase the standard of living of the country as a whole.

In the face of the failure of the 1980s policies to promote investment, conservatives came up with a new explanation of why the economy was so sluggish: the deficit. Ironically, the conservative policies mentioned above were largely responsible for the public debt, but nonetheless Republicans, along with many Democrats galvanized by billionaire Ross Perot, latched onto deficit reduction as the most important fiscal policy of the 1990s.

The deficit, they argued, kept long-term interest rates high because it created competition for precious funds. The result was that federal borrowing, necessitated by debt-financed government spending and tax cuts, "crowded out" private investment. The best solution, they said, was to reduce the deficit and bring down long-term interest rates so that private investment would thrive.

Identifying Influence

Economist Steven Fazzari tackled these assumptions in a study of the influence of the federal government's taxing and spending policies on private investment. Using a large data base from Standard and Poor on over 5,000 manufacturing firms from 1971 to 1990, Fazzari tested three different factors for their effects on levels of investment in plant and equipment: interest rates, the business cycle, and the financial conditions of the firms.

According to Fazzari, these three "channels of influence" shape patterns of investment. First, he takes on the traditionalists, by addressing the costs associated with investment: the price of borrowing money (i.e., interest rates), depreciation (how fast the new piece of equipment or building will lose its value), and taxes affecting both corporate profits and dividends. To measure this channel, Fazzari employs the interest rate on one type of corporate bond.

Next, he considers the influence of the business cycle by looking at sales growth. Traditional economic theory tends to assume a ready market, but Fazzari suggests instead that firms make investment decisions based on their perception of their ability to sell their products. The more robust current sales are and are expected to be, the more likely firms will be willing to risk new investment—regardless of the interest rate. Since the general condition of the economy influences sales levels, it also has an impact on investment.

In Fazzari's examination of the third channel of influence—the financial condition of firms—he again questions conventional wisdom, this time about the supply and demand for loans. Most economists assume that if the expected return on an investment exceeds the interest rate, then the project is profitable and will be undertaken. This is most likely to be true when the firm in question has enough cash on hand from prior profits to make the investment without asking a bank for a loan. Many firms, though, need to borrow money, and some are unable to persuade banks to loan it to them. Banks often refuse loan applications from new businesses with few assets, or charge them prohibitively high interest rates. Even if a young firm finds a potentially profitable investment, severe constraints on raising capital may prevent the firm from pursuing it. A firm's financial condition—not the projected rate of return on the new investment—can thus end up determining whether or not investment takes place.

Perfecting Policy

After looking at the importance of interest rates, the business cycle, and the financial conditions of firms in determining investment, Fazzari found that interest rates exert the weakest influence of the three factors. He concludes that there is no evidence that interest rates significantly affect investment for the fastest growing firms in his sample. Based on these findings, Fazzari claims that "it would be speculative to base policy on the assumption that interest rates drive investment to an important extent, especially for growing firms."

So, what kinds of fiscal policies should we adopt? If we believe Fazzari's results, we should be looking for those that attend to the financial conditions of firms and stimulate demand for products.

A tax cut targeted not at the very rich but at the "middle class" would probably give investment at least a temporary boost by generating increased consumption. Increased sales from a temporary tax cut create the illusion of a permanent increase in demand, and the multiplier and accelerator effects discussed earlier come into play. In order to meet what firms believe is a permanent increase in demand for their goods, they make investments in more equipment, more factories, and more employees.

Another means of encouraging investment that Fazzari evaluates is cutting corporate income taxes. Such cuts increase firms' after-tax profits, leaving them with a larger pool of funds to invest if they so choose. Since there is no guarantee that they will invest the savings from reduced taxes, though, Fazzari prefers investment tax credits (ITCs) to cuts in taxes for all firms. Only if firms invested would they be able to reduce their corporate tax bills. In Fazzari's view, ITCs will effectively encourage investment whether it is sensitive to interest rates or not.

The most important lesson from Fazzari's analysis is that concerns about investment should not stand in the way of policy initiatives that are important for society, such as spending on education and job training, simply because they may increase the federal budget deficit and cause interest rates to rise. Government investments in public works and education will likely increase productivity in the long run, and this can only be good for investment. Moreover, if investment is not sensitive to interest rates, then the much-discussed "crowding out" effect of deficit spending on private business is bound to be very small. And as Fazzari points out, when unemployment is high, the stimulative effects of deficit spending on sales may far outweigh the impacts of increased interest rates.

The focus on balanced budgets should be tempered by a thorough analysis of what this policy implies for society's immediate and long-term welfare. When we underinvest in the economy during a recession by eliminating educational and social investments, the foregone technical innovation resulting from this underinvestment may lead to less efficient workers, and lower productivity, for many years.

Fazzari's results not only repudiate the traditional answer to lagging investment—tax cuts for the wealthy and the lowering of interest rates. Instead, the government should be trying to stimulate the economy through improved physical and social infrastructure, which will boost not only sales but investment and incomes.

Article 3.2

THE DOW HIGH AND STOCK OWNERSHIP

BY SYLVIA ALLEGRETTO
March/April 2007

In April 2007 the Dow Jones Industrial Average rose above 13,000 for the first time ever, an event marked with great fanfare in some quarters. "Dow 13,000" may be a milestone on Wall Street, but it is a relatively insignificant blip on the radar screen of average working families. Fostered by the constant focus and widespread attention given to the performance of the stock market, conventional wisdom has it that everyone in the United States is heavily invested in the stock market—and so is poised to benefit when stock prices rise. However, the data tell a different story.

In recent decades the share of U.S. households owning any stock, whether directly (owning shares in a particular company) or indirectly (owning shares through a mutual fund or a retirement account) has indeed increased. But the most recent triennial data from the Survey of Consumer Finances show that this trend has actually reversed course: just over half of households (51.9%) owned any stock in 2001, but just under half (48.6%) in 2004—the first such decline on record (see Figure 1). In 2004, only about a third of U.S. households had stock holdings valued at more than $5,000.

The distribution of stocks by value is heavily tilted to the wealthiest Americans, as shown in Figure 2. In 2004, the wealthiest 1% of households owned 36.9% of the value of all stocks, while the next 9% owned 41.9%. Hence, the wealthiest 10% owned about 80% of all wealth in stocks. Between 2001 and 2004, while the

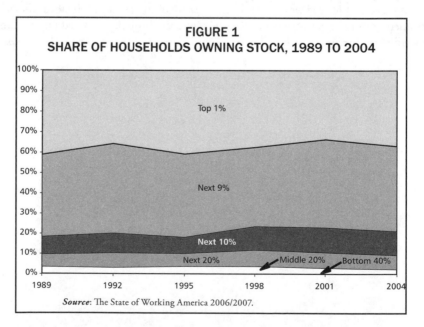

FIGURE 1
SHARE OF HOUSEHOLDS OWNING STOCK, 1989 TO 2004

Top 1%

Next 9%

Next 10%

Next 20%

Middle 20% Bottom 40%

Source: The State of Working America 2006/2007.

wealthiest 1% of households increased their share of total stock value, the share held by the bottom 80% fell from just above 10% (10.7%) to just below (9.4%).

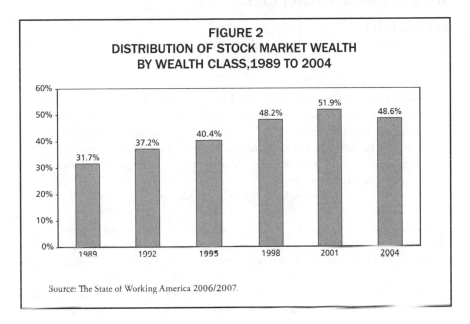

FIGURE 2
DISTRIBUTION OF STOCK MARKET WEALTH
BY WEALTH CLASS,1989 TO 2004

Source: The State of Working America 2006/2007.

For the most part, lower-, middle-, and even upper-middle-income working-age households depend on their paychecks, not stock portfolios, to meet their everyday needs. Typical working families that own stock do so in retirement plans that are costly to turn into cash. So higher stock prices do little to help them make ends meet at a time when inflation-adjusted wages for most workers have been stagnant for many years now.

Article 3.3

WHO DECIDES STOCK PRICES?

BY ELLEN FRANK
May/June 2002

> Dear Dr. Dollar:
> *During the course of a single day, a stock can go up and down frequently. These changes supposedly reflect the changing demand for that stock (and its potential resale value) or changing expectations of a company's profitability. But this seems too vague to me. How can these factors be so volatile? Who actually decides, or what is the mechanism for deciding, when a stock price should go up or down and by how much?*
> —Joseph Balszak, Muskegon, Mich.

Let's start with your last question first—how are stock prices determined? Shares in most large established corporations are listed on organized exchanges like the New York or American Stock Exchanges. Shares in most smaller or newer firms are listed on the NASDAQ—an electronic system that tracks stock prices.

Every time a stock is sold, the exchange records the price at which it changes hands. If, a few seconds or minutes later, another trade takes place, the price at which that trade is made becomes the new market price, and so on. Organized exchanges like the New York Stock Exchange will occasionally suspend trading in a stock if the price is excessively volatile, if there is a severe mismatch between supply and demand (many people wanting to sell, no one wanting to buy) or if they suspect that insiders are deliberately manipulating a stock's price. But in normal circumstances, there is no official arbiter of stock prices, no person or institution that "decides" a price. The market price of a stock is simply the price at which a willing buyer and seller agree to trade.

Why then do prices fluctuate so much? The vast bulk of stock trades are made by professional traders who buy and sell shares all day long, hoping to profit from small changes in share prices. Since these traders do not hold stocks over the long haul, they are not terribly interested in such long-term considerations as a company's profitability or the value of its assets. Or rather, they are interested in such factors mostly insofar as news that would affect a company's long-term prospects might cause *other traders* to buy the stock, causing its price to rise. If a trader believes that others will buy shares (in the expectation that prices will rise), then she will buy as well, hoping to sell when the price rises. If others believe the same thing, then the wave of buying pressure will, in fact, *cause* the price to rise.

Back in the 1930s, economist John Maynard Keynes compared the stock market to a contest then popular in British tabloids, in which contestants had to look at photos and choose the faces that *other contestants* would pick as the prettiest. Each contestant had to look for photos "likeliest to catch the fancy of the other competitors, all of whom are looking at the problem from the same point of view." Similarly, stock traders try to guess which stocks other traders will buy. The successful trader is the one who anticipates and outfoxes the market, buying before a stock's price rises and selling before it falls.

Financial firms employ thousands of market strategists and technical analysts who spend hours poring over historical stock data, trying to divine the logic behind these price changes. If they could unlock the secret of stock prices, they could arm their traders with the ability to always buy low and sell high. So far, no one has found this particular holy grail. And by continuing to guess and gamble, traders send prices gyrating.

For small investors, who do hold stock for the long term and will need to cash in their stocks at some point to finance their retirements, the volatility of the market can be a source of constant anxiety. Every time a share in, say, General Electric is traded, the new price is used to revalue *all* outstanding shares—just as the value of your home appreciates when the house down the block sells for more than a similar house sold last week. But the value of your home wouldn't be so high if every house on your block were suddenly put up for sale. Similarly, if all ten billion outstanding shares of General Electric—or even a small fraction of them—were put up for sale, they wouldn't fetch anywhere near the current market price. Small investors need to keep in mind that the gains and losses on their 401(k) statements are just hypothetical paper gains and losses. You won't know the true value of your stocks until you actually try to sell them.

Article 3.4

PRIVATE EQUITY EXPOSED

An insider gives a peek at a notoriously secretive industry.

BY ORLANDO SEGURA, JR.

July/August 2008

Today, private equity seems to be everywhere. Enter a Dunkin' Donuts, and you experience private equity. Scan your radio dial, and you're likely to encounter private equity. Purchase gifts for your children at Toys "R" Us, and you engage with private equity. The private equity industry, like other alternative investment industries that have risen to prominence over the last two decades, exerts tremendous economic and political influence in the United States and globally. It is important, then, to understand how this industry works and thrives. For the past three years, I have had the opportunity to see firsthand the inner workings of the industry—first as a consultant to large buyout firms, and then as a financial analyst for one of the firms themselves. Drawing on these experiences, I will try to shed some light on this notoriously secretive industry and answer three important questions: How do private equity firms make money? How do private equity firms affect the distribution of financial risk in society as a whole? And how does the regulatory landscape in the United States give private equity firms an advantage in the market?

How Do Private Equity Firms Make Money?

Specialized transactions called leveraged buyouts are central to what private equity firms do, and it is important to be familiar with the mechanics of these transactions in order to understand how these firms generate profit. Private equity firms are private partnerships that raise money from large investors—pension funds, other investment funds, and wealthy individuals (often the same people who are running the private equity firms)—and use that money to purchase other companies. This is the "buyout" part.

The "leveraged" part is the more important one, however. Private equity firms do not simply employ the money they raise on their own to buy companies. They borrow money from investment banks to complete the transactions. In most instances, this borrowed money constitutes the majority of the funding needed to pay for the company. At one point in the industry's infancy, firms were able to borrow 90% or more of the purchase price of the "target" companies. Today, as credit markets have tightened, that number is lower, but on average it still exceeds 50% of purchase price. When the buyout transaction is completed, the payback for this debt becomes the responsibility of the acquired company and is placed on its balance sheet as a liability. Most private equity firms retain ownership of the businesses they buy for three to five years and then sell them for a profit, often to other private equity firms.

The ability to use such leverage vastly increases the potential returns on private equity firms' investments. A simple analogy helps show how this works. Imagine you decide to buy a house that costs $100,000 in a neighborhood where property values are appreciating. You put a very small $1,000 down payment on the house and borrow the other $99,000 from the bank. In three years' time, the house has doubled in value and you are now able to sell it for $200,000. After you repay the loan, you have $100,000 in profit—a return of 100 times your original $1,000 investment. Now, imagine if you had only been able to borrow $1,000 from the bank; you would have had to make a $99,000 down payment. The house still appreciates to a value of $200,000, but in this scenario you have turned your original $99,000 investment into a $100,000 profit, generating only a return roughly equal to your original investment. In the first scenario, you put much less of your own equity at risk, yet you generate the same absolute profit as in the second scenario. This simple example illustrates the power of leverage, and why private equity firms would want to maximize the share of borrowed money they invest.

Why have investment banks been willing to lend private equity firms so much money? Part of the reason is that they are able to pass the debt along by selling, or "syndicating," it. Banks package the debt into securities called collateralized debt obligations, or CDOs, which they sell on the open market. CDOs have existed since 1987, but did not achieve prominence in the markets until 2001, when banks began devising sophisticated models that allowed them to rapidly price and sell these securities.

The benefit banks derive from their ability to segment and distribute the risks associated with the debt they underwrite for private equity firms cannot be overstated. They lower their downside risk associated with default on these loans because they only hold onto a small portion of the entire loan package, or "facility." So banks can underwrite more debt than they would be able to if they held onto the loans in full. And they can take in more lucrative fees, too. The banks get most of their revenues from fees for originating the loans, generally 2% to 3% of the amount of the loan.

All told, such large amounts of capital being used to purchase companies creates hefty profits for the investment banks and the private equity firms, not to mention the ancillary professional service industries required to complete the deals, including accountants, lawyers, and consultants.

This is simply the tip of the profit iceberg for private equity firms, however. The real money comes in what is called "carry"—the share of profits that the funds' managers are entitled to when they sell a business. Remember, the more these firms borrow for a transaction—the more they "leverage"—the more any increase in value translates into equity profit. The industry norm is for private equity partnerships to keep 20% of the profit that they make when they sell a company.

And apart from the über-profits they "earn" from selling the highly leveraged businesses they own, private equity firms charge hefty management fees to *both* the investors in the fund and to the companies they buy. The "market" management fee that private equity firms charge their investors ranges between 2% and 2.5% of the total fund size. The companies they purchase must likewise pay a quarterly "management fee," usually around 2% of the purchase price of the company. Effectively, private equity firms earn money in return for being given money *and* for spending money. As the value of many of the companies that private equity firms buy can soar into the hundreds of millions, or even billions, of dollars, this represents a low-risk, assured stream of income. On a fund of $10 billion, these fees alone can translate into hundreds of millions of dollars in revenue a year.

How do private equity firms affect the distribution of financial risk in society?

The profits that financial players like private equity firms and investment banks enjoy come at a price. Today, there are hundreds of billions of dollars in CDOs that are spread throughout the economy, most owned by individual investors. Of course, it is the businesses private equity firms own that are carrying the underlying loans that were bundled to create the CDOs. These businesses risk default if they are not able to make the payments on these debts. And the more the private equity firm was able to borrow to purchase the company, the greater the risk the business faces because it will have to manage larger debt payments on an ongoing basis. An ordinary business downturn that the business might have been able to weather may now thrust it into default if it cannot manage the high debt payments resulting from the leveraged buyout. And if enough of these businesses get into trouble, the holders of the CDOs will see the value of their investments tumble. We are seeing this happen now with the subprime crisis, which was fueled by devaluation in mortgage-backed securities.

The ability of banks and private equity firms to siphon the benefits while distributing the risks of leverage is rooted in the legal frameworks that "incentivize" such behavior (to use the industry jargon). Private equity firms are shielded from the extreme downside financial risks because of their peculiar form of corporate governance. Private equity firms set up each company they buy as a separate corporation with limited liability. This means that if one of the highly leveraged businesses experiences a downturn and is unable to pay its loans, the only equity that is at stake is what was used to purchase that business. Thus, a private equity fund can still post healthy returns even if some businesses in its portfolio go bankrupt.

As we've seen, private equity firms have an incentive to leverage their business buyouts as much as possible. But this increases the risk of default for the individual businesses they own because they are forced to pay such large principal and interest payments to support the debt that has been placed on their shoulders. Thus, not only do private equity firms increase the systemic risk across the economy by issuing publicly traded CDOs that provide their leverage, they also increase the more immediate risk for those who work for the businesses they own by saddling them with heavy debt obligations.

The "loosening" of the credit markets, fueled partly through the ascendance of CDOs, predictably led private equity firms to execute ever-larger transactions. In 2007, the Blackstone Group purchased Equity Office Properties for $39 billion and in one fell swoop became one of the largest holders of real estate in the world. Currently, Bain Capital is in the process of completing the purchase of Clear Channel Communications, the largest owner of radio stations in the United States. These are but two of many multi-billion dollar transactions by private equity firms that have occurred over the past decade, and which until now have largely gone unnoticed by the general public. These colossal companies, like all businesses bought up by private equity firms, are now at an increased risk should their profit margins weaken or interest rates rise in a cyclical downturn of the economy. To ensure that their requisite loan payments are made, the new managers of these companies, appointed by and acting on behalf of the private equity firm owner, may cut costs by simply laying off workers and offshoring certain functions. The market implications of contractions in the economy are thus amplified by the actions of private equity firms.

How does the regulatory landscape give private equity firms a market advantage?

With the profits that can be earned in private equity, it is no surprise that the industry has grown as much as it has recently, and it is no surprise that private equity firms are able to attract some of the brightest business minds in the market. Predictably, self-interested individuals are drawn to these firms, aiming to maximize the amount of money they can earn. But that is not the whole story. The regulatory landscape in the United States has given private equity firms a number of advantages in the market—limited transparency into the business dealings of the firms and the businesses they own, capital-gains tax advantages, a lack of consumer protection in the credit markets, lax antitrust law enforcement, among others. In effect, the legal landscape is ripe for private equity firms to thrive.

Since private equity firms have at their disposal all these levers for generating profit so seamlessly, one would imagine that the government would tax their earnings at an effectively higher tax rate than normal business earnings. This could not be further from the truth. Owners of corporations in the United States are afforded numerous tax breaks and incentives from writing off "losses" or deducting "business expenses" from taxable earnings. On this front, private equity firms have cleverly found ways to go above and beyond the call of duty. Virtually all private equity firms are structured as limited liability partnerships, or LLPs. This confers two explicit benefits to the partners. First, they are protected from any downside in their equity investments, meaning that if one of their investments goes bust, they will only lose the equity that they put into that specific business. Second, they are protected under a tax shelter that allows the majority of their profits to be taxed at a very low rate. Because they are partnerships that technically earn "capital gains" on the profitable sale of a business, they are taxed at a flat 15% rate, as opposed to the 28% to 33% income tax rate that ordinary individuals pay. Thanks to this loophole, private equity managers are taxed at lower rates than their secretaries and administrative assistants who make as much money in a year as their bosses make in a day.

Many European countries have recently instituted laws in recognition of the legal and regulatory advantages that private equity owners have enjoyed since the industry's inception. In the UK this past year, for example, Parliament passed a law that took away private equity firms' tax advantages, which incidentally were very similar to what currently exists in the United States. Here, House Democrats recently introduced a bill to do away with the capital gains tax structure for private equity firms and tax them at ordinary income tax rates. This would have raised private equity firms' tax rates on their carry from a flat 15% to a flat 35%. But Charles

Schumer (D-N.Y.), head of the Senate Finance Committee, came out against the bill, killing it for now.

It is no coincidence that, as a senator from New York, Schumer receives tens of thousands of dollars from private equity bosses and relies on their support for an ever-increasing portion of his campaign funding. Of course, he is not alone. The private equity industry created its own PAC in 2007, the Private Equity Council, to lobby against efforts to increase taxes on the industry. To date, they have succeeded; there is every reason to believe they will continue to succeed. Schumer's fellow senator from New York, Hillary Clinton, is a loyal recipient of private equity money and joined him in opposing the bill. On the Republican side, former New York City mayor Rudy Giuliani has taken a predictable pro-private-equity stance, as did his competitor in the Republican presidential primaries, Mitt Romney, who made hundreds of millions of dollars as a partner of Bain Capital, one of the leading private equity firms in the world. The political muscle of the industry is as strong as its economic success.

The legal framework that actively encourages this industry to thrive has spawned a new breed of capitalism, one in which businesses are treated as assets to be bought and sold rather than as social institutions that are sources of people's livelihood. Perhaps we should ask: What value do these firms confer upon the economy, and through it, on society? Private equity firms do not foster innovation in the economy, they do not create jobs, and for the most part they do not actively manage the businesses they own. Rather, they redirect the benefits of equity ownership to a small and insular group of people instead of creating social value for everyone. It is time to learn more about how and why these institutions exert their power and, at the very least, to demand more transparency, thoughtful regulation, and fairer taxation in return for the privilege of being able to operate in our economy.

Sources: Tomas Krüger Andersen, "Legal Structure of Private Equity and Hedge Funds," 2007 (available at isis.ku.dk/kurser/blob.aspx?feltid= 155330); Martin Arnold, "Doubt Cast on Buy-Out Firms' Huge Profits," *Financial Times*, November 23, 2007; Neil Hodge, "Private Equity: A Debt to Society?" *Financial Management*, September 2007.

Article 3.5

FROM TULIPS TO MORTGAGE-BACKED SECURITIES

BY GERALD FRIEDMAN
January/February 2008

Thirty years ago, economist Charles Kindleberger published a little book, *Manias, Panics, and Crashes,* describing the normal tendency of capitalist financial markets to fluctuate between speculative excess (or "irrational exuberance" in the words of a recent central banker) and panic. Kindleberger describes about 40 of these panics over the nearly 260 years from 1720–1975, or one every seven years. Following Kindleberger's arithmetic, we were due for a panic because it had been seven years since the high-tech bubble burst and the stock market panic of 2000-01. And the panic came, bringing in its wake a tsunami of economic woe, liquidity shortages, cancelled investments, rising unemployment, and economic distress.

Of course, more than mechanics and arithmetic are involved in the current financial panic. But there is a sense of inevitability about the manias and panics of capitalist financial markets, a sense described by writers from Karl Marx to John Maynard Keynes, Hyman Minsky, John Kenneth Galbraith, and Robert Shiller. The problem is that financial markets trade in unknown and unknowable future returns. Lacking real information, they are inevitably driven by the madness of crowds.

Unlike tangible commodities whose price should reflect its real value and real cost of production, financial assets are not priced according to any real returns, nor even according to some expected return, but rather according to expectations of what others will pay in the future, or, even worse, expectations of future expectations that others will have of assets' future return. Whether it is Dutch tulips in 1637, the South Sea Bubble of 1720, Florida real estate in the 1920s, or mortgage-backed securities today, it is always the same story of financial markets floating like a manic-depressive from euphoria to panic to bust. When unregulated, this process is made still worse by market manipulation, and simple fraud. Speculative markets like these can make some rich, and can even be exciting to watch, like a good game of poker; but this is a dangerous and irresponsible way to manage an economy.

There was a time when governments understood. Learning from past financial disasters, the United States established rules to limit the scope of financial euphoria and panic by strictly segregating different types of banks, by limiting financial speculation, and by requiring clear accounting of financial transactions. While they were regulated, financial markets contributed to the best period of growth in American history, the "glorious thirty" after World War II. To be sure, restrictions on speculative behavior and strict regulations made this a boring time to be a banker, and they limited earnings in the financial services sector. But, limited to a secondary role, finance served a greater good by providing liquidity for a long period of steady and relatively egalitarian economic growth.

Of course, over time we forgot why we had regulated financial markets, memory loss helped along by the combined efforts of free-market economists and self-interested bankers and others on Wall Street. To promote "competition," we lowered the barriers between different types of financial institutions, widening the scope of financial markets. We moved activities such as home mortgage lending onto national markets and allowed a rash of bank mergers to create huge financial institutions too large to be allowed to fail, but never too large to operate irresponsibly. Despite the growing scope and centralization of financial activity, the government accepted arguments that we could trust financial firms to self-regulate because it was in their interest to maintain credible accounting.

So we reap the whirlwind with a market collapse building to Great Depression levels. Once again, we learn history's lesson from direct experience: capitalist financial markets cannot be trusted. It is time to either re-regulate or move beyond.

Article 3.6

WHO GETS THOSE TRILLIONS?

BY ARTHUR MacEWAN
January/February 2009

Dear Dr. Dollar:
As housing prices have fallen, it seems that people have lost a huge amount in terms of the value of their homes. We are told that, over the whole country, trillions of dollars in home equity have been lost. Who gets those trillions? And, likewise, what about the trillions lost in the stock market?
—Carlos Rafael Alicea Negrón, Bronx, N.Y.

The simple answer to your question is that no one gets the lost trillions; they are simply gone. But, like all simple answers, this one doesn't explain very much.

Suppose that seven years ago, you bought your house for $200,000. Housing prices continued to rise, and at the beginning of 2007 you saw that other people in your neighborhood were selling houses similar to yours for $400,000. So you, quite reasonably, figured that your house was worth $400,000.

But now the housing bubble has burst. Similar houses in your neighborhood are selling for "only" $300,000 and thus it is now quite reasonable to figure that the value of your house has dropped by $100,000 as compared to the beginning of 2007. (Multiply this $100,000 by roughly 75 million homes across the country, and you have losses of $7.5 trillion.)

Your house, however, was not involved in any actual transaction at this lower value. So no one has gained the value you lost. If, for example, last year one of your neighbors had sold an equivalent house for $400,000 and now buys your house for $300,000 this neighbor would have gained what you lost. But most houses are not bought and sold in any given year. Their value is determined by those equivalent (or similar) houses that are actually bought and sold.

Moreover, even if someone bought your house at $300,000, that person would gain the value you lost only in the special case of the example above, where the person was lucky enough to have sold an equivalent house at $400,000. If instead that person was a new entrant to the housing market or a person who had just sold a similar house elsewhere for $300,000, then no one would be gaining what you lost.

Thus in the great majority of cases, the $100,000 value would simply be gone, and no one would have gotten it.

The situation on the stock market is similar. The values of stocks are determined by the sales that actually take place. When we hear that today the value of Mega Corporation's stock fell from $100 a share to $75 dollars a share, this means that the price of shares that were traded today were selling at $75 while those that were traded yesterday were selling for $100. But most shares of Mega Corporation were not actually traded either day. Their value fell—just like the value of your house fell when neighbors sold their houses—but no one gained this lost value. As in the housing market, the values of stocks have declined by trillions, but the trillions are simply gone.

Of course as with the situation in the housing market, some actual gains of value can take place when stock prices fall. If someone sold a share of Mega Corporation yesterday for $100 and bought it today for $75, this person obtained a gain. But with most of the declines in stock values, no one gets a gain.

To understand what has happened recently, it is useful to keep in mind that the high housing values of recent years were the result of a speculative bubble. The values increased not because there was some real change in the houses themselves. The houses were not providing more living services to the degree that their prices rose. The prices of housing rose because people expected them to rise more. The situation was a speculative bubble, and housing prices rose far above their historical trend.

And just as, in general, the loss of value when prices fell was not balanced by a gain, the gains that people saw when the bubbles expanded were not balanced by losses. As the bubble grew and the value of your house rose from $200,000 to $400,000, no one experienced an equivalent loss. Virtually all home buyers and owners were winners.

But speculative bubbles do not last.

Article 3.7

THE NEW WORLD OF HOME LOANS

BY AMY GLUCKMAN AND HOWARD KARGER

September/October 2007

Buying a home is the largest purchase most families will make in their lifetimes, the largest expenditure in a family budget, and the single largest asset for two-thirds of homeowners. It's also the most fraught with danger—in large part thanks to the growing chasm between ever-higher home prices and stagnant lower- and middle-class incomes. The last decade has seen an unprecedented surge in home prices to levels that current incomes simply do not support. For example, only 18% of Californians can afford the median house in the state using traditional loan-affordability calculations.

This disparity might have put a dent in the mortgage finance business. But no: in 2005, Americans owed $5.7 trillion in mortgages, a 50% increase in just four years. Over the past decade the mortgage finance industry has developed creative schemes designed to squeeze potential homebuyers, albeit often temporarily, into houses they cannot afford.

Most of the new mortgage products fall into the category of subprime mortgages —those offered to people whose problematic credit drops them into a lower lending category. They are generally adjustable-rate mortgages (ARMs) with some kind of a twist. Here are a few of these "creative" (read: confusing and risky) mortgage options.

Option ARM: With this loan, borrowers choose each month which of three or four different—and fluctuating—payments to make:

• full (principal+interest) payment based on a 30-year or 15-year repayment schedule.

• interest-only payment—does not reduce the loan principal or build homeowner equity. Borrowers who pay only interest for a period of time then face a big jump in the size of monthly payments or else are forced to refinance.

• minimum payment—may be lower than one month's interest; if so, the shortfall is added to the loan balance. The result is "negative amortization": over time, the principal goes up, not down. Eventually the borrower may have an "upside down" mortgage where the debt is greater than the market value of the home.

According to the credit rating firm Fitch Ratings, up to 80% of all option ARM borrowers choose the minimum monthly payment option. So it's no surprise that in 2005, 20% of option ARMs were "upside down." When a negative amortization limit is reached, the minimum payment jumps up to fully amortize the loan for the remaining loan term. In other words, borrowers suddenly have to start paying the real bill.

Even borrowers who pay more than the monthly minimums can face payment shocks. Option ARMs often start with a temporary super-low teaser interest rate (and correspondingly low monthly payments) that allows borrowers to qualify for "more house." The catch? Since the low initial monthly payment, based on interest rates as low as 1.25%, is not enough to cover the real interest rate, the borrower eventually faces a sudden increase in monthly payments.

Balloon Loan: This loan is written for a short 5- to 7-year term during which the borrower pays either interest and principal each month or, in a more predatory form, interest only. At the end of the loan term, the borrower must pay off the entire loan in a lump sum—the "balloon payment." At that point, buyers must either refinance or lose their homes. Balloon loans are known to real estate pros as "bullet loans," since if the loan comes due—forcing the owner to refinance—during a period of high interest rates, it's like getting a bullet in the heart. According to the national organizing and advocacy group ACORN, about 10% of all subprime loans are balloons.

Balloon loans are sometimes structured with monthly payments that fail to cover the interest, much less pay down the principal. Although the borrower makes regular payments, her loan balance increases each month: negative amortization. Many borrowers are unaware that they have a negative amortization loan until they have to refinance.

Shared Appreciation Mortgage (SAM): These are fixed-rate loans for up to 30 years that have easier credit qualifications and lower monthly payments than conventional mortgages. In exchange for a lower interest rate, the borrower relinquishes part of the future value of the home to the lender. Interest rate reductions are based on how much appreciation the borrower is willing to give up. SAMs discourage "sweat equity" since the homeowner receives only some fraction of the appreciation resulting from any improvements. Not surprisingly, these loans have been likened to sharecropping.

Stated-Income Loan: Aimed at borrowers who do not draw regular wages from an employer but live on tips, casual jobs that pay under the table, commissions, or investments, this loan does not require W-2 forms or other standard wage documentation. The trade-off: higher interest rates.

No-Ratio Loan: The debt-income ratio (the borrower's monthly payments on debt, including the planned mortgage, divided by her monthly income) is a standard benchmark that lenders use to determine how large a mortgage they will write. In return for a higher interest rate, the no-ratio loan abandons this benchmark; it is aimed at borrowers with complex financial lives or those who are experiencing divorce, the death of a spouse, or a career change.

Article 3.8

FINANCIALIZATION: A PRIMER

BY RAMAA VASUDEVAN
November/December 2008

Y ou don't have to be an investor dabbling in the stock market to feel the power of finance. Finance pervades the lives of ordinary people in many ways, from student loans and credit card debt to mortgages and pension plans.

And its size and impact are only getting bigger. Consider a few measures:

- U.S. credit market debt—all debt of private households, businesses, and government combined—rose from about 1.6 times the nation's GDP in 1973 to over 3.5 times GDP by 2007.

- The profits of the financial sector represented 14% of total corporate profits in 1981; by 2001-02 this figure had risen to nearly 50%.

These are only a few of the indicators of what many commentators have labeled the "financialization" of the economy—a process University of Massachusetts economist Gerald Epstein succinctly defines as "the increasing importance of financial markets, financial motives, financial institutions, and financial elites in the operation of the economy and its governing institutions."

In recent years, this phenomenon has drawn increasing attention. In his latest book, pundit Kevin Phillips writes about the growing divergence between the real (productive) and financial economies, describing how the explosion of trading in myriad new financial instruments played a role in polarizing the U.S. economy. On the left, political economists Harry Magdoff and Paul Sweezy had over many years pointed to the growing role of finance in the operations of capitalism; they viewed the trend as a reflection of the rising economic and political power of "rentiers"—those whose earnings come from financial activities and from forms of income arising from ownership claims (such as interest, rent, dividends, or capital gains) rather than from actual production.

From Finance to Financialization

The financial system is supposed to serve a range of functions in the broader economy. Banks and other financial institutions mop up savings, then allocate that capital, according to mainstream theory, to where it can most productively be used. For households and corporations, the credit markets facilitate greatly increased borrowing, which should foster investment in capital goods like buildings and machinery, in turn leading to expanded production. Finance, in other words, is supposed to facilitate the growth of the "real" economy—the part that produces useful goods (like bicycles) and services (like medical care).

In recent decades, finance has undergone massive changes in both size and shape. The basic mechanism of financialization is the transformation of future streams of income (from profits, dividends, or interest payments) into a tradable asset like a stock or a bond. For example, the future earnings of corporations are transmuted into equity stocks that are bought and sold in the capital market. Likewise, a loan, which involves certain fixed interest payments over its duration, gets a new life when it is converted into marketable bonds. And multiple loans, bundled together then "sliced and diced" into novel kinds of bonds ("collateralized debt obligations"), take on a new existence as investment vehicles that bear an extremely complex and opaque relationship to the original loans.

The process of financialization has not made finance more effective at fulfilling what conventional economic theory views as its core function. Corporations are not turning to the stock market as a source of finance for their investments, and their borrowing in the bond markets is often not for the purpose of productive investment either. Since the 1980s, corporations have actually spent more money buying back their own stock than they have taken in by selling newly issued stock. The granting of stock options to top executives gives them a direct incentive to have the corporation buy back its own shares—often using borrowed money to do so—in order to hike up the share price and allow them to turn a profit on the sale of their personal shares. More broadly, instead of fostering investment, financialization reorients managerial incentives toward chasing short-term returns through financial trading and speculation so as to generate ballooning earnings, lest their companies face falling stock prices and the threat of hostile takeover.

What is more, the workings of these markets tend to act like an upper during booms, when euphoric investors chase the promise of quick bucks. During downturns these same mechanisms work like downers, turning euphoria into panic as investors flee. Financial innovations like collateralized debt obligations were supposed to "lubricate" the economy by spreading risk, but instead they tend to heighten volatility, leading to amplified cycles of boom and bust. In the current crisis, the innovation of mortgage-backed securities fueled the housing bubble and encouraged enormous risk-taking, creating the conditions for the chain reaction of bank (and other financial institution) failures that may be far from over.

Financialization and Power

The arena of finance can at times appear to be merely a casino—albeit a huge one—where everyone gets to place her bets and ride her luck. But the financial system carries a far deeper significance for people's lives. Financial assets and liabilities represent claims on ownership and property; they embody the social relations of an economy at a particular time in history. In this sense, the recent process of financialization implies the increasing political and economic power of a particular segment of the capitalist class: rentiers. Accelerating financial transactions and the profusion of financial techniques have fuelled an extraordinary enrichment of this elite.

This enrichment arises in different ways. Financial transactions facilitate the reallocation of capital to high-return ventures. In the ensuing shake-up, some sectors of capital profit at the expense of other sectors. More important, the capitalist class as a whole is able to force a persistent redistribution in its favor, deploying its newly expanded wealth to bring about changes in the political-economy that channel even more wealth its way.

The structural changes that paved the way for financialization involved the squashing of working-class aspirations during the Reagan-Thatcher years; the defeats of the miners' strike in England and of the air traffic controllers' (PATCO) strike in the United States were perhaps the most symbolic instances of this process. At the same time, these and other governments increasingly embraced the twin policy mantras of fighting inflation and deregulating markets in place of creating full employment and raising wages. Corporations pushed through legislation to dismantle the financial regulations that inhibited their profitmaking strategies.

Financialization has gathered momentum amid greater inequality. In the United States, the top 1% of the population received 14.0% of the national after-tax income in 2004, nearly double its 7.5% share in 1979. In the same period the share of the bottom fifth fell from 6.8% to 4.9%.

And yet U.S. consumption demand has been sustained despite rising inequality and a squeeze on real wages for the majority of households. Here is the other side of the financialization coin: a massive expansion of consumer credit has played an important role in easing the constraints on consumer spending by filling the gap created by stagnant or declining real wages. The credit card debt of the average U.S. family increased by 53% through the 1990s. About 67% of low-income families with incomes less than $10,000 faced credit card debt, and the debt of this group saw the largest increase—a 184% rise, compared to a 28% increase for families with incomes above $100,000. Offered more and more credit as a privatized means of addressing wage stagnation, then, eventually, burdened by debt and on the edge of insolvency, the working poor and the middle class are less likely to organize as a political force to challenge the dominance of finance. In this sense, financialization becomes a means of social coercion that erodes working-class solidarity.

As the structures created by financial engineering unravel, the current economic crisis is revealing the cracks in this edifice. But even as a growing number of U.S. families are losing their homes and jobs in the wake of the subprime meltdown, the financial companies at the heart of the crisis have been handed massive bailouts and their top executives have pocketed huge pay-outs despite their role in abetting the meltdown—a stark sign of the power structures and interests at stake in this era of financialization.

Sources: Robin Blackburn, "Finance and the Fourth Dimension," *New Left Review* 39 May-June 2006; Robert Brenner, "New Boom or Bubble," *New Left Review* 25 Jan-Feb 2004; Tamara Draut and Javier Silva, "Borrowing to make ends meet," *Demos*, Sept 2003; Gerald Epstein, "Introduction" in G. Epstein, ed., *Financialization and the World* Economy, 2006; John Bellamy Foster, "The Financialization of Capitalism," *Monthly Review*, April 2007; Gretta Krippner, "The financialization of the US economy," *Socio-Economic Review* 3, Feb. 2005; Thomas Palley, "Financialization : What it is and why it matters," Political Economy Research Institute Working Paper #153, November 2007; A. Sherman and Arin Dine, "New CBO data shows inequality continues to widen," Center for Budget Priorities, Jan. 23, 2007; Kevin Phillips, *Bad Money: Reckless Finance, Failed Politics, and the Global Crisis of American Capitalism*, 2008.

Chapter 4

FISCAL POLICY, DEFICITS, AND DEBT

INTRODUCTION

Most textbooks depict a macroeconomy stabilized by government intervention. Reflecting the influence of Keynes, they look at ways the government can use fiscal policy—government spending and taxation—to bolster a flagging economy. Today's economy, mired in the worst economic crisis since the Great Depression, is surely flagging. Worse yet, that crisis comes on the heels of a feeble economic expansion that created fewer jobs and did less to raise wages than any other economic expansion since World War II (see Article 1.1).

What is the role of fiscal policy in this context? As the crisis worsened in the fall of 2008, the federal government dramatically increased spending. First Congress passed the Troubled Asset Recovery Program (TARP), which bailed out giant investment banks and insurance companies. It then passed the Obama stimulus package and budget, which provided some much-needed domestic spending but also boosted military spending. At the same time, the Federal Reserve and the Federal Deposit Insurance Corporation (which insures bank deposits) issued loans, lines of credit, and loan guarantees and pledged an emergency fund to clean up losses on Wall Street. All told, the federal government, the Fed, and the FDIC sunk nearly the value of a year's total U.S. national output into propping up the failed financial sector and rescuing the economy. (See Chapter 6 for more on the financial bailout.)

That spending, along with the Bush administration's 2001 and 2003 tax cuts and military spending to prosecute wars in Iraq and Afghanistan pushed the federal budget far into the red, ringing up a deficit of $1.4 trillion, or 9.9% of GDP, in 2009. That record "peacetime" deficit and those in the next few years will swell federal government debt to 67% of GDP by 2020, according to the latest estimates.

Our coverage begins with economist John Miller's provocative article "How I Learned to Stop Worrying and Love the Deficit" (Article 4.3). Miller maintains that deficit-financed stimulus spending was what stood between us and a complete economic collapse. He calls for yet more domestic spending and yet larger deficits to alleviate the economic suffering that continues unabated. In Article 4.4, economist Marty Wolfson tackles two persistent myths about budget deficits: that the government should never spend more than it takes in, and that doing so creates a burden on future generations. Deficit spending that puts unemployed people to work and boosts productivity, he argues, is the right policy during a recession and need not burden our grandchildren. In Article 4.5, economist Arthur MacEwan spells out why the private spending that would counteract an economic downturn is unlikely to be forthcoming, rendering government action in the form of deficit spending necessary to get a stalled economy going again. State governments are facing massive revenue shortfalls as well, reports economist Marianne Hill. Federal support and budget slashing will not close those gaps in a sustained way, she argues, so state governments must expand their tax base beyond regressive sales taxes and stop multi-state corporations from avoiding state taxes (Article 4.4).

Economist Ryan Dodd makes the case for the government acting as the economy's employer of last resort, arguing that direct job creation is the ultimate cure to catastrophic economic slumps (Article 4.1). Economist Gerald Friedman debunks the claim that direct job creation and other government spending failed to pull the economy out of the Great Depression. Friedman shows that the U.S. economy slumped in the late 1930s precisely because the federal government cut back on its stimulus spending and direct job creation (Article 4.2). Heidi Garrett-Peltier, an economist at the Political Economy Research Institute, makes the case that dollar per dollar, government spending on clean energy, health care, and education creates more jobs than military spending (Article 4.6). Jeannette Wicks-Lim, also at the Political Economy Research Institute, argues that transforming our fossil-fuel economy to a clean-energy economy presents us with an opportunity to make real headway integrating women into male-dominated workplaces. That can happen if federal spending goes to construction projects that are most successful at meeting affirmative action goals (Article 4.7).

Economist Paul Krugman's essay (Article 4.8) explains that the 2001–2003 tax cuts can only be sustained by shredding the social safety net, the kind of spending which adds far more to economic growth than the Bush tax cuts. Unfortunately, as Krugman shows, that was exactly the point (Article 4.8). Miller makes the case for a financial transaction tax on trading stocks and other securities as a way to reduce speculation in financial markets and to restore a focus on longer-term planning and job creation in the economy (Article 4.9).

With record budget deficits, attention has turned to the long-term solvency of Social Security, and conservatives are once again issuing calls for privatization. Economist Doug Orr examines the merits of their proposals and finds them wanting. Orr shows that, left alone, Social Security is unlikely to suffer a shortfall in revenues, let alone a crisis (Article 4.10). Finally, medical researcher Joel Harrison demonstrates that American families, even those who have no health coverage and get little or no care, spend dramatic sums on a health care system that fails to provide care to millions. Each health insurer adds its bureaucracy, profits, high corporate salaries, advertising, and sales commissions to the actual cost of providing care. Unlike a universal single-payer system, the health care reform of 2010 will not eliminate these costs (Article 4.11).

Discussion Questions

1. (Article 4.1) What is the case for making the federal government the "employer of last resort"? Why is Dodd convinced a modern WPA program will work?

2. (Article 4.2) What evidence does Friedman marshall to make the case that federal spending, especially if it had been applied in larger and continuing doses, could have brought the Great Depression to an end by 1940?

3. (Article 4.3) Are today's record-setting "peacetime" federal government budget deficits a problem? Why or why not? Should we aim to balance the budget over the next few years as the economy emerges from its financial crisis? If so, how should this be accomplished?

4. (Article 4.4) According to Wolfson, what factors are important in determining whether the government debt is affordable? Why does he claim that such debt does not necessarily impose a burden on future generations; under what circumstances does he argue it can be a burden?

5. (Article 4.5) How large are the budget gaps faced by state governments and how might they go about durably closing those gaps?

6. (Article 4.6) According to MacEwan, why is a shortfall in private spending unlikely to be self-correcting?

7. (Article 4.8) What factors make government spending on clean energy an effective economic stimulus and a promising opportunity to promote equal opportunity for women workers?

8. (Article 4.9) What does Krugman think is the hidden agenda of those currently pushing for tax cuts? Do you agree with his analysis? Explain why or why not.

9. (Article 4.10) What evidence does Miller present to make the case that U.S. financial markets are inefficient and that a financial transaction tax would improve their efficiency?

10. (Article 4.11) What convinces Orr that the Social Security system is not suffering a crisis? What is the looming bond market crisis that Orr says is the real concern of those who want to privatize Social Security?

11. (Article 4.12) How does Harrison support his claim that Americans already spend far more on health care than is typically recognized?

Article 4.1

A NEW WPA?

National governments, by serving as "employers of last resort," could guarantee full employment by providing a job for anyone ready, willing and able to work.

BY RYAN A. DODD
March/April 2008

D ark clouds are now looming over America's economic future. As first the stock market boom and then the housing boom have come to an end, along with the fountains of cheap credit that were their mainspring, the perennial gale of unemployment is blowing in. The president and Congress have addressed the downturn with tax rebates and talk of "debt relief." Meanwhile, public infrastructure is crumbling. Workers' wages are stagnating while their work hours are rising. Health insurance is becoming less and less affordable for the typical family. And as U.S. military spending escalates, government spending on essential services is drastically reduced.

All of these facts serve to remind us that capitalist economies are inherently unstable and structurally incapable of creating full employment at decent wages and benefits. While tax rebates and debt relief may provide some minor protection from the coming economic storm, these measures are temporary—and inadequate—responses to a perpetual problem. As an alternative to these ad hoc policies or, worse yet, the free-market fundamentalism still widely preached in Washington, some economists and policymakers, in the United States and abroad, are touting a policy that seeks to end unemployment via a government promise to provide a job to anyone ready, willing, and able to work.

Argentina's Experiment in Direct Job Creation

In early December 2001, following nearly two decades of neoliberal restructuring, the Argentine economy collapsed. Apparently, two decades of privatization, liberalization, and government austerity, ushered in by Argentina's brutal military junta (in power from 1976 to 1983), were not enough to sate the appetites of global financial capital: earlier that year the International Monetary Fund had withheld $1.3 billion in loans the country needed to service its $142 billion external debt. In response to the IMF's action, the government froze all bank accounts (although many wealthy Argentines managed to relocate their funds abroad before the freeze) and drastically cut government spending. As a consequence, the economy experienced a severe depression as incomes and expenditures fell through the floor. The unemployment rate shot up to a record 21.5% by May 2002, with over 50% of the population living in poverty.

The popular response to the crisis was massive. Protests and demonstrations erupted throughout the country. The government went through five presidents in the course of a month. Workers eventually reclaimed dozens of abandoned factories and created democratically run cooperative enterprises, many of which are still in operation today and are part of a growing coop movement.

Reclaiming factories was a lengthy and difficult process, however, and the immediate problem of unemployment remained. In response, in April 2002 the Argentine government put into place a direct job creation program known as *Plan Jefes de Hogar* ("Heads-of-Household Plan"), which promised a job to all heads of households satisfying certain requirements. In order to qualify, a household had to include a child under the age of 18, a person with a disability, or a pregnant woman; the household head had to be unemployed; and each household was generally limited to only one participant in the program. The program provided households with 150 pesos a month for four hours of work a day, five days a week. Program participants mainly engaged in the provision of community services and/or participated in worker training programs administered by local nonprofits.

While limited in scope and viewed by many in the government as an emergency measure, the program was incredibly successful and popular with its workers. It provided jobs and incomes to roughly two million workers, or 13% of Argentina's labor force, as well as bringing desperately needed goods and services—from community gardens to small construction projects—to severely depressed neighborhoods. The entry of many women into the program, while their husbands continued to look for jobs in the private sector, had a liberating effect on traditional family structures. And by some accounts, the program helped facilitate the cooperative movement that subsequently emerged with the takeover of abandoned factories. Not surprisingly, as Argentina's economy has recovered from the depths of the crisis, the government has recently made moves to discontinue this critical experiment in direct job creation.

"Employer of Last Resort"

The Argentine experience with direct job creation represents a real-world example of what is often referred to as the *employer of last resort* (ELR) proposal by a number of left academics and public policy advocates. Developed over the course of the past two decades, the ELR proposal is based on a rather simple idea. In a capitalist economy, with most people dependent on private employment for their livelihoods, the government has a unique responsibility to guarantee full employment. This responsibility has been affirmed in the U.N. Universal Declaration of Human Rights, which includes a right to employment. A commitment to full employment is also official U.S. government policy as codified in the Employment Act of 1946 and the Humphrey-Hawkins Act of 1976.

Although many versions of the ELR proposal have been put forward, they all revolve around the idea that national governments could guarantee full employment by providing a job to anyone ready, willing, and able to work. The various proposals differ mainly on the wage and benefit packages they would provide to participants. The most common proposal calls for paying all participants a universal basic wage and benefit package, regardless of skills, work experience, or prior earnings. This wage and benefit package would then form the effective minimum for both the public and private sectors of the economy. After fixing a wage and benefit package, the government would allow the quantity of workers in the program to float, rising and falling in response to cyclical fluctuations in private-sector employment.

As with Argentina's program, ELR proposals typically call for participants to work in projects to improve their local communities—everything from basic infrastructure projects to a Green Jobs Corps. Most ELR proponents also advocate a decentralized approach similar to Argentina's, with local public or nonprofit institutions planning and administering the projects, though it is essential that the program be funded at the national level.

This raises an important question: How will governments pay for such a large-scale program? Wouldn't an ELR program require significantly raising taxes or else result in exploding budget deficits? Can governments really afford to employ everyone who wants a job but cannot find one in the private economy? Advocates of ELR address the issue of affordability in different ways, but all agree that the benefits to society vastly outweigh the expense. Many ELR advocates go even further, arguing that any talk of "costs" to society misrepresents the nature of the problem of unemployment. The existence of unemployed workers represents a net cost to society, in terms of lost income and production as well as the psychological and social stresses that result from long spells of unemployment. Employing them represents a net benefit, in terms of increased incomes *and* enhanced individual and social wellbeing. The real burden of an ELR program, from the perspective of society, is thus effectively zero.

Most estimates of the direct cost of an ELR program are in the range of less than 1% of GDP per year. For the United States, this was less than $132 billion in 2006, or about 5% of the federal budget. (By way of comparison, in 2006 the U.S. government spent over $120 billion on the wars in Iraq and Afghanistan—and that figure does not include the cost of lives lost or ruined or the future costs incurred, for example, for veterans' health care.) Furthermore, an ELR program provides benefits to society in the form of worker retraining, enhanced public infrastructure, and increased social output (e.g., cleaner parks and cities, free child care, public performances, etc.). By increasing the productivity of those participants who attend education or training programs, an ELR program would also decrease real costs throughout the economy. Estimates of program costs take into account a reduction in other forms of social assistance such as food stamps, cash assistance, and unemployment insurance, which would instead be provided to ELR participants in the form of a wage and benefit package. Of course, those who cannot work would still be eligible for these and other forms of assistance.

Today, the ELR idea is mostly confined to academic journals and conferences. Still, proponents can point to a number of little known real-world examples their discussions have helped to shape. For example, the Argentine government explicitly based its *Jefes de Hogar* program on the work of economists associated with the Center for Full Employment and Price Stability (CFEPS) at the University of Missouri-Kansas City. Daniel Kostzer, an economist at the Argentine Ministry of Labor and one of the main architects of the program, had become familiar with the CFEPS proposal and was attempting to create such a program in Argentina a few years before the collapse provided him with the necessary political support. Similar experiments are being considered or are currently underway in India, France, and Bolivia. Advocates of ELR proposals can also be found at the Levy Economics Institute (U.S.), the Center for Full Employment and Equity (Australia), and the National Jobs for All Coalition (U.S.).

The Case for Direct Job Creation

Involuntary unemployment is a fundamental and inherent feature of a capitalist economy left to its own devices. In a society where most people depend on employment in the private sector for their livelihood, the inability of a capitalist economy to consistently create enough jobs for all who seek work is deeply troubling, pointing to the need for intervention from outside of the private sector. ELR advocates view national governments—with their unique spending abilities, and with their role as, in principle, democratically accountable social institutions—as the most logical institutions for collective action to bring about full employment. In addition, government job creation is viewed as the simplest and most direct means for overcoming the problem of involuntary unemployment in a capitalist economy.

The standard mainstream response to the problem of unemployment is to blame the victims of capitalism for lacking the necessary talents, skills, and effort to get and keep a job. Hence, the mainstream prescription is to promote policies aimed at enhancing the "human capital" of workers in order to make them more "competitive" in a rapidly globalizing economy. The response of ELR advocates is that such policies, if they accomplish anything at all, simply redistribute unemployment and poverty more equitably. For example, according to the Bureau of Labor Statistics, the number of unemployed workers (including so-called "discouraged" and "underemployed" workers) in August 2007 was 16.4 million, while the number of job vacancies was 4.1 million. No amount of investment in human capital is going to change the fact that there simply aren't enough jobs to go around.

Advocates of ELR also consistently reject the Keynesian rubric, with its focus on demand-management strategies—that is, policies aimed at increasing aggregate demand for the output of the economy. This approach has been pursued either directly, through government spending on goods and services (including transfer payments to households), or indirectly, largely through policies intended to increase private investment. Such an approach exacerbates inequality by biasing policy in favor of the already well-to-do, through tax cuts and investment credits to wealthy individuals and powerful corporations. These policies also tend to privilege the more highly skilled and better-paid workers found in the industries that generally benefit from the government's largesse (often arms manufacturers and other military-related companies). For example, much of the increase in government spending during the Cold War era went into the high-tech, capital-intensive, and oligopolized sectors of the economy. Capital-intensive industries require relatively small amounts of labor, and, thus, produce little employment growth per dollar of government expenditure. Under this policy approach, the most that lower-paid or unemployed workers could hope for would be to snatch a few crumbs from the great corporate feast as the economy expanded over time.

In contrast to both the human-capital and demand-management approaches, ELR provides a means for rapidly achieving zero involuntary unemployment. By definition, anyone who is unemployed and chooses not to accept the ELR offer would be considered voluntarily unemployed. Many individuals with sufficient savings and decent job prospects may forgo the opportunity to participate in the ELR program, but ELR always provides them with a backup option.

In addition to the immediate effects of ELR on employment, the program acts as an "automatic stabilizer" in the face of cyclical fluctuations in the private sector of the economy. During a recession, the number of participants in the program can be expected to grow as people are laid off and/or find it increasingly difficult to find private-sector employment. The opposite happens during the recovery phase of the business cycle, as people find it easier to find private-sector employment at wages above the ELR minimum. As a result, ELR advocates argue, the existence of such a program would dampen fluctuations in private-sector activity by setting a floor to the decline in incomes and employment.

A final and less discussed benefit of the program is its socializing effect. The example of Argentina is instructive in this respect. The nature of employment in the *Jefes* program, oriented as it was toward community rather than market imperatives, created a sense of public involvement and responsibility. Participants reported increases in morale and often continued to work beyond the four hours a day for which they were getting paid; they appreciated the cooperative nature of most of the enterprises and their focus on meeting essential community needs as opposed to quarterly profit targets. By expanding the public sphere, the *Jefes* program created a spirit of democratic participation in the affairs of the community, unmediated by the impersonal relations of market exchange. These are the kinds of experiences that are essential if capitalist societies are to move beyond the tyranny of the market and toward more cooperative and democratic forms of social organization.

Some economists and advocates have pressed for a similar proposal, the *basic income guarantee* (BIG). Instead of guaranteeing jobs, under this proposal the government would guarantee a minimum income to everyone by simply giving cash assistance to anyone earning below that level, in an amount equal to the gap between his or her actual income and the established basic income. (Hence this proposal is sometimes referred to as a "negative income tax.") BIG is an important idea deserving wider discussion than it has so far received. But ELR advocates have a number of concerns. One is that a BIG program is inherently inflationary: by providing income without putting people to work, it creates an additional claim on output without directly increasing the production of that output. Another is that BIG programs are less politically palatable—and hence less sustainable—than ELR schemes, which benefit society at large through the provision of public works and other social goods, and which avoid the stigma attached to "welfare" programs. Finally, a job offers social and psychological benefits that an income payment alone does not: maintaining and enhancing work skills, keeping in contact with others, and having the satisfaction of contributing to society. When, for instance, participants in Argentina's *Jefes* program were offered an income in place of a job, most refused; they preferred to work. Consequently, ELR programs meet the same objectives as basic income guarantee schemes and more, without the negative side effects of inflation and stigmatization. Nonetheless, a BIG program may be appropriate for those who should not be expected to work.

Learning from the Past

The idea that the government in a capitalist economy should provide jobs for the unemployed is not new. In the United States, the various New Deal agencies created during the Great Depression of the 1930s offer a well-known example. Organizations such as the Works Progress Administration and the Civilian Conservation Corps were designed to deal with the massive unemployment of that period. Unemployment peaked at almost 25% of the civilian labor force in 1933 and averaged over 17% for the entire decade. These programs were woefully inadequate, largely due to their limited scale. It ultimately took the massive increases in government expenditure precipitated by the Second World War to pull the U.S. economy out of depression.

The onset of the postwar "Golden Age" and the dominance of Keynesian economics sounded the death knell of direct job creation as a solution to unemployment. The interwar public employment strategy was replaced with a "demand-management" strategy—essentially a sort of trickle-down economics in which various tax incentives and government expenditure programs, mainly military spending, were used to stimulate private investment. Policymakers believed that this would spur economic growth. The twin problems of poverty and unemployment would then be eliminated since, according to President Kennedy's famous aphorism, "a rising tide lifts all boats."

In the mid 1960s, the civil rights movement revived the idea of direct job creation as a solution to the problems of poverty and unemployment. Although the Kennedy and Johnson administrations had declared a so-called War on Poverty, the movement's call for direct job creation fell on deaf ears as the Johnson administration, at the behest of its Council of Economic Advisers, pursued a more conservative approach based on the standard combination of supply-side incentives to increase private investment and assorted strategies to "improve" workers' "human capital" so as to make them more attractive to private employers.

The rise to dominance of neoliberalism since the mid-1970s has resulted in a full-scale retreat from even the mildly social democratic policies of the early postwar period. While a commitment to full employment remains official U.S. policy, the concerns of central bankers and financial capitalists now rule the roost in government circles. This translates into a single-minded obsession with fighting inflation at the expense of all other economic and social objectives. Not only is fighting inflation seemingly the only concern of economic policy, it is seen to be in direct conflict with the goal of full employment (witness the widespread acceptance among economists and policymakers of the NAIRU, or "non-accelerating inflation rate of unemployment" theory, which posits that the economy has a set-point for unemployment, well above zero, below which rapidly rising inflation must occur). Whenever falling unemployment leads to concerns about "excessive" wage growth, central banks are expected to raise interest rates in an attempt to force slack on the economy and thereby decrease inflationary pressures. The resulting unemployment acts as a kind of discipline, tempering the demands of working-class people for higher wages or better working conditions in favor of the interests of large commercial and financial institutions. The postwar commitment to full employment has finally been sacrificed on the altar of price stability.

ELR and Capitalism

As demonstrated by the history of public employment programs in the United States and the example of Argentina, direct job-creation programs do not happen absent significant political pressure from below. This is the case whether or not those calling for change explicitly demand an ELR program. Given the hegemonic position of neoliberal ideology, there are many powerful forces today that would be hostile to the idea of governments directly creating jobs for the unemployed. These forces represent a critical barrier to the implementation of an ELR program. In fact, these forces represent a critical barrier to virtually any project for greater social and economic justice. The purpose of initiating a wider discussion of ELR proposals is to build them into more comprehensive programs for social and economic justice. As is always the case, this requires the building of mass-based social movements advocating for these and other progressive policies.

A significant objection to the ELR proposal remains: it's capitalism, stupid. If you don't like unemployment, poverty, and inequality—not to mention war, environmental destruction, and alienating and exploitative work—then you don't like capitalism, and you should seek alternatives instead of reformist employment policies. ELR advocates would not disagree. In the face of the overlapping and myriad problems afflicting a capitalist economy, the achievements of even a full-scale ELR program would be limited. The political difficulties involved in establishing an ELR program in the first place, in the face of opposition from powerful elements of society, would be immense. And certainly, the many experiments in non-capitalist forms of economic and social organization currently being carried out, for example, in the factories of Argentina and elsewhere, should be championed. But it is fair to ask: shouldn't we also champion living wage laws, a stronger social safety net for those who cannot or should not be expected to work, and universal health care—as well as an end to imperialist wars of aggression, environmentally unsustainable practices, and the degradation of work? In sum, shouldn't we seek to alleviate all of the symptoms of capitalism, even as we work toward a better economic system?

Sources: Joseph Halevi, "The Argentine Crisis," *Monthly Review*, April 2002; Pavlina Tcherneva, "Macroeconomic Stabilization Policy in Argentina: A Case Study of the 2002 Currency Collapse and Crisis Resolution through Job Creation," Bard College Working Paper, 2007; L. Randall Wray, *Understanding Modern Money: The Key to Full Employment and Price Stability*, Edward Elgar, 1998; Congressional Research Service, "The Cost of Iraq, Afghanistan and Other Global War on Terror Operations Since 9/11," www.fas.org/sgp/crs/natsec/RL33110.pdf, update 7/07; National Jobs for All Coalition, "September 2007 Unemployment Data," www.njfac.org/jobnews.html; Nancy Rose, "Historicizing Government Work Programs: A Spectrum from Workfare to Fair Work," Center for Full Employment and Price Stability, Seminar Paper No. 2, March 2000; Judith Russell, *Economics, Bureaucracy and Race: How Keynesians Misguided the War on Poverty*, Columbia Univ. Press, 2004; Fadhel Kaboub, "Employment Guarantee Programs: A Survey of Theories and Policy Experiences," Levy Econ. Inst., Working Paper No. 498, May 2007.

Article 4.2

RESPONDING TO REVISIONISM

Fiscal stimulus and recovery during the Great Depression

BY GERALD FRIEDMAN
May/June 2009

"THERE IS NO DISAGREEMENT THAT WE NEED ACTION BY OUR GOVERNMENT,
A RECOVERY PLAN THAT WILL HELP TO JUMPSTART THE ECONOMY."

—PRESIDENT-ELECT BARACK OBAMA, JANUARY 9, 2009

With all due respect, Mr. President, that is not true.

*Notwithstanding reports that all economists are now Keynesians and that we
all support a big increase in the burden of government, we the undersigned do
not believe that more government spending is a way to improve economic performance. More government spending by Hoover and Roosevelt did not pull the
United States economy out of the Great Depression in the 1930s. More government spending did not solve Japan's "lost decade" in the 1990s. As such, it is a
triumph of hope over experience to believe that more government spending will
help the U.S. today. To improve the economy, policymakers should focus on
reforms that remove impediments to work, saving, investment and production.
Lower tax rates and a reduction in the burden of government are the best ways
of using fiscal policy to boost growth*
   —Full-page Cato Institution ad in the *New York Times* and other
major newspapers, signed by 200 economists, late January 2009.

In the 1930s, the Great Depression discredited laissez-faire capitalism, and President Franklin Roosevelt's New Deal showed the world how an active government
could restore economic vitality and improve life. Since then, the claim that the New
Deal failed to end the Great Depression of the 1930s has become central to conservative attacks on government fiscal policy. "More government spending by Hoover
and Roosevelt," the Cato Institute claims in a recent advertisement, "did not pull
the United States economy out of the Great Depression in the 1930s."

   Such claims have some superficial credibility; official statistics, not including workers on federal emergency employment, report an unemployment rate of
over 9% at the end of Roosevelt's first term, and over 12% in 1938. Indeed, economic historians have long recognized that New Deal fiscal policy did not end
the Great Depression; E. Cary Brown concluded in 1956, for example, that fiscal
policy "seems to have been an unsuccessful recovery device in the 'thirties." But
he adds that this was "not because it did not work but because it was not tried."
Christina D. Romer, now head of the President's Council of Economic Advisers,
reached similar conclusions, also finding that fiscal policy was applied too timidly
to end the Depression.

It is a nice piece of rhetoric for the Cato Institute and other conservatives to equate FDR with the failed policies of Herbert Hoover. Yes, FDR was not fiscally aggressive enough, but Hoover did not try to stimulate the economy with government spending at all. Instead, he greeted the onset of the Great Depression by trimming government spending to maintain budget balance. He ran surpluses during the early Depression years, 1929–30, only reversing course in 1932 when plunging revenues, which fell to half the 1930 level, forced a significant deficit. On the spending side, federal consumption and investment remained stuck at 1.8% of Gross Domestic Product (GDP) throughout the Hoover years.

Thus Cato is right: Hoover's policy of budget balance and spending restraint did not stem economic collapse. Instead, under Hoover, investment fell by 81%, consumption by 18%, and the GDP by over 25%. Unemployment rose from 2.9% of the civilian labor force to 23% and 8 million jobs disappeared. By the end of his term, collapse had spread to the banking system. The economy spiraled down when banks, fearing insolvency due to mortgages and loans unlikely to be repaid in a collapsing economy, further cut back on their lending. Depositors lined up to withdraw their money, driving the banks another step towards insolvency, and dragging the economy down further.

Arriving in office in March 1933, Roosevelt intervened aggressively in financial markets, averting further panic by closing all banks for a week. Eventually, only the stronger banks were allowed to reopen, and they were backed with a new federal system of depositor insurance to prevent further bank panics. Roosevelt pressed the Federal Reserve to inaugurate a policy of monetary ease. He also significantly increased government spending, running deficits that averaged 4.8% of GDP throughout his first term. Unlike Hoover's inadvertent 1932 deficit, Roosevelt's New Deal deficits reflected significantly increased spending even with rising revenues. During FDR's first term, real federal spending was over twice the Hoover level.

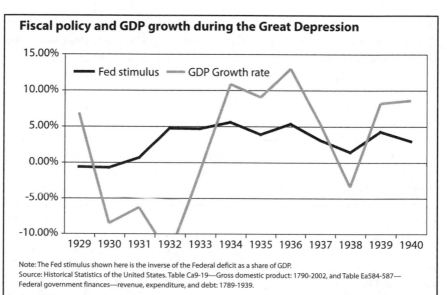

Fiscal policy and GDP growth during the Great Depression

Note: The Fed stimulus shown here is the inverse of the Federal deficit as a share of GDP.
Source: Historical Statistics of the United States. Table Ca9-19—Gross domestic product: 1790-2002, and Table Ea584-587—Federal government finances—revenue, expenditure, and debt: 1789-1939.

Critics who charge that Roosevelt's fiscal policy failed to cure the Depression ignore the very rapid economic recovery that came with the New Deal. Stimulated by his aggressive fiscal policy, the economy boomed during Roosevelt's first term at rates about double the size of the federal deficit. GDP growth averaged over 10% a year from 1934 to 1936, and the economy grew from 62% of its trend level in 1933 to 76% in 1936. By 1937, FDR's stimulus policies had lowered unemployment to 9%, less than half the rate when he assumed office.

While the New Deal did not end the Depression, had FDR remained on course through his second term, the Depression may have ended by 1940. But instead of continuing aggressive fiscal policy, FDR reversed course in 1937, dramatically reducing the federal deficit after 1936. This plunged the economy back into a severe depression. Unemployment shot up three points to 12% in 1938. Roosevelt quickly reversed course with enough deficit spending from 1939 to 1941 to revive the economy after the 1938 dip. But it was the massive Keynesian stimulus of WWII, with deficits as high as 27% of GDP in 1943, that finally ended the Great Depression.

Even this casual examination of the 1930s discredits conservative claims about the New Deal. But there are positive lessons here as well. Far from contradicting Keynesian expectations, the New Deal shows the power of fiscal policy, both to promote recovery (1933–37 and 1939–45) and to exacerbate depression (1929–30 and 1938). The New Deal could have done better with a larger deficit. Nonetheless, when combined with reform of the financial sector and the banks, the New Deal produced four years of rapid growth that by 1937 had more than halved the unemployment rate.

Cato is right that there are lessons for the Obama administration in the New Deal experience. But the lessons are the opposite of those they would preach. First, we will need a very large stimulus, probably significantly larger than the deficit of 6–8% of GDP planned for now. Between a sharp drop in consumption with falling housing and stock market prices, falling exports, and declining investment due to the financial crisis, we may have a decline in aggregate demand of as much 20% of GDP. This would suggest the need for a deficit of between 10% and 14% of GDP, significantly more than is currently planned by the administration.

Lesson two: facing a serious economic downturn, don't declare victory prematurely. An economic collapse builds a great deal of depressing inertia that may require a long period of sustained stimulus to overcome. By prematurely moving towards budget balance in 1937–38, the Roosevelt administration prolonged the Great Depression by several years. We may hope that the Obama administration will be in a position to make that mistake in 2010 or 2011; and let us hope that they learn from the past.

Sources: E. Cary Brown, "Fiscal Policy in the 'Thirties: A Reappraisal," *The American Economic Review* 46:5 (Dec. 1956), 857–79; John K. Galbraith, *The Great Crash of 1929* (New York, Harpers, 1955); Charles Kindleberger, *The World in Depression* (Berkeley, University of California Press, 1986); Christina D. Romer, "What Ended the Great Depression?" *The Journal of Economic History* 52:4 (Dec 1993), 757–84; Herbert Stein, *The Fiscal Revolution in America* (Chicago, University of Chicago Press, 1969); Peter Temin and Barrie Wigmore, "The End of One Big Deflation," *Explorations in Economic History* 27 (Oct. 1990), 483–502; Peter Temin, *Did Monetary Forces Cause the Great Depression?* (New York, Norton, 1976); Peter Temin, *Lessons from the Great Depression* (Cambridge, MIT Press, 1989).

Article 4.3

HOW I LEARNED TO STOP WORRYING AND LOVE THE DEFICIT

BY JOHN MILLER
November/December 2009

> THE PELOSI-OBAMA DEFICITS
>
> [C]urrent U.S. fiscal policy is "borrow and spend" on a hyperlink. The ... deficit for 2009 will be "only" $1.58 trillion ... . But the Obama fiscal plan envisions $9 trillion in new borrowing over the next decade.
>
> We've never fretted over budget deficits, at least if they finance tax cuts to promote growth or spending to win a war. But these deficit estimates are driven entirely by more domestic spending and already assume huge new tax increases.
>
> [T]he White House still hasn't ruled out another fiscal stimulus. ... Obamanomics has turned into an unprecedented experiment in runaway government with no plan to pay for it, save, perhaps, for a big future toll on the middle class such as a value-added tax.
>
> —from an op-ed in the *Wall Street Journal*, 9/26/09

You would have thought the federal budget deficit had morphed into Dr. Strangelove's doomsday machine from the howling that followed the publication of the Congressional Budget Office (CBO) projections in August. The *Wall Street Journal* editors were happy to join in despite assuring readers that they are not deficit-phobic.

But the truth is, government spending and the budget deficit it engendered are what stood between us and an economic doomsday that would have rivaled the Great Depression of the 1930s. In that context, the Obama budget deficits are neither all that big nor all that bad, although they sure could have been better had the spending priorities been more progressive. And even larger deficits could have done—and still could do—more to alleviate the economic suffering that continues unabated even as the economy begins to stabilize.

How Big Is It?

Even after correcting for inflation, $1.58 trillion is a record federal budget deficit. But this eye-popping number needs to be seen in context.

A trillion and a half dollar deficit will equal 11.2% of Gross Domestic Product (GDP) for 2009, according to CBO estimates. That too is a record for "peacetime" deficits. The Reagan deficits in their worst year reached 6% of GDP. During World War II, however, military spending pushed the federal deficit to qualitatively different levels, reaching 31.3% of GDP and never dropping below 14.5% during the war years 1942 to 1945.

Whatever its size, before pinning the 2009 deficit on runaway government spending, it's important to assess how much the collapsing economy contributed to the deficit. Big government bashers like the *Journal* editors would have you believe that the entire budget deficit was brought on by reckless government spending.

That is hardly the case. The collapsing economy added more to the deficit from 2007 to 2009 than any other factor. As economic activity dried up, personal and corporate income tax revenues plummeted: this year government revenues will drop to 14.9% of GDP, their lowest level since 1950. Plus, the crashing economy automatically pushed government spending on unemployment insurance and food stamps up, further widening the deficit. Even the financial-sector bailout and the Obama stimulus package taken together did less to swell the deficit than the economic collapse did.

To control for the effect of the business cycle on the budget deficit, economists look at the so-called standardized, or cyclically adjusted, deficit—the deficit that would occur if the economy was always operating at the peak of the business cycle, in other words, at its "potential GDP." Standardized deficit figures indicate that the 2009 budget is highly stimulative but hardly disproportionate to the economic emergency it confronted. In 2009 the cyclically adjusted deficit will reach 8.6% of potential GDP, and then shrink to 3.4% by 2011, according to CBO estimates. The previous high was 4.7% in 1986 (with data back to 1962), in the midst of the "borrow and squander" Reagan years when the only emergencies facing the nation were the desire of the rich for a tax cut and the drive to expand cold-war military spending. Under George W. Bush, tax cutter to the rich *extraordinaire*, the cyclically adjusted deficit reached 3.1% in 2004, the near equal of the projected 2011 figure.

The CBO projected deficits will add $9 trillion in the next decade to the national debt, the cumulative amount of money the government will have borrowed to finance its annual deficits.

That is another frightening number, but it too needs to be seen in context. For instance, publicly held federal-government debt will reach 67.8% of GDP in 2019, according to CBO projections. That number would be the largest ratio of debt to national output since 1952, but still not in the same ballpark as the 120% figure at the end of World War II.

But absent the stimulus, the federal government would face yet larger deficits as the economy and federal tax revenues fell further. And unlike World War II spending that sparked a 20-year economic boom, a do-nothing strategy would be followed by a depression that would impose far greater costs than escalating government debt.

Domestic Spending Gone Wild?

The *Journal*'s editors are correct that it is not the size of the deficit that is worrisome, but its content—the spending and taxing policies that brought it about. But on that count they really should not be complaining, because it was the tax cuts and military spending they favor that played a decisive role in pushing the federal budget out of the black and into the red.

When the Bush administration took office in 2001, the CBO projected the federal government would run a budget *surplus* of $710 billion in FY 2009. The CBO now projects a $1.6 trillion budget deficit. The Economic Policy Institute found that the bad economy (slow growth and then the crisis) and Bush administration tax and spending policies (from the 2001 and 2003 tax cuts, to spending on Afghanistan and Iraq, to Medicare prescription drug coverage) each caused about 42% of that $2.3 trillion budget swing. Following by quite a distance were the Obama stimulus package and the TARP bailout, accounting for 7.6% and 7.7% of the budget swing respectively. Supplemental defense allocations for the Iraq and Afghanistan wars accounted for more of the increase in the deficit (9.3%) than either program.

Nor do the CBO numbers justify the editors' claim that we are about to enter a period of runaway government and deficits "driven entirely by more domestic spending." Discretionary domestic spending (federal government spending on education, housing, infrastructure, and the like) will average 3.7% of GDP over the 2010 to 2019 period—no higher than in 2008, the last year of the Bush administration. Mandatory domestic spending (including Social Security, Medicare, Medicaid, and unemployment insurance) will average 12.8% of GDP over the next ten years, 1.6 percentage points more than in 2008. Even that jump in what is, after all, already-obligated spending will account for just two-fifths of the federal deficits that the CBO projects for the next ten years. That is hardly domestic spending gone wild.

The True Test

Obama administration policies might not have been the chief cause of the 2009 deficit or the $2.3 trillion budget swing from black to red ink over this decade, nor will they commission runaway domestic spending as the editors allege.

But that alone does not make the president's policies successful. The true test of any deficit spending policy is whether it makes people better off. The policies endorsed by the editors have failed that test miserably. Worse yet, they saddled us with large deficits that now block the very spending proposals that might pass that test. Whether it is spending for universal health care, green technology, infrastructure repair, or school renovations—or help for those who have lost their homes—the new refrain is that spending must not add one dime to "the deficit."

A second dose of deficit-financed stimulus spending, a notion the editors dismiss out of hand, would create jobs desperately needed as even official unemployment rates are likely remain at double-digit levels through much of 2010.

In a very real way, our jobs and our prospects for living in a fair society depend upon learning to stop worrying and love the deficit.

Sources: The Pelosi-Obama Deficits," *Wall Street Journal,* Sept. 26, 2009; "The Budget and Economic Outlook: An Update," Congressional Budget Office, August 2009; "Measuring the Effects of the Business Cycle on the Federal Budget: An Update," Congressional Budget Office, September 1, 2009; John Irons, Kathryn Edwards, and Anna Turner, "The 2009 Budget Deficit: How did we get here?" Economic Policy Institute, August 20, 2009.

Article 4.4

MYTHS OF THE DEFICIT

BY MARTY WOLFSON
May/June 2010

Nearly 15 million people are officially counted as unemployed in the United States, and more than 6 million of these have been unemployed for more than 26 weeks. Another 11 million are the "hidden" unemployed: jobless workers who have given up looking for work and part-time workers who want full-time jobs. Unemployment has especially affected minority communities; the official black teenage unemployment rate, for example, stands at 42%.

The *moral* case for urgently addressing the unemployment issue is clear. The costs of unemployment, especially prolonged unemployment, are devastating. Self-worth is questioned, homes are lost, families stressed, communities disrupted. Across the land, the number one issue is jobs, jobs, jobs.

The *economic* case for how to address the jobs issue is also clear. As Keynes argued during the Great Depression, federal government spending can directly create jobs. And the $787 billion stimulus package approved by Congress in February 2009 did help pull the economy back from disaster, when it was shedding 20,000 jobs *a day* in late 2008 and early 2009.

But we still have a long way to go. To get back just to where we were when the recession began in December 2007, the economy would need to create 11.1 million jobs: 8.4 million to replace the jobs lost and 2.7 million to absorb new workers who have entered the labor market since then.

Despite a pickup of economic activity recently, long-term projections are that the unemployment rate will fall only gradually over the next several years. The Congressional Budget Office forecast for the unemployment rate for 2012 is a stubbornly high 8%. So why are we not moving more aggressively to reduce unemployment?

The *ideological* opposition to government spending remains a major obstacle. There are those who see an increase in the role of government as something to be avoided at all costs—even if the cost is the jobs of the unemployed.

Even among those who are not subject to such ideological blinders, there is still a *political* argument that resonates strongly. The argument is that government spending to create jobs will create large budget deficits, which will have terrible consequences for the American people. Politicians, pundits, and other commentators—in a frenzied drumbeat of speeches, op-eds, and articles—have asserted that the most urgent priority *now* is to reduce the budget deficit.

It is important to note that this argument is focused on current policy, not just the long-term budgetary situation. There is room for debate about long-term budget deficits, but these are affected more by the explosive growth of health-care costs than by government discretionary spending to create jobs.

Why, then, are people taken in by an argument that says it is more important to reduce the budget deficit now than for the government to spend money to create jobs? Two myths constantly repeated in the public debate have contributed to this situation:

1) Families can't spend more than they have; neither should the government.

It seems to be common sense that a family can't spend more than it has. But of course that is exactly what the family does when it takes out a car loan or a student loan, or does any other kind of borrowing. The government, just like families, should be able to borrow. The real issue is whether or not the debt is affordable. For families, and for the government, that depends on the size of the debt relative to the income available to service the debt; it also depends on the nature of the borrowing.

For the federal government, the relevant debt-income measure is the ratio of outstanding debt of the federal government to gross domestic product. (*Outstanding debt* is the total amount owed at a particular time, roughly the result of debt accumulated over time by annual budget deficits; GDP, the value of goods and services produced, is equal to total income.) In 2009, this ratio was 53%. Although higher than the recent low point of 33% at the end of the 1990s expansion, the ratio in 2009 was still far lower than the record peak of 109% in 1946—after which the U.S. economy in the post-World War II period experienced the strongest economic growth in its history.

The U.S. ratio of 53% actually compares favorably to those of other advanced industrial countries. For example, IMF data indicate the following debt-to-GDP ratios for 2009: France (67%), Germany (70%), Japan (105%), and Italy (113%).

The nature of the borrowing also affects affordability. If a family runs up credit-card debt to finance a lavish lifestyle, after the fancy dinners are eaten the family still needs to figure out how to pay its debt. But if a family member borrows to buy a car to get to work, presumably the job will help provide the income to service the debt.

Likewise for the federal government: If the government borrows to finance tax cuts for the rich, and the rich use their tax cuts to purchase imported luxury goods, then the government still needs to figure out how to pay its debt. On the other hand, if the government borrows to put people to work creating long-term investments that increase the productivity of the U.S. economy, like infrastructure and education, then it is in a much better situation. The income generated by the more productive economy, as well as by the newly employed workers, can help to provide the tax revenue to service the debt.

So it is a myth to say that families can't spend more than they have. They can, and so can the government. And both are justified in borrowing if the size of the debt is manageable and if so doing helps to provide the income necessary to service the debt.

2) Large budget deficits create a burden for our grandchildren.

This is the issue that probably resonates most forcefully with public opinion. If we in the current generation run up a big debt, it may be left to our grandchildren to repay. The only difficulty with this reasoning is that the grandchildren who may be asked to repay the debt are paying it to other grandchildren. When the government incurs a debt, it issues a bond, an obligation to repay the debt to the holder of the bond. If the holders of the bond are U.S. residents, then paying off the debt means paying money to U.S. residents. In other words, debt that is an obligation of future

U.S. taxpayers is also a source of income to the U.S. holders of that debt. Thus there is not a generational burden that we today are imposing on "our grandchildren" as a collective entity.

Of course, the obvious exception to this reasoning is the debt held by non-U.S. residents. In that case, it is indeed true that future generations of Americans will need to pay interest to foreign holders of U.S. debt. But the basic reason for this situation is the trade deficit, not the budget deficit. When we pay more for imports than we receive from exports, and when U.S. multinational companies ship production abroad to take advantage of low-cost labor, foreigners are provided with dollars that they can use to invest in U.S. assets. And the real burden that this causes is the same whether foreigners invest in U.S. government debt or whether they invest in U.S. companies, real estate, the U.S. stock market, etc.

Borrowing by the federal government can in some situations create a real burden, but it has less to do with generational transfers and more to do with distributional issues and the nature of economic growth (discussed above). If the grandchildren who are taxed in the future to pay off government debt are poorer than the grandchildren who are paid, the distribution of income becomes more unequal.

Also, cutting taxes for the rich and spending money on wars in Iraq and Afghanistan do not lead to the kind of productive economic growth that generates strong tax revenue. So financing these by debt *does* create a real distributional burden: The rich and military contractors benefit, but the losers are those who might be taxed, or those whose government programs might be squeezed out of the budget, because of the need to pay interest on the debt.

Borrowing money to put people back to work does make sense. It helps people most in need, the unemployed. It provides them with income that they can use to pay taxes and to buy goods and services that create more jobs, more income, and more tax revenue. Indeed, our inability thus far to seriously tackle the unemployment problem is what has worsened the budget problem, as tax receipts have fallen and spending for unemployment benefits and food stamps have risen. An analysis by the Economic Policy Institute reveals that the largest source of the 2009 budget deficit (42%) was actually the recession itself.

We *will* leave a burden for our grandchildren if we don't address the urgent problem of unemployment, if we let parents and grandparents suffer the indignities and financial hardships of lost jobs. We *will* leave a burden for our grandchildren if we don't rebuild our aging infrastructure, break our reliance on fossil fuels, and provide all our children with an excellent education. It makes perfect sense to borrow money now to address these problems, and we shouldn't let myths about budget deficits get in the way of meeting these real needs.

Sources: Congressional Budget Office, "The Budget and Economic Outlook: Fiscal Years 2010 to 2020," January 2010; John Irons, Kathryn Edwards, and Anna Turner, "The 2009 Budget Deficit: How Did We Get Here?" Economic Policy Institute, August 20, 2009; Dean Baker, "The Budget Deficit Scare Story and the Great Recession," Center for Economic and Policy Research, February 2010; Office of Management and Budget, "The President's Budget For Fiscal Year 2011, Historical Tables: Table 7.1, Federal Debt at the End of Year: 1940-2015," February 2010.

Article 4.5

STATE BUDGET BLUES

Looking for funds in all the wrong places

BY MARIANNE HILL
November/December 2009

California's fiscal woes may have grabbed the national headlines, but states across the nation are slashing budgets to close gaps that are averaging a jaw-dropping 24% this year. Even before the economy nose-dived in late 2008, the Government Accountability Office (GAO) was warning states to expect growing revenue shortfalls over the coming decade. The recession and the staggering increase in the federal debt have worsened the GAO's predictions.

The GAO now estimates that, if programs are maintained at current levels, state and local revenues will fall short by an average of 7.6% annually over the coming decade.

To close the yawning gaps in their budgets, states are currently relying on stimulus funds and budget cuts. But fewer federal funds will be there to help as the country begins to pay down the huge national debt. Experts anticipate that federal dollars going to state programs will be scaled back, with funding levels increasing only in targeted areas such as health care and energy. So shortfalls in state budgets will continue for years to come unless states either enact more cuts or update their antiquated tax systems.

In fact, it is past time to overhaul current tax systems. Neither the federal government nor state and local governments are adequately capturing revenue from the high-income, high-growth segments of the economy. At the same time, lower- and middle-income families are unfairly burdened.

Trends in expenditures account for part of the problem. State and local spending on health care for Medicaid, employees, and retirees is projected to significantly outpace revenues. Federal grants-in-aid, which finance about 20% of state and local budget outlays, are dominated by grants to Medicaid. Half of federal grants-in-aid go to Medicaid and this proportion has been increasing with rising enrollment and the growing cost of health care. By 2012, 60% of grants-in-aid will be going to Medicaid, leaving fewer federal dollars for other programs.

Health care reform that succeeds in reducing the cost of medical services while expanding coverage could improve the states' budgetary outlook, but the outlook for revenue collections would remain problematic. The major factor is the erosion of state tax bases, particularly of the sales tax, which accounts for about a third of state and local revenues.

The fiscal crisis in the states will have a long-term impact on our quality of life since state and local governments, with federal assistance, provide most of the public services we receive. They employ almost seven times as many people as does the federal government, and state and local expenditures on public services are greater than federal expenditures, if Medicare and military spending are excluded.

The growing demands on the states are not taken into account by the GAO study, by the way, which only considers the cost of maintaining current service levels. The future scenario for state budgets, then, is likely to be more dire than the GAO predicts. Even with health care reform and improvements in revenue collection and program efficiency, the states will need new revenue sources, better aligned with their income bases, to carry out their vital role in the economy.

Traditionally, states have turned to the sales tax when seeking additional funds. The sales tax is the largest single revenue source for state and local budgets, accounting for a third of tax receipts. Statewide sales tax rates range from a low of 0% in the five states with no general sales tax to 7.25% in California. Recent expansions of the sales tax include the increased taxation of services and of Internet sales.

This reliance on the sales tax is increasingly a liability, however, since the most rapidly expanding industries are in services that are often not subject to the sales tax, such as health care, education, and financial services (credit cards, loans, etc.). A few states are now taxing gross receipts of all businesses to capture service industries, but economists are generally appalled: firms with high input costs but low profit margins can be crippled by a tax on receipts rather than on income net of costs.

Personal and corporate incomes, other potential revenue sources, offer an expanding tax base, but increases in exemptions and deductions have cut into taxable income. (Personal income taxes accounted for about 24% of state and local tax receipts, corporate income taxes 5%, and property taxes 30%, in 2007.)

How states raise needed revenues can be as critical as how they are spent. Equity —basing taxes on the ability to pay—is a prime concern: equity aids both revenue collections and the economic well-being of families. It is especially urgent given recent income trends.

Since the 1980s, progress in raising living standards has been hindered both in the states and nationally by rising income inequality. Output per employee more than doubled in the United States from 1960 to 2005, but earnings did not. In fact, real hourly earnings in 2005 were lower than in 1967, after adjusting for inflation.

The picture is very different for those at the top of the corporate ladder. The typical S&P 500 CEO had an income about 42 times as high as that of the average worker in 1980, but now this CEO gets 344 times as much, according to the Institute for Policy Studies. The top 5% of families currently have incomes about 20 times as high as the bottom 20% at present, up from 11 times as high in 1979.

These figures help to explain why the poverty rate in 1988, 1998, and 2008 remained stubbornly at 13%, despite rising average incomes.

Taxes can increase inequality. Sales taxes, for example, absorb a greater percentage of the income of low-income families than of high-income families, and so increase inequality. Figures on federal corporate taxation are especially disturbing for this reason: 30% of U.S. corporations with gross receipts of $50 million or more paid no taxes over the 1998-2005 period, according to the GAO. If smaller corporations are included as well, 65% paid no U.S. corporate income tax.

Corporations also avoid state taxes. The Multistate Tax Commission found that large, multi-state corporations avoided about $7 billion in state corporate taxes, due to such tactics as shifting their reported profits from high-tax states to low-tax states.

To combat such problems, 20-plus states have banded together and use combined reporting. This requires a multi-state corporation to add together the profits of all its subsidiaries, regardless of their location, into one report. The report provides each state with information needed to levy the appropriate tax, based on individual state tax provisions.

Combined reporting also makes it more difficult for companies to avoid reporting income altogether: one study of 252 large corporations found that in 2003 those companies on average failed to include two-thirds of their actual U.S. pretax profits on their state tax returns. The study found, for example, that Wal-Mart reported $77 billion in pretax profits to its shareholders but paid state income taxes on about half that sum.

The National Association of State Budget Officers suggests another reform: monitoring tax breaks offered to corporations. It notes that some states impose a surcharge on tax breaks offered under business incentive programs if the return to the state from these tax breaks is not as great as expected.

Other reforms could improve the states' revenue outlook. Currently, the personal income tax rate paid by those in the top bracket ranges from Vermont's 9.5% to zero: there are nine states with no personal income tax. An increase in the number of brackets and in rates could boost revenues, while increasing basic exemptions at the same time would protect middle-income families. The tax break on capital gains should be examined.

There are nontraditional means of raising funds as well. For example, penalties and fines for fraud and violations of labor and environmental regulations can be imposed or increased. A carbon emissions tax could be a major revenue source.

Stable, equitable revenue sources are found when taxes are levied in line with the distribution of income and wealth in a state. Taxes like the sales tax that push low-income families further into poverty don't make sense when alternative revenue sources are available that are both more lucrative and more equitable. It is time to look to these sources to close shortfalls in state and local budgets.

Sources: Center for Budget and Policy Priorities; Citizens for Tax Justice; Economic Policy Institute, Institute on Taxation and Economic Policy, *State of Working America 2007*; *Economic Report of the President 2008*; Federation of Tax Administrators; GAO documents GAO-09-210T, GAO-08-957 and GAO-07-1080SP.

Article 4.6

WHY ARE THINGS GETTING WORSE AND WORSE?

BY ARTHUR MacEWAN
March/April 2009

> Dear Dr. Dollar:
>
> *I learned in my economics classes that in a market economy, problems tend to be self-correcting: when a recession starts, demand weakens; then prices drop, people and firms start to buy more and the economy picks up again. So why don't we see this kind of self-correction now? Why does it seem as if things are getting worse and worse?* —Corina Chio, Los Angeles, Calif.

Life, it turns out, is more complicated than the way it is presented in many economics classes. "More complicated" means different.

One of the key differences between reality and the standard fare of some economics classes is that the standard fare does not take sufficient account of the time lapses between one event and another. These time lapses don't simply mean that adjustments take longer; they mean that the nature of those adjustments can be very different from what one learns in class.

When demand weakens, prices do tend to drop, but they don't drop immediately. So, for example, when demand weakens and people buy fewer cars, candy, cardigans, and computers, the prices of these goods don't fall right away. But, facing the fall-off in purchases, the firms that make these products cut back on production and lay off workers. So demand falls further because the unemployed have less money to buy all these products. In this situation, things can get worse and worse instead of being turned around by the falling prices. Which way things go is not automatic, but depends on the seriousness of the initial fall-off in demand and the speed with which that fall-off occurs.

A further problem with the simplistic analysis presented in some classes is that people's buying decisions are based on expectations about the future as well as on current prices. If auto dealers try to get me to buy a new car by lowering the price, I am not likely to respond positively if I think I may well lose my job soon and be unable to make the monthly payments. And if my main use for a car is to get to and from work, my expectation of lack of work will make me even less likely to buy a new car regardless of the price.

Firms behave similarly. Why should a firm hire more labor or invest in new plants and equipment if the firm expects that people will be cutting back on demand for the firm's products? Even if interest rates and the prices of labor and raw materials are all falling, firms are unlikely to expand operations if they do not think the demand will be there. Indeed, it is precisely the falling prices that signal to firms that a recession is developing—which means that demand will not be there.

Worse: as prices fall, both consumers and firms are likely to delay purchases, expecting that things will be even cheaper if they wait. But by waiting (i.e., by not spending) they create even more downward pressure. So falling prices (deflation) can make things worse, not better.

And even worse still: because consumers and firms act quite rationally in this manner—cutting back expenditures because they expect things to get worse—things do get worse! When each firm and consumer acts rationally in response to negative expectations, as a group they tend to insure that those negative expectations will become reality. Individual rationality and social rationality come in conflict with one another. This phenomenon is often referred to as "the paradox of thrift." People respond to the situation by being thrifty, doing what is good for them individually. But the outcome for society as a whole is bad. Under these circumstances, there is a need for collective action—that is, government action.

This collective action—this government action—will be most effective when it takes the form of deficit spending. And this is exactly what is meant when people talk about a "stimulus package." By engaging in deficit spending the government is increasing demand more by its spending than it is reducing demand through taxes. The difference is made up by borrowing, and the "stimulus" is greatest when the borrowed money would not have been spent—and it would not have been spent precisely because the private firms and individuals who have the money (the money the government is borrowing) also have poor expectations about the future.

Not every economic downturn gets worse and worse. There can be a process of self-correction. But when a serious downturn develops—as is the case right now—self-correction is not going to solve our problems. The collective action that we can take through government is essential to avoid economic disaster.

Article 4.7

IS MILITARY KEYNESIANISM THE SOLUTION?
Why war is not a sustainable strategy for economic recovery.

BY HEIDI GARRETT-PELTIER
March/April 2010

The United States is currently preparing to send 30,000 additional troops to Afghanistan by summer 2010. Military contractors, deeply integrated into the U.S. economy, will continue to prosper and profit from increased military spending resulting from this surge of troops. At a time when unemployment in the domestic economy remains near 10%, it may seem convenient to fall back on the principle of military Keynesianism: War is good for the economy.

John Maynard Keynes, the British economist whose work has once again become popular in the wake of this most recent economic crisis, advocated increased government spending to lift an economy out of recession or depression. When consumers and businesses slow their spending, the government can step in to increase demand for goods and services so that businesses can continue to produce and people can remain employed. This fiscal stimulus could take the form of infrastructure projects, healthcare, education, or other productive endeavors. By this logic, military spending can lift an economy out of recession by creating demand for goods and services provided by military contractors, such as the production of tanks and ammunition or the provision of security services. Advocates of this strategy point not only to the widespread employment created by military spending, but also claim that military spending creates well-paying, stable jobs.

It is true that military spending creates jobs throughout the economy, and that many of those jobs are well-paying. But at a time when our jobless rate is high, infrastructure is crumbling, and global climate change is becoming an increasingly urgent matter, we must ask whether military spending is truly a solution to our economic woes or whether we might be able to create more jobs in productive areas that also help us meet longer-term goals.

In a recent paper that I co-authored with Robert Pollin, we show that dollar per dollar, more jobs are created through spending on clean energy, health care, and education than on the military. Further, we show that more middle-income and well-paying jobs are created in all of these areas. For each $1 billion of spending, over 17,000 jobs would be created in clean energy, close to 20,000 in health care, and over 29,000 in education. That same $1 billion would create only 11,600 jobs as a result of military spending. If we look at well-paying jobs, those that pay over $64,000 per year, these alternative domestic spending areas also outperform military spending. The same $1 billion would create 1,500 well-paying jobs in clean energy and just over 1,000 in the military—clean energy creates 50% *more* good jobs than military spending. Education, which is labor-intensive and creates many well-paying jobs per dollar of expenditure, creates close to 2,500 jobs paying over $64,000—that's 2.5 times as many as the military.

According to the National Priorities Project, military spending on the Iraq and Afghanistan wars has reached approximately $1 trillion since 2001, not including the cost of the surge of 30,000 troops. In fiscal year 2009, federal government outlays on the military were 17% of all outlays. Meanwhile, energy, resource conservation, and the environment accounted for only 1% of federal outlays, while education, training, and social services made up only 2%. Military spending is therefore *eight to seventeen times* as high as federal education- and energy-related spending.

The Obama administration is facing increased pressure to reduce the size of the fiscal deficit and the national debt, both of which have grown partly as a result of military spending. At the same time, there is an urgent need to put people back to work and to move the country toward a low-carbon future. While military Keynesianism offers one strategy for recovering from the recession, it is by no means the most effective, even putting aside the other reasons for objecting to a war economy. By reducing military spending, we can channel some of those savings to clean energy, healthcare, education, and other matters of national and global importance.

Sources: "The U.S. Employment Effects of Military and Domestic Spending Priorities: An Updated Analysis", by Robert Pollin and Heidi Garrett-Peltier, available at www.peri.umass.edu; National Priorities Project, www.nationalpriorities.org.

Article 4.8

HOW THE GREEN ECONOMY CAN PROMOTE EQUAL OPPORTUNITIES FOR WOMEN

BY JEANNETTE WICKS-LIM
July/August 2009

Create jobs. End the recession. Save the environment. What else can transforming our fossil fuel economy to a clean energy economy do? How about create unprecedented employment opportunities for women? Readers of Linda Hirshman's recent *New York Times* editorial may think this is a dubious claim. She sparked a debate over the gender bias in Obama's stimulus plan by asking, "Where are the new jobs for women?" She makes a good point. Transitioning to a clean-energy economy has the makings of a decent jobs program. Unfortunately, many of these jobs are in male-dominated industries such as construction.

Therefore, the next question we should ask is: "How do we get women into these new jobs?" Women would benefit significantly from gaining access to these male-dominated jobs that pay decent wages. Take for example the $18.72 average wage of carpenters, 99% of whom are men. This wage can cover the basic needs of a small family. Compare this to the $11.48 average wage of preschool teachers, 98% of whom are women. At this wage, a preschool teacher would have to work in excess of 25 hours more per week to support a similar living standard.

In fact, transforming our fossil-fuel economy to a clean-energy economy presents us with an unprecedented opportunity to make real headway in integrating male-dominated workplaces. This is precisely because so many federal dollars will be injected into the male-dominated construction industry.

First, the billions of dollars being injected into the construction industry through the American Recovery and Reinvestment Act (ARRA) can come with strings attached. Currently, construction contracts involving more than $10,000 in federal funds are covered by Executive Order 11246, which requires that contractors adopt affirmative-action goals to reduce the under-representation of women and minorities in their workforce. In other words, the ARRA dollars can be used to coax employers into adopting affirmative-action policies—the only policies that attack workplace segregation head-on.

Second, the federal government's deep pockets can support the very type of construction projects that are most successful at meeting affirmative action goals: large, long-term projects. Large construction projects have the capacity to absorb new workers while keeping adequate numbers of journey-level workers on a construction site. Long-term projects better accommodate the training needs of new workers who need time to develop their skills. An excellent example is the government's funding of high-speed rail corridors; over $8 billion have been committed to creating hundreds of miles of new rail service over the next several years.

Securing increased opportunities for women, however, requires more than just an increase in the reach of federal regulations into industries with a history of discrimination. We also need better enforcement of these regulations by the Office of Federal Contract Compliance Program. More adequate staffing would be a good place to start. We must also fund pre-apprenticeship and outreach programs, as well as wrap-around services (e.g., child care subsidies, mentoring) to increase the supply of qualified women.

It would, of course, be cheaper to simply re-hire currently unemployed male construction workers—not an insignificant fact in the midst of the worst recession since the Great Depression. However, programs such as the Apprenticeship Opportunities Project in Seattle have taught us that publicly funded construction projects can successfully raise the number of female apprentices in their workforce while remaining profitable. In other words, although buying into a tradition of discrimination may stretch our tax dollars further, it is not our only option.

We should not ignore other challenges that women face in the current recession, such as the severe cuts in funding to the female-dominated education industry. At the same time, the Obama administration's commitment to constructing a clean energy economy has put before us the best opportunity yet to integrate women into decent-paying male-dominated jobs. We must seize this opportunity.

Article 4.9

THE TAX-CUT CON

BY PAUL KRUGMAN
September 2003

Bruce Tinsley's comic strip, "Mallard Fillmore," is, he says, "for the average person out there: the forgotten American taxpayer who's sick of the liberal media." In June 2003, that forgotten taxpayer made an appearance in the strip, attacking his TV set with a baseball bat and yelling: "I can't afford to send my kids to college, or even take 'em out of their substandard public school, because the federal, state and local governments take more than 50% of my income in taxes. And then the guy on the news asks with a straight face whether or not we can 'afford' tax cuts."

Nobody likes paying taxes, and no doubt some Americans are as angry about their taxes as Tinsley's imaginary character. But most Americans also care a lot about the things taxes pay for.

All politicians say they're for public education; almost all of them also say they support a strong national defense, maintaining Social Security and, if anything, expanding the coverage of Medicare. When the "guy on the news" asks whether we can afford a tax cut, he's asking whether, after yet another tax cut goes through, there will be enough money to pay for those things. And the answer is no.

But it's very difficult to get that answer across in modern American politics, which has been dominated for 25 years by a crusade against taxes.

I don't use the word "crusade" lightly. The advocates of tax cuts are relentless, even fanatical. An indication of the movement's fervor—and of its political power—came during the Iraq war. War is expensive and is almost always accompanied by tax increases. But not in 2003. "Nothing is more important in the face of a war," declared Tom DeLay, the House majority leader, "than cutting taxes." And sure enough, taxes were cut, not just in a time of war but also in the face of record budget deficits.

A result of the tax-cut crusade is that there is now a fundamental mismatch between the benefits Americans expect to receive from the government and the revenues government collects. This mismatch is already having profound effects at the state and local levels: teachers and policemen are being laid off and children are being denied health insurance. The federal government can mask its problems for a while by running huge budget deficits, but it, too, will eventually have to decide whether to cut services or raise taxes. And we are not talking about minor policy adjustments. If taxes stay as low as they are now, government as we know it cannot be maintained. In particular, Social Security will have to become far less generous; Medicare will no longer be able to guarantee comprehensive medical care to older Americans; Medicaid will no longer provide basic medical care to the poor.

How did we reach this point? What are the origins of the antitax crusade? And where is it taking us?

Supply-Siders, Starve-the-Beasters, and Lucky Duckies

It is often hard to pin down what antitax crusaders are trying to achieve. The reason is not, or not only, that they are disingenuous about their motives—though as we will see, disingenuity has become a hallmark of the movement in recent years. Rather, the fuzziness comes from the fact that today's antitax movement moves back and forth between two doctrines. Both doctrines favor the same thing: big tax cuts for people with high incomes. But they favor it for different reasons.

One of those doctrines has become famous under the name "supply-side economics." It's the view that the government can cut taxes without severe cuts in public spending. The other doctrine is often referred to as "starving the beast," a phrase coined by David Stockman, Ronald Reagan's budget director. It's the view that taxes should be cut precisely in order to force severe cuts in public spending. Supply-side economics is the friendly, attractive face of the tax-cut movement. But starve-the-beast is where the power lies.

The starting point of supply-side economics is an assertion that no economist would dispute: taxes reduce the incentive to work, save and invest. A businessman who knows that 70 cents of every extra dollar he makes will go to the IRS is less willing to make the effort to earn that extra dollar than if he knows that the IRS will take only 35 cents. So reducing tax rates will, other things being the same, spur the economy.

This much isn't controversial. But the government must pay its bills. So the standard view of economists is that if you want to reduce the burden of taxes, you must explain what government programs you want to cut as part of the deal. There's no free lunch.

What the supply-siders argued, however, was that there was a free lunch. Cutting marginal rates, they insisted, would lead to such a large increase in gross domestic product that it wouldn't be necessary to come up with offsetting spending cuts. What supply-side economists say, in other words, is, "Don't worry, be happy and cut taxes." And when they say cut taxes, they mean taxes on the affluent: reducing the top marginal rate means that the biggest tax cuts go to people in the highest tax brackets.

The other camp in the tax-cut crusade actually welcomes the revenue losses from tax cuts. Its most visible spokesman today is Grover Norquist, president of Americans for Tax Reform, who once told National Public Radio: "I don't want to abolish government. I simply want to reduce it to the size where I can drag it into the bathroom and drown it in the bathtub." And the way to get it down to that size is to starve it of revenue. "The goal is reducing the size and scope of government by draining its lifeblood," Norquist told *U.S. News & World Report*.

What does "reducing the size and scope of government" mean? Tax-cut proponents are usually vague about the details. But the Heritage Foundation, ideological headquarters for the movement, has made it pretty clear. Edwin Feulner, the foundation's president, uses "New Deal" and "Great Society" as terms of abuse, implying that he and his organization want to do away with the institutions Franklin Roosevelt and Lyndon Johnson created. That means Social Security, Medicare, Medicaid—most of what gives citizens of the United States a safety net against economic misfortune.

The starve-the-beast doctrine is now firmly within the conservative mainstream. George W. Bush himself seemed to endorse the doctrine as the budget surplus evaporated: in August 2001 he called the disappearing surplus "incredibly positive news" because it would put Congress in a "fiscal straitjacket."

Like supply-siders, starve-the-beasters favor tax cuts mainly for people with high incomes. That is partly because, like supply-siders, they emphasize the incentive effects of cutting the top marginal rate; they just don't believe that those incentive effects are big enough that tax cuts pay for themselves. But they have another reason for cutting taxes mainly on the rich, which has become known as the "lucky ducky" argument.

Here's how the argument runs: to starve the beast, you must not only deny funds to the government; you must make voters hate the government. There's a danger that working-class families might see government as their friend: because their incomes are low, they don't pay much in taxes, while they benefit from public spending. So in starving the beast, you must take care not to cut taxes on these "lucky duckies." (Yes, that's what the *Wall Street Journal* called them in a famous editorial.) In fact, if possible, you must raise taxes on working-class Americans in order, as the *Journal* said, to get their "blood boiling with tax rage."

So the tax-cut crusade has two faces. Smiling supply-siders say that tax cuts are all gain, no pain; scowling starve-the-beasters believe that inflicting pain is not just necessary but also desirable. Is the alliance between these two groups a marriage of convenience? Not exactly. It would be more accurate to say that the starve-the-beasters hired the supply-siders—indeed, created them—because they found their naive optimism useful.

A look at who the supply-siders are and how they came to prominence tells the story. The supply-side movement likes to present itself as a school of economic thought like Keynesianism or monetarism—that is, as a set of scholarly ideas that made their way, as such ideas do, into political discussion. But the reality is quite different. Supply-side economics was a political doctrine from Day 1; it emerged in the pages of political magazines, not professional economics journals.

That is not to deny that many professional economists favor tax cuts. But they almost always turn out to be starve-the-beasters, not supply-siders. And they often secretly—or sometimes not so secretly—hold supply-siders in contempt. N. Gregory Mankiw, now chairman of George W. Bush's Council of Economic Advisers, is definitely a friend to tax cuts; but in the first edition of his economic-principles textbook, he described Ronald Reagan's supply-side advisers as "charlatans and cranks."

It is not that the professionals refuse to consider supply-side ideas; rather, they have looked at them and found them wanting. A conspicuous example came earlier this year when the Congressional Budget Office tried to evaluate the growth effects of the Bush administration's proposed tax cuts. The new CBO head, Douglas Holtz-Eakin, is a conservative economist who was handpicked for his job by the administration. But his conclusion was that unless the revenue losses from the proposed tax cuts were offset by spending cuts, the resulting deficits would be a drag on growth, quite likely to outweigh any supply-side effects.

But if the professionals regard the supply-siders with disdain, who employs these people? The answer is that since the 1970s almost all of the prominent supply-siders have been aides to conservative politicians, writers at conservative publications like *National Review*, fellows at conservative policy centers like Heritage or economists at private companies with strong Republican connections. Loosely speaking, that is, supply-siders work for the vast right-wing conspiracy. What gives supply-side economics influence is its connection with a powerful network of institutions that want to shrink the government and see tax cuts as a way to achieve that goal.

Supply-side economics is a feel-good cover story for a political movement with a much harder-nosed agenda.

A Planned Crisis

Right now, much of the public discussion of the Bush tax cuts focuses on their short-run impact. Critics say that the 2.7 million jobs lost since March 2001 prove that the administration's policies have failed, while the administration says that things would have been even worse without the tax cuts and that a solid recovery is just around the corner.

But this is the wrong debate. Even in the short run, the right question to ask isn't whether the tax cuts were better than nothing; they probably were. The right question is whether some other economic-stimulus plan could have achieved better results at a lower budget cost. And it is hard to deny that, on a jobs-per-dollar basis, the Bush tax cuts have been extremely ineffective. According to the Congressional Budget Office, half of this year's $400 billion budget deficit is due to Bush tax cuts. Now $200 billion is a lot of money; it is equivalent to the salaries of four million average workers. Even the administration doesn't claim its policies have created four million jobs. Surely some other policy—aid to state and local governments, tax breaks for the poor and middle class rather than the rich, maybe even WPA-style public works—would have been more successful at getting the country back to work.

Meanwhile, the tax cuts are designed to remain in place even after the economy has recovered. Where will they leave us?

Here's the basic fact: partly, though not entirely, as a result of the tax cuts of the last three years, the government of the United States faces a fundamental fiscal shortfall. That is, the revenue it collects falls well short of the sums it needs to pay for existing programs. Even the U.S. government must, eventually, pay its bills, so something will have to give.

The numbers tell the tale. This year and next, the federal government will run budget deficits of more than $400 billion. Deficits may fall a bit, at least as a share of gross domestic product, when the economy recovers. But the relief will be modest and temporary. As Peter Fisher, undersecretary of the treasury for domestic finance, puts it, the federal government is "a gigantic insurance company with a sideline business in defense and homeland security." And about a decade from now, this insurance company's policyholders will begin making a lot of claims. As the baby boomers retire, spending on Social Security benefits and Medicare will steadily rise, as will spending on Medicaid (because of rising medical costs). Eventually, unless there are sharp cuts in benefits, these three programs alone will consume a larger share of GDP than the federal government currently collects in taxes.

Alan Auerbach, William Gale, and Peter Orszag, fiscal experts at the Brookings Institution, have estimated the size of the "fiscal gap"—the increase in revenues or reduction in spending that would be needed to make the nation's finances sustainable in the long run. If you define the long run as 75 years, this gap turns out to be 4.5% of GDP. Or to put it another way, the gap is equal to 30% of what the federal government spends on all domestic programs. Of that gap, about 60% is the result of the Bush tax cuts. We would have faced a serious fiscal problem even if those tax cuts had never happened. But we face a much nastier problem now that they are in place.

And more broadly, the tax-cut crusade will make it very hard for any future politicians to raise taxes.

So how will this gap be closed? The crucial point is that it cannot be closed without either fundamentally redefining the role of government or sharply raising taxes.

Politicians will, of course, promise to eliminate wasteful spending. But take out Social Security, Medicare, defense, Medicaid, government pensions, homeland security, interest on the public debt, and veterans' benefits—none of them what people who complain about waste usually have in mind—and you are left with spending equal to about 3% of gross domestic product. And most of that goes for courts, highways, education, and other useful things. Any savings from elimination of waste and fraud will amount to little more than a rounding-off error.

So let's put a few things back on the table. Let's assume that interest on the public debt will be paid, that spending on defense and homeland security will not be compromised, and that the regular operations of government will continue to be financed. What we are left with, then, are the New Deal and Great Society programs: Social Security, Medicare, Medicaid and unemployment insurance. And to close the fiscal gap, spending on these programs would have to be cut by around 40%.

It's impossible to know how such spending cuts might unfold, but cuts of that magnitude would require drastic changes in the system. It goes almost without saying that the age at which Americans become eligible for retirement benefits would rise, that Social Security payments would fall sharply compared with average incomes, that Medicare patients would be forced to pay much more of their expenses out of pocket—or do without. And that would be only a start.

All this sounds politically impossible. In fact, politicians of both parties have been scrambling to expand, not reduce, Medicare benefits by adding prescription drug coverage. It's hard to imagine a situation under which the entitlement programs would be rolled back sufficiently to close the fiscal gap.

Yet closing the fiscal gap by raising taxes would mean rolling back all of the Bush tax cuts, and then some. And that also sounds politically impossible.

For the time being, there is a third alternative: borrow the difference between what we insist on spending and what we're willing to collect in taxes. That works as long as lenders believe that someday, somehow, we're going to get our fiscal act together. But this can't go on indefinitely.

Eventually—I think within a decade, though not everyone agrees—the bond market will tell us that we have to make a choice.

In short, everything is going according to plan.

For the looming fiscal crisis doesn't represent a defeat for the leaders of the tax-cut crusade or a miscalculation on their part. Some supporters of President Bush may have really believed that his tax cuts were consistent with his promises to protect Social Security and expand Medicare; some people may still believe that the wondrous supply-side effects of tax cuts will make the budget deficit disappear. But for starve-the-beast tax-cutters, the coming crunch is exactly what they had in mind.

What Kind of Country?

The astonishing political success of the antitax crusade has, more or less deliberately, set the United States up for a fiscal crisis. How we respond to that crisis will determine what kind of country we become.

If Grover Norquist is right—and he has been right about a lot—the coming crisis will allow conservatives to move the nation a long way back toward the kind of limited government we had before Franklin Roosevelt. Lack of revenue, he says, will make it possible for conservative politicians—in the name of fiscal necessity—to dismantle immensely popular government programs that would otherwise have been untouchable.

In Norquist's vision, America a couple of decades from now will be a place in which elderly people make up a disproportionate share of the poor, as they did before Social Security. It will also be a country in which even middle-class elderly Americans are, in many cases, unable to afford expensive medical procedures or prescription drugs and in which poor Americans generally go without even basic health care. And it may well be a place in which only those who can afford expensive private schools can give their children a decent education.

But that's a choice, not a necessity. The tax-cut crusade has created a situation in which something must give. But what gives—whether we decide that the New Deal and the Great Society must go or that taxes aren't such a bad thing after all—is up to us. The American people must decide what kind of a country we want to be.

Excerpted from the *New York Times Magazine*, September 14, 2003.

Article 4.10

SAND IN THE WHEELS, NOT IN THE FACE
Why a transaction tax is a really good *idea.*

BY JOHN MILLER
March/April 2010

> WHY TAXING STOCK TRADES IS A REALLY BAD IDEA
>
> [S]urely it is "socially useful" to let free people transact freely, without regula-
> tors and legislators micromanaging them. ... It's Economics 101 that the free
> actions of market participants cause supply and demand to reach equilibrium.
> And isn't that what investors—indeed even speculators—do? Can they do it as
> well when facing the dead-weight costs of a transaction tax?
>
> If not, then trading volume in our stock markets will fall. Beyond the tax,
> everyone— investors and speculator, great and small—who buys or sells stocks
> will pay more to transact in markets that are less liquid. In such a world, mar-
> kets would necessarily be more risky, and the cost of capital for business would
> necessarily rise. The consequence of that is that innovation, growth, and jobs
> would necessarily fall. That would be the full and true cost of the trading tax.
>
> —Donald L. Luskin and Chris Hynes, "Why Taxing Stock Trades Is a Really
> Bad Idea," *Wall Street Journal,* January 5, 2010

"Some financial activities which proliferated over the last 10 years were socially useless," Britain's Finance Service Authority Chairman Adiar Turner
told a black-tie gathering of financial executives in London in September 2009. That
is why he had proposed a transaction tax for the United Kingdom and why British
Prime Minister Gordon Brown would propose an international transaction tax at
the November G-20 summit.

The gathered bankers "saw red," as one report described their reaction. Investment bankers Donald L. Luskin and Chris Hynes are still irate.

In some ways their reaction is surprising. A financial transaction tax is nothing
other than a sales tax on trading stocks and other securities. Transaction taxes are
already in place in about 30 countries, and a transaction tax applied to the sale of
stock in the United States from 1914 to 1964.

In addition, the transaction tax rates on a single trade are typically quite low. For
instance, the "Let Wall Street Pay for the Restoration of Main Street Act of 2009,"
proposed by U.S. Representative Peter DeFazio (D-Ore.), would assess a one quarter
of one percent (.25%) tax on the value of stock transactions, and two one hundredths
of one percent (.02%) tax on the sale on a variety of derivative assets—including credit
default swaps, which played such a large role in the mortgage crisis. To target speculators, the bill exempts retirement accounts, mutual funds, education and health savings
accounts, and the first $100,000 of transactions annually.

In other ways, Luskin's and Hynes's reaction is not surprising at all. At its heart, a transaction tax is a radical measure. Its premise is that faster-acting financial markets driven by speculation don't bring relief to the economy—instead, they loot the economy. Its purpose, as Nobel Prize-winning economist James Tobin put it when he proposed his original transaction tax on international money markets during the 1970s, is to "throw sand in the wheels" of our financial markets.

Also, while its tax rate is low, the burden of a transaction tax adds up as securities are repeatedly traded, as is the practice on Wall Street today. For instance, even after accounting for its exemptions and allowing for a sizable decline in trading, the DeFazio bill would still raise $63.5 billion annually, according to the estimates of Dean Baker, co-director of the Center for Economic Policy Research.

Luskin and Hynes have two main objections to the transaction tax. The first is that a transaction tax would affect every single person who owns and invests in stocks, not just speculators. Customers would not have to pay a tax to buy or sell mutual funds, but, as Luskin and Hynes emphasize, the mutual funds themselves would have to pay a tax every time they trade stocks. So everyone holding mutual funds would still end up paying the tax.

What Luskin and Hynes don't say is this: Mutual funds that actively trade stocks would pay three times the transaction taxes of an average fund, as the Investment Company Institute, the fund industry trade group, reports. And stock index funds, which hold a sample of all stocks but seldom trade them, are taxed the least. Those funds have historically outperformed other mutual funds. So a transaction tax would work to push mutual fund customers to invest their savings more wisely, providing some with higher rates of return with a transaction tax than their previous funds provided without it. And that would mean fewer broker fees and lower profits for the fund industry.

But what really sticks in Luskin's and Hynes's craw is the assertion that financial trading is not socially useful. That claim flies in face of the long-held contention, buttressed by much of finance theory, that the equilibrium outcomes of financial markets are efficient. And if financial markets are efficient, there is no need for a tax that will reduce trading.

But much of what Luskin and Hynes have to say is not right. First, as anyone who *paid attention* in Economics 101 would know, reaching an equilibrium is not in and of itself desirable. To endorse the outcomes of today's speculative financial markets as desirable because they reach an equilibrium is the equivalent of describing a gambler in a poker game raking in a big pot as desirable because it clears the table. And the gamblers in our financial markets did rake in some awfully big pots betting that subprime borrowers would default on their loans. The last few years show us just how undesirable that equilibrium turned out to be.

Second, speculation dwarfs financing investment in U.S. stock markets. During the 1970s, for every dollar of new investment in plants and equipment, $1.30 in stocks were traded on the U.S. exchanges, reports Robert Pollin, co-director of the Political Economy Research Institute. But from 1998 to 2007, $27 in stocks were traded on the U.S. exchanges for every dollar of corporate investment in plant equipment. Such a rapid stock turnover has diverted the attention of managers of enterprises from long-term planning. Whatever damage that churning caused on Main Street, it paid off handsomely on Wall Street. From 1973 to 2007, the size of the financial (and insurance) sector relative to the economy doubled, financial sector profits went from one-quarter to two-fifths of domestic profits, and compensation in the finance industry went from just about average to 180% of the private industry average.

By counteracting these trends, a transactions tax can actually enhance, not diminish, the efficiency of financial markets. If it forces the financial sector to fulfill its function of transferring savings to investment with less short-term churning, then the tax will have freed up resources for more productive uses.

A transaction tax would surely be a step in the right direction toward reducing the bloat of the finance industry, righting the balance of speculation over enterprise, and restoring the focus on long-term planning and job-creation in the economy.

None of that will happen unless every last grain of the decades' worth of sand the bullies on Wall Street have kicked in our faces gets thrown into the wheels of finance. That is a tall order. But as DeFazio's and Turner's example shows, some of today's policymakers are up to the task.

Sources: "The Benefits of a Financial Transaction Tax," by Dean Baker, Center For Economic and Policy Research, December 2008; ""Public Investment, Industrial Policy, and U.S. Economic Renewal," by Robert Pollin and Dean Baker, Political Economy Research Institute, December 2009; "Turner Plan on 'Socially Useless' Trades Make Bankers See Red," by Caroline Binham, Bloomberg.com; "Taxing Wall Street Today Wins Support for Keynes Idea (Update 1)," by Yaiman Onaran, Bloomberg.com; "The Potential Revenue from Financial Transactions Taxes, by Dean Baker, Robert Pollin, Travis McArthur, and Matt Sherman, Political Economy Research Institute, Working paper no. 212, December 2009; "Why Taxing Stock Trades Is a Really Bad Idea," by Donald L. Luskin and Chris Hynes, *Wall Street Journal*, January 5, 2010; "Lawmakers Weigh A Wall Street Tax," by John McKinnon, *Wall Street Journal*, December 19, 2009; Tobin Tax, freerisk. org/wiki/index.php/Tobin_tax; text of HR 4191—"Let Wall Street Pay for the Restoration of Main Street Act of 2009," www.govtrack.us.

Article 4.11

SOCIAL SECURITY ISN'T BROKEN
So why the rush to "fix" it?

BY DOUG ORR
November/December 2004

Federal Reserve Chairman Alan Greenspan told Congress earlier this year that everyone knows there's a Social Security crisis. That's like saying "everyone knows the earth is flat."

Starting with a faulty premise guarantees reaching the wrong conclusion. The truth is there is no Social Security crisis, but there is a potential crisis in retirement income security and there may be a crisis in the future in U.S. financial markets. It's this latter crisis that Greenspan actually is worried about.

Social Security is the most successful insurance program ever created. It insures millions of workers against what economists call "longevity risk," the possibility they will live "too long" and not be able to work long enough, or save enough, to provide their own income. Today, about 10% of those over age 65 live in poverty. Without Social Security, that rate would be almost 50%.

Social Security was originally designed to supplement, and was structured to resemble, private-sector pensions. In the 1930s, all private pensions were defined-benefit plans. The retirement benefit was based on a worker's former wage and years of service. In most plans, after 35 years of service the monthly benefit, received for life, would be at least half of the income received in the final working year.

Congress expected that private-sector pensions eventually would cover most workers. But pension coverage peaked at 40% in the 1960s. Since then, corporations have systematically dismantled pension systems. Today, only 16% of private-sector workers are covered by defined-benefit pensions. Rather than supplementing private pensions, Social Security has become the primary source of retirement income for almost two-thirds of retirees. Thus, Congress was forced to raise benefit levels in 1972.

What has happened to private-sector defined benefit pensions? They've been replaced with defined-contribution (DC) savings plans such as 401(k)s and 403(b)s. These plans provide some retirement income but offer no real protection from longevity risk. Once a retiree depletes the amount saved in the plan, their retirement income is gone.

In a generous DC plan, a firm might match the worker's contribution up to 3% of his or her pay. With total contributions of 6%, average wage growth of 2% a year, and an average return on the investment portfolio of 5%, after 35 years of work, a retiree would exhaust the plan's savings in just 8.5 years even if her annual spending is only half of her final salary. If she restricts spending to just one-third of the final salary, the savings can stretch to 14 years.

At age 65, life expectancy for women today is about 20 years, and for men about 15 years, so DC savings plans will not protect the elderly from longevity risk. The conversion of defined-benefit pensions to defined-contribution plans is the source of the real potential crisis in retirement income. Yet Greenspan did not mention this in his testimony to Congress.

No Crisis

Opponents of Social Security have hated it since its creation in 1935. The first prediction of a Social Security crisis was published in 1936! The Heritage Foundation and Cato Institute are home to many of the program's opponents today, and they fixate on the concept of a "demographic imperative." In 1960, the United States had 5.1 workers per retiree, in 1998 we had 3.4, and by 2030 we will have only 2.1. Opponents claim that with these demographic changes, revenues will eventually be insufficient to pay Social Security retirement benefits.

The logic is appealingly simple, but wrong for two reasons. First, this "old-age dependency" ratio in itself is irrelevant. No amount of financial manipulation can change this fact: all current consumption must come from current physical output. The consumption of all dependents (non-workers) must come from the output produced by current workers. It's the overall dependency ratio—the number of workers relative to all non-workers, including the aged, the young, the disabled, and those choosing not to work—that determines whether society can "afford" the baby boomers' retirement years. In the 1960s we had only 0.62 workers for each dependent, and we were building new schools and the interstate highway system and getting ready to put a man on the moon. No one bemoaned a demographic crisis or looked for ways to cut the resources allocated to children; in fact, the living standards of most families rose rapidly. In 2030, we will have 0.98 workers per dependent. We'll have more workers per dependent in the future than we did in the past. While it is true a larger share of total output will be allocated to the aged, just as a larger share was allocated to children in the 1960s, society will easily produce adequate output to support all workers and dependents, and at a higher standard of living.

Second, the "demographic imperative" ignores productivity growth. Average worker productivity has grown by about 2% per year, adjusted for inflation, for the past half-century. That means real output per worker doubles every 36 years. This productivity growth is projected to continue, so by 2040, each worker will produce twice as much as today. Suppose each of three workers today produces $1,000 per week and one retiree is allocated $500 (half of his final salary)—then each worker gets $833. In 2040, two such workers will produce $2,000 per week each (after adjusting for inflation). If each retiree gets $1,000, each worker still gets $1,500. The incomes of both workers and retirees go up. Thus, paying for the baby boomers' retirement need not decrease their children's standard of living. A larger share of output going to retirees does not imply that the standard of living of those still working will be lower. Those still working will have a slightly smaller share of a much larger pie.

So why the talk of a Social Security crisis? Social Security always has been a pay-as-you-go system. Current benefits are paid out of current tax revenues. But in the 1980s, a commission headed by Greenspan recommended raising payroll taxes to expand the trust fund in order to supplement tax revenues when the baby boom generation retires. Congress responded in 1984 by raising payroll taxes significantly. As a result, the Social Security trust fund, which holds government bonds as assets, has grown every year since. As the baby boom moves into retirement, these assets will be sold to help pay their retirement benefits.

Each year, Social Security's trustees must make projections of the system's status for the next 75 years. In 1996, they projected the trust fund balance would go to zero in 2030. In 2000, they projected a zero balance in 2036 and today they project a zero balance in 2042. The projection keeps changing because the trustees continue to make unrealistic assumptions about future economic conditions. The current projections are based on the assumption that annual GDP growth will average 1.8% for the next 75 years. In no 20-year period, even including the Great Depression, has the U.S. economy grown that slowly. Each year the economy grows faster than 1.8%, the zero balance date moves further into the future. But the trustees continue to suggest that if we return to something like the Great Depression, the trust fund will go to zero.

Opponents of Social Security claim the system will then be "bankrupt." Bankruptcy implies ceasing to exist. But if the trust fund goes to zero, Social Security will not shut down and stop paying benefits. It will simply revert to the pure pay-as-you-go system that it was before 1984 and continue to pay current benefits using current tax revenues. Even if the trustees' worst-case assumptions come true, the payroll tax paid by workers would need to increase by only about two percentage points, and only in 2042, not today.

If the economy grows at 2.4%—which is still slower than the stagnant growth of the 1980s—the trust fund never goes to zero. The increase in real output and real incomes will generate sufficient revenues to pay promised benefits. By 2042, we will need to lower payroll taxes or raise benefits to reduce the surplus.

The claim that benefits of future retirees must be reduced in order to not reduce the standard of living of future workers is simply wrong. It is being used to drive a wedge between generations and panic younger workers into supporting Bush's plan to destroy Social Security. Under the most likely version of his privatization proposal, according to Bush's own Social Security Commission, the guaranteed benefits from Social Security of a 20-year-old worker joining the labor force today would be reduced by 46%. That Commission also admitted that private accounts are unlikely to make up for this drop in benefits. An estimate made by the Goldman Sachs brokerage firm suggests that even with private accounts, retirement income of younger workers would be reduced by 42% compared to what they would receive if nothing is done to change the Social Security system. Private accounts are a losing proposition for younger workers.

The Real Fear: An Oversupply of Bonds

So why did Greenspan claim cutting benefits would become necessary? To understand the answer, we need to take a side trip to look at how bonds and the financial markets affect each other. It turns out that rising interest rates reduce the selling price of existing financial assets, and falling asset prices push up interest rates (see box "How Does the Bond Market Work?").

For example, in the 1980s, President Reagan cut taxes and created the largest government deficits in history up to that point. This meant the federal government had to sell lots of bonds to finance the soaring government debt; to attract enough buyers, the Treasury had to offer very high interest rates. During the 1980s, real interest rates (rates adjusted for inflation) were almost four times higher than the historic average. High interest rates slow economic growth by making it more expensive for consumers to buy homes or for businesses to invest in new infrastructure. The GDP growth rate in the 1980s was the slowest in U.S. history apart from the Great Depression.

But high interest rates also depress financial asset prices. A five percentage point rise in interest rates reduces the selling price of a bond (loan) that matures in 10 years by 50%. It was the impact of the record-high interest rates of the 1980s on the value of the loan portfolios of the savings and loan industry that caused the S&L crisis and the industry's collapse.

Greenspan is worried because he sees history repeating itself in the form of President Bush's tax cuts. In his testimony, Greenspan expressed concern over a potentially large rise in interest rates. This is his way of warning about an excess supply of bonds. Starting in 2020, Social Security will have to sell about $150 billion (in 2002 dollars) in trust fund bonds each year for 22 years. At the same time, private-sector pension funds will be selling $100 billion per year of financial assets to make their pension payments. State and local governments will be selling $75 billion per year to cover their former employees' pension expenses, and holdings in private mutual funds will fall by about $50 billion per year as individual retirees cash in their

HOW DOES THE BOND MARKET WORK?

A bond is nothing more than an IOU. A company or government borrows money and promises to pay a certain amount of interest annually until it repays the loan. When you buy a newly issued bond, you are making a loan. The amount of the loan is the "face value" of the bond. The initial interest rate at which the bond is issued, the "face rate," multiplied by this face value determines the amount of interest paid each period. Until the debt is paid back, events in the financial markets affect the bond's value.

If market interest rates fall, prices of existing bonds rise. Why? Suppose you buy a bond with a face value of $100 that pays 10%. You then collect $10 per year. If the current interest rate falls to 5%, newly issued bonds will pay that new rate. Since your bond pays 10%, people would rather buy that one than one paying 5%. They are willing to pay more than the face value to get it, so the price will be bid up until interest rates equalize. The price at which you could sell your bond will rise to $200, since $10 is 5% of $200.

But changes in bond prices also affect interest rates. If more people are selling bonds than buying them, an excess supply exists, and prices will fall. If you need to sell your bond to get money to pay your rent, you might have to lower the price of the bond you hold to $50. Because the bond still pays $10 per year to the owner, the new owner gets a 20% return on the $50 purchase. Anyone trying to issue new bonds will have to match that return, so the new market interest rate becomes 20%.

401(k) assets. Private firms will still need to issue about $100 billion of new bonds a year to finance business expansion. Combined, these asset sales could total $475 billion per year.

This level of bond sales is more than double the record that was set in the 1980s following the Reagan tax cuts. But back then, the newly issued bonds were being purchased by "institutional investors" such as private-sector pension funds and insurance companies. After 2020, these groups will be net sellers of bonds. The financial markets will strain to absorb this level of asset sales. It's unlikely they will be able to also absorb the extra $400 billion per year of bond sales needed to cover the deficit spending that will occur if the new Bush tax cuts are made permanent. This oversupply of bonds will drive down the value of all financial assets.

In a 1994 paper, Sylvester Schieber, a current advisor to President Bush on pension and Social Security reform, predicted this potential drop in asset prices. After 2020, the value of assets held in 401(k) plans, already inadequate, will be reduced even more. More importantly, at least to Greenspan, the prices of assets held by corporations to fund their defined benefit pension promises will fall. Thus, pension payments will need to come out of current revenues, reducing corporate profits and, in turn, driving down stock prices.

It's this potential collapse in the prices of financial assets that worries Greenspan most. In order to reduce the run-up of long-term interest rates, some asset sales must be eliminated. Greenspan said, "You don't have the resources to do it all." But rather than rescinding Bush's tax cuts, Greenspan favors reducing bond sales by the Social Security trust fund. Doing that requires a reduction in benefits and raising payroll taxes even more.

Framing a question incorrectly makes it impossible to find a solution. The problem is not with Social Security, but rather with blind reliance on financial markets to solve all economic problems. If the financial markets are likely to fail us, what is the solution? The solution is simple once the question is framed correctly: where will the real output that baby boomers are going to consume in retirement come from?

The federal budget surplus President Bush inherited came entirely from Social Security surpluses resulting from the 1984 payroll tax increase. Bush gave away revenues meant to provide for workers' retirement as tax cuts for the wealthiest 10% of the population.

We should rescind Bush's tax cuts and use the Social Security surpluses to really prepare for the baby boom retirement. Public investment or targeted tax breaks could be used to encourage the building of the hospitals, nursing homes, and hospices that aging baby boomers will need. Such investment in public and private infrastructure would also stimulate the real economy and increase GDP growth. Surpluses could be used to fund the training of doctors, nurses and others to staff these facilities, and of other high skilled workers more generally. The higher wages of skilled labor will help generate the payroll tax revenues needed to fund future benefits. If baby boomers help to fund this infrastructure expansion through their payroll taxes while they are still working, less output will need to be allocated when they retire. These expenditures will increase the productivity of the real economy, which will help keep the financial sector solvent to provide for retirees.

Destroying Social Security in order to "save" it is not a solution.

Sources: Dean Baker and Mark Weisbrot, *Social Security: The Phony Crises*, University of Chicago Press, 1999; William Wolman and Anne Colamosca, *The Great 401(k) Hoax*, Perseus Publishing, 2002; Sylvester J. Schieber and John B. Shoven, "The Consequences of Population Aging on Private Pension Fund Saving and Asset Markets," National Bureau of Economic Research, Working Paper No. 4665, 1994.

Article 4.12

PAYING MORE, GETTING LESS

How much is the sick U.S. health care system costing you?

BY JOEL A. HARRISON
March/April 2008

By any measure, the United States spends an enormous amount of money on health care. Here are a few of those measures. Last year, U.S. health care spending exceeded 16% of the nation's GDP. To put U.S. spending into perspective: the United States spent 15.3% of GDP on health care in 2004, while Canada spent 9.9%, France 10.7%, Germany 10.9%, Sweden 9.1%, and the United Kingdom 8.7%. Or consider per capita spending: the United States spent $6,037 per person in 2004, compared to Canada at $3,161, France at $3,191, Germany at $3,169, and the U.K. at $2,560.

By now the high overall cost of health care in the United States is broadly recognized. And many Americans are acutely aware of how much they pay for their own care. Those without health insurance face sky-high doctor and hospital bills and ever more aggressive collection tactics—when they receive care at all. Those who are fortunate enough to have insurance experience steep annual premium hikes along with rising deductibles and co-pays, and, all too often, a well-founded fear of losing their coverage should they lose a job or have a serious illness in the family.

Still, Americans may well *underestimate* the degree to which they subsidize the current U.S. health care system out of their own pockets. And almost no one recognizes that even people without health insurance pay substantial sums into the system today. If more people understood the full size of the health care bill that they as individuals are already paying—and for a system that provides seriously inadequate care to millions of Americans—then the corporate opponents of a universal single-payer system might find it far more difficult to frighten the public about the costs of that system. In other words, to recognize the advantages of a single-payer system, we have to understand how the United States funds health care and health research and how much it actually costs us today.

Paying through the Taxman

The U.S. health care system is typically characterized as a largely private-sector system, so it may come as a surprise that more than 60% of the $2 trillion annual U.S. health care bill is paid through taxes, according to a 2002 analysis published in *Health Affairs* by Harvard Medical School associate professors Steffie Woolhandler and David Himmelstein. Tax dollars pay for Medicare and Medicaid, for the Veterans Administration and the Indian Health Service. Tax dollars pay for health coverage for federal, state, and municipal government employees and their families, as well as for many employees of private companies working on government contracts. Less visible but no less important, the tax deduction for employer-paid health insurance, along with other health care-related tax deductions, also represents a form of government spending on health care. It makes little difference whether the government gives taxpayers (or their employers) a deduction for their health care spending, on the one hand, or collects their taxes then pays for their health care, either directly or via a voucher, on the other. Moreover, tax dollars also pay for critical elements of the health care system apart from direct care—Medicare funds much of the expensive equipment hospitals use, for instance, along with all medical residencies.

All told, then, tax dollars already pay for at least $1.2 trillion in annual U.S. health care expenses. Since federal, state, and local governments collect about $3.48 trillion annually in taxes of all kinds—income, sales, property, corporate—that means that *more than one third (34.4%)* of the aggregate tax revenues collected in the United States go to pay for health care.

Beyond their direct payments to health care providers and health insurance companies, then, Americans already make a sizeable annual payment into the health care system via taxes. How much does a typical household contribute to the country's health care system altogether? Of course, households pay varying amounts in taxes depending on income and many other factors. Moreover, some households have no health insurance coverage; others do have coverage for which they may pay some or all of the premium cost. What I aim to do here is to estimate the average size of the health care cost burden for households at different income levels, both those with job-based health coverage and those with no coverage.

Note that the estimates in the table (next page) *do not include* out-of-pocket expenses. For those with health insurance, these include co-pays, deductibles, and uncovered expenses (consider, for example, that even my high-end policy does not cover commonly used home medical equipment such as oxygen). For those without insurance, of course, out-of-pocket expenses include their full hospital, doctor, and pharmacy bills.

The first row ("Share and Amount of Income Going to Health Care via Taxes Alone") shows how much of the total tax burden on households at three income levels goes into the nation's health care system. In other words, a family with an annual income of $50,000 that has no health insurance nonetheless contributes nearly 10% of its income to health care merely by paying typical income, payroll, sales, excise, and other taxes. A person who earns about $25,000 a year and has no health coverage already contributes over $2,400 a year to the system—enough for a healthy young adult to purchase a year's worth of health insurance.

The next two rows add in, for individuals and for families, the cost of employer-based health insurance. So, a household at the $50,000 income level with family health insurance coverage is paying *over a quarter* of its income into the health care system.

How were these figures derived? The tax component of the figures represents 34.4% of the total tax burden (federal, state, and local) on households at the three income levels. Of course, estimating average combined federal, state, and local taxes paid by households at different income levels is not a simple matter. The most comprehensive such estimates come from the Tax Foundation, a conservative think tank. Other analysts, however, including the liberal Center on Budget and Policy Priorities, view the Tax Foundation's figures as overestimating the total tax burden. The center has published its own estimates, based on figures from the Congressional Budget Office and Congress's Joint Committee on Taxation. The figures in the table are based on the CBO's numbers, which fall in between the Tax Foundation's estimates and the JCT-based estimates. (Estimates based on the Tax Foundation and JCT figures, along with details of the analysis, can be found at www.dollarsandsense.org.) It is worth noting that using the Tax Foundation's numbers, which show a larger share of income going to taxes at every income level, would have made the story even worse. For a family with health insurance earning $50,000 a year, for instance, the share of income going into health care would have been 28.7% rather than 26.4%.

For insurance premiums: in 2007, the average annual premiums for health insurance policies offered through employers were $4,479 for individuals and $12,106 for families, according to the Kaiser Family Foundation's annual survey of health benefits. Of course, some employers pay all or a large share of that premium while others pay half or less, leaving much of the premium cost to the worker. Either way, however, the full premium cost represents a bite taken out of the worker's total "wage packet"—the cost of wages plus benefits. This becomes evident when premiums go up: workers either see their own premium payments rise directly, or else face cuts or stagnation in their wages and non-health benefits. For that reason, economists typically view the entire premium as a cost imposed on the worker regardless of variations in employer contribution.

These figures are not meant to be exact, but do offer reasonable estimates of how much U.S. families are actually paying into the country's health care system today. Again, they do not include out-of-pocket expenses, which averaged 13.2% of all health care expenditures in 2005. Moreover, they do not include the risk of bankruptcy that health care costs impose: 50% of consumer bankruptcies in the United

What Americans Pay into the U.S. Health Care System Today		Household Income Level		
		$25,000	$50,000	$75,000
Share and Amount of Income Going to Health Care via Taxes Alone		9.0% ($2,425)	9.8% ($5,300)	10.7% ($8,633)
Share and Amount of Total Wage Packet Going to Health Care for Households with Insurance	Individual	22.0% ($6,904)	16.8% ($9,779)	15.4% ($13,112)
	Family	37.2% ($14,531)	26.4% ($17,406)	22.3% ($20,749)

Note: The share of total wage packet going to health care was calculated as follows:

$$\frac{(amount\ of\ total\ tax\ burden\ going\ to\ health\ +\ annual\ health\ insurance\ premium)}{(annual\ salary\ +\ payroll\ tax\ [FICA\ and\ Medicare]\ +\ annual\ health\ insurance\ premium)}$$

Further details of the calculations are available at www.dollarsandsense.org/harrison.

States stem from medical bills, including a surprising number among households that do have some kind of health coverage. Nor do they include the approximately 20% of auto insurance premiums or the 40% of workers' compensation premiums that pay for medical expenses.

Where Does All the Money Go?

After you've finished gasping in surprise at the share of your income that is already going into health care, you may wonder where all that money goes. One answer is that the United States has the most bureaucratic health care system in the world, including over 1,500 different companies, each offering multiple plans, each with its own marketing program and enrollment procedures, its own paperwork and policies, its CEO salaries, sales commissions, and other non-clinical costs—and, of course, if it is a for-profit company, its profits. Compared to the overhead costs of the single-payer approach, this fragmented system takes almost 25 cents more out of every health care dollar for expenses other than actually providing care.

Of the additional overhead in the current U.S. system, approximately half is borne by doctors' offices and hospitals, which are forced to maintain large billing and negotiating staffs to deal with all the plans. By contrast, under Canada's single-payer system (which is run by the provinces, not by the federal government), each medical specialty organization negotiates once a year with the nonprofit payer for each province to set fees, and doctors and hospitals need only bill that one payer.

Of course, the United States already has a universal, single-payer health care program: Medicare. Medicare, which serves the elderly and people with disabilities, operates with overhead costs equal to just 3% of total expenditures, compared to 15% to 25% overhead in private health programs. Since Medicare collects its revenue through the IRS, there is no need to collect from individuals, groups, or businesses. Some complexity remains—after all, Medicare must exist in the fragmented world that is American health care—but no matter how creative the opponents of single-payer get, there is no way they can show convincingly how the administrative costs of a single-payer system could come close to the current level.

Some opponents use current U.S. government expenditures for Medicare and Medicaid to arrive at frightening cost estimates for a universal single-payer health care system. They may use Medicare's $8,568 per person, or $34,272 for a family of four (2006). But they fail to mention that Medicare covers a very atypical, high-cost slice of the U.S. population: senior citizens, regardless of pre-existing conditions, and people with disabilities, including diagnoses such as AIDS and end-stage renal disease. Or they use Medicaid costs—forgetting to mention that half of Medicaid dollars pay for nursing homes, while the other half provide basic health care coverage, primarily to children in low-income households, at a cost of only about $1,500 a year per child.

Getting What We've Already Paid For

Americans spend more than anyone else in the world on health care. Each health insurer adds its bureaucracy, profits, high corporate salaries, advertising, and sales commissions to the actual cost of providing care. Not only is this money lost to health care, but it pays for a system that often makes it more difficult and complicated to receive the care we've already paid for. Shareholders are the primary clients of for-profit insurance companies, not patients.

Moreover, households' actual costs as a percentage of their incomes are far higher today than most imagine. Even families with no health insurance contribute substantially to our health care system through taxes. Recognizing the hidden costs that U.S. households pay for health care today makes it far easier to see how a universal single-payer system—with all of its obvious advantages—can cost most Americans less than the one we have today.

Sources: Center on Budget and Policy Priorities, "The Debate Over Tax Levels: How Much Does a Typical Family Pay?" March 11, 1998; Center on Budget and Policy Priorities, "Tax Foundation Figures Do Not Represent Middle-Income Tax Burdens: Figures May Mislead Policymakers, Journalists, and the Public," April 13, 2006; Center on Budget and Policy Priorities, "Clearing Up Confusion on the Cost of Covering Uninsured Children Eligible for Medicaid or SCHIP," March 13, 2007; Gary Claxton et al., "Health Benefits in 2007: Premium Increases Fall to an Eight-Year Low, While Offer Rates and Enrollment Remain Stable," *Health Affairs* 26(5), 2007 [based on "Employer Health Benefits 2007 Annual Survey" by the Kaiser Family Foundation]; Congressional Research Service, "U.S. Health Care Spending: Comparison with Other OECD Countries," September 17, 2007; Andrés de Francisco and Stephen Matlin, eds., *Monitoring Financial Flows for Health Research 2006* (Global Forum for Health Research, 2006); Tax Foundation, "Who Pays America's Tax Burden, and Who Gets the Most Government Spending?" March 2007; Public Citizen Congress Watch, "Rx R&D Myths: The Case Against the Drug Industry's R&D 'Scare Card'," July 2001; Steffie Woolhandler et al., "Health Care Administration in the United States and Canada: Micromanagement, Macro Costs," *Int'l Journal of Health Services* 34(1), 2004; Steffie Woolhandler and David Himmelstein, "Paying for National Health Insurance—And Not Getting It," *Health Affairs* 21(4), July/August 2002.

Chapter 5

MONETARY POLICY AND FINANCIAL MARKETS

INTRODUCTION

Ben Bernanke replaced Alan Greenspan as the man behind the curtain of the Federal Reserve Board just in time to oversee the worst financial crisis since the Great Depression.

Bernanke needed all the wizard-like powers the business press sometimes attributed to Greenspan, given it was his job to pull the economy's fat out of the fire. And those powers were in awfully short supply when Greenspan himself confessed before Congress in October 2008 that the financial crisis had left him "in a state of shocked disbelief" and that he had "made a mistake in presuming that banks ... were capable of protecting their own shareholders."

For now Bernanke seems to have averted complete economic meltdown. But little has been done to resolve the nearly intractable mortgage debt crisis or to put in place the measures that might prevent another financial crisis. Working people have fared no better under Bernanke than they did under maestro Greenspan. Even before the financial crisis, Greenspan worried that, under his tenure, inequality had worsened to levels that threatened our democratic institutions, and that the unprecedented level of U.S. reliance on foreign borrowing had become unsustainable. Bernanke has acknowledged the seriousness of both problems as well, but seems just as incapable as his predecessor of remedying them.

But why should it matter who chairs the Federal Reserve Board? The Fed is charged with using monetary policy to keep inflation in check and provide liquidity to keep the economy going (or bolster a flagging economy). The Fed is supposed to use its three tools—the reserve requirement, the discount and federal funds rates, and open market operations—to manipulate banking activity, control the money supply, and direct the economy to everyone's benefit.

It all sounds value-free. But what the Fed really does is serve those who hold financial assets. And that is just what's wrong with Fed monetary policy. When it comes to making monetary policy, the Fed puts the interests of bondholders first, well before those of job seekers and workers. Investors look to the Fed to protect the value of their stocks and bonds by keeping inflation low—and if that means keeping a cap on employment growth, so be it.

That is why monetary policy is not just a matter for financial market junkies, but for anyone concerned with the social policies it holds hostage. As Doug Orr and Ellen Frank argue in this chapter, "Whenever any policy is proposed, be it in health care, housing or transportation, the first question politicians ask is, 'What will the bond market think about it?'" The authors go on to show just how monetary policy under Greenspan has worked against most of us and even helped push the economy into a slowdown in 2000 (Article 5.2).

Other articles in this chapter look closely at diverse aspects of Fed policy making. Doug Orr explains in everyday language what money is and how the Fed attempts to control the money supply (Article 5.1). Arthur MacEwan compares monetary and fiscal policy, highlighting the greater powers of fiscal policy to counteract recessions (Article 5.3). The explosion in the excess reserves held by U.S. banks, as economist Gerald Friedman shows, confirms that using conventional monetary policy, the Fed can do little to get the economy going if banks won't make loans (Article 5.4). In a second article Friedman argues that Fed chief Bernanke responded to the crisis of 2008 and 2009 solely with repeated increases in the money supply not only due to his belief that the economy is self-correcting, but also because of the misreading of the cause of the Great Depression propagated by his teachers (Article 5.5).

The Fed is also charged with overseeing the regulation of U.S. financial institutions, including the stock market and home mortgage lending as well as the banking industry. But with the blessing of most economists, in recent decades Congress and the Fed have done more to deregulate these institutions than to regulate them in a way that promotes the public interest. In a thoroughgoing article, economist and one-time bank regulator William K. Black tells the story of how deregulation promoted dysfunction in the banking industry and enabled the current subprime mortgage crisis (Article 5.6).

The remainder of the chapter tallies up the damage inflicted by the financial crisis. Arthur MacEwan explicates the role that a giant pool of money (actually, financial assets) played in the home mortgage crisis (Article 5.7). Marty Wolfson gives a down-to-earth description of the financial instruments and deregulatory measures at the heart of the crisis. He calls for a regulatory structure that puts limits on financial risk and manipulation (Article 5.8).

Wolfson and two other economists, Fred Moseley and Robert Pollin, close the chapter with proposals for what to do about the home mortgage crisis, the banking industry, and the Fed. Moseley analyzes the bailout of the public mortgage lending agencies, Fannie Mae and Freddie Mac. He makes the case for a public home mortgage agency whose sole purpose would be to provide affordable housing (Article 5.10). Wolfson describes what was wrong with the bailout of the financial industry and describes how we can do better than just throwing money at banks (Article 5.9). Pollin makes the case for transforming the Fed into a democratically controlled investment bank that serves the interests of all of us (Article 5.11).

Discussion Questions

1. (Article 5.1) What are the mechanisms the Fed uses to "control" the creation of money by the banking system. Why, according to Orr, is the Fed's control over

the creation of money "limited"?

2. (Article 5.2) According to Orr and Frank, monetary policy serves the interests of bondholders at the expense of people seeking work and of everyone who benefits from social spending. What evidence do they provide to demonstrate this? Do you find it convincing?

3. (Article 5.3) What advantage is there in using monetary policy to slow down the economy? Why might fiscal policy be a more effective tool for lifting the economy out of a recession?

4. (Article 5.4) Why does Friedman, like others before him, liken monetary policy to "pushing on a string"? What evidence does Friedman offer to show that this analogy is an apt description of monetary policy today?

5. (Article 5.6) After reading Black's article, describe the measures that have led to the deregulation of the U.S. banking industry and the impact this deregulation has had.

6. (Article 5.10) Who is to blame for the financial troubles of Fannie Mae and Freddie Mac? How should Fannie and Freddie be reformed? Should the provision of affordable housing be their sole focus?

7. (Article 5.11) What are the chief elements of Pollin's proposal to transform the Fed? How would the Fed's focus and decision-making change? Do you think Pollin's proposal would be effective?

Article 5.1

WHAT IS MONEY?

BY DOUG ORR
November/December 1993

We all use money every day. Yet many people do not know what money actually is. There are many myths about money, including the idea that the government "prints" all of it and that it has some intrinsic value. But actually, money is less a matter of value, and more a matter of faith.

Money is sometimes called the universal commodity, because it can be traded for all other commodities. But for this to happen, everyone in society must believe that money will be accepted. If people stop believing that it will be accepted, the existing money ceases to be money. Recently in Poland, people stopped accepting the zloty, and used vodka as money instead.

In addition to facilitating exchanges, money allows us to "store" value from one point in time to another. If you sell your car today for $4,000, you probably won't buy that amount of other products today. Rather, you store the value as money, probably in a bank, until you want to use it.

The "things" that get used as money have changed over time, and "modern" people often chuckle when they hear about some of them. The Romans used salt (from which we get the word "salary"), South Sea Islanders used shark's teeth, and several societies actually used cows. The "Three Wise Men" brought gold, frankincense and myrrh, each of which was money in different regions at the time.

If money does not exist, or is in short supply, it will be created. In POW camps, where guards specifically outlaw its existence, prisoners use cigarettes instead. In the American colonies, the British attempted to limit the supply of British pounds, because they knew that by limiting the supply of money, they could hamper the development of independent markets in the colonies. Today, the United States uses a similar policy, through the International Monetary Fund, in dealing with Latin America.

To overcome this problem, the colonists began to use tobacco leaves as money. This helped the colonies to develop, but it also allowed the holders of large plots of land to grow their own money! When the colonies gained independence, the new government decreed gold to be money, rather than tobacco, much to the dismay of Southern plantation owners. Now, rather than growing money, farmers had to find or buy it.

To aid the use of gold as money, banks would test its purity, put it in storage, and give the depositor paper certificates of ownership. These certificates, "paper money," could then be used in place of the gold itself. Since any bank could store gold and issue certificates, by the beginning of the Civil War, over 7,000 different types of "paper money" were in circulation in the United States, none of it printed by the government.

While paper money is easier to use than gold, it is still risky to carry around large amounts of cash. It is safer to store the paper in a bank and simply sign over its ownership to make a purchase. We sign over the ownership of our money by writing a check. Checking account money became popular when the government outlawed the printing of paper money by private banks in 1864.

How Banks Create Money

Banks are central to understanding money, because in addition to storing it, they help to create it. Bankers realize that not everyone will withdraw their money at the same time, so they loan out much of the money that has been deposited. It is from the interest on these loans that banks get their profits, and through these loans the banking system creates new money.

If you deposit $100 cash in your checking account at Chase Manhattan Bank, you still have $100 in money to use, because checks are also accepted as money. Chase must set aside some of this cash as "reserves," in case you or other depositors decide to withdraw money as cash. Current regulations issued by the Federal Reserve Bank (the Fed) require banks to set aside three cents out of each dollar. So Chase can make a loan of $97, based on your deposit. Chase does not make loans by handing out cash but instead by putting $97 in the checking account of the person, say Emily, taking out the loan. So from your initial deposit of $100 in cash, the economy now has $197 in checking account money.

The borrower, Emily, pays $97 for some product or service by check, and the seller, say Ace Computers, deposits the money in its checking account. The total amount of checking account money is still $197, but its location and ownership have changed. If Ace Computer's account is at Citibank, $97 in cash is transferred from Chase to Citibank. This leaves just $3 in cash reserves at Chase to cover your original deposit. However, Citibank now has $97 in "new" cash on hand, so it sets aside three cents on the dollar ($2.91) and loans out the rest, $94.09, as new checking account money. Through this process, every dollar of "reserves" yields many dollars in total money.

If you think this is just a shell game and there is only $100 in "real" money, you still don't understand money. Anything that is accepted as payment for a transaction is "real" money. Cash is no more real than checking account money. In fact, most car rental companies will not accept cash as payment for a car, so for them, cash is not money!

Today, there is $292 billion of U.S. currency, i.e. "paper money," in existence. However, somewhere between 50% to 70% of it is held outside the United States by foreign banks and individuals. The vast majority of all money actually in use in the United States is not cash, but rather checking account money. This type of money, $726 billion, was created by private banks, and was not "printed" by anyone. In fact, this money exists only as electronic "bits" in banks' computers. (The less "modern" South Sea Islanders could have quite a chuckle about that!)

The amount of money that banks can create is limited by the total amount of reserves, and by the fraction of each deposit that must be held as reserves. Prior to 1914, bankers themselves decided what fraction of deposits to hold as reserves. Since then, this fraction has been set by the main banking regulator, the Fed.

Until 1934, gold was held as reserves, but the supply of gold was unstable, growing rapidly during the California and Alaska "gold rushes," and very slowly at other times. As a result, at times more money was created than the economy needed, and at other times not enough money could be created. Starting in 1934, the U.S. government decided that gold would no longer be used as reserves. Cash, now printed by the Fed, could no longer be redeemed for gold, and cash itself became the reserve asset.

Banks, fearing robberies, do not hold all of their cash reserves in their own vaults. Rather, they store it in an account at a regional Fed bank. These accounts count as reserves. What banks do hold in their vaults is their other assets, such as Treasury bonds and corporate bonds.

The Fed and Bank Reserves

The only role of the government in creating money is through the Fed. If the Fed wants to expand the money supply, it must increase bank reserves. To do this, the Fed buys Treasury bonds from a bank, and pays with a check drawn on the Fed itself. By depositing the check in its reserve account at the Fed, the bank now has more reserves, so the bank can now make more loans and create new checking account money.

By controlling the amount of reserves, the Fed attempts to control the size of the money supply. But as recent history has shown, this control is limited. During the recent recession, the Fed created reserves, but many banks were afraid to make loans, so little new money was created. During the late 1970s, the Fed tried to limit the amount of money banks could create by reducing reserves, but banks simply created new forms of money, just like the POW camp prisoners. In 1979, there was only one form of checking account money. Today, there are many, with odd names such as NOWs, ATSs, repos, and money market deposit accounts.

These amorphous forms of money function only because we believe they will function, which is why the continued stability of the banking system is so critical. Banks do not have cash reserves to cover all checking account money. If, through a replay of the savings & loan debacle, we lose faith in the commercial banking system and all try to take out our "money" as cash, the banks will become insolvent (fail), and the money they have created will simply disappear. This would create a real crisis, since no market economy can function without its money.

Article 5.2

FOCUS ON THE FED
The bond barket versus the rest of us

BY DOUG ORR AND ELLEN FRANK
October 1999

Why should anyone involved in environmental issues, or education reform efforts, or efforts to house the homeless, or anyone else, care about monetary policy? After all, it only affects the financial markets, right? *Wrong*. Monetary policy is holding all other social policy hostage, and is part of the cause of the rapid increase in income inequality in the United States. Whenever any policy change is proposed, be it in health care, housing or transportation, the first question politicians ask is, "What will the bond market think about this?"

"The bond market" is a euphemism for the financial sector of the U.S. economy and the Federal Reserve Bank (the Fed), which regulates that sector. The Fed is the central bank of the U.S. government. It controls monetary policy, and has been using its power to help the banking industry and the holders of financial assets, while thwarting government attempts to deal with pressing social problems.

Since 1979, the Fed has had an unprecedented degree of independence from government control. This independence had put it in a position to veto any progressive fiscal policy that the Congress might propose. To understand how this situation developed, we must understand the function of banks, the structure of the Fed, and the role of monetary policy.

Banks and Instability

Government regulates the banking industry because private sector, profit-driven banking is inherently unstable. Banks do more than just store money—they help create it. If you deposit a dollar in the bank, you still have that dollar. Commercial banks will set aside three cents as "reserves" to "cover" your deposit, and the remaining 97 cents is loaned out to someone else who now has "new money." By making loans, banks create new money and generate profit. The drive to maximize profits often leads banks to become overextended: making too many loans and holding too few reserves. This drive for profits can undermine a bank's stability.

If depositors think the bank is holding too few reserves, or is making overly speculative loans, they might try to withdraw their money as cash. Large numbers of depositors withdrawing cash from a bank at the same time is called a "run on the bank." Since banks only hold 3% of their deposit liabilities as cash, even a moderate-sized "run" would be enough to drain the bank of its cash reserves. If a bank has no reserves, it is insolvent and is forced to close. At that point, all remaining deposits in the bank cease to exist, and depositors lose their money.

The failure of a bank affects more than just that bank's depositors. One bank's excesses tend to shake people's faith in other banks. If the run spreads, "bank panics" can occur. During the 1800s, such panics erupted every 10 to 15 years, bankrupting between 10% and 25% of the banks in the United States and creating a recession each time.

The Creation of the Fed

The panic of 1907 bankrupted some of the largest banks and led to demands for bank reforms that would stabilize the system. Reform proposals ranged from doing almost nothing to nationalizing the entire banking industry. As a compromise, the Federal Reserve was created in 1913. The U.S. government saw the Fed as a way for bankers to regulate themselves, and structured the Federal Reserve System so that it could be responsive to its main constituents: banks and other financial-sector businesses that are now called, euphemistically, "the bond market." While ideally it should serve the interests of the general public when it conducts monetary policy, in reality the Fed balances two, occasionally conflicting goals: maintaining the stability of "the bond market" and maximizing financial-sector profits. Over time, Congress and the President have varied the degree of independence that they have given to the Fed to choose between these goals.

Initially, the Fed enjoyed a high degree of independence. Unfortunately, it was more successful in aiding bank profits than in stabilizing the system. During the 1920s, the Fed allowed member banks to engage in highly speculative activities, including using depositor's money to play the stock market. While many banks were very profitable, speculative excesses caused almost 20% of the banks in existence in 1920 to fail during the following decade. With the onset of the Great Depression, between 1929 and 1933, more than 9,000 banks, 38% of the total, failed. Since the Fed had not achieved its first goal, in 1935 Congress responded with laws that put many new regulations on banks, and reduced the Fed's independence.

Fed Independence Lost

Under the new regulations, commercial banks were restricted to taking deposits and making commercial loans. Thus, the only opportunity for making a profit was to maintain a "spread" between the interest rate paid on deposits and that charged on loans. Loans are made for relatively long terms, and deposits are not. If the short-term interest rate on deposits varies widely, the spread will grow and shrink, which makes bank profits unstable. In order to stabilize bank profits, during the 30 years after 1935, the Treasury mandated that the Fed keep this rate approximately constant.

Under this arrangement, Congress indirectly controlled monetary policy. If Congress wanted to stimulate the economy it could increase government spending or cut taxes. Both led to an increase in spending and an increase in the demand for money. To keep interest rates, which are the price of money, from rising, the Fed must increase the supply of money. Thus, the Fed "accommodated" fiscal policy decisions made by Congress and the President.

During most of this period, growth was moderate and prices were stable. The Fed went along because this arrangement did not threaten bank profits. Starting in the mid-1960s, however, stimulative fiscal policy started to push up the inflation rate, which did threaten bank profits. A confrontation over Fed independence ensued and grew in intensity throughout the 1970s.

Inflation's Impact

Contrary to the view commonly propagated by the media, inflation does not affect everyone equally. In fact, there are very clear winners and losers. Inflation is an increase in the average level of prices, but some prices rise faster than average and some rise slower. If the price of something you are selling is rising faster than average, you win. Otherwise, you lose. Inflation redistributes income, but in an arbitrary manner. This uncertainty makes inflation unpopular, even to the winners. However, one industry always loses from unexpected inflation, and that industry is finance.

Banks make loans today that will be repaid, with interest, in the future. If inflation reduces the value of those future payments, the banks' profits will be reduced. So bankers are interested in the "real interest rate," that is, the actual (nominal) interest rate on the loan minus the rate of inflation. If the interest rate on commercial bank loans is 7% and the rate of inflation is 3%, the real rate of interest is 4%. In the early postwar period, real interest rates were relatively stable at about 2%.

From 1965 on, unexpected increases in inflation reduced the real interest rate. This cheap credit was a boon to home buyers, farmers, and manufacturers, but it greatly reduced bank profits. Banks wanted inflation cut. The Keynesian view of monetary policy offered a simple but unpopular solution: raise interest rates enough to cause a recession. High unemployment and falling incomes would take the steam out of inflation.

Putting people out of work to help bankers would be a hard sell. The Fed needed a different story to justify shifting its policy from stabilizing interest rates to fighting inflation. That story was monetarism, a theory that claims that changes in the money supply affect prices, but nothing else in the economy.

The Monetarist Experiment

On October 6, 1979, Fed Chair Paul Volcker, using monetarist theory as a justification, announced that the Fed would no longer try to keep interest rates at targeted levels. He argued that Fed policy should concentrate on controlling inflation, and to do so he would now focus on limiting the money supply growth rate. Since neither Congress nor the President attempted to overrule Volcker, this change ushered in an era of unprecedented independence for Fed monetary policy.

During the next three years, the Fed reduced the rate of growth in the money supply, but this experiment did not yield the results predicted by the monetarists. Instead of a swift reduction in the rate of inflation, the most immediate outcome was a rapid rise in the real interest rate and the start of the worst recession since the Great Depression.

As the Keynesian view predicted, the recession occurred because high interest rates slowed economic growth and increased unemployment. In 1979, the unemployment rate was 5.8%. By 1982 it had reached 10.7%, the first double-digit rate since the Depression. With fewer people working and buying products, the inflation rate, which had been 8.7% in 1979, finally started to slow in 1981 and was approaching 4% by the end of 1982. Tight money policies by the Fed kept nominal interest rates from falling as fast as inflation. This raised real interest rates (nominal rates minus inflation) on commercial loans from 0.5% in 1979 to 10% in 1982.

The Fed's fight against inflation had a severe impact on the entire economy. All businesses, especially farming and manufacturing, run on credit. The rise in interest rates, combined with lower prices, squeezed the profits of farmers and manufacturers.

Both of these industries rely heavily on exports, and so were also hurt by the negative effect of high interest rates on the competitiveness of U.S. exports. Real interest rates in the United States were the highest in the world, thereby attracting financial investment from abroad. In order for foreigners to buy financial assets in the United States, they first had to buy dollars. This demand for dollars drove up their value in international markets. While a "strong" dollar means imports are relatively cheap, it also means that U.S. exports are expensive. Foreign countries could not afford to buy our "costly" agricultural and manufactured exports. As a result, during this period, bankruptcy rates in these two industries were massive, higher than during the 1930s.

Despite its high cost to the rest of the economy, the monetarist experiment did not benefit many banks. Initially, the high real interest rates appeared to help bank profits. Regulations capped the interest rates banks could pay on deposits, but rates charged on loans were not regulated. This increased the profit on loans. Many investors, however, started moving their deposits to less regulated financial intermediaries, such as mutual funds, that could pay higher rates on deposits. In addition, the recession forced many borrowers to declare bankruptcy and default on their loans. Both of these factors pushed banks toward insolvency.

Reversing Course

It was bank losses, rather than the pain in the rest of the economy, that led Volcker to announce in September 1982 that he was abandoning monetarism. His new policy aimed to provide enough reserves to keep most banks solvent and to allow a *slow* recovery from the recession. Unemployment remained high for the next five years, so inflation continued to slow. Real interest rates stayed near 8% through 1986, so interest-sensitive industries, such as farming and manufacturing, did not take part in the recovery.

Volcker made his allegiance to the banking industry very clear during a meeting, in February 1985, with a delegation of state legislators, laborers, and farmers who were demanding easier money and lower interest rates. He told them, "Look, your constituents are unhappy, mine aren't."

Yet by 1985, the crisis in the savings and loan industry was spreading into commercial banking. To provide cash ("liquidity") to the banks, Volcker allowed the money supply to grow by 12% during 1985 and by 17% in 1986. Monetarists raised the specter of a return to double-digit inflation. Instead, the rate of inflation continued to slow, demonstrating that a simple link between the money supply and inflation does not exist.

The Veto

Despite the failure and subsequent abandonment of monetarist policies, the Fed still uses monetarist *theory* to justify its continued focus on "fighting inflation." The myth that monetary policy only affects inflation provides a convenient "cover" that allows the Fed to serve its narrow constituency: "the bond market." During 1998, nominal interest rates appeared low, but because inflation is so low, real interest rates on commercial loans were 6.8%—3.2 times the post-World War II average. Real interest rates remain high because "the bond market" worries about any possible increase in future inflation.

Fighting inflation benefits the bond market. However, despite the near-depression that monetarism caused in the 1980s and the extremely slow rate of economic growth that has occurred in the 1990s, the Fed continues to claim that fighting inflation serves the interests of the entire country. The public's widespread belief in this myth denies progressives in Congress the support they need to force the Fed back into accommodating fiscal policy. It also provides support for those in Congress that want to block any expansion of social programs.

If Congress decides to spend more for environmental clean-up, housing the homeless, or education, "the bond market" will raise the specter of renewed inflation. The Fed will then raise interest rates, as it did in June 1999, as a "preemptive strike" to prevent inflation. The increase in interest rates, if large enough, will slow the economy, increase unemployment, reduce government revenues, and return the federal budget to a deficit. Since Congress is aware of this probable outcome, and knows it will be incorrectly blamed for it, Congress won't pass any legislation "the bond market" doesn't like. This is how the bond market holds Congress hostage. As long as Congress and the President allow the Fed to follow an inflation-fighting policy, the Fed can maintain a veto threat over the elected government.

The Fed has also played a large role in the rapid increase in income and wealth inequality that started in the 1980s and has accelerated in the 1990s. The two decades following World War II are often called the "golden age" of the U.S. economy. On average, Gross Domestic Product (GDP) grew 4.2% each year, unemployment averaged 4.6%, and real commercial interest rates averaged 2.1%. Average real wages, that is, wages adjusted for inflation, grew at an annual rate of 2.1%, rising from $8.34 an hour in 1950 to $12.75 in 1970 (both measured in 1998 dollars). This period saw the creation of a true middle class in the United States.

In the two decades since 1980, GDP growth has averaged 2.6% each year, unemployment has averaged 6.6%, and real interest rates have averaged 5.9%. Average real wages *declined* every year from 1980 to 1996. In fact, the real wage in 1996 was exactly the same as in 1968. If wages had continued to grow at 2.1%, the average wage today would be almost twice what it is. Without the slow growth policies of the Fed and the anti-labor policies started under Reagan, the average income of the majority of the people in the United States would be twice as large. Instead, we've seen a hollowing out of the middle class, and a rapid transfer of wealth and income to those already wealthy.

By focusing on inflation rather than interest rates, the media deflect attention from a critical social issue—how high interest rates transfer income from the indebted middle class to the very rich. The social consequences of high interest rates can be gauged by looking at the share of interest income in total U.S. personal income. Between 1980 and 1989, real interest rates rose from 1.8% to 6.1%. The share of income received as interest rose from 11% to 15.2%. As rates came back down slightly in the mid-1990s, so did the share of income going to interest.

Where Do Interest Payments Go?

If ownership of financial assets was evenly distributed among households, the growth in interest income would not be of much importance. When increases in interest rates outstripped wage and salary gains, the typical household would simply gain on the asset side what they were losing on the liability side. An increase in the size of their mortgage payment would be matched by an increase in their interest income.

But ownership of financial assets is heavily concentrated. A mere 7% of families with incomes of $100,000 or more control nearly half of total household net worth. Yet this number understates the concentration of financial wealth. Almost 80% of families in the United States have almost no assets, outside the equity in their homes and vehicles. As a result, despite the massive increase in financial asset values during the 1990s, median net worth was no higher in 1995 than it was in 1989. Almost all of the growth in net worth accrued to the few owners of financial assets.

Detailed studies of wealth data collected by the Fed report that in 1995 the wealthiest 10% of households owned 89.8% of all bonds, 88.4% of all stocks, 88.5% of financial trusts, and 91% of other business equity. Despite the media hype about the "democratization" of the stock market, between 1989 and 1995 the concentration of stock ownership increased. In 1995 only 15.3% of households held stocks directly and only 12% owned shares in mutual funds outside of their retirement accounts.

The "poorest" nine-tenths of the U.S. population—that is, most of us—have virtually no financial assets. Such families gain little from rising interest rates. But the higher mortgage, credit card, and auto payments that result take a real toll on living standards. Each uptick in the real interest rate entails a transfer of income from the lowest 90% of the population to the highest 10%. And most of that income goes to the very, very wealthy who are yet another part of "the bond market" served by the Fed.

Economist James Galbraith has called today's high interest rates a form of taxation without representation. The term is apt. Tax increases are passed by Congress, which has at least some public oversight. Interest rate hikes are decided by the Fed, an institution over which the President, Congress and the public have virtually no control.

Like taxes, rising interest rates are a drain on the resources and income of the vast majority of U.S. households. But unlike tax revenues that can be used to provide education, environmental clean-up, homeless shelters, roads, airports, and other infrastructure, interest payments flow into the pockets of the very rich, who become ever so much richer.

Resources: Arthur B. Kennickell, Martha Starr-McCluer, and Annika E. Sunden, "Family Finances in the U.S.: Recent Evidence from the Survey of Consumer Finances," *Federal Reserve Bulletin* (Jan. 1997); Lawrence Mishel, Jared Bernstein, and John Schmitt, *The State of Working America 1998-99*, 1999.

Article 5.3

HOW DO FISCAL AND MONETARY POLICY COMPARE?

BY ARTHUR MacEWAN

July/August 1997

The Federal Reserve influences the economy through monetary policy—the actions the Fed takes to affect the cost and availability of credit. For example, in March of this year, the Fed, led by its chairman Alan Greenspan, decided that it was time to slow economic growth. So it induced banks and other lenders to raise their interest rates. Higher interest rates mean fewer businesses and individuals will take out loans and spend the borrowed money. Lower spending means slower economic growth.

The federal government can also influence economic growth and the demand for goods and services through fiscal policy—the way it taxes and spends. If the government wants to slow down the economy, for example, it can raise taxes and reduce its own spending. Less money ends up in people's hands if the government hires fewer construction workers to build roads, or if it cuts back on education programs.

One problem with fiscal policy is that changing the budget takes time—except for programs whose spending levels change automatically when the economy does, like unemployment compensation. To slow down the economy, Congress has to pass new laws raising taxes—certainly a "no no" these days—or cutting spending. Then the President has to accept Congress's new law, which might require negotiations, or more legislative action. All this is to say that the political process involves considerable delays and might result in no action at all.

Monetary policy is different because the Fed does not have to bother with this messy political process that we call democracy. It is "independent" since its members, appointed by the President, serve long terms. They decide whether to ease or tighten the availability of credit, without any role for Congress or the President. To be sure, the "independence" of the Fed is not enshrined in the Constitution. Yet for Congress and the President to pass new laws which directed or restricted the Fed's action would be a serious disruption of well-established policy.

The law governing the Fed says that it should pursue both stable prices (low inflation) and full employment. In fact, the Fed focuses almost exclusively on the goal of stable prices. If unemployment has to rise to meet this goal, well, too bad. It is easy to see why the Fed does its work best when it doesn't have to worry about getting democratic approval.

Fiscal policy is somewhat more constrained by democratic processes than is monetary policy. For example, conservative attacks on Medicare and Social Security have not gotten very far because these programs are very popular.

But the recent mania to balance the budget makes it difficult to use fiscal policy to stimulate economic expansion by increasing spending. This may present some serious problems during economic downturns. The monetary policy of the Fed, it turns out, is not nearly so effective in stimulating economic expansion during a recession as it is in slowing growth during relatively good times. In a recession, the Fed can induce commercial banks to lower their interest rates. But if the recession leads investors to worry that demand for products and services will fall, the lower interest rates might not reignite economic growth. What's the point, for example, in building a new office building when it doesn't look like it will be possible to rent out the space in existing buildings for quite a while?

In a recession, then, trying to use monetary policy to get the economy going can be like pushing on a string. It simply won't do any good. Fiscal policy, however, might directly create demand, present businesses with the reality of a new expansion, and generate a new period of investment and growth.

Article 5.4

PUSHING ON STRINGS

*The explosion of U.S. banks' excess reserves since last fall
illustrates the dramatic failure of monetary policy.*

BY GERALD FRIEDMAN
May/June 2009

Monetary policy is not working. Since the economic crisis began in July 2007, the Federal Reserve has dramatically cut interest rates and pumped out over a trillion dollars, increasing the money supply by over 15% in less than two years. These vast sums have failed to revive the economy because the banks have been hoarding liquidity rather than lending.

The Federal Reserve requires that banks hold money on reserve to back up deposits and other bank liabilities. In the past, beyond these required reserves, banks would hold very small amounts of excess reserves, holdings that they minimized because reserves earn very little or no interest. Between the 1950s and September 2008, U.S. banks held over $5 billion in total excess reserves only once, after the September 11 attacks. This changed with the collapse of Lehman Brothers. Beginning with less than $2 billion in August 2008, excess reserves soared to $60 billion in September and then to $559 billion in November before peaking at $798 billion in January 2009. (They have since dropped to $644 billion in the last accounting month.)

This explosion of excess reserves represents a signal change in bank policy that threatens the effectiveness of monetary policy in the current economic crisis. Aware of their own financial vulnerability, even insolvency, frightened bank managers re-

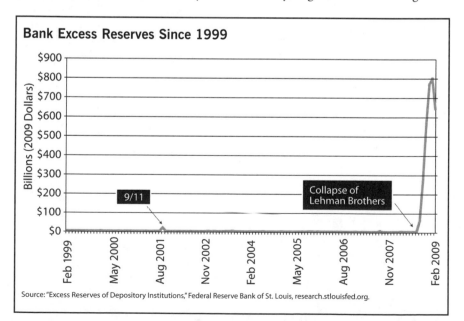

Bank Excess Reserves Since 1999

Source: "Excess Reserves of Depository Institutions," Federal Reserve Bank of St. Louis, research.stlouisfed.org.

sponded to the collapse of major investment houses like Lehman Brothers by grabbing and hoarding all the cash that they could get. At the same time, a general loss of confidence and spreading economic collapse persuaded banks that there are few to whom they could lend with confidence that the loans would be repaid. Clearly, our banks have decided that they need, or at least want, the money more than consumers and productive businesses do.

Banks could have been investing this money by lending to businesses needing liquidity to buy material inputs or pay workers. Had they done so, monetarist economists would be shouting from the rooftops, or at least in the university halls, about how monetary policy prevented another Great Depression. Instead, even the *Wall Street Journal* is proclaiming that "We're All Keynesians Again" because monetary policy has failed. Monetary authorities, the *Journal* explains, can create money but they cannot force banks to lend or to invest it in productive activities. The Federal Reserve confronts a reality shown in the graph above: it can't "push on a string," as Fed Chair Marriner Eccles famously put it in testimony before Congress in 1935, in the depths of the Great Depression.

If the banks won't lend, then we need more than monetary policy to get out of the current crisis. No bailout, no TARP program, can revive the economy if banks hoard all the cash they receive. The Obama stimulus was an appropriate response to the failure of string-pushing. But much more government stimulus will be needed to solve a crisis this large, and we will need programs to move liquidity from bank vaults to businesses and consumers. It may be time to stop waiting on the banks, and to start telling them what to do with our money.

Article 5.5

BERNANKE'S BAD TEACHERS

BY GERALD FRIEDMAN
July/August 2009

Addressing a conference honoring Milton Friedman on his 90th birthday in 2002, the future chairman of the Federal Reserve Board, Ben Bernanke, praised Friedman's 1963 book, written with Anna J. Schwartz, *A Monetary History of the United States.* Before Friedman and Schwartz, most economists saw the Great Depression of the 1930s as proof that capitalist economies do not tend towards full-employment equilibrium. But Friedman and Schwartz restored the prior orthodoxy by blaming the Great Depression on bad monetary policy by the Federal Reserve while exonerating American capitalism. The Great Depression was "the product of the nation's monetary mechanism gone wrong."

It is significant that Friedman and Schwartz never use the phrase "the Great Depression"; instead, they speak of "the Great Contraction" of the 1930s, addressing the reduction in the money supply while treating the fall in employment and output as a secondary matter, the consequence of bad government policy that caused "the Great Contraction." By flattering the prejudices of economists who want to believe in the natural stability of free markets, Friedman and Schwartz's story has become the accepted explanation of America's worst economic disaster.

Bernanke, for one, confesses that he was inspired by their work; "hooked" in graduate school, "I have been a student of monetary economics and economic history ever since." Pushing on an open door, Friedman and Schwartz persuaded most orthodox economists, and that part of the political elite that listens to economists, that the economic collapse that began in 1929 was an accident that would have been avoided by reliance on free markets and competent Federal Reserve monetary policy.

Bernanke closed his 2002 remarks with a promise. "Let me end my talk," he said, "by abusing slightly my status as an official representative of the Federal Reserve. I would like to say to Milton and Anna: Regarding the Great Depression. You're right, we did it. We're very sorry. But thanks to you, we won't do it again."

Bernanke had five years to ponder this promise before he faced a worthy challenge; and then he acted with the vigor of a Friedman/Schwartz acolyte. When this decade's housing bubble began to deflate in early 2007, major financial firms like New Century Financial and Bear Stearns reported major losses, and confidence in the U.S. financial system began to collapse as swiftly as in 1929–33. In early August, the rising tide reached tsunami dimensions when the International Monetary Fund warned of a trillion dollars in bank losses from bad mortgages. This was Bernanke's moment. Channeling Friedman and Schwartz, careful to avoid the mistakes of 1929–33, the Federal Reserve moved quickly in early August 2007 to provide liquidity to financial markets. It acted again on August 17 by cutting mortgage rates. More cuts came on September 18, on October 31, and on December 11. Then, on December 12, the Fed announced the creation of a new facility formed with the Europeans (Term Auction Facility, or TAF) to provide $24 billion in additional liquidity to financial markets. After still more interest-rate cuts in January 2008, a new special lending facility, with $100 billion, was established on March 2, along with another $75 billion for the TAF. Then, on March 11, another new facility was created, the Term Securities Lending Facility, with $200 billion. And all this was long before the bailouts of Fannie Mae, Freddie Mac, AIG, or the federal government's trillion-dollar Troubled Asset Relief Program (TARP).

If insanity consists of doing the same thing over and over again and expecting different results, then the Federal Reserve went insane after the summer of 2007. Never before has it acted this aggressively in trying to get ahead of a financial market meltdown. Under Bernanke, the Fed has increased the money supply by over 16% in less than two years, nearly mirroring the 18% drop in the money supply in the same period after the stock market collapse of 1929. Had he lived, Milton Friedman would have been proud.

The one thing that has not changed between the crisis of 1929 and the crisis of 2007 has been the behavior of the real economy. Bernanke has avoided his predecessors' monetary policy mistakes, but he has not prevented a sharp economic downturn. Since 2007, the economy has lost nearly 6 million jobs, including over half a million in the last month. At 8.9%, the April 2009 unemployment rate unnervingly equals the 1930 figure. We have a long way to go before we hit Great Depression level unemployment; but we are only in the second year of this collapse. And monetary policy is not helping.

Here, then, we see the legacy of Friedman and Schwartz. Confident that capitalist free markets naturally move towards a full-employment equilibrium, Bernanke and his allies saw the need for only one type of government action: providing liquidity to the banks in order to strengthen confidence in the financial markets. Guided by Friedman and Schwartz, Bernanke has provided nearly unlimited aid to the Wall Street bankers and financiers responsible for our current economic collapse. And he has starved the real economy—businesses, workers, and homeowners—to avoid interfering in free markets.

Bernanke has conducted an economic policy as cruel as it has been ineffective. But the blame here goes beyond Milton Friedman and Anna Schwartz. It lies squarely on the economics profession.

(MIS)UNDERSTANDING A BANKING INDUSTRY IN TRANSITION

Under deregulation the industry became dysfunctional—but economists still won't revise their anti-regulation script.

BY WILLIAM K. BLACK
November/December 2007

The U.S. financial system is, once again, in crisis. Or, more precisely, twin crises—first, huge numbers of defaults among subprime mortgage borrowers, and second, massive losses for the holders of new-fangled investments comprised of bundles of loans of varying risk, including many of those subprime mortgages.

These crises should shock the nation. Our largest, most sophisticated financial institutions have followed business practices that were certain to produce massive losses—practices so imprudent, in precisely the business task (risk management) that is supposed to be their greatest expertise, that they have created a worldwide financial crisis.

Why? Because their CEOs, acting on the perverse incentives created by today's outrageous compensation systems, engaged in practices that vastly increased their corporations' risk in order to drive up reported corporate income and thereby secure enormous increases in their own individual incomes. And those perverse incentives follow them out the door: CEOs Charles Prince, at Citicorp, and Stanley O'Neal, at Merrill Lynch, had dismal track records of similar failures prior to the latest disasters, but they collected massive bonuses for their earlier failures and will receive obscene termination packages now. Pay and productivity (and integrity) have become unhinged at U.S. financial institutions.

As this goes to print, Treasury Department officials are working with large financial institutions to cover up the scale of the growing losses. This is the same U.S. Treasury that regularly prates abroad about the vital need for transparency. And a former Treasury Secretary, Robert Rubin, who failed utterly in his fiduciary duty as lead board member at Citicorp to prevent the series of recent abuses, will become Citicorp's new CEO.

To even begin to understand events in the U.S. and global banking industries, you have to look back at the seismic shifts in the industry over the past 30 to 40 years, and at the interplay between those shifts and government policy. The story that continues to unfold is one of progressively worse policies that make financial crises more common and more severe.

These policies have their boosters, though. Chief among them are neoclassical banking and finance economists, whose ideology and methodologies lead them into blatant misreadings of the realities of the industry and the causes of its failures. When the history of this crisis-ridden era in global finance is written, the economists will no doubt be given a significant share of the blame.

A New Era of Crisis

The changes in the U.S. banking industry in recent decades have been so great that a visitor from the 1950s would hardly recognize the industry. Over two decades of intense merger and acquisition activity has left a far smaller number of banks, with assets far more concentrated in the largest ones. Between 1984 and 2004, the number of banks on the FDIC's rolls fell from 14,392 to 7,511; the share of the U.S. banking industry's assets held by the ten largest banks rose from 21% in 1960 to nearly 60% in 2005. At the same time, nonbank businesses that lend, save, and invest money have proliferated, as have the products they sell: a vast array of new kinds of loans and exotic savings and investment vehicles. And the lines have blurred between all of the different players in the industry—between banks and thrifts (e.g., savings and loans), between commercial banks and investment banks.

These changes were made possible by the deregulation of the industry. Bit by bit, beginning in the 1970s, the banking regulations put into place in the wake of the Great Depression were repealed, culminating in the Gramm-Leach-Bliley Act in 1999, which removed the remaining legal barriers to combining commercial banking, investment banking, and insurance under one corporate roof. The

Deposit Insurance Spreads Despite Economists' Protests

Banking economists now overwhelmingly criticize deposit insurance. This represents a major change. The prior consensus, shared by Milton Friedman and John Kenneth Galbraith alike, praised deposit insurance for ending the periodic runs on uninsured banks that helped cause the Great Depression. Today, however, the conventional economic wisdom is that deposit insurance may stop runs, but at the expense of encouraging banks to make imprudent loans and take excessive risks. (Neoclassical economists widely view insurance as inherently creating an incentive for insured parties to act in unduly risky ways because of the safety net that insurance provides—a phenomenon termed "moral hazard.")

This claim is dubious: economists do not offer a credible mechanism whereby deposit insurance could lead to the ills they claim it causes. Deposit insurance does not protect the shareholders or the CEO—the two groups (the first, in theory; the second, in practice) that control a bank. It is the depositors who are insured. Thus, they must be the ones who are subject to moral hazard—in other words, the argument against deposit insurance must be based on the claim that it reduces the incentive of depositors to exercise "private market discipline" by pulling their money out of a bank they believe is being poorly run or looted. But there is no credible evidence that depositors are capable of either discerning frauds or avoiding runs on healthy banks based on false rumors. Indeed, studies have shown that even private-sector financial experts who specialize in evaluating the health of banks cannot do so effectively.

Proponents of the view that deposit insurance causes banking failures display an unrecognized logical inconsistency. Their proposed reform is to rely on private market discipline to prevent management from looting the bank or lending imprudently in a bubble. But, if we assume hypothetically that private market discipline is effective against CEOs who would be so inclined, then it should normally be effective despite the presence of deposit insurance. Deposit insurance does not remove private market discipline where the bank is owned by shareholders (unless the CEO owns all the stock) or where the bank issues uninsured subordinated debt. Yet during the S&L crisis, control fraud (the looting of an institution by its own managers or owners) was most common in S&Ls owned in stock form, with the largest losses overwhelmingly among stock S&Ls. In these cases deposit insurance did not new world of combined financial services is exemplified by the deal, inked (but ostensibly illegal) before the 1999 law was passed, that merged the insurance and investment-banking giant Travelers with Citibank, at the time the nation's number-one commercial bank.

These transformational changes in domestic banking, along with the related effects of economic globalization both in the United States and abroad, have produced recurrent crises in the financial sector. Indeed, the current era has seen over 100 major banking crises, in countries around the globe. Thomas Hoenig, head of the Kansas City Federal Reserve Bank, emphasized the remarkable and disturbing facts in a meeting with fellow heads of supervision:

> A 1996 survey by the IMF [International Monetary Fund] … found that 73 percent [133 of 181] of their member countries had experienced significant banking problems during the preceding 15 years. Many of these problems led to substantial declines in GDP [and] serious disruptions in credit and capital markets. …

To date none of these crises has led to a global Great Depression. Only a few were larger in absolute terms than the 1980s S&L debacle in the United States. Yet

---

preclude private market discipline; market discipline was simply inadequate to prevent control fraud. Some opponents of deposit insurance proclaim the S&L debacle to be their primary example—a flat misreading of the facts.

The empirical evidence economists use to support their critique of deposit insurance is inconsistent. Moreover, even where the adoption of deposit insurance is correlated with a rise in bank failures, the causal relationship may be just the opposite of what economists claim. Nations with early signs of an impending banking crisis may adopt deposit insurance to reduce the risks of runs. Developing nations tend to adopt deposit insurance in conjunction with privatization—which itself often prompts a banking crisis. More broadly, in part because of the fall of the Soviet Union and the rise of the neoliberal "Washington Consensus," the number of nations adopting deposit insurance increased sharply in the last two decades. Banking crises have indeed been far more common over this same period—precisely because these radical transitions have been occurring in nations with weak institutions, too few regulators with too little experience, patterns of bank ownership that maximize conflicts of interest, and substantial corruption.

In addition, empirical studies rely on subjective coding of different countries' deposit insurance policies, often done by economists who oppose deposit insurance. In countries with no formal deposit insurance, implicit government guarantees for banks are common. There are good theoretical and historical reasons to argue that such implicit guarantees—common in crony capitalism and kleptocracies—create greater moral hazard than explicit deposit insurance does because they can be structured to bail out a bank's shareholders and CEO as well as its creditors (as was done in Chile). But there is no way to code accurately for whether there was an implicit guarantee (or whether bank CEOs believed there was an implicit guarantee) in a particular country at a particular time.

Despite these weaknesses in both evidence and analysis, World Bank economists draw firm conclusions, opposing the adoption of deposit insurance in any nation and clearly hoping for its elimination. But the world has rejected their advice. By 2006, 95 countries had deposit insurance, over four times the number in 1983. Moreover, economists' suggestions on how to "improve" deposit insurance (require banks to issue subordinated debt, charge variable rates for deposit insurance, or require private insurance of accounts) are rarely adopted and have proven unsuccessful in practice.

many imposed a much greater relative cost, measured as a percentage of the country's GDP. Some caused severe, depression-like economic problems in the affected nation. Some produced contagion effects that caused severe crises in other nations. And acute banking crises can cause long-term harm. Japan is a rich nation and can afford a 15-year banking crisis—but the world economy cannot. The crisis cut Japan's economic growth to near-zero for a decade, in turn creating contagion effects in the many countries for whom Japan was a major trading partner or a significant source of capital investment. Tens of millions of people remain in poverty in Asia and Africa as a result.

The recurrent banking crises have come as a shock to the United States, given the dearth of bank failures over the first three decades after World War II. The first severe postwar U.S. banking crisis was stemmed from the large loans that top U.S. banks made to sovereign borrowers (i.e., nations), largely in Latin America. The banks had claimed that sovereign loans offered high returns with minimal default risk because the nation could always repay the loan by printing more money. Citibank head Walter Wriston notoriously implied that countries could not go broke. The claim was absurd. However, banking regulators took no effective action to restrain this lending.

The 1982 Mexican default led to contagion and fears of an international meltdown, but the Federal Reserve and the Bank for International Settlements (BIS) took effective action. Brazil experienced a long economic slowdown that contributed to an imminent default on its loans from major U.S. banks. A Brazilian default could have rendered several of our largest banks insolvent. The banks were rescued by a combination of bailouts to Brazil through the IMF and the World Bank and flawed (albeit permissible under so-called Generally Accepted Accounting Principles, or GAAP) "troubled-debt restructuring" to cover up the losses. Brazil used the bailouts to pay minimal interest on the U.S. bank loans and ultimately recovered; while several U.S. banks took serious losses, none failed.

On the heels of this crisis came the savings and loan crisis, an unprecedented debacle which saw the collapse of some 1,000 S&Ls and which cost U.S. taxpayers about $125 billion dollars—primarily the cost of repaying to depositors money that criminal S&L heads had literally stolen from their institutions.

The causes of these crises are varied. They typically occur, however, when large banks are in essence looted by their owners and managers (a phenomenon known as "control fraud") or when there are financial bubbles in which assets become massively overvalued.

Economists who conduct case studies of banking crises commonly report the existence of substantial control fraud. Looting played a prominent role in the S&L debacle. Here is the conclusion of the National Commission on Financial Institution Reform, Recovery and Enforcement (NCFIRRE):

> The typical large failure was a stockholder-owned, state-chartered institution
> in Texas or California where regulation and supervision were most lax. ... The
> failed institution typically had experienced a change of control and was tightly
> held, dominated by an individual with substantial conflicts of interest. ... In
> the typical large failure, every accounting trick available was used to make the
> institution look profitable, safe, and solvent. Evidence of fraud was invariably

present as was the ability of the operators to "milk" the organization through high dividends and salaries, bonuses, perks and other means. In short, the typical large failure was one in which management exploited virtually all the perverse incentives created by government policy.

Looting has played a significant role in banking crises around the world. It became so prevalent in the states of the former Soviet Union that it inspired a new term of art, "tunneling," to describe the process of the CEO and owners converting a company's funds to their private benefit.

In addition to the national banking crises, fraud has caused spectacular failures of large banks. The Bank for Credit and Commerce International (BCCI—known informally as the "Bank for Crooks and Criminals International"), Barings Bank, and Continental Bank all stunned the public when they failed. BCCI was the largest bank in the developing world, Barings was England's oldest bank, and Continental was America's third largest bank. Each one collapsed with minimal public warning.

And, of course, more recently control fraud played a role in a number of spectacular business failures outside of the banking industry including Enron, WorldCom, and Tyco. This fact makes it obvious that the conventional economic wisdom, which blames this era's wave of bank failures and banking crises on regulation and deposit insurance (which are specific to the banking industry) is just wrong. Despite this, mainstream economists persist in their diagnosis, rarely scrutinizing the deregulation and privatization that many observers believe in fact triggered these crises.

...They First Make Proud

Economists have dominated the creation of public policies to prevent banking crises. Their track record has been abysmal. They designed and implemented the disastrous deregulation that produced the U.S. S&L debacle, they praised Japan's and East Asia's banking structures just before they collapsed, and they designed the IMF's crisis intervention strategy that intensified losses and human misery. They also designed and praised privatization programs in many transition economies that led to banking crises; they planned (and in some cases profited from) the catastrophic failure of "shock therapy" in Russia. The irony is that when financial experts were

---

Offshore Banks

One particularly dark side of globalization is the rise of new offshore banks. While Switzerland now has reasonably workable procedures for tracking the funds of kleptocrats and drug traffickers, several small nations have adopted extreme forms of bank secrecy designed to cater to the needs of criminals and tax evaders. Corporations often incorporate in a tax haven because of the extremely low tax rates. In the late 1990s, the Organisation for Economic Co-operation and Development, an organization of the world's industrialized countries, created an initiative to try to curtail these abuses. Conservative think tanks sought to kill the OECD plan and convinced President Bush to block its implementation as one of his earliest actions. The administration reduced its opposition to the OECD initiative after the 9/11 attacks, when it became clear that terrorists used the offshore banks as their preferred means to move funds.

most confident in their consensus, they erred the most grievously. As Mark Twain remarked: "It's not the things you *don't* know that cause disasters; it's the things you *do* know, *but aren't true.*"

This record of failure is disappointing and has caused great human suffering. Remarkably, the economists' hubris is unaffected by it. They are now engaged in a war against deposit insurance and regulation. At this juncture, they are losing that war, but they are persevering in their effort to reclaim their domination over banking policy.

Neoclassical banking economists are failing in this arena for three reasons. First, they neither study nor understand fraud mechanisms and the institutions that are essential to limit fraud and corruption. Second, they are shackled by an ideology that *presumes* that unfettered markets always produce the best outcomes and that government intervention is always bad. For instance, in their writings many of the World Bank's banking economists display a passionate contempt for democratic government and banking regulators. Third, they are mono-disciplinary. They rarely cite (and no doubt rarely examine) the literature in other relevant fields such as political science, sociology, and white-collar criminology.

Indeed, although it should be central to their study of crisis prevention, they rarely even cite the work of economist and 2001 Nobel Prize winner George Akerlof. Based on their study of the S&L crisis, which found that looting was a major cause of total S&L losses, Akerlof and Paul Romer developed an economic model of the looting control fraud.

Looters use accounting fraud to make a company *appear* extraordinarily profitable. Consider the S&L crisis. The worst S&L control frauds were the ones report-

---

They Just Never Learn

Today's financial crisis offers a superb example of how their methods lead mainstream economists to endorse both private practices and public policies that are perverse. The current crisis exemplifies a variant of accounting control frauds—one in which the CEO and top managers "skim" rather than loot the company—and demonstrates the unrecognized economic costs of obscenely high CEO pay. The incentives created by typical CEO compensation packages in the financial services industry produce bad investment decisions, decisions that increase the CEO's ability to skim, but that expose the financial institution to losses and the nation and world to recurrent financial crises.

Consider the plight of the honest chief financial officer (CFO) in the modern financial world. His counterparts at rival firms are earning record returns by investing in subprime mortgages. Economists trumpet studies showing that banks' income is boosted by practices he questions, including:

- Making more subprime mortgages
- Making more of the worst mortgages such as "Ninja" loans (no verification of income, job or assets), also known as "liars' loans"
- Making subprime loans at particularly high interest rates—which draws in the riskiest borrowers because only the worst credit risks and frauds will apply
- Making loans as quickly as possible
- Growing as quickly as possible
- Reducing internal controls against fraud
- Making loans in cities known to be "hot spots" for mortgage fraud
- Qualifying borrowers by offering "teaser" interest rates that will soon increase substantially

ing the highest profitability. Moreover, the control frauds were routinely able to get a Big 8 audit firm to give them "clean" GAAP (or Generally Accepted Accounting Principles, the official standard of review in the U.S. accounting industry) opinions for false financial statements.

Economists, in turn, relied on *reported* accounting profits and share prices (which rose along with reported profits) to determine whether a given S&L was well run. But relying on reported accounting earnings or stock prices *must* lead to perverse results when a wave of looting control frauds is expanding. Thanks to their fraudulent accounting, whatever strategies control frauds follow will look profitable, and hence praiseworthy. In the S&Ls, this led economists to praise (1) domination by an owner/CEO; (2) extremely rapid growth; (3) changes of control; and (4) large investments in acquisition, development, and construction (ADC) loans and direct investments. Lo and behold, these factors turned out to characterize the worst failures. In other words, standard econometrics techniques led economists to praise that which was fraudulent and fatal. The error was so great that they identified the worst S&L in the nation as the best.

Worse, economists persist in the same error. During the recent expansion of the even larger wave of looting control frauds such as Enron, economists touted (1) conflicts of interest at the top audit firms (which they euphemistically restyled as "synergies"); (2) using a top-tier auditor; (3) rapid growth; and (4) granting the CEO greater stock options as positive factors that were leading to increased profits and higher share prices. It was only after the looters began to collapse that variables like these reversed their sign (from a positive to a negative correlation) and displayed their true relationship to business failure. Economists are doomed to repeat

---

- Making loans in areas with rapidly inflating housing bubbles
- Purchasing and holding in portfolio high-yield CDOs (collateralized debt obligations, the investment instruments backed by bundles of mortgages and other loans, often of high risk)
- Keeping minimal reserves against losses

When a housing bubble is expanding, these practices dramatically increase fees and other noninterest income, minimize expenses, and produce relatively few losses. (Losses remain low as long as house prices are rising because borrowers who get in trouble can sell their house for more than they owe or else refinance based on its market value.) Note that this pretty income picture requires accounting and securities fraud, though: reserving properly for the future losses inherent in subjecting the financial institution to this vastly increased default risk would remove the fictional accounting gain.

The combination of dramatically increased revenue, moderately reduced expenses, and minimal loss means that financial institutions that invest heavily in subprime mortgages and CDOs must report record profits while the bubble is hyperinflating.

So what is our honest CFO to do? If she does not follow the pack, her company will report substantially lower income. Its stock price will fall relative to its rivals. The CEO's and CFO's compensation and wealth will fall sharply as raises disappear, bonuses decline, and the value of their shares and stock options falls. The CFO may be fired.

The upshot is that modern compensation systems and the short-term perspective of investors and senior managers all result in perverse incentives to make grossly imprudent investments in those assets experiencing the worst bubbles. This creates a destructive cycle in which large numbers of financial institutions follow the same dysfunctional strategy, which in turn extends and inflates the bubble and produces even more accounting control frauds.

these mistakes until they adopt statistical techniques that cannot be gamed by accounting fraud.

The Economists' War against Banking Regulation

In keeping with their skewed analysis of the recent wave of bank failures and banking crises, banking economists, including those at the World Bank and the IMF, have been waging a war against banking regulation. It is a curious assault that rests on implicit and false dichotomies between market and regulation and between types of regulation.

The World Bank economists recognize that regulation is vital to mandate accurate disclosure of corporate financial information and aid private market enforcement, but appear to believe that regulatory strength is unnecessary to induce banks to provide accurate information. That view is illogical and incorrect. Obtaining accurate information about banks is the heart of banking examination. Regulators use their powers primarily to pry out accurate information from the fraudulent; control frauds do not cooperate voluntarily.

Economists' rationale for opposing strong banking regulators typically rests on public choice theory, which holds that the actors in political systems act to maximize their own self-interest. This analysis paints politicians as corrupt and regulators as "captured" by the industries they are supposed to be regulating. World Bank economist Thorsten Beck and his colleagues summed up this view in 2003 and 2006 working papers:

> Politicians may induce banks to divert the flow of credit to politically connected firms, or powerful banks may "capture" politicians and induce official supervisors to act in the best interest of banks ... .

> Government solutions to overcome market failures ... have been proven wrong in Bangladesh as across the developed and developing world. ... Indeed, powerful regulators are worse than futile—they are corrupt and harmful.

Again, this analysis is nonsensical. If banks can dominate politicians and strong regulators, they can certainly dominate the design of the disclosure standards they face. In that case, pursuant to the economists' own logic, the banks will submit, and politicians beholden to them will permit, deceptive financial reports that grossly overstate banks' value. (This has, in fact, been done in many cases.) Accounting fraud, in turn, renders markets deeply inefficient and causes private market discipline to become perverse. The looters report record profits. Credit is supposed to flow to the most profitable banks. So private markets *aid* the CEOs looting their banks by providing them with the funds to expand rapidly. Again, the failure to understand bank accounting fraud mechanisms, which have been well explained by Akerlof and Romer, leads to a deeply flawed analysis. (In lieu of Akerlof and Romer, the anti-regulation economists frequently cite work sponsored by Michael Milken's institute. Milken was the notorious junk-bond king and looter who caused large losses during the S&L crisis by recruiting and funding several of the worst control frauds, such as Charles Keating. Today,

Milken's institute blames the S&L debacle on regulation and seeks to rehabilitate his reputation.)

This overarching logical error, their hostility to democracy, and their view of public officials as inevitably rapacious leads economists to a claim that only *private* parties should exert discipline against banks. The view has a number of problems. First, it is overstated. Regulators in some nations do resist political pressure. In the S&L crisis, many regulators did their job despite intense political pressure and saved over a trillion dollars in the process. On the other hand: if, over time, people are taught to believe that it is normal and rational for public officials to be rapacious, this can become a self-fulfilling prophecy as those who aim to enrich themselves sign on to become officials.

Moreover, the argument proves too much. If the banks (or politicians) are powerful enough to act illegitimately *through* regulators, they are powerful enough to act illegitimately *without* regulators to achieve the same result. The argument is also based on a fundamental misunderstanding of control frauds. It is not the "powerful banks" Beck and his coauthors refer to that put pressure on regulators or politicians—it is the CEOs or their agents who do. They do not coerce regulators "to act in the best interest of banks." They coerce them in an attempt to act to help the CEO loot the bank.

In fact, the evidence shows that private parties are *more* subject to capture than public officials. Looting control frauds are routinely able to get top-tier audit firms to give their blessing to massive accounting fraud. The ratings agencies do no better against control fraud. Our most prestigious law firms have helped CEOs loot and destroy their clients. Private deposit insurance funds for thrifts used to exist in many states. None do now. The Maryland, Ohio, and Utah funds were each destroyed by the very first thrift that collapsed in their state thanks to control fraud. No private insurer made more than a feeble effort to exercise discipline. Instead, they acted as boosters for the CEOs who looted and destroyed their own thrifts and brought down the insurance funds with them.

Finally, the empirical studies on banking regulation rely on coding of data by economists who typically oppose regulation, rendering the results unreliable. The risks of subjective bias are acute. There is no objective measure of "strong" regulation, or capture, or "rent seeking behavior." We know that economists have claimed that the Bank Board under Chairman Edwin Gray was captured during the S&L crisis. Not so. In fact, *private* experts were routinely captured by the S&L control frauds. Plus, the studies focus on formal supervisory power, yet informal banking supervision is widespread and often a regulator's most effective tool.

Overall, empirical studies find that better quality regulation (again, to be fair, a subjective concept) reduces banking losses.

International Convergence

Despite the flawed logic and lack of empirical support for their views, conventional banking economists, including those at the World Bank, continue to voice opposition to the creation of strong supervisory agencies. For now, however, their call has been rejected.

In the 1980s, the U.S. government reacted to Japan's emergence as the new (apparent) dominant financial power by claiming that Japan gained an unfair advantage because its banks were permitted to operate with lower capital reserves. If all other factors are held constant, a bank held to a lower capital reserve requirement can grow more quickly, lend more cheaply, and finance greater economic growth. Complaining that the playing field was not level, the United States insisted on an international agreement to set minimum bank capital standards. The U.S. effort succeeded in 1988, when the largest industrial nations adopted the Basel Accord. More recently, the accord was revised and expanded ("Basel II") to include more closely calibrated minimum capital requirements as well as a supervisory strategy of "prompt corrective action" against banks that fail to meet the capital requirements and a strategy to make private market discipline more effective by requiring banks to disclose more information.

The Basel Accord was a major step towards greater international uniformity of banking regulation ("convergence") among developed nations. The expansion of the European Union is another major force for convergence, as candidate nations must adopt modern banking laws and regulatory structures meeting the EU's minimum standards.

Banks are also subject to an increasing number of international treaties designed to restrict money laundering and bribery. There are, however, very few enforcement actions or prosecutions, so enforcement does not appear to be effective at this time. In addition, offshore banks remain an enormous loophole limiting the effectiveness of convergence.

New banking crises have diminished substantially in nations complying with the Basel accords. Of course, it is too early to judge whether the Basel process is responsible for this success. However, we do have cross-country evidence showing that weak regulation leads to recurrent waves of control fraud. Tests of Basel's effectiveness by one of the World Bank economists find positive relationships between stronger regulation and bank health. (These tests employed a methodology that posed less risk of subjective bias by the economists conducting the studies, but they remain inherently subjective.)

The economists' frustration, however, is understandable. They are skilled research scientists for whom econometric studies are the epitome of proof. Contrary case studies are mere "anecdotal evidence" that are fully encompassed within their data and, therefore, require no refutation. Moreover, their worldview is shaped by public choice theory. They view banking regulators as corrupt, "rent seeking" parasites who merely pretend to virtue. Alternatively, in their "capture" model, regulators are cowards who roll over to aid the control frauds. They have not been banking regulators, so they are uncontaminated and can see the truth as the empirical data reveal it to them.

Regulators, however, dominate much of the Basel process. They view the economists' disdain as an inaccurate and insulting caricature that indicates their ignorance of the real-world banking business. Regulators tend to believe in their experiences, which overwhelmingly teach that control frauds exploit regulatory weaknesses and that normally honest, sober bankers act like frat boys on spring break during financial bubbles. Imprudent lending is the norm in bubbles. Regulators have seen many econometric "proofs" of propositions they know to be false from experience. Some of them have a reasonably sophisticated understanding of the illusion of precision in empirical work and the many opportunities for subjective coding to lead even the best scholars into error. To date, the regulators have staved off the economists' war against banking regulation, and even the World Bank's economists have had to concede that the *initial* results of the Basel process are extremely positive.

Basel II does have a worrying component. It encourages the large banks to value their assets (which implicitly means evaluating their risk) using their own proprietary models. It is easy for these models to be designed so as to dramatically overstate asset values. The problem is compounded by the nature of proprietary models: they are secret, complex, and (perhaps) subject to frequent adjustment. That makes them a nightmare to try to regulate. And in what is essentially a form of control fraud, modern compensation systems, especially in the United States, create powerful incentives for top managers to overstate banks' asset values in order to puff up their own pay packages. Such abuse is so common that instead of "mark to market," the usual term for bringing the valuation of an asset into line with its market price, the process is often known to insiders as "mark to myth."

In the United States, the word "deregulation" still has a positive ring for many despite the disastrous results of this country's experiment in loosening the reins on the banking industry. So perhaps it is ironic that it was the United States that instigated an international effort to develop convergent banking regulations worldwide. International convergence is moving forward, and for now the pace of new financial crises has slowed. The Basel process is indeed leveling the playing field among financial services companies around the world. But what kind of field will emerge? Does the Basel process offer any hope of reshaping the new world of banking into one that better meets consumer needs and better serves the broader public interest? If the banking economists, with their ideological commitment to oppose any regulation, are kept at bay, then at least we may find out.

Sources. C.E.V Borio and R. Filosa, "The Changing Borders of Banking: Trends and Implications," *BIS Working Paper* 23, 10/94; Center for International Private Enterprise, "Financial Reform: Paving the Way for Growth and Democracy," *Economic Reform Today*, 1995; J. Bisignano, "Precarious Credit Equilibria: Reflections on the Asian Financial Crisis," *BIS Working Papers*, 3/99; W. K. Black, The Best Way to Rob a Bank is to Own One, 2005; L.J. White, T*he S&L Debacle: Public Policy Lessons for Bank and Thrift Regulation*, 1991; Federal Home Loan Bank Board, "Agenda for Reform: A Report on Deposit Insurance," 1983; K. Calavita et al., *Big Money Crime: Fraud and Politics in the Savings and Loan Industry*, 1997; W. K. Black et al., "The Savings and Loan Debacle of the 1980's: White-Collar Crime or Risky Business?" *Law & Policy* 17; G. Akerlof and P. M. Romer, "Looting: The Economic Underworld of Bankruptcy for Profit," *Brookings Papers on Econ Activity*, 1993; M. Mayer, *The Greatest-Ever Bank Robbery*, 1990; T. Curry and L. Shibut, "The Cost of the Savings and Loan Crisis: Truth and Consequences," *FDIC Banking Review*, Fall 2000; W. K. Black, "Reexamining the Law-and-Economics Theory of Corporate Governance," *Challenge*, 1993; C-J Lindgren et al., "Bank Soundness and Macroeconomic Policy," IMF, 1996; T. M. Hoenig, "Exploring the Macro-Prudential Aspects of Financial Sector Supervision," speech to the Meeting for Heads of Supervision, BIS, Basel, Switzerland, 4/27/04; V. A. Atanasov et al., "The Anatomy of Financial Tunneling in an Emerging Market," McCombs

School of Business, Research Paper Fin-04-06; N. Passas, "The Genesis of the BCCI Scandal," *J Law and Soc*, 3/66; P. L. Zweig, *Belly Up: The Collapse of the Penn Square Bank*, 1986; R. J. Herring, "BCCI & Barings: Bank Resolutions Complicated by Fraud and Global Corporate Structure"; H.R. Davia et al., *Accountant's Guide to Fraud Detection and Control* (2nd ed.), 2000; P. Blustein, "The Chastening: Inside the Crisis that Rocked the Global Financial System and Humbled the IMF," *Public Aff*, 2001; W. K. Black, "A Tale of Two Crises," Kravis Leadership Inst Rvw, Fall 2002; Federal Reserve Bank of San Francisco, *Economic Letter*, 3/06; B. H. Soral et al., "Fraud, banking crisis, and regulatory enforcement: Evidence from micro-level transactions data," *European Journal of Law and Econ*, 4/06; J. L. Pierce, *The Future of Banking*, 1991; E. J. Kane, *The Gathering Crisis in Federal Deposit Insurance*, MIT Univ Press, 1985; A. Demirguc-Kunt and E. Detragiache, "Does Deposit Insurance Increase Banking System Stability? An Empirical Investigation," *J Monetary Econ*, 10/02; D. Pyle, review of "The Gathering Crisis in Federal Deposit Insurance" in *J Econ Lit*, 9/86; J. Santos, "Bank Capital Regulation in Contemporary Banking Theory: A review of the literature," in *Financial Markets, Institutions & Instruments*, 2001; A.B. Ashcraft, "Does the Market Discipline Banks? New Evidence from Regulatory Capital Mix," 10/2/06; T. Beck et al., "Bank Supervision and Corporate Finance," *World Bank Policy Research Working Paper*, 5/03; D. R. Brumbaugh, Jr, *Thrifts Under Siege: Restoring Order to American Banking*, 1988; T. Beck et al., "Bank Supervision and Corruption in Lending," 9/3/05; A. Demirguc Kunt et al., "Banking on the Principles: Compliance with Basel Core Principles and Bank Soundness," *IMF Working Paper* 10/06; R. La Porta et al., "Related Lending," *Quarterly J Econ*, 2003; S. Johnson et al., "Tunnelling," Am Econ Assoc Papers & Proceedings, 2000; R. Haselmann et al., "How Law Affects Lending," *Columbia Law and Economics Working Paper*, 9/06; J. D. Edwards and J. H. Godwin, "Why Sound Accounting Standards Count," *Econ Reform Today*, 1995; J. R. Barth, *The Great Savings and Loan Debacle*, 1991.

Article 5.7

THE GIANT POOL OF MONEY

BY ARTHUR MacEWAN
September/October 2009

> Dear Dr. Dollar:
> *On May 9, the public radio program* This American Life *broadcast an expla-nation of the housing crisis with the title: "The Giant Pool of Money." With too much money looking for investment opportunities, lots of bad investments were made—including the bad loans to home buyers. But where did this "giant pool of money" come from? Was this really a source of the home mortgage crisis?*
> —Gail Radford, Buffalo, N.Y.

The show was both entertaining and interesting. A good show, but maybe a bit more explanation will be useful.

There was indeed a "giant pool of money" that was an important part of the story of the home mortgage crisis—well, not "money" as we usually think of it, but financial assets, which I'll get to in a moment. And that pool of money is an impor-tant link in the larger economic crisis story.

The giant pool of money was the build-up of financial assets—U.S. Treasury bonds, for example, and other assets that pay a fixed income. According to the pro-gram, the amount of these assets had grown from roughly $36 trillion in 2000 to $70 trillion in 2008. That's $70 *trillion*, with a T, which is a lot of money, roughly the same as total world output in 2008.

These financial assets built up for a number of reasons. One was the doubling of oil prices (after adjusting for inflation) between 2000 and 2007, largely due to the U.S. invasion of Iraq. This put a lot of money in the hands of governments in oil-producing countries and private individuals connected to the oil industry.

A second factor was the large build up of reserves (i.e., the excess of receipts from exports over payments for imports) by several low-income countries, most no-tably China. One reason some countries operated in this manner was simply to keep the cost of their currency low in terms of U.S. dollars, thus maintaining demand for their exports. (Using their own currencies to buy dollars, they were increasing both the supply of their currencies and the demand for dollars; this pushed the price of their currencies down and of dollars up.) But another reason was to protect them-selves from the sort of problems they had faced in the early 1980s, when world reces-sion cut their export earnings and left them unable to meet their import costs and pay their debts—thus the debt crisis of that era.

This build-up of dollar reserves by governments (actually, central banks) of other countries was also a result of the budgetary deficits of the Bush adminis-tration. Spending more than it was taking in as taxes (after the big tax cuts for the wealthy and with the heavy war spending), the Bush administration needed to borrow. Foreign governments, by buying the U.S. securities, were providing the loans.

Still a third factor explaining the giant pool of financial assets was the high level of inequality within the United States and elsewhere in the global economy. Since 1993, half of all income gains in the United States have gone to the highest-income 1% of households. While the very rich spend a good share of their money on mansions, fancy cars, and other luxuries, there was plenty more money for them to put into investments—the stock market but also fixed-income securities (i.e., bonds).

So there is the giant pool of money or, again, of financial assets.

The financial assets became a problem for two connected reasons. First, in the recovery following the 2001 recession, economic growth was very slow; there were thus very limited real investment opportunities. Between 2001 and 2007, private fixed investment (adjusted for inflation) grew by only 11%, whereas in the same number of years following the recession of the early 1990s, investment grew by 59%.

Second, in an effort to stimulate more growth, the Federal Reserve kept interest rates very low. But the low interest rates meant low returns on financial assets—U.S. government bonds in particular, but financial assets in general. So the holders of financial assets went searching for new investment opportunities, which, as the radio program explained, meant pushing money into high-risk mortgages. The rest, as they say, is history.

So the giant pool of money was the link that tied high inequality, the war, and rising financial imbalances in the world economy (caused in large part by the U.S. government's budgetary policies) to the housing crisis and thus to the more general financial crisis.

Article 5.8

DERIVATIVES AND DEREGULATION

BY MARTY WOLFSON

November/December 2008

It has become commonplace to describe the current financial crisis as the most serious since the Great Depression. Although we have more tools now to avoid a depression, the current crisis presents in some ways more significant challenges than did the banking crises of the 1930s.

And it's not over.

The form of the current crisis is similar to others we have seen in the past: a speculative increase in asset prices, overly optimistic expectations, and an expansion of debt sustainable only if the speculative bubble continues. Then the bubble pops, debt can't be repaid, and losses mount at financial institutions. The risk of bank failures rises and lenders get scared. They panic, refuse to lend to anyone that seems at all risky, and seek safety in cash or super-safe assets.

In the early 1930s, there was no federal deposit insurance and little federal government intervention. Depositor runs took down the banking system.

In more recent crises, though, the Federal Reserve successfully developed and used its powers as a lender of last resort. Deposit insurance helped to reassure small depositors and, if needed, the Federal Deposit Insurance Corporation stepped in and bailed out threatened banks. It could guarantee all liabilities of a failing bank and arrange mergers with healthier banks. These tools generally worked to reduce panicked reactions and prevent the freezing up of credit.

But this time, after the collapse of the speculative bubble in housing prices, the course of events has been different. The Federal Reserve was forced to expand the concept of a lender of last resort in unprecedented ways. It has lent to investment banks and insurance companies, not just regulated depository institutions. It has taken all kinds of assets as collateral for its loans, not just the high-grade securities it traditionally accepted. It has even lent to nonfinancial corporations (by buying their commercial paper).

What is surprising is that these dramatic actions and expensive bailouts of financial institutions, such as American International Group (AIG) and even Fannie Mae and Freddie Mac, were insufficient to reassure lenders about the ability of financial institutions to honor their repayment commitments. Treasury Secretary Paulson's plan to use $700 billion to buy "toxic assets" from financial institutions, signed into law by President Bush on October 3rd, failed to stop what had become by then a generalized panic and freeze-up of credit. It took a coordinated global initiative to inject capital directly into financial institutions, plus a federal guarantee on bank debt and unlimited FDIC insurance on non-interest-bearing (mostly business) accounts at banks, announced on October 12th, to begin to have an effect on unfreezing credit markets.

The "TED spread," a widely watched measure of credit risk that had spiked sharply during the panic, began to reverse its path following the October 12 announcement. The TED spread measures the difference between an interest rate that banks charge when lending to each other (the London Interbank Offered Rate, or LIBOR) and the interest rate on U.S. Treasury bills. Because the Treasury is assumed to be "risk-free," the difference between it and LIBOR measures the perceived relative risk of lending to banks.

Why has this panic been so much more difficult to control? The answer has to do with the widespread use of complicated and opaque securities, known as derivatives, in a deregulated, interconnected, and global financial system.

A derivative is a financial contract that derives its value from something else, such as an asset or an index. At the root of the current crisis are derivatives known as mortgage-backed securities (MBSs). MBSs are claims to payments from an underlying pool of mortgages. The ability of MBS issuers to repay their debt, and thus the value of the MBS, is derived from the ability of homeowners to meet their mortgage payments.

In the process leading up to the crisis, a mortgage broker typically extended a mortgage to a borrower, and then turned to a commercial bank to fund the loan. The bank might sell the loan to Fannie Mae, which would pool a group of mortgages together and sell the resulting MBS to an investment bank like Lehman Brothers. Lehman, in turn, repackaged the MBS in various ways, and issued even more complicated derivatives called collateralized debt obligations (CDOs). Buyers of the CDOs might be other banks, hedge funds, or other lenders.

At the base of this complicated pyramid of derivatives might be a subprime borrower whose lender did not explain an adjustable-rate loan, or another borrower whose ability to meet mortgage payments depended on a continued escalation of home prices. As subprime borrowers' rates reset, and especially as housing price speculation collapsed, the whole house of cards came crashing down.

Why were mortgage loans made that could not be repaid? And why did supposedly sophisticated investors buy MBSs and CDOs based on these loans? First of all, the mortgage brokers and commercial banks that made and funded these loans quickly sold them off and no longer had any responsibility for them. Second, rating agencies like Moody's and Standard & Poor's gave these derivatives stellar AAA ratings, signifying a credit risk of almost zero. Recent Congressional hearings have highlighted the conflict of interest that these rating agencies had: they were being paid by the issuers of the derivatives they were rating. Third, financial institutions up and down the line were making money and nobody was limiting what they could do. In the deregulated financial environment, federal regulators stood aside as housing speculation spun out of control and did little to regulate, or even document, the growth of complicated derivatives.

Finally, financial institutions' concerns about the creditworthiness of the derivatives they held were eased because they thought they could protect themselves against possible loss. For example, by using another type of derivative known as a credit default swap, holders of MBSs and CDOs could make periodic premium payments to another financial institution, like American International Group (AIG), to insure themselves against default by the issuers of the MBSs and CDOs. (This insurance contract was technically classified as a derivative rather than insurance in order to escape regulation.) However, if an insurer like AIG is unable to honor all its insurance contracts, then the protection against loss is illusory.

The total value of all the securities insured by credit default swaps at the end of 2007 was estimated by the Bank of International Settlements to be $58 trillion, and by the International Swaps and Derivatives Association to be $62 trillion. (The estimates could vary by as much as $4 trillion because unregulated credit default swaps do not have to be officially reported to regulatory agencies. Moreover, even greater ambiguity surrounds these contracts because insurers can transfer their liability to other parties, and the insured party may be unaware of the creditworthiness or even the identity of the new insurer.)

Surprisingly, though, the value of the actual securities that form the basis of these credit default swaps was only about $6 trillion. How could $6 trillion worth of assets be insured at ten times that amount? The discrepancy is due to the fact that it is possible to speculate on the likelihood of default of a security without actually owning the security: all the speculator has to do is enter into a credit default swap contract with an insurer. The total volume of "insured securities" can thus escalate dramatically.

Because derivatives are so complex, because so much speculation and debt are involved, and because it is so hard to know how much is at risk (and exactly who is at risk), regulators are unsure of the implications of the failure of a particular financial institution. That is why they have been so fearful of the consequences of letting a troubled institution fail.

The exception that did indeed prove the rule was Lehman Brothers. The Federal Reserve and Treasury did not bail it out, and its failure led to an intensification of the problems in credit markets. A money market fund, the Reserve Primary Fund, announced that it would only pay 97 cents on the dollar to its investors, because its investments in Lehman Brothers could not be redeemed. The Treasury moved quickly to announce that it would insure money market funds, in order to prevent a run on the funds. However, the Lehman failure raised further concerns that lenders had about the derivatives portfolios of other banks, and about the possibility that the banks would not have enough capital to cover potential losses.

Secretary Paulson's initial plan to buy "toxic" assets (including MBSs and CDOs) from financial institutions was designed to address these concerns about bank capital. However, his plan was probably also negatively affected by uncertainty. Because these "toxic" assets are complex and nobody wants to buy them, there is no market for them and their value is uncertain. And because the Paulson plan's unstated objective was to boost bank capital by overpaying for these assets, the difficulties in pricing the assets raised the prospects of long delays and questions about whether the plan to increase bank capital would be successful. Lenders continued to hold back. They may also have hesitated because of concern about a political backlash against a taxpayer subsidy for the very banks that many people blamed for the crisis.

By injecting capital directly into the banks, the global initiative announced on October 12th raised the prospect of returns on the capital investment for taxpayers. It also avoided the uncertainties of buying individual assets and helped to reduce the panic.

But the crisis isn't over. Reducing the panic is only the first step. There is now likely to be a longer-term credit crunch that will continue to threaten the broader economy. Banks and other lenders will be wary for quite some time. Losses on mort-gage-related assets will continue as years of housing speculation—financed with heaps of borrowed money—continues to unwind. Bank lending will lag as banks rebuild their capital and overcome their pessimistic expectations.

It will be up to the federal government to pick up the slack that the banks will leave. We will need programs to enable people to stay in their homes and stabilize their communities. We will need to create jobs by investing in infrastructure, re-newable energy, and education. We will need a "trickle-up" approach that puts peo-ple first and raises living standards and opportunities.

At the same time, we need a regulatory structure for the financial system that puts limits on risk and manipulation. It is clear that deregulation, and the entire neoliberal model that has dominated economic policy for the past 30 years, has run aground. It has sown the seeds of financial crisis, and this crisis has led us to the edge of an abyss. Only by dramatically reorienting our economic and financial structure can we avoid the abyss and create the kind of society that meets our needs. The na-ture of that new structure should be the subject of intensive democratic discussion and debate in the days to come.

Article 5.9

THE BAILOUTS REVISITED

Who gets bailed out and why? Is there any alternative to "Too Big to Fail"?

BY MARTY WOLFSON
September/October 2009

Bank of America got bailed out, but Lehman Brothers was allowed to fail. The insurance company American International Group (AIG) was rescued, but in July federal authorities refused to bail out a significant lender to small and medium-sized businesses, the CIT Group (not to be confused with Citigroup, which did get bailed out).

What is the logic behind these decisions? Who is being bailed out—and who should be? The AIG story offers an instructive case study, one that sheds light on these and other questions.

Last September, the Federal Reserve Board announced that it was lending AIG up to $85 billion to prevent the firm's collapse. Unless it bailed out AIG, the Fed warned, financial markets could panic, loans could become more difficult to get, and many more businesses, jobs, and homes could be lost. To counter public anger over the bailout, the Fed argued that the ultimate beneficiaries would be the American people.

Citing proprietary information, AIG initially released few details about how it paid out the money it received. But this March, AIG's plan to pay $165 million in bonuses to employees at its Financial Products unit hit the headlines. An angry firestorm erupted: why should public bailout money be used to pay excessive bonuses to the very people who had caused the problem? U.S. officials and AIG CEO Edward Liddy denounced the payments as outrageous, but claimed they could not rescind the bonuses because they were bound by legal contracts. As it turned out, many AIG employees returned the bonuses voluntarily. And in a rare display of bipartisanship, the House of Representatives voted 328 to 93 to enact a 90% tax on bonuses paid to executives at companies that had received at least $5 billion in bailout money.

But the AIG bailout involved billions of dollars. The Financial Products employees only got millions. Who got the rest of the money? Under mounting public pressure, and after consulting with the Federal Reserve, AIG finally revealed who the beneficiaries were.

It's the Banks!

Yes, the money went primarily to large banks, those same banks that took their own large risks in the mortgage and derivatives markets and that are already receiving billions of dollars in federal bailout money. The banks are using AIG's bailout money to avoid taking losses on their contracts with the company.

Why did AIG, an insurance company, have such extensive dealings with the large banks, and why did those transactions cause so much trouble for AIG?

The story begins with AIG's London-based Financial Products unit, which issued a large volume of derivatives contracts known as credit default swaps (CDSs).

These were essentially insurance contracts that provided for payments to their purchasers (known as "counterparties") in the event of losses on collateralized debt obligations (CDOs), another kind of derivative. Many of the CDOs were based in complicated ways on payments on home mortgages. When the speculative housing bubble popped, mortgages could not be repaid, the CDOs lost value, and AIG was liable for payment on its CDSs.

By September 2008, AIG's situation had deteriorated to the point where its credit ratings were downgraded; this meant the company was required to post collateral on its CDS contracts, i.e., to make billions of dollars in cash payments to its counterparties to provide some protection for them against possible future losses. Despite its more than $1 trillion in assets, AIG did not have the cash. Without assistance it would have had to declare bankruptcy. After attempts to get the funding from private parties, including Goldman Sachs and JPMorgan Chase, failed, the Federal Reserve stepped in. The initial $85 billion credit line was followed by an additional $52.5 billion in credit two months later. By March 2009 the Treasury had invested $70 billion directly in the company, after which the Fed cut back its initial credit line to $25 billion.

AIG paid out those billions in several categories. Between September and December of 2008, $22.4 billion went to holders of CDSs as cash collateral. This cash was paid not only to those who sought insurance for CDOs they actually held, but also to speculators who purchased CDSs without owning the underlying securities. (Data to evaluate the extent of speculation involved have not been published.)

The largest beneficiaries of these payments were Société Générale, Deutsche Bank, Goldman Sachs, and Merrill Lynch.

Second, in an effort to stop the collateral calls on these CDSs, AIG spent $27.1 billion to purchase insured CDOs from its counterparties in return for their agreement to terminate the CDSs. Again, the largest beneficiaries of this program were Société Générale, Goldman Sachs, Merrill Lynch, and Deutsche Bank.

Third, it turned out that a significant cash drain on AIG was its securities lending program. Counterparties borrowed securities from AIG and in turn posted cash collateral with AIG. When AIG got into trouble, though, the counterparties decided that they wanted their cash back and sought to return the securities they had borrowed. However, AIG had used the cash to buy mortgage-backed securities, the same securities that were falling in value as the housing market crashed. So $43.7 billion of AIG's bailout money went to those counterparties—chiefly Barclays, Deutsche Bank, BNP Paribas, Goldman Sachs, and Bank of America, with Citigroup and Merrill Lynch not too far behind.

Necessary Bailouts?

Without all that bailout money going to the banks via AIG, wouldn't the financial system have crashed, the banks have stopped lending, and the recession have gotten worse? Well, no.

At least, the banks did not need to receive all the money they did. If a regulatory agency such as the Federal Reserve or the Federal Deposit Insurance Corporation had taken over AIG, it could have used the appropriate tools to, as Fed chair Ben Bernanke told a House committee this March, "put AIG into conservatorship or receivership, unwind it slowly, protect policyholders, and impose haircuts on creditors and counterparties as appropriate. That outcome would have been far preferable to the situation we find ourselves in now." (A haircut in this context is a reduction in the amount a claimant will receive.)

A sudden and disruptive bankruptcy of AIG could indeed have caused a crash of the financial system, especially as it would have come just one day after the sudden fall of Lehman Brothers on September 15. It is the element of surprise and uncertainty that leads to panic in financial markets. On the other hand, an orderly takeover of AIG such as Bernanke described, with clear information on how much counterparties would be paid, likely could have avoided such a panic.

So why didn't the Federal Reserve take over AIG? It said it did not have the legal authority to take over a nonbank financial institution like AIG. Indeed, to his credit, Bernanke frequently asks for such authority when he testifies to Congress. So why didn't the Fed demand it last September? Wasn't such authority important enough to make it a condition of the bailout? And couldn't Congress have passed the necessary legislation as quickly as it passed the bank bailout bill last fall and the tax on AIG bonuses? Even if that took a few weeks, the Fed could have lent money to AIG to keep it from failing until it had the authority to take the company over.

Of course, the Fed already has the authority to take over large troubled banks—but refuses to use it. Now, Fed and Treasury officials claim that since all the major banks passed the recently administered "stress test," such takeovers are unnecessary. However, even some of the banks that passed the test were judged to be in need of more capital. If they can't get it from private markets then, according to Treasury Secretary Timothy Geithner, the government is prepared to supply them with the capital they need.

In other words, the federal government's strategy of transferring extraordinary amounts of public money to large banks that lose money on risky deals will continue. In fact, the same strategy is evident in the Treasury's proposed Public Private Investment Program, which uses public money to subsidize hedge funds and other private investors to buy toxic assets from the banks. The subsidy allows the private investors to pay a higher price to the banks for their toxic assets than the banks could have received otherwise.

Bail Out the People

The consistent principle behind this strategy is that no large bank can fail. This is why the relatively small CIT Group wasn't rescued from potential bankruptcy but Bank of America was. The decision not to bail out Lehman Brothers, which led to panic in financial markets, is now considered a mistake. However, policymakers drew the wrong lesson from the Lehman episode: that all large bank failures must be prevented. They failed to recognize the important distinction between disruptive and controlled failures.

Yes, there are banks that are too big to fail suddenly and disruptively. However, any insolvent bank, no matter what its size, should be taken over in a careful and deliberative way. If this means nationalization, then so be it. Continental Illinois National Bank, at the time the 11th largest bank in the United States, was essentially nationalized in 1984, ending the turmoil in financial markets that Continental's difficulties had created.

This "too big to fail" strategy equates stabilizing the financial system and promoting the people's welfare with saving the corporate existence of individual large banks. Likewise the auto companies: while GM and Chrysler have been treated much more harshly than the banks, the auto bailout was similarly designed to keep these two corporate entities alive above all else, even at the expense of thousands of autoworker jobs.

The federal government's current bank-bailout strategy may be well-meaning, but there are four problems with it. It uses public money unnecessarily and is unfair to taxpayers. It may not work: it risks keeping alive "zombie banks" that are really insolvent and unwilling to lend, a recipe for repeating Japan's "lost decade" experience. It makes financial reform going forward much more difficult. Protecting the markets for derivative products like CDOs and CDSs allows for a repeat of the risky practices that got us into the current crisis. And finally, by guaranteeing the corporate existence of large banks, we are maintaining their power and priorities and thus are not likely to see gains on predatory lending, foreclosure abuse, and other areas where reform is sorely needed.

If we want to help the people who are suffering in this crisis and recession, then we should make financial policies with them directly in mind. Just throwing money at the banks will not get the job done.

Article 5.10

THE BAILOUT OF FANNIE MAE AND FREDDIE MAC

BY FRED MOSELEY
September/October 2008

On Sunday, September 7 [2008], Treasury Secretary Henry Paulson announced that the U.S. government was taking control of Fannie Mae and Freddie Mac, the two giant home mortgage companies, which together either own or guarantee almost half of the mortgages in the United States. This takeover stands in striking contrast to the generally laissez-faire philosophy of the U.S. government, especially the Republican Party. Why did Paulson take this highly unusual action? And what will be the future of Fannie and Freddie? To delve into these questions is to underscore the critical fault line between private profits and public aims—in this case, the aim of making homeownership affordable—a fault line that ran right through the hybrid structure of Fannie and Freddie.

A Brief History

Fannie Mae (short for the Federal National Mortgage Association) was created as an agency of the federal government in 1938 in an attempt to provide additional funds to the home mortgage market and to help the housing industry recover from the Great Depression. Fannie Mae purchased approved mortgages from commercial banks, which could then use the funds to originate additional mortgages. It continued to fulfill this function on a modest scale in the early postwar years.

Fannie Mae was privatized in 1968, in part to help reduce the budget deficit caused by the Vietnam War (a short-sighted goal, if ever there was one). In 1970, Freddie Mac (Federal Home Loan Mortgage Corporation) was created as a private company in order to provide competition for Fannie Mae. Chartered by the federal government, both are (or were, until the takeover) so-called government-sponsored enterprises: private enterprises whose main goal is to maximize profit for the shareholders who own them, but also quasi-public enterprises with a mandated goal of increasing the availability of affordable mortgages to families in the United States. In the end, this dual mandate proved to be untenable.

In order to obtain funds to purchase mortgages, Fannie and Freddie sell short-term bonds. In other words, their business plan involves borrowing short-term and lending long-term, because interest rates are higher on long-term loans than on short-term loans. However, such "speculative finance" is risky because it depends on the willingness of short-term creditors to continue to loan to Fannie and Freddie by rolling over or refinancing their short-term loans. If creditors were to lose confidence in Fannie and Freddie and refuse to do so, then they would be in danger of bankruptcy. This is what almost happened in the recent crisis.

Beginning in the 1970s, Fannie and Freddie began to develop and sell "mortgage-backed securities"—hundreds of mortgages bundled together and sold to investors as a security, similar to a bond. They also guaranteed these securities (so that if a mortgage defaulted, they would repurchase it from the investors) and made money by charging a fee for this guarantee (like an insurance premium). This major financial innovation enabled the two companies to buy more mortgages from commercial banks, thereby increasing the supply of credit in the home mortgage market, which in turn was supposed to push mortgage interest rates lower, making houses more affordable. These early mortgage-backed securities consisted entirely of "prime" mortgages—that is, loans at favorable interest rates, typically made to creditworthy borrowers with full documentation and a substantial down payment.

The securities that Fannie and Freddie sold were widely perceived by investors to carry an implicit government guarantee: if Fannie or Freddie were ever in danger of bankruptcy, then the federal government would pay off their debts (even though this government guarantee was explicitly denied in legislation and in the loan agreements themselves). This perceived guarantee enabled Fannie and Freddie to borrow money at lower interest rates because loans to them were viewed as less risky.

In the 1980s, Wall Street investment banks also began to package and sell mortgage-backed securities. In the 1990s and 2000s, these "private label" mortgage-backed securities expanded rapidly in volume and also in reach, coming to include "subprime" mortgages—loans at higher interest rates with less favorable terms, geared toward less credit-worthy borrowers and typically requiring little or no documentation and little or no down payment.

The subprime innovation was entirely the work of the investment banks; as of 2000, Fannie and Freddie owned or guaranteed almost no subprime mortgages. This innovation greatly increased the supply of credit for home mortgages and led to the extraordinary housing boom of the last decade, and also eventually to the crisis. As a result of these changes, the share of mortgage-backed securities sold by Fannie and Freddie fell to around 40% by 2005.

In the recent housing boom, the companies—especially Freddie—began to take greater risks. While continuing to bundle prime mortgages into securities and sell them to investors, Fannie and Freddie began to buy mortgage-backed securities issued by investment banks, including some based on subprime and Alt-A (between prime and subprime) mortgages. Why did they begin buying as well as selling mortgage-backed securities? Buying these private-label securities gave Fannie and Freddie a way to get in on the subprime action—while still avoiding direct purchases of subprime mortgages from the banks and mortgage companies that originated them. It was a way both to increase their profits at the behest of their shareholders, and, in response to pressure from the government, to make more mortgages available to low- and middle-income families. Of course, it also opened them up to the risks of the subprime arena. Moreover, the prime mortgages they continued to buy and guarantee were increasingly at inflated, bubble prices, making them vulnerable to the eventual bust and the decline of housing prices.

Anatomy of a Crisis

When the subprime crisis began in the summer of 2007, Fannie and Freddie at first appeared to be relatively unaffected, and were even counted on to increase their purchases of mortgages in order to support the mortgage market and help overcome the crisis. Congress facilitated this by relaxing some of its regulations on the two companies: the maximum value of mortgages that they could purchase was increased substantially; their reserve capital requirements, already much lower than for commercial banks, were reduced further; and restrictions on their growth were lifted. As a result of these changes and the drying up of private label mortgage-backed securities, the share of all mortgage-backed securities sold by Fannie and Freddie doubled to approximately 80%. Without Fannie and Freddie, the mortgage and housing crises of the last year would have been much worse.

As the overall crisis unfolded, however, the financial situation of Fannie and Freddie deteriorated. Delinquency and foreclosure rates for the mortgages they own or guarantee, while lower than for the industry as a whole, increased rapidly and beyond expectations. The two companies together reported losses of $14 billion in the last year. Their actual losses have been much worse. As of mid-2008, the two had lost about $45 billion due to the decline in the value of their mortgage-backed securities, mostly those backed by subprime and Alt-A mortgages. But by labeling that decline "temporary," they could leave the losses off their balance sheets. If these losses were counted, as they should be, then Freddie's capital would be completely wiped out (a value of -$5.6 billion), and Fannie's would be reduced to a razor-thin margin of $12.2 billion (less than 2% of its assets), likely becoming negative in the coming quarters. In addition, both Fannie and Freddie count as assets "tax deferred losses" that can be used in future years to offset tax bills—if they make a profit. Without this dubious (but legal) accounting trick, the net assets of both Fannie and Freddie would be below zero, -$20 billion and -$32 billion respectively.

The financial crisis of Fannie and Freddie worsened in early July. The price of their stock, which had already fallen by more than half since last summer, declined another 50% in a few weeks, for a total decline of over 80%. Fear spread that Fannie and Freddie's creditors would refuse to roll over their short-term loans to the two. If that were to happen, then the U.S. home mortgage market and the housing construction industry probably would have collapsed completely, and the U.S. economy would have fallen into an even deeper recession. Furthermore, approximately 20% of the mortgage-backed securities and debt of Fannie and Freddie are owned by foreign investors. Mainly these are foreign governments, most significantly China. If these foreign investors became unwilling to continue to lend Fannie and Freddie money, this would have precipitated a steep fall in the value of the dollar which, on top of recent significant declines, would have dealt another blow to the U.S. economy. Clearly, the potential crisis here was serious enough to spur government action.

In late July, Congress passed a law authorizing the Treasury to provide unlimited amounts of money to Fannie and Freddie, either by buying new issues of stock or by making loans, and also to take over the companies in a conservator arrangement if necessary.

Government Takeover

Through August [2008] the financial condition of Fannie and Freddie continued to deteriorate (especially Freddie), and confidence in their ability to survive waned. Foreign investors in particular reduced their purchases of the companies' debt, and mortgage rates increased. The Treasury concluded that it had to implement a takeover in order to reassure creditors and restore stability to the home mortgage market.

The Treasury plan has three main components:

• It commits up to $200 billion over the next 15 months for purchases of preferred shares of Fannie and Freddie as necessary to keep the companies solvent;

• It establishes a special lending facility that will provide emergency loans in case of a liquidity crisis;

• It commits to purchase unspecified amounts of Fannie and Freddie's mortgage-backed securities "as deemed appropriate."

The day after Paulson's announcement, William Poole, ex-president of the Federal Reserve Bank of St. Louis, estimated that the total cost to taxpayers would be in the neighborhood of $300 billion.

The top managers and the boards of directors of both companies will be dismissed and replaced by new, government-appointed managers. Other than that, the Treasury hopes that day-to-day operations at Fannie and Freddie will be "business as usual." They will continue to borrow money from creditors, now reassured by the government's intervention and more willing to lend to them, and they will continue to purchase and guarantee prime mortgages. In fact, Treasury Department plans call for the volume of mortgages purchased by the two companies to increase over the next year in order to push the supply of mortgage loans up and mortgage interest rates down.

The Treasury plan is a complete bailout of the creditors of Fannie and Freddie, who will be repaid in full, with taxpayer money if necessary. In contrast, owners of Fannie or Freddie stock will lose to some degree: dividends will be suspended for the foreseeable future, and their stock is now worth very little. But their stock was not expropriated. Nor was it wiped out entirely; it could regain value in the future as the home mortgage market recovers. Without the intervention, both companies would have gone bankrupt and the stockowners would have lost everything. So the intervention does represent at least a modest bailout for shareholders.

The most controversial issue in the months ahead will be the future of Fannie and Freddie. Should they become public enterprises permanently? Should they be re-privatized? Should they be sold off in pieces and cease to exist? Secretary Paulson made it clear that the government's current conservatorship is a holding action, and that decisions about the companies' ultimate status will only be made once the next administration and the next Congress are in office. Paulson said that Fannie and Freddie's current structure is unworkable because of its dual and conflicting goals of making housing affordable and maximizing profit—a radical statement, if you think about it! And he suggested that the two should either be fully public enterprises, or else they should be fully private enterprises without any government backing.

In the upcoming debate, the left should advocate forcefully for a public home mortgage agency, one whose sole purpose is to provide affordable housing without the conflicting purpose of maximizing profit. This would stabilize the home mortgage market and help it avoid the boom/bust cycle of private mortgage markets that has brought on the current crisis.

More fundamentally, because decent affordable housing is a basic economic right, providing credit for home purchases should be a function of the government rather than of private businesses whose primary goal is maximum profit. The provision of credit for housing should not be an arena where enormous profits are made, as has been the case in recent years. Without these huge profits, mortgages would be cheaper and houses more affordable. Plus, the kinds of fraudulent lending practices that played a significant role in the recent housing boom would be minimized.

With the presidential election just weeks away, the crisis of Fannie, Freddie, and the whole home lending market is poised to become a major campaign issue. McCain has said that he wants Fannie and Freddie to "go away"—i.e., to be broken up and disappear, leaving the mortgage market entirely to private enterprises. Obama has emphasized the conflict between the public aim of making housing widely affordable and the private aim of making a profit, but so far he has not come down on one side or the other. Now he will have to decide. I hope that he will be a strong advocate of a public home mortgage agency, and I think this would help him to get elected.

Article 5.11

TRANSFORMING THE FED

BY ROBERT POLLIN
November 1992

The U.S. financial system faces deep structural problems. Households, businesses, and the federal government are burdened by excessive debts. The economy favors short-term speculation over long-term investment. An unrepresentative and unresponsive elite has extensive control over the financial system. Moreover, the federal government is incapable of reversing these patterns through its existing tools, including fiscal, monetary, and financial regulatory policies.

I propose a dramatically different approach: transforming the Federal Reserve System (the "Fed") into a public investment bank. Such a bank would have substantial power to channel credit in ways that counter financial instability and support productive investment by private businesses. The Fed would use its powers to influence how and for what purposes banks, insurance companies, brokers, and other lenders loan money.

The U.S. government has used credit allocation policies, such as low-cost loans, loan guarantees, and home mortgage interest deductions, extensively and with success. Its primary accomplishment has been to create a home mortgage market that, for much of the period since World War II, provided non-wealthy households with unprecedented access to home ownership.

I propose increasing democratic control over the Federal Reserve's activities by decentralizing power to the 12 district Fed banks and instituting popular election of their boards of directors. This would create a mechanism for extending democracy throughout the financial system.

My proposal also offers a vehicle for progressives to address two separate but equally serious questions facing the U.S. economy:

- how to convert our industrial base out of military production and toward the development and adoption of environmentally benign production techniques; and
- how to increase opportunities for high wage, high productivity jobs in the United States. The U.S. needs such jobs to counteract the squeeze on wages from increasingly globalized labor and financial markets.

Transforming the Federal Reserve system into a public investment bank will help define an economic path toward democratic socialism in the United States.

My proposal has several strengths as a transitional program. It offers a mechanism for establishing democratic control over finance and investment—the area where capital's near-dictatorial power is most decisive. The program will also work within the United States' existing legal and institutional framework. We could implement parts of it immediately using existing federal agencies and with minimal demands on the federal budget.

At the same time, if an ascendant progressive movement put most of the program in place, this would represent a dramatic step toward creating a new economic system. Such a system would still give space to market interactions and the pursuit of greed, but would nevertheless strongly promote general well-being over business profits.

How the Fed Fails

At present the Federal Reserve focuses its efforts on managing short-term fluctuations of the economy, primarily by influencing interest rates. When it reduces rates, it seeks to increase borrowing and spending, and thereby stimulate economic growth and job opportunities. When the Fed perceives that wages and prices are rising too fast (a view not necessarily shared by working people), it tries to slow down borrowing and spending by raising interest rates.

This approach has clearly failed to address the structural problems plaguing the financial system. The Fed did nothing, for example, to prevent the collapse of the savings and loan industry. It stood by while highly speculative mergers, buyouts, and takeovers overwhelmed financial markets in the 1980s. It has failed to address the unprecedented levels of indebtedness and credit defaults of private corporations and households.

New Roles for the Fed

Under my proposal, the Federal Reserve would shift its focus from the short to the long term. It would provide more and cheaper credit to banks and other financiers who loan money to create productive assets and infrastructure—which promote high wage, high productivity jobs. The Fed would make credit more expensive for lenders that finance speculative activities such as the mergers, buyouts, and takeovers that dominated the 1980s.

The Fed would also give favorable credit terms to banks that finance decent affordable housing rather than luxury housing and speculative office buildings. It would make low-cost credit available for environmental research and development so the economy can begin the overdue transition to environmentally benign production. Cuts in military spending have idled many workers and productive resources, both of which could be put to work in such transformed industries.

Finally, the Fed would give preferential treatment to loans that finance investment in the United States rather than in foreign countries. This would help counter the trend of U.S. corporations to abandon the domestic economy in search of lower wages and taxes.

The first step in developing the Fed's new role would be for the public to determine which sectors of the economy should get preferential access to credit. One example, suggested above, is industrial conversion from military production to investment in renewable energy and conservation.

Once the public establishes its investment goals, the Fed will have to develop new policy tools and use its existing tools in new ways to accomplish them. I propose that a transformed Federal Reserve use two major methods:

- set variable cash ("asset reserve") requirements for all lenders, based on the social value of the activities the lenders are financing; and

- increase discretionary lending activity by the 12 district Federal Reserve banks.

Varying Banks' Cash Requirements

The Fed currently requires that banks and other financial institutions keep a certain amount of their assets available in cash reserves. Banks, for example, must carry three cents in cash for every dollar they hold in checking accounts. A bank cannot make interest-bearing loans on such "reserves." I propose that the Fed make this percent significantly lower for loans that finance preferred activities than for less desirable investment areas. Let's say the public decides that banks should allocate 10% of all credit to research and development of new environmental technologies, such as non-polluting autos and organic farming. Then financial institutions that have made 10% of their loans in environmental technologies would not have to hold any cash reserves against these loans. But if a bank made no loans in the environmental area, then it would have to hold 10% of its total assets in reserve. The profit motive would force banks to support environmental technologies without any direct expenditure from the federal budget.

All profit-driven firms will naturally want to avoid this reserve requirement. The Fed must therefore apply it uniformly to all businesses that profit through accepting deposits and making loans. These include banks, savings and loans, insurance companies, and investment brokerage houses. If the rules applied only to banks, for example, then banks could circumvent the rules by redefining themselves as another type of lending institution.

Loans to Banks That Do the Right Thing

The Federal Reserve has the authority now to favor some banks over others by making loans to them when they are short on cash. For the most part, however, the Fed has chosen not to exercise such discretionary power. Instead it aids all banks equally, through a complex mechanism known as open market operations, which increases total cash reserves in the banking system. The Fed could increase its discretionary lending to favored banks by changing its operating procedures without the federal government creating any new laws or institutions. Such discretionary lending would have several benefits.

First, to a much greater extent than at present, financial institutions would obtain reserves when they are lending for specific purposes. If a bank's priorities should move away from the established social priorities, the Fed could then either refuse to make more cash available to it, or charge a penalty interest rate, thereby discouraging the bank from making additional loans. The Fed, for example, could impose such obstacles on lenders that are financing mergers, takeovers, and buyouts.

In addition, the Fed could use this procedure to more effectively monitor and regulate financial institutions. Banks, in applying for loans, would have to submit to the Fed's scrutiny on a regular basis. The Fed could more closely link its regulation to banks' choices of which investments to finance.

Implementing this procedure will also increase the authority of the 12 district banks within the Federal Reserve system, since these banks approve the Fed's loans. Each district bank will have more authority to set lending rates and monitor bank compliance with regulations.

The district banks could then more effectively enforce measures such as the Community Reinvestment Act, which currently mandates that banks lend in their home communities. Banks that are committed to their communities and regions, such as the South Shore Bank in Chicago, could gain substantial support under this proposed procedure.

Other Credit Allocation Tools

The Fed can use other tools to shift credit to preferred industries, such as loan guarantees, interest rate subsidies, and government loans. In the past the U.S. government has used these techniques with substantial success. They now primarily support credit for housing, agriculture, and education. Indeed, as of 1991, these programs subsidized roughly one-third of all loans in the United States.

Jesse Jackson's 1988 Presidential platform suggested an innovative way of extending such policies. He proposed that public pension funds channel a portion of their money into a loan guarantee program, with the funds used to finance investments in low cost housing, education, and infrastructure.

There are disadvantages, however, to the government using loan guarantee programs and similar approaches rather than the Fed's employing asset reserve requirements and discretionary lending. Most important is that the former are more expensive and more difficult to administer. Both loan guarantees and direct government loans require the government to pay off the loans when borrowers default. Direct loans also mean substantial administrative costs. Interest subsidies on loans are direct costs to government even when the loans are paid back.

In contrast, with variable asset reserve requirements and discretionary lending policies, the Fed lowers the cost of favored activities, and raises the cost of unfavored ones, without imposing any burden on the government's budget.

Increasing Public Control

The Federal Reserve acts in relative isolation from the political process at present. The U.S. president appoints seven members of the Fed's Board of Governors for 14 year terms, and they are almost always closely tied to banking and big business. The boards of directors of the 12 district banks appoint their presidents, and these boards are also composed of influential bankers and business people within each of the districts.

The changes I propose will mean a major increase in the central bank's role as an economic planning agency for the nation. Unless we dramatically improve democratic control by the public over the Fed, voters will correctly interpret such efforts as an illegitimate grasp for more power by business interests.

Democratization should proceed through redistributing power downward to the 12 district banks. When the Federal Reserve System was formed in 1913, the principle behind creating district banks along with the headquarters in Washington was to disperse the central bank's authority. This remains a valuable idea, but the U.S. government has never seriously attempted it. Right now the district banks are highly undemocratic and have virtually no power.

One way to increase the district banks' power is to create additional seats for them on the Open Market Committee, which influences short-term interest rates by expanding or contracting the money supply.

A second method is to shift authority from the Washington headquarters to the districts. The Board of Governors would then be responsible for setting general guidelines, while the district banks would implement discretionary lending and enforcement of laws such as the Community Reinvestment Act.

The most direct way of democratizing the district banks would be to choose their boards in regular elections along with other local, regional, and state-wide officials. The boards would then choose the top levels of the banks' professional staffs and oversee the banks' activities.

Historical Precedents

Since World War II other capitalist countries have extensively employed the types of credit allocation policies proposed here. Japan, France, and South Korea are the outstanding success stories, though since the early 1980s globalization and deregulation of financial markets have weakened each of their credit policies. When operating at full strength, the Japanese and South Korean programs primarily supported large-scale export industries, such as steel, automobiles, and consumer electronics. France targeted its policies more broadly to coordinate Marshall Plan aid for the development of modern industrial corporations.

We can learn useful lessons from these experiences, not least that credit allocation policies do work when they are implemented well. But substantial differences exist between experiences elsewhere and the need for a public investment bank in the United States.

In these countries a range of other institutions besides the central bank were involved in credit allocation policies. These included their treasury departments and explicit planning agencies, such as the powerful Ministry of International Trade and Industry (MITI) in Japan. In contrast, I propose to centralize the planning effort at the Federal Reserve.

We could create a new planning institution to complement the work of the central bank. But transforming the existing central banking system rather than creating a new institution minimizes both start-up problems and the growth of bureaucracies.

A second and more fundamental difference between my proposal and the experiences in Japan, France, and South Korea is that their public investment institutions were accountable only to a business-oriented elite. This essentially dictatorial approach is antithetical to the goal of increasing democratic control of the financial system.

The challenge, then, is for the United States to implement effective credit allocation policies while broadening, not narrowing, democracy. Our success ultimately will depend on a vigorous political movement that can fuse two equally urgent, but potentially conflicting goals: economic democracy, and equitable and sustainable growth. If we can meet this challenge, it will represent a historic victory toward the construction of a democratic socialist future.

Resources: Robert Pollin, "Transforming the Federal Reserve into a Public Investment Bank: Why it is Necessary; How it Should Be Done," in G. Epstein, G. Dymski and R. Pollin, eds., *Transforming the U.S. Financial System,* M.E. Sharpe, 1993.

Chapter 6

UNEMPLOYMENT AND INFLATION

INTRODUCTION

In June of 2009, with the economy still in the throes of its worst crisis since the Great Depression, supply-side economist Arthur Laffer warned of the threat of inflation. In an op-ed piece in the *Wall Street Journal* Laffer wrote that "we can expect rapidly rising prices over the next four or five years." He argued that the Fed's unprecedented expansion of the money supply during the crisis has the potential to unleash an inflation spiral more virulent than that in the 1970s.

There might be something to Laffer's concerns about price stability over the longer term. But why voice those concerns just three days after the economy had registered its highest unemployment rate in 26 years? Do conservative economists think it is more important to address a threat of inflation that will not manifest itself for another year or more than to deal with record-setting unemployment today?

In short, the answer is yes. This is hardly a surprise when considering that investors and stockholders feel precisely the same way because rising prices eat into their real rate of return or profits, after accounting for inflation.

Why is that? The explanation comes down to the trade-off between inflation and unemployment. Standard macroeconomics textbooks depict that trade-off as a "Phillips curve" in which rising employment pushes up prices.

Why does this textbook trade-off affect the returns of stockholders and other investors? The answer, as economist Robert Pollin points out, is "all about class conflict." Wall Street investors, out to protect the value of their assets and their investment profits, are hyper-concerned with price stability, and this pits them against workers on Main Street, who care about employment and wage growth. Higher unemployment rates and fewer jobs eat away at the bargaining power of workers, keeping wage growth and inflation in check and corporate profit margins wide.

Pollin captures that dynamic in "The 'Natural Rate' of Unemployment." As he sees it, the unemployment rate consistent with price stability —the so-called "natural rate"—declined dramatically in the 1990s because workers' economic power eroded during the decade (Article 6.1). John Miller supplements Pollin's class-conflict analysis by looking at why stock prices on Wall Street improved while unemployment rates on Main Street worsened through much of 2009 (Article 6.2).

Economist Chris Tilly attributes the long-term decline in pay, benefits, and working conditions for U.S. workers to slower economic growth; the business offensive against workers' protections, such as unions and the minimum wage; and businesses pushing more risks onto workers in the form of temporary work, mass layoffs, and reduced benefits (Article 6.3). That the share of unemployed workers who receive benefits has shrunk since the 1970s only makes things worse for workers. Economist Marianne Hill reports on the broken unemployment compensation system and some promising initiatives that might fix it (Article 6.5).

U.S. labor markets are also haunted by offshore outsourcing, which began with manufacturing jobs and has now spread to back office work and a wide swath of service-sector jobs. In his second article, John Miller notes that the alarming estimates of the scope of offshore outsourcing have given even some inveterate free-traders second thoughts (Article 6.4).

What can be done to raise wages and get workers a better deal? Economist Arthur MacEwan's answer is to reverse the declines in workers' political muscle and bargaining power of the last four decades, declines that result from weakened unions and social support programs (Article 6.6). Fellow economist Jeannette Wicks-Lim agrees. She argues that pushing U.S. workers' unionization rate back up is a key strategy for creating jobs with decent compensation in the coming decade (Article 6.7).

Economist Ramaa Vasudevan takes a careful look at the macroeconomics between inflation and unemployment and how that trade-off changed during the stagflation of the 1970s and the productivity boom of the 1990s. Like Pollin, she attributes the combination of sustained low inflation and low unemployment during the 1990s to the relatively weak bargaining position of workers (Article 6.8).

Research analyst Ben Collins closes out the chapter by looking at the forces driving the rise of food prices across the globe. Food and other commodities have become a hot new target for investment as housing and stocks turn sour. The financialization of food, just another in a long list of ills visited upon the global economy by unregulated financial markets, has not only contributed to economic instability but is also changing how people around the world eat and who doesn't eat at all (Article 6.9).

Discussion Questions

1. (Article 6.1) What is the concept of the non-accelerating inflation rate of unemployment (the NAIRU, or "natural rate of unemployment")? Is there a natural rate? What is it?

2. (Article 6.1) Given the class conflict inherent in the trade-off between inflation and unemployment, what policies might lead to improved standards of living for workers in today's economy?

3. (Article 6.2) Why would investors on Wall Street benefit from rising unemployment on Main Street?

4. (Article 6.3) What forces have led to a "raw deal" for workers in the long run?

5. (Article 6.3) How have the "paradox of corporate thrift," the "neoliberal paradox," and the "Arkansas paradox" complicated the task of winning a fair deal for workers?

6. (Article 6.4) Just how big a problem is offshore outsourcing? For whom?

7. (Article 6.4) What policies would best address the negative impacts of offshore outsourcing?

8. (Article 6.5) What are the current initiatives to reform the unemployment compensation system? Do you agree with Hill that they hold promise?

9. (Articles 6.6, 6.7) How might strengthening unions raise wages and help to create decent jobs?

10. (Article 6.8) What are the costs of higher inflation and who bears those costs? According to Vasudevan's evidence, what is the relationship between inflation and growth?

11. (Article 6.1, 6.8) What forces led to sustained low inflation and low unemployment during the 1990s? How are those conditions changing today?

12. (Article 6.9) What forces have transformed food commodities into a hot speculative investment? What steps, if any, do you think governments should take to regulate speculation in food commodities and its dangerous consequences for the world's food supply?

Article 6.1

THE "NATURAL RATE" OF UNEMPLOYMENT
It's all about class conflict.

BY ROBERT POLLIN
September/October 1998

In 1997, the official U.S. unemployment rate fell to a 27-year low of 4.9%. Most orthodox economists had long predicted that a rate this low would lead to uncontrollable inflation. So they argued that maintaining a higher unemployment rate—perhaps as high as 6%—was crucial for keeping the economy stable. But there is a hitch: last year the inflation rate was 2.3%, the lowest figure in a decade and the second lowest in 32 years. What then are we to make of these economists' theories, much less their policy proposals?

Nobel prize-winning economist Milton Friedman gets credit for originating the argument that low rates of unemployment would lead to accelerating inflation. His 1968 theory of the so-called "natural rate of unemployment" was subsequently developed by many mainstream economists under the term "Non-Accelerating Inflation Rate of Unemployment," or NAIRU, a remarkably clumsy term for expressing the simple concept of a threshold unemployment rate below which inflation begins to rise.

According to both Friedman and expositors of NAIRU, inflation should accelerate at low rates of unemployment because low unemployment gives workers excessive bargaining power. This allows the workers to demand higher wages. Capitalists then try to pass along these increased wage costs by raising prices on the products they sell. An inflationary spiral thus ensues as long as unemployment remains below its "natural rate."

Based on this theory, Friedman and others have long argued that governments should never actively intervene in the economy to promote full employment or better jobs for workers, since it will be a futile exercise, whose end result will only be higher inflation and no improvement in job opportunities. Over the past generation, this conclusion has had far-reaching influence throughout the world. In the United States and Western Europe, it has provided a stamp of scientific respectability to a whole range of policies through which governments abandoned even modest commitments to full employment and workers' rights.

This emerged most sharply through the Reaganite and Thatcherite programs in the United States and United Kingdom in the 1980s. But even into the 1990s, as the Democrats took power in the United States, the Labour Party won office in Britain, and Social Democrats won elections throughout Europe, governments remained committed to stringent fiscal and monetary policies, whose primary goal is to prevent inflation. In Western Europe this produced an average unemployment rate of over 10% from 1990-97. In the United States, unemployment rates have fallen sharply in the 1990s, but as an alternative symptom of stringent fiscal and monetary policies, real wages for U.S. workers also declined dramatically over the past generation. As of 1997, the average real wage for nonsupervisory workers in the United States was 14% below its peak in 1973, even though average worker productivity rose between 1973 and 1997 by 34%.

Why have governments in the United States and Europe remained committed to the idea of fiscal and monetary stringency, if the natural rate theory on which such policies are based is so obviously flawed? The explanation is that the natural rate theory is really not just about predicting a precise unemployment rate figure below which inflation must inexorably accelerate, even though many mainstream economists have presented the natural rate theory in this way. At a deeper level, the natural rate theory is bound up with the inherent conflicts between workers and capitalists over jobs, wages, and working conditions. As such, the natural rate theory actually contains a legitimate foundation in truth amid a welter of sloppy and even silly predictions.

The "Natural Rate" Theory Is about Class Conflict

In his 1967 American Economic Association presidential address in which he introduced the natural rate theory, Milton Friedman made clear that there was really nothing "natural" about the theory. Friedman rather emphasized that: "by using the term 'natural' rate of unemployment, I do not mean to suggest that it is immutable and unchangeable. On the contrary, many of the market characteristics that determine its level are man-made and policy-made. In the United States, for example, legal minimum wage rates ... and the strength of labor unions all make the natural rate of unemployment higher than it would otherwise be."

In other words, according to Friedman, what he terms the "natural rate" is really a social phenomenon measuring the class strength of working people, as indicated by their ability to organize effective unions and establish a livable minimum wage.

Friedman's perspective is supported in a widely-read 1997 paper by Robert Gordon of Northwestern University on what he terms the "time-varying NAIRU." What makes the NAIRU vary over time? Gordon explains that, since the early 1960s, "The two especially large changes in the NAIRU... are the increase between the early and late 1960s and the decrease in the 1990s. The late 1960s were a time of labor militancy, relatively strong unions, a relatively high minimum wage and a marked increase in labor's share in national income. The 1990s have been a time of labor peace, relatively weak unions, a relatively low minimum wage and a slight decline in labor's income share."

In short, class conflict is the spectre haunting the analysis of the natural rate and NAIRU: this is the consistent message stretching from Milton Friedman in the 1960s to Robert Gordon in the 1990s.

Stated in this way, the "Natural Rate" idea does, ironically, bear a close family resemblance to the ideas of two of the greatest economic thinkers of the left, Karl Marx and Michal Kalecki, on a parallel concept—the so-called "Reserve Army of Unemployed." In his justly famous Chapter 25 of Volume I of *Capital*, "The General Law of Capitalist Accumulation," Marx argued forcefully that unemployment serves an important function in capitalist economies. That is, when a capitalist economy is growing rapidly enough so that the reserve army of unemployed is depleted, workers will then utilize their increased bargaining power to raise wages. Profits are correspondingly squeezed as workers get a larger share of the country's total income. As a result, capitalists anticipate further declines in profitability and they therefore reduce their investment spending. This then leads to a fall in job creation, higher unemployment, and a replenishment of the reserve army. In other words, the reserve army of the unemployed is the instrument capitalists use to prevent significant wage increases and thereby maintain profitability.

Kalecki, a Polish economist of the Great Depression era, makes parallel though distinct arguments in his also justly famous essay, "The Political Aspects of Full Employment." Kalecki wrote in 1943, shortly after the 1930s Depression had ended and governments had begun planning a postwar world in which they would deploy aggressive policies to avoid another calamity of mass unemployment. Kalecki held, contrary to Marx, that full employment can be beneficial to the profitability of businesses. True, capitalists may get a smaller share of the total economic pie as workers gain bargaining power to win higher wages. But capitalists can still benefit because the size of the pie is growing far more rapidly, since more goods and services can be produced when everyone is working, as opposed to some significant share of workers being left idle.

But capitalists still won't support full employment, in Kalecki's view, because it will threaten their control over the workplace, the pace and direction of economic activity, and even political institutions. Kalecki thus concluded that full employment could be sustainable under capitalism, but only if these challenges to capitalists' social and political power could be contained. This is why he held that fascist social and political institutions, such as those that existed in Nazi Germany when he was writing, could well provide one "solution" to capitalism's unemployment problem, precisely because they were so brutal. Workers would have jobs, but they would never be permitted to exercise the political and economic power that would otherwise accrue to them in a full-employment economy.

Broadly speaking, Marx and Kalecki do then share a common conclusion with natural rate proponents, in that they would all agree that positive unemployment rates are the outgrowth of class conflict over the distribution of income and political power. Of course, Friedman and other mainstream economists reach this conclusion via analytic and political perspectives that are diametrically opposite to those of Marx and Kalecki. To put it in a nutshell, in the Friedmanite view mass unemployment results when workers demand more than they deserve, while for Marx and Kalecki, capitalists use the weapon of unemployment to prevent workers from getting their just due.

From Natural Rate to Egalitarian Policy

Once the analysis of unemployment in capitalist economies is properly understood within the framework of class conflict, several important issues in our contemporary economic situation become much more clear. Let me raise just a few:

1. Mainstream economists have long studied how workers' wage demands cause inflation as unemployment falls. However, such wage demands never directly cause in-

flation, since inflation refers to a general rise in prices of goods and services sold in the market, not a rise in wages. Workers, by definition, do not have the power to raise prices. Capitalists raise prices on the products they sell. At low unemployment, inflation occurs when capitalists respond to workers' increasingly successful wage demands by raising prices so that they can maintain profitability. If workers were simply to receive a higher share of national income, then lower unemployment and higher wages need not cause inflation at all.

2. There is little mystery as to why, at present, the so-called "time-varying" NAIRU has diminished to a near vanishing point, with unemployment at a 25-year low while inflation remains dormant. The main explanation is the one stated by Robert Gordon—that workers' economic power has been eroding dramatically through the 1990s. Workers have been almost completely unable to win wage increases over the course of the economic expansion that by now is seven years old.

3. This experience over the past seven years, with unemployment falling but workers showing almost no income gains, demonstrates dramatically the crucial point that full employment can never stand alone as an adequate measure of workers' well-being. This was conveyed vividly to me when I was working in Bolivia in 1990 as part of an economic advising team led by Keith Griffin of the University of California-Riverside. Professor Griffin asked me to examine employment policies.

I began by paying a visit to the economists at the Ministry of Planning. When I requested that we discuss the country's employment problems, they explained, to my surprise, that the country *had no employment problems*. When I suggested we consider the situation of the people begging, shining shoes, or hawking batteries and Chiclets in the street just below the window where we stood, their response was that these people *were* employed. And of course they were, in that they were actively trying to scratch out a living. It was clear that I had to specify the problem at hand far more precisely. Similarly, in the United States today, we have to be much more specific as to what workers should be getting in a fair economy: jobs, of course, but also living wages, benefits, reasonable job security, and a healthy work environment.

4. In our current low-unemployment economy, should workers, at long last, succeed in winning higher wages and better benefits, some inflationary pressures are likely to emerge. But if inflation does not accelerate after wage increases are won, this would mean that businesses are not able to pass along their higher wage costs to their customers. Profits would therefore be squeezed. In any case, in response to *either* inflationary pressures or a squeeze in profitability, we should expect that many, if not most, segments of the business community will welcome a Federal Reserve policy that would slow the economy and raise the unemployment rate.

Does this mean that, as long as we live in a capitalist society, the control by capitalists over the reserve army of labor must remain the dominant force establishing the limits of workers' strivings for jobs, security, and living wages? The challenge for the progressive movement in the United States today is to think through a set of policy ideas through which full employment at living wages can be achieved and sustained.

Especially given the dismal trajectory of real wage decline over the past generation, workers should of course continue to push for wage increases. But it will also be crucial to advance these demands within a broader framework of proposals. One important component of a broader package would be policies through which labor and capital bargain openly over growth of wages and profits after full employment is achieved. Without such an open bargaining environment, workers, with reason, will push for higher wages once full employment is achieved, but capitalists will then respond by either raising prices or favoring high unemployment. Such open bargaining policies were conducted with considerable success in Sweden and other Nordic countries from the 1950s to the 1980s, and as a result, wages there continued to rise at full employment, while both accelerating inflation and a return to high unemployment were prevented.

Such policies obviously represent a form of class compromise. This is intrinsically neither good nor bad. The question is the terms under which the compromise is achieved. Wages have fallen dramatically over the past generation, so workers deserve substantial raises as a matter of simple fairness. But workers should also be willing to link their wage increases to improvements in productivity growth, i.e., the rate at which workers produce new goods and services. After all, if the average wage had just risen at exactly the rate of productivity growth since 1973 and not a penny more, the average hourly wage today for nonsupervisory workers would be $19.07 rather than $12.24.

But linking wages to improvements in productivity then also raises the question of who controls the decisions that determine the rate of productivity growth. In fact, substantial productivity gains are attainable through operating a less hierarchical workplace and building strong democratic unions through which workers can defend their rights on the job. Less hierarchy and increased workplace democracy creates higher morale on the job, which in turn increases workers' effort and opportunities to be inventive, while decreasing turnover and absenteeism. The late David Gordon of the New School for Social Research was among the leading analysts demonstrating how economies could operate more productively through greater workplace democracy.

But improvements in productivity also result from both the public and private sector investing in new and better machines that workers put to use every day, with the additional benefit that it means more jobs for people who produce those machines. A pro-worker economic policy will therefore also have to be concerned with increasing investments to improve the stock of machines that workers have at their disposal on the job.

In proposing such a policy approach, have I forgotten the lesson that Marx and Kalecki taught us, that unemployment serves a purpose in capitalism? Given that this lesson has become part of the standard mode of thinking among mainstream economists ranging from Milton Friedman to Robert Gordon, I would hope that I haven't let it slip from view. My point nevertheless is that through changing power relationships at the workplace and the decision-making process through which investment decisions get made, labor and the left can then also achieve a more egalitarian economy, one in which capitalists' power to brandish the weapon of unemployment is greatly circumscribed. If the labor movement and the left neglect issues of control over investment and the workplace, we will continue to live amid a Bolivian solution to the unemployment problem, where full employment is the by-product of workers' vulnerability, not their strength.

Sources: A longer version of this article appears as "The 'Reserve Army of Labor' and the 'Natural Rate of Unemployment': Can Marx, Kalecki, Friedman, and Wall Street All Be Wrong?," *Review of Radical Political Economics*, Fall 1998. Both articles derive from a paper originally presented as the David Gordon Memorial Lecture at the 1997 Summer Conference of the Union for Radical Political Economics. See also Robert Pollin and Stephanie Luce, *The Living Wage: Building a Fair Economy*, 1998; David Gordon, *Fat and Mean*, 1997; David Gordon, "Generating Affluence: Productivity Gains Require Worker Support," *Real World Macro*, 15th ed., 1998.

Article 6.2

BAD NEWS, GOOD NEWS, AND CLASS CONFLICT

BY JOHN MILLER
January/February 2010

SOFT ECONOMY? NO PROBLEM
Stocks have surged despite a steady increase in the unemployment rate.

First the bad news: The economy is weak. And now the good news: The economy is weak... Oddly, the same problem that worries many investors over the longer term is what encourages some for the short term: a soft economy. The reason is that an ailing economy requires the Federal Reserve to keep its short-term interest-rate targets near zero and continue pumping billions of dollars into the financial system.

—E. S. Browning, "For Stock Investors, Bad Economy Isn't Bad," *Wall Street Journal*, November 9, 2009

So the *Journal* has noticed that bad news on Main Street is good news on Wall Street. What's next—will the *Journal* report that "the history of all hitherto existing societies is the history of class struggle"?

But the *Journal* reporters still have some work to do before they earn their merit badges in Marxism. First off, any economist worth her salt will tell you that stock prices are a leading economic indicator that goes up ahead of an economic recovery. Stock prices (measured in the chart to the right as the change in the Dow Jones Industrial Average) rise in anticipation of improved corporate profits, as investors want to buy in early. And the unemployment rate is a lagging economic indicator that goes down only after the economy heats up.

Employment lags because employers do not want to hire more workers until they are sure that the expansion will hold, and in the meantime they push the existing workforce harder and expand hours. So it's not surprising to see stock prices and unemployment rates moving together as the economic recovery is just getting under way.

Second, the *Journal* attributes the correlation between rising stock prices and unemployment rates to the Fed's prodigious expansion of the money supply that pushed down interest rates. With few other good investment outlets, the plentiful supply of funds found its way into the stock market igniting a speculative boom.

There is something to that. Low interest rates have especially benefited hard-hit financial corporations. Cheap money brought these banks back to life. Rock-bottom interest rates widened their margins, the gap between short-term rates at which banks borrow and long-term interest rates at which they lend, boosting bank profits. And the price of their stocks has risen at twice the rate of the nearly year-long upswing in the market.

But that is only part of the story. As any class-conflict theorist would quickly add, the Fed could not have cut interest rates so drastically unless the threat of inflation had been tamed —especially the threat of higher wages, the largest cost of most corporations. Stock prices are up because the weak economy has put a damper on wage increases and allowed corporate cost-cutting to boost profits. As the 1970s demonstrated, inflation wipes out stock market gains.

Nothing knocks the stuffing out of workers' ability to push for higher wages more than a weak economy. Double-digit official unemployment rates have battered workers' bargaining power. As of October 2009, there were 6.3 officially unemployed workers for every job opening, the highest number since the Bureau of Labor Statistics began tracking that ratio in 2000. This is surely not the time to be asking the boss for a raise.

Don't expect the economic recovery to break the correlation between rising stock market gains and unemployment rates anytime soon by lowering unemployment rates—unless the stock market boom fizzles. A jobless recovery, a hallmark of the economic downturns of the last two decades, has transformed the correlation between rising unemployment rates and stock market prices to something other than a statistical oddity.

Even though the economy has begun growing again, the prospects for more jobs anytime soon remain bleak. Following the 2001 economic downturn, the U.S. economy continued to lose jobs for another two years and it took more than three years before the economy had replaced the jobs lost in the recession. If the current sluggish recovery creates jobs at the same pace as the last recovery, it would take 86 months, or more than 7 years, to replace the far greater number of jobs lost in this downturn than in the 2001 recession.

Now that's enough to make anyone, even a *Journal* reporter, a Marxist.

Sources: E. S. Browning, "For Stock Investors, Bad Economy Isn't Bad," *WSJ*, 12/9/09; Tom Lauricella, "For Bank-Stock Gains, Hope for a Slow Recovery," *WSJ*, 11/29/09; Connor Dougherty, "Jobs Data Cloud Recovery," *WSJ*, 11/3/09; Heidi Shierholz, "6.3 job seekers per job opening in October," Economic Policy Institute, 12/08/09.

Article 6.3

RAW DEAL FOR WORKERS

BY CHRIS TILLY
July/August 2003

F ew people have seen the inside of a "secondary meat processor"—a factory where large cuts of beef are turned into hamburger patties, roast beef, and other beef products. The workers who process beef do not have it easy. Many stand for long hours on wet floors. They are in constant contact with raw meat. In a typical plant the temperature ranges from 50° down to 3°F. Some workers rake 30-pound beef slabs from a huge bin onto a scale. Others heave giant roasts from one transmission belt to another. The work is repetitive and boring, but at the same time requires extreme attention to detail because of the potential for injury as well as food safety regulations. At one typical plant, entry-level pay is $7.75 an hour, or $16,000 a year—a poverty-level wage. There is no question that meat processors are getting a raw deal.

But the raw deal for workers is not limited to those workers who deal with raw meat. Pay, opportunities, and job quality have gotten worse for most workers in the United States over the past 30 years, across most sectors of the economy.

Obviously, the 2001 recession and the current jobless recovery have meant two-plus years of severe job shortages. But the deterioration of U.S. labor market conditions is a longer-term phenomenon. The spread of second-class jobs in the past three decades relates to fundamental changes in the economy and society, including sluggish productivity growth and employer assaults on workers' rights and protections.

The strongest evidence for the raw deal comes from looking at how workers were doing at the peak of the 1990s boom, three years ago. It was the longest boom in recorded U.S. history (lasting from March 1991 to March 2001). The expansion drove unemployment down to its lowest level in 30 years and spurred talk about a "new economy" that would turn productivity growth into endless prosperity. It should have been the best of times. But as a glance at the numbers reveals, it was not the best of times for working people.

Why the Raw Deal?

Why are workers getting such a raw deal? First, the economic pie is growing more slowly. Productivity growth during the "new economy" 1990s was only two-thirds as fast as in the "old economy" 1960s. That reflects the fact that companies have not invested as much in upgrading their equipment and training their workers as they once did—although the numbers are up compared to the 1980s, when productivity growth was even slower.

Why are these investments down? Businesses make an investment when they expect a payoff. But total global demand for goods and services grew only about half as fast in the 1980s and 1990s as it did in the 1960s and 1970s, and the increasing globalization of trade and investment meant that businesses were much more likely to face new competitors.

Second, over the last 20 years, businesses have aggressively attacked the protections that workers had built up for themselves. They have busted and blocked unions, shredded the unspoken agreements that governed many non-union workplaces, and lobbied to weaken pro-worker legislation. One consequence of these efforts: private sector workers are now less than one-third as likely to belong to a union now as they were in the mid-1950s. The minimum wage is only worth about two-thirds as much as it was at its high point in the late 1960s (after taking inflation into account). Because the low-wage workforce includes disproportionate numbers of women and people of color, the minimum wage and unions particularly benefit these groups.

Republican presidents have joined in the attacks on these protections. Every Republican administration since Ronald Reagan has doggedly opposed minimum wage increases. When Reagan fired striking air traffic controllers in 1981, he set a precedent for the permanent replacement of strikers. George W. Bush out-did Reagan in 2002 when he demanded that the Department of Homeland Security not have civil service protections and announced plans to privatize half of the federal workforce. Republicans in the White House have also stacked the National Labor Relations Board (NLRB), other federal agencies, and the courts with anti-labor appointees. As a result, these agencies offer at best weak enforcement of labor protections. To provide two recent examples: the NLRB recently ruled that unions have no right to hand out leaflets in company parking lots, and the Supreme Court ruled in 2002 that if a company terminates an undocumented worker, it need not pay the worker his or her back pay. Further, under-funding of the Occupational Safety and Health Administration (OSHA) has reduced inspections in hazardous workplaces—like meat processors. Self-styled New Democrats have backed many of these changes in the name of aiding business.

Of course, at the same time as corporations have attacked rank-and-file workers' protections, they have increased the rewards to top executives and stockholders. CEO pay kept growing through 2001, even while profits and stock values declined.

The third reason for the raw deal is that businesses have pushed more and more risk onto workers. The most extreme example of this is the growth of temporary work, which has expanded more than twenty-fold since the late 1960s. (Temporary work has been shrinking for the last two years—which of course is exactly the point: you hire temporary workers so you can dump them when the economy goes south.) But beyond the temps themselves, the frequency of mass layoffs highlights the fact that really, almost all jobs are temporary today.

Benefits are another area where workers bear more and more risk. Twenty-five years ago, most workers with pensions had "defined benefit" plans which specified the amount they would be paid upon retirement. Today, fewer than half of all workers are covered by any retirement plan, and fewer than one in five has a defined-benefit pension plan. Businesses prefer to offer defined-contribution plans like 401(k)s which require employee contributions and tie retirement income to market returns. In the last two years, we saw the results for those who had invested their 401(k) savings in Wall Street. Similarly, employers who offer health insurance have made workers take on more and more of the cost of health benefits—with the result that a growing number of workers decide they can't afford their health plan and go without coverage.

Because They Can

Why are businesses attacking worker protections and demanding that workers bear more risk? The first answer that many people give is "globalization"—and the increased competition that comes with it. Globalization has certainly had an important impact, but it does not offer an adequate explanation for business's newly combative stance. After all, it is the National Restaurant Association—representing an industry that experiences absolutely no global competition—that has fought hardest to keep the minimum wage low. To a large extent, businesses have gone on the offensive not because they *must*, but because they *can*.

Of course, businesses have always had the ability to lobby against the minimum wage, to cut health benefits, and to run anti-union campaigns. What has changed is the social acceptability of such actions. Princeton economist Paul Krugman recently argued that this is what accounts for the stratospheric rise of CEO pay: businesses have torn up the old social contract that placed important restraints on corporate self-seeking. Once a few large companies did this, the pressure mounted for other companies to go along or else face a competitive disadvantage, both in the stock market and in the market for goods and services. And as the social contract got rewritten, the government stopped enforcing the old rules. Cases in point are recent changes by the Supreme Court, the NLRB, and OSHA, mentioned earlier.

What can be done about this raw deal? It's tempting to think about the Arnold Schwarzenegger solution. In the 1986 movie *Raw Deal* ("They gave him a raw deal. *Nobody* gives him a raw deal."), Schwarzenegger used fists, guns, and explosives to wipe out the Chicago mob. But leveling the playing field for workers is no Hollywood action film. Complicating the task of winning a fairer share are three paradoxes.

Three Paradoxes

The first is the *paradox of corporate thrift*. Again, businesses are spending less on investments in equipment and training, and are also doing their best to keep wages and benefits low, all because the demand for the goods and services they sell is not growing very fast. For any business individually, this kind of thrift makes sense. But the paradox is that for businesses taken as a whole, it's counterproductive. Because if businesses are keeping down their own spending, and giving workers as little as possible, the overall result is to keep down the demand for goods and services. It's a vicious circle.

Handing another million dollars to a CEO is not a good way to stimulate the economy. True, some CEOs, like Tyco's Dennis Kozlowski, found creative ways to spend the money—on art, furniture, boats, and travel. But in general, rich people save most of their income. If you took a million dollars of executive pay and divided it among 1,000 poor families, you would get a lot more economic impact.

The second paradox is what University of Massachusetts economist James Crotty calls the *neoliberal paradox*. With slow global growth and increased global competition, it's become harder for most businesses to keep profits up. But at the same time, changes in the stock market mean that investors now demand consistently high profits. The growth of large institutional investors and the invention of the hostile takeover have made it possible for investors to threaten companies with takeover or destruction unless they generate high returns. Crotty points out that profit for nonfinancial corporations actually peaked in 1997. But corporations knew what would happen if they told their shareholders this bad news. In this context, the pressures for accounting games and even fraud became irresistible.

These first two paradoxes point out that the economy is far too important to let businesses run it. But when we think about how to take more control away from businesses, we run into the third paradox, the *Arkansas Traveler paradox*, named for an old song in which a traveler comes upon a man whose roof is leaking in a rainstorm. When the traveler asks him why he doesn't fix the roof, he says, "I can't fix it when it's raining." Asked why he doesn't then repair the roof when it's sunny, he replies, "When it's sunny, there's no need to fix it."

Similarly, when the economy is booming, workers have more economic leverage. Businesses run up against labor shortages, so they're more willing to make concessions to in order to ensure they can get the workers they need. It's a good time to organize a union, push for a higher minimum wage, or demand that employers provide a training program. Governments have the money to enforce regulations or to help pay for training.

But when the economy is booming, many workers don't see as much need to band together to defend their interests. Why form a union or lobby for a higher minimum wage when you can hop to a better paying job? Why push for a training program when even unskilled workers are getting jobs? The 1990s may not have amounted to a workers' paradise, but employment rates and wages were relatively edenic compared to the two decades that came before.

On the other hand, when the economy crashes, all of a sudden even the corporate media and mainstream politicians begin to focus on all the ways that business falls short. But when businesses are struggling for survival, they will fight desperately against any attempt to give workers a bigger share. The large numbers of unemployed job seekers put a damper on any attempts to organize unions or boost minimum wages. Governments face budget shortfalls, so they are not inclined to take on new activities.

The only way out of this box is not economic, but political. We have to build a movement that sees beyond the current situation in any given year. In the boom years, we have to remember all the problems of a business-dominated economy and use our economic leverage to strengthen institutions and business practices that help workers. In the bust years, like now, we have to keep in mind that economic resources will soon enough be growing again, and put in place rules that will more equitably distribute and effectively use them. We know what rules make a difference: the most important are strong wage floors and collective bargaining protections. By making businesses work under a better set of rules, we can actually help grow those resources by steering the economy out of the paradox of thrift and the neoliberal paradox.

If the problem is a raw deal, the solution is a new New Deal. The New Deal of the 1930s and 1940s saved U.S. capitalism from itself. It looks like we're going to have to do it again.

Article 6.4

OUTSIZED OFFSHORE OUTSOURCING

The scope of offshore outsourcing gives some economists and the business press the heebie-jeebies.

BY JOHN MILLER
September/October 2007

A t a press conference introducing the 2004 *Economic Report of the President*, N. Gregory Mankiw, then head of President Bush's Council of Economic Advisors, assured the press that "Outsourcing is probably a plus for the economy in the long run [and] just a new way of doing international trade."

Mankiw's comments were nothing other than mainstream economics, as even Democratic Party-linked economists confirmed. For instance Janet Yellen, President Clinton's chief economist, told the *Wall Street Journal*, "In the long run, outsourcing is another form of trade that benefits the U.S. economy by giving us cheaper ways to do things." Nonetheless, Mankiw's assurances were met with derision from those uninitiated in the economics profession's free-market ideology. Sen. John Edwards (D-N.C.) asked, "What planet do they live on?" Even Republican House Speaker Dennis Hastert (Ill.) said that Mankiw's theory "fails a basic test of real economics."

Mankiw now jokes that "if the American Economic Association were to give an award for the Most Politically Inept Paraphrasing of Adam Smith, I would be a leading candidate." But he quickly adds, "the recent furor about outsourcing, and my injudiciously worded comments about the benefits of international trade, should not eclipse the basic lessons that economists have understood for more than two centuries."

In fact Adam Smith never said any such thing about international trade. In response to the way Mankiw and other economists distort Smith's writings, economist Michael Meeropol took a close look at what Smith actually said; he found that Smith used his invisible hand argument to favor domestic investment over far-flung, hard-to-supervise foreign investments. Here are Smith's words in his 1776 masterpiece, *The Wealth of Nations*:

> By preferring the support of domestic to that of foreign industry, he [the investor] intends only his own security; and by directing that industry in such a manner as its produce may be of the greatest value, he intends only his own gain, and he is in this, as in many other cases, led by an invisible hand to promote an end, which was no part of his intention.

Outsized offshore outsourcing, the shipping of jobs overseas to take advantage of low wages, has forced some mainstream economists and some elements of the business press to have second thoughts about "free trade." Many are convinced that the painful transition costs that hit before outsourcing produces any ultimate benefits may be the biggest political issue in economics for a generation. And some recognize, as Smith did, that there is no guarantee unfettered international trade will leave the participants better off even in the long run.

Keynes's Revenge

Writing during the Great Depression of the 1930s, John Maynard Keynes, the preeminent economist of the twentieth century, prescribed government spending as a means of compensating for the instability of private investment. The notion of a mixed private/government economy, Keynes's prosthesis for the invisible hand of the market, guided U.S. economic policy from the 1940s through the 1970s.

It is only fitting that Paul Samuelson, the first Nobel Laureate in economics, and whose textbook introduced U.S. readers to Keynes, would be among the first mainstream economist to question whether unfettered international trade, in the context of massive outsourcing, would necessarily leave a developed economy such as that of the United States better off—even in the long run. In an influential 2004 article, Samuelson characterized the common economics wisdom about outsourcing and international trade this way:

> Yes, good jobs may be lost here in the short run. But ...the gains of the winners from free trade, properly measured, work out to exceed the losses of the losers. ... Never forget to tally the real gains of consumers alongside admitted possible losses of some producers. ... The gains of the American winners are big enough to more than compensate the losers.

Samuelson took on this view, arguing that this common wisdom is "dead wrong about [the] *necessary* surplus of winning over losing" [emphasis in the original]. In a rather technical paper, he demonstrated that free trade globalization can sometimes give rise to a situation in which "a productivity gain in one country can benefit that country alone, while permanently hurting the other country by reducing the gains from trade that are possible between the two countries."

OFFSHORED? OUTSOURCED? CONFUSED?

The terms "offshoring" and "outsourcing" are often used interchangeably, but they refer to distinct processes:

Outsourcing – When a company hires another company to carry out a business function that it no longer wants to carry on in-house. The company that is hired may be in the same city or across the globe; it may be a historically independent firm or a spinoff of the first company created specifically to outsource a particular function.

Offshoring or *Offshore Outsourcing* – When a company shifts a portion of its business operation abroad. An offshore operation may be carried out by the same company or, more typically, outsourced to a different one.

ATTRIBUTES OF JOBS OUTSOURCED

- No Face-to-Face Customer Servicing Requirement
- High Information Content
- Work Process is Telecommutable and Internet Enabled
- High Wage Differential with Similar Occupation in Destination Country
- Low Setup Barriers
- Low Social Networking Requirement

Many in the economics profession do admit that it is hard to gauge whether intensified offshoring of U.S. jobs in the context of free-trade globalization will give more in winnings to the winners than it takes in losses from the losers. "Nobody has a clue about what the numbers are," as Robert C. Feenstra, a prominent trade economist, told *BusinessWeek* at the time.

The empirical issues that will determine whether offshore outsourcing ultimately delivers, on balance, more benefits than costs, and to whom those benefits and costs will accrue, are myriad. First, how wide a swath of white-collar workers will see their wages reduced by competition from the cheap, highly skilled workers who are now becoming available around the world? Second, by how much will their wages drop? Third, will the U.S. workers thrown into the global labor pool end up losing more in lower wages than they gain in lower consumer prices? In that case, the benefits of increased trade would go overwhelmingly to employers. But even employers might lose out depending on the answer to a fourth question: Will cheap labor from abroad allow foreign employers to out-compete U.S. employers, driving down the prices of their products and lowering U.S. export earnings? In that case, not only workers, but the corporations that employ them as well, could end up worse off.

Bigger Than A Box

Another mainstream Keynesian economist, Alan Blinder, former Clinton economic advisor and vice-chair of the Federal Reserve Board, doubts that outsourcing will be "immiserating" in the long run and still calls himself "a free-trader down to his toes." But Blinder is convinced that the transition costs will be large, lengthy, and painful before the United States experiences a net gain from outsourcing. Here is why.

First, rapid improvements in information and communications technology have rendered obsolete the traditional notion that manufactured goods, which can generally be boxed and shipped, are tradable, while services, which cannot be boxed, are not. And the workers who perform the services that computers and satellites have now rendered tradable will increasingly be found offshore, especially when they are skilled and will work for lower wages.

Second, another 1.5 billion or so workers—many in China, India, and the former Soviet bloc—are now part of the world economy. While most are low-skilled workers, some are not; and as Blinder says, a small percentage of 1.5 billion is nonetheless "a lot of willing and able people available to do the jobs that technology will move offshore." And as China and India educate more workers, offshoring of high-skill work will accelerate.

Third, the transition will be particularly painful in the United States because the U.S. unemployment insurance program is stingy, at least by first-world standards, and because U.S. workers who lose their jobs often lose their health insurance and pension rights as well.

How large will the transition cost be? "Thirty million to 40 million U.S. jobs are potentially offshorable," according to Blinder's latest estimates. "These include scientists, mathematicians and editors on the high end and telephone operators, clerks and typists on the low end."

Blinder arrived at these figures by creating an index that identifies how easy or hard it will be for a job to be physically or electronically "offshored." He then used the index to assess the Bureau of Labor Statistics' 817 U.S. occupational categories. Not surprisingly, Blinder classifies almost all of the 14.3 million U.S. manufacturing jobs as offshorable. But he also classifies more than twice that many U.S. service sector jobs as offshorable, including most computer industry jobs as well as many others, for instance, the 12,470 U.S. economists and the 23,790 U.S. multimedia artists and animators. In total, Blinder's analysis suggests that 22% to 29% of the jobs held by U.S. workers in 2004 will be potentially offshorable within a decade or two, with nearly 8.2 million jobs in 59 occupations "highly offshorable." Table 1 provides a list of the broad occupational categories with 300,000 or more workers that Blinder considers potentially offshorable.

Mankiw dismissed Blinder's estimates of the number of jobs at risk to offshoring as "out of the mainstream." Indeed, Blinder's estimates are considerably larger than earlier ones. But these earlier studies either aim to measure the number of U.S. jobs that will be outsourced (as opposed to the number at risk of being outsourced), look at a shorter period of time, or have shortcomings that suggest they underestimate the number of U.S. jobs threatened by outsourcing. (See "Studying the Studies.")

Global Arbitrage

Low wages are the reason U.S. corporations outsource labor. Table 2 shows just how large the international wage differentials were for computer programmers in 2002. Programmers in the United States make wages nearly *ten times* those of their counterparts in India and the Philippines, for example.

Today, more and more white-collar workers in the United States are finding themselves in direct competition with the low-cost, well-trained, highly educated workers in Bangalore, Shanghai, and Eastern and Central Europe. These workers often use the same capital and technology and are no less productive than the U.S. workers they replace. They just get paid less.

This global labor arbitrage, as Morgan Stanley's chief economist Stephen Roach calls it, has narrowed international wage disparities in manufacturing, and now in services too, by unrelentingly pushing U.S. wages down toward international norms. ("Arbitrage" refers to transactions that yield a profit by taking advantage of a price differential for the same asset in different locations. Here, of course, the "asset" is wage labor of a certain skill level.) A sign of that pressure: about 70% of laid-off workers in the United States earn less three years later than they did at the time of the layoff; on average, those reemployed earn 10% less than they did before.

TABLE 1: MAJOR OCCUPATIONS RANKED BY OFFSHORABILITY

Occupation	Category	Index Number	Number of Workers
Computer programmers	I	100	389,090
Telemarketers	I	95	400,860
Computer systems analysts	I	93	492,120
Billing and posting clerks and machine operators	I	90	513,020
Bookkeeping, accounting, and auditing clerks	I	84	1,815,340
Computer support specialists	I and II	92/68	499,860
Computer software engineers: Applications	II	74	455,980
Computer software engineers: Systems software	II	74	320,720
Accountants	II	72	591,311
Welders, cutters, solderers, and brazers	II	70	358,050
Helpers—production workers	II	70	528,610
First-line supervisors/managers of production and operating workers	II	68	679,930
Packaging and filling machine operators and tenders	II	68	396,270
Team assemblers	II	65	1,242,370
Bill and account collectors	II	65	431,280
Machinists	II	61	368,380
Inspectors, testers, sorters, samplers, and weighers	II	60	506,160
General and operations managers	III	55	1,663,810
Stock clerks and order fillers	III	34	1,625,430
Shipping, receiving, and traffic clerks	III	29	759,910
Sales managers	III	26	317,970
Business operations specialists, all other	IV	25	916,290

Source: Alan Blinder, "How Many U.S. Jobs Might Be Offshorable?" *CEPS Working Paper* #142, March 2007, figures from Bureau of Labor Statistics and author's judgments.

And it's not only laid-off workers who are hurt. A study conducted by Harvard labor economists Lawrence F. Katz, Richard B. Freeman, and George J. Borjas finds that every other worker with skills similar to those who were displaced also loses out. Every 1% drop in employment due to imports or factories gone abroad shaves 0.5% off the wages of the remaining workers in that occupation, they conclude.

Global labor arbitrage also goes a long way toward explaining the poor quality and low pay of the jobs the U.S. economy has created this decade, according to Roach. By dampening wage increases for an ever wider swath of the U.S. workforce, he argues, outsourcing has helped to drive a wedge between productivity gains and wage gains and to widen inequality in the United States. In the first four years of this decade, nonfarm productivity in the United States has recorded a cumulative increase of 13.3%—more than double the 5.9% rise in real compensation per hour over the same period. ("Compensation" includes wages, which have been stagnant for the average worker, plus employer spending on fringe benefits such as health insurance, which has risen even as, in many instances, the actual benefits have been cut back.) Roach reports that the disconnect between pay and productivity growth during the current economic expansion has been much greater in services than in manufacturing, as that sector weathers the powerful forces of global labor arbitrage for the first time.

Doubts in the Business Press?!

Even in the business press, doubts that offshore outsourcing willy-nilly leads to economic improvement have become more acute. Earlier this summer, a *BusinessWeek* cover story, "The Real Cost of Offshoring," reported that government statistics have underestimated the damage to the U.S. economy from offshore outsourcing. The problem is that since offshoring took off, *import* growth, adjusted for inflation, has been faster than the official numbers show. That means improvements in living standards, as well as corporate profits, depend more on cheap imports, and less on improving domestic productivity, than analysts thought.

Growing angst about outsourcing's costs has also prompted the business press to report favorably on remedies for the dislocation brought on by offshoring that deviate substantially from the non-interventionist, free-market playbook. Even the most unfazed pro-globalization types want to beef up trade adjustment assistance for displaced workers and strengthen the U.S. educational system. But both proposals are inadequate.

More education, the usual U.S. prescription for any economic problem, is off the mark here. Cheaper labor is available abroad up and down the job-skill ladder, so even the most rigorous education is no inoculation against the threat of offshore outsourcing. As Blinder emphasizes, it is the need for face-to-face contact that stops jobs from being shipped overseas, not the level of education necessary to perform them. Twenty years from now, home health aide positions will no doubt be plentiful in the United States; jobs for highly trained IT professionals may be scarce.

Trade adjustment assistance has until now been narrowly targeted at workers hurt by imports. Most new proposals would replace traditional trade adjustment assistance and unemployment insurance with a program for displaced workers that offers wage insurance to ease the pain of taking a lower-paying job and provides for portable health insurance and retraining. The pro-globalization research group McKinsey Global Institute (MGI), for example, claims that for as little as 4% to 5% of the amount they've saved in lower wages, companies could cover the wage losses of all laid-off workers once they are reemployed, paying them 70% of the wage differential between their old and new jobs (in addition to health care subsidies) for up to two years.

While MGI confidently concludes that this proposal will "go a long way toward relieving the current anxieties," other globalization advocates are not so sure. They recognize that economic anxiety is pervasive and that millions of white-collar workers now fear losing their jobs. Moreover, even if fears of actual job loss are overblown, wage insurance schemes do little to compensate for the downward pressure offshoring is putting on the wages of workers who have not been laid off.

STUDYING THE STUDIES

When economist Alan Blinder raised alarm bells in 2006 about the potentially large-scale offshoring of U.S. jobs, his results were inevitably compared to earlier research on offshore outsourcing. Three studies have been especially influential. The 2002 study (revised in 2004) by Forrester Research, a private, for-profit market research firm, which estimated that 3.3 million U.S. service sector jobs would move offshore by 2015, caused perhaps the biggest media stir. It was picked up by *BusinessWeek* and the *Wall Street Journal*, and hyped by Lou Dobbs, the CNN business-news anchor and outspoken critic of offshoring.

Forrester researcher John McCarthy developed his estimate by poring over newspaper clippings and Labor Department statistics on 505 white-collar occupations and then making an educated guess about how many jobs would be shipped offshore by 2015.

The Forrester study projects actual offshoring, not the number of jobs at risk of offshoring, so its estimate is rightfully lower than Blinder's. But the ample possibilities for technological change between now and 2015 convince Blinder that the Forrester estimate is nonetheless too low.

A 2003 study by University of California economists Ashok Bardhan and Cynthia Kroll estimated that about 11% of all U.S. jobs in 2001 were vulnerable to offshoring. Bradhan and Kroll applied the "outsourceability attributes" listed in "Attributes of Jobs Outsourced" to occupations where at least some outsourcing either has already taken place or is being planned.

Blinder considers the Bardhan and Kroll estimate for 2001 to be comparable to his estimate that 20% to 30% of the employed labor force will be at risk of offshore outsourcing within the next ten to twenty years, especially considering that Bardhan and Kroll do not allow for outsourcing to spread beyond the occupations it is currently affecting. This is like "looking only slightly beyond the currently-visible tip of the iceberg," according to Blinder.

The McKinsey Global Institute (MGI), a research group known for its unabashedly favorable view of globalization, has done its best to put a positive spin on offshore outsourcing. Its 2003 study, which relied on the Forrester offshoring estimates, concluded

Other mainstream economists and business writers go even further, calling for not only wage insurance but also taxes on the winners from globalization. And globalization has produced big winners: on Wall Street, in the corporate boardroom, and among those workers in high demand in the global economy.

Economist Matthew Slaughter, who recently left President Bush's Council of Economic Advisers, told the *Wall Street Journal*, "Expanding the political support for open borders [for trade] requres making a radical change in fiscal policy." He proposes eliminating the Social Security-Medicare payroll tax on the bottom half of workers—roughly, those earning less than $33,000 a year—and making up the lost revenue by raising the payroll tax on higher earners.

The goal of these economists is to thwart a crippling political backlash against trade. As they see it, "using the tax code to slice the apple more evenly is far more palatable than trying to hold back globalization with policies that risk shrinking the economic apple."

---

that offshoring is already benefiting the U.S. economy. For instance, MGI calculates that for every dollar spent on a business process outsourced to India, the U.S. economy gains at least $1.12. The largest chunk—58 cents—goes back to the original employer in the form of cost savings, almost exclusively in the form of lower wages. In addition, 30% of Indian offshoring is actually performed by U.S. companies, so the wage savings translate into higher earnings for those companies. The study also argues that offshore outsourcing frees up U.S. workers to do other tasks.

A second MGI study, in 2005, surveyed dozens of companies in eight sectors, from pharmaceutical companies to insurers. The study predicted that multinational companies in the entire developed world will have located only 4.1 million service jobs in low-wage countries by 2008—a figure equal to only 1% of the total number of service jobs in developed countries.

But the MGI outsourcing studies have serious limitations. For instance, Blinder points out that MGI's analysis looks at a very short time frame, and that the potential for outsourcing in English-speaking countries such as the United States is higher than elsewhere, a fact lost in the MGI studies' global averages.

In their 2005 book *Outsourcing America*, published by the American Management Association, public policy professors Ron Hira and Anil Hira argue that MGI's 2003 report "should be viewed as a self-interested lobbying document that presents an unrealistically optimistic estimate of the impact of offshore outsourcing." For instance, most of the data for the report came from case studies conducted by MGI that are unavailable to the public and unsupported by any model. Moreover, the MGI analysis assumes that the U.S. economy will follow its long-term trend and create 3.5 million jobs a year, enough to quickly reemploy U.S. workers displaced by offshoring. But current U.S. job creation falls far short of that trend. A recent White House fact sheet brags that the U.S. economy has created 8.3 million jobs since August 2003. Still, that is less than 2.1 million jobs a year, and only 1.8 million jobs over the last 12 months.

MGI's Farrell is right about one thing. "If the economy were stronger," she says, "there wouldn't be such a negative feeling" about work getting offshored. But merely assuming high job growth doesn't make it so.

Some even call for extending global labor arbitrage to CEOs. In a June 2006 *New York Times* op-ed, equity analyst Lawrence Orlowski and New York University assistant research director Florian Lengyel argued that offshoring the jobs of U.S. chief executives would reduce costs and release value to shareholders by bringing the compensation of U.S. CEOs (on average 170 times greater than the compensation of average U.S. workers in 2004) in line with CEO compensation in Britain (22 times greater) and in Japan (11 times greater).

Yet others focus on the stunning lack of labor mobility that distinguishes the current era of globalization from earlier ones. Labor markets are becoming increasingly free and flexible under globalization, but labor enjoys no similar freedom of movement. In a completely free market, the foreign workers would come here to do the work that is currently being outsourced. Why aren't more of those workers coming to the United States? Traditional economists Gary Becker and Richard Posner argue the answer is clear: an excessively restrictive immigration policy.

Onshore and Offshore Solidarity

Offshoring is one of the last steps in capitalism's conversion of the "physician, the lawyer, the priest, the poet, the man of science, into its paid wage laborers," as Marx and Engels put it in the *Communist Manifesto* 160 years ago. It has already done much to increase economic insecurity in the workaday world and has become, Blinder suggests, the number one economic issue of our generation.

Offshoring has also underlined the interdependence of workers across the globe. To the extent that corporations now organize their business operations on a global scale, shifting work around the world in search of low wages, labor organizing must also be global in scope if it is to have any hope of building workers' negotiating strength.

Yet today's global labor arbitrage pits workers from different countries against each other as competitors, not allies. Writing about how to improve labor standards, economists Ajit Singh and Ann Zammit of the South Centre, an Indian non-governmental organization, ask the question, "On what could workers of the world unite" today? Their answer is that faster economic growth could indeed be a positive-sum game from which both the global North and the global South could gain. A pick-up in the long-term rate of growth of the world economy would generate higher employment, increasing wages and otherwise improving labor standards in both regions. It should also make offshoring less profitable and less painful.

The concerns of workers across the globe would also be served by curtailing the ability of multinational corporations to move their investment anywhere, which weakens the bargaining power of labor both in advanced countries and in the global South. Workers globally would also benefit if their own ability to move between countries was enhanced. The combination of a new set of rules to limit international capital movements and to expand labor mobility across borders, together with measures to ratchet up economic growth and thus increase worldwide demand for labor, would alter the current process of globalization and harness it to the needs of working people worldwide.

Sources: Alan S. Blinder, "Fear of Offshoring," CEPS Working Paper #119, Dec. 2005; Alan S. Blinder, "How Many U.S. Jobs Might Be Offshorable?" CEPS Working Paper #142, March 2007; N. Gregory Mankiw and P. Swagel, "The Politics and Economics of Offshore Outsourcing," Am. Enterprise Inst. Working Paper #122, 12/7/05; "Offshoring: Is It a Win-Win Game?" McKinsey Global Institute, August 2003; Diane Farrell et al., "The Emerging Global Labor Market, Part 1: The Demand for Talent in Services," McKinsey Global Institute, June 2005; Ashok Bardhan and Cynthia Kroll, "The New Wave of Outsourcing," Research Report #113, Fisher Center for Real Estate and Urban Economics, Univ. of Calif., Berkeley, Fall 2003; Paul A. Samuelson, "Where Ricardo and Mill Rebut and Confirm Arguments of Mainstream Economists Supporting Globalization," *J Econ Perspectives* 18:3, Summer 2004; Alan S. Blinder, "Free Trade's Great, but Offshoring Rattles Me," *Wash. Post,* 5/6/07; Michael Mandel, "The Real Cost of Offshoring," *BusinessWeek*, 6/18/07; Aaron Bernstein, "Shaking Up Trade Theory," *BusinessWeek,* 12/6/04; David Wessel, "The Case for Taxing Globalization's Big Winners," *WSJ,* 6/14/07; Bob Davis, "Some Democratic Economists Echo Mankiw on Outsourcing," *WSJ;* N. Gregory Mankiw, "Outsourcing Redux," gregmankiw. blogspot.com/2006/05/outsourcing-redux; David Wessel and Bob Davis, "Pain From Free Trade Spurs Second Thoughts," *WSJ,* 3/30/07; Ajit Singh and Ann Zammit, "On What Could Workers of the World Unite? Economic Growth and a New Global Economic Order," from *The Global Labour Standards Controversy: Critical Issues For Developing Countries,* South Centre, 2000; Michael Meeropol, "Distorting Adam Smith on Trade," *Challenge,* July/Aug 2004.

Article 6.5

UNEMPLOYMENT INSURANCE: A BROKEN SYSTEM

BY MARIANNE HILL
September/October 2009

Millions of workers have lost their jobs in the current recession. Employment is down 12% in manufacturing, 7% in professional and business services, and more than 5% overall in the private sector compared to last year. Over 5.6 million people have lost their jobs since last June. The ranks of the unemployed are continuing to grow; the unemployment rate in June hit 9.5%. Good thing that unemployment insurance provides income to help tide these workers over this rough patch, right? Not so fast.

The share of unemployed workers receiving benefits has gradually shrunk since the 1970s. In 1975, over half of unemployed workers received regular benefits. But in 2008, only 37% of the unemployed did; in some states the figure was less than 25%. And so-called "discouraged workers," those who want but are not actively seeking employment, are not considered part of the labor force and so are not even included in these figures.

Unemployment insurance, in short, is not a benefit that everyone who loses a job can count on. Several groups are working to change this. The American Recovery and Reinvestment Act (ARRA), better know as the Obama stimulus package, provides temporary funding for states that expand their unemployment coverage, and so far this year 25 states have done so. Others, however, are resisting even a temporary expansion of coverage that would be fully federally funded.

Why Unemployment Compensation?

When unemployment insurance was established as a nationwide program in 1935, it was hailed as a means of enabling workers to protect their standard of living between jobs. With it, workers are better able to keep their homes and their health. It helps to stabilize family well-being and maintain the labor force in a region. By enabling workers to engage in longer job searches, unemployment compensation also improves workers' job choices. It even enhances employers' flexibility in hiring by making lay-offs less painful.

Unemployment insurance is also an important countercyclical tool: it bolsters consumer spending during economic downturns and then automatically drops off as the economy recovers and unemployment falls. Because it reduces the need for other forms of government intervention to raise demand in a downturn, the program has supporters across the ideological spectrum.

Coverage and benefits vary by state. The average weekly benefit in 2008 was $300—about 35% of the average weekly wage. Benefits are paid from state funds that are financed by a payroll tax on employers. This tax is levied on anywhere from the first $7,000 to the first $35,300 of each worker's annual earnings depending on the state; the national average is $11,482. The tax rate ranges from 0.83% to 5% of the taxable portion of wages, with a national average of 2.42%. (Who bears the cost of this tax is debated: economists have shown that whether or not a company is able to pass the cost of payroll taxes forward to customers or back to employees depends on conditions in its particular product and labor markets.)

Shifts in employment patterns and a tightening of eligibility requirements are behind the nationwide reduction in effective unemployment insurance coverage. Today almost 30% of the U.S. work force is employed in nonstandard work arrangements, including part-time, temporary, contract or on-call work, and self-employment. Most of these jobs are subject to the payroll tax that funds unemployment benefits—yet these workers often find they are ineligible. For instance, persons who are seeking only part-time employment do not qualify for unemployment benefits in many states. This affects women in particular, including heads of households, who often work part time due to dependent care responsibilities. People who work full time but only for part of the year may also find it difficult to qualify for unemployment benefits.

Many workers who are not eligible for benefits provide income that is critical to their families. In 2007, 41% of workers worked only part-time or part-year. Among heads of households, this figure, though lower, is still sizeable: in 2007, it was 32% overall and 42% for female family heads. Besides child care, elder care can also mean part-time or part-year work for many. Nearly one-third of working adults with older parents report missing some work to care for them.

Who Are the Unemployed?

Certain industries, regions, and workers are being hit harder than others this recession. In June, 15 states and the District of Columbia had unemployment rates of over 10%, but only one, North Dakota, had an unemployment rate below 5%. Michigan, Oregon, South Carolina and Rhode Island all had seasonally adjusted jobless rates of 12% or more.

Unemployment hits some population groups much harder than others—young people, people of color, and anyone with relatively few years of education. Among workers over 20 years of age, black men had the highest jobless rate in June at 16.4%. The rate for Hispanic women was 11.5%, for black women 11.3%, and for Hispanic men 10.7%. In contrast, the jobless rate was under 10% for both white men (9.2%) and white women (6.8%).

A combination of factors including occupational segregation, lower educational levels, and discrimination result in lower incomes for women and for black and Latino men, exacerbating the impact of higher unemployment. Data from 2005-2007 show that black women working year-round, full-time earned $15,900 a year less than white men; for Hispanic women the wage gap was $21,400. Lower-income families have fewer assets to see them through rough economic times, and their extended families are also hard-pressed as demands upon them increase. Nonprofits, another part of the social safety net, suffer from increased demand for services and decreased donations during recession. As a result, families of blacks, women and Hispanics suffer severe setbacks during a period of recession, and unemployment insurance can be especially critical to them.

Families in which one or more wage earners lose their jobs bear costs greater than just the lost wages. Savings are exhausted; rates of illness, both mental and physical, increase; debt levels often rise (inadequate medical insurance coverage is a major factor—in 2008, 60% of the unemployed lacked health insurance); and the pursuit of a college education or other training may be postponed. Studies have documented a rise in suicide rates, mental and physical illnesses, and domestic and other violence among the unemployed. These problems become widespread during recessions and become a burden on society, not just on individual families.

Promising Initiatives

Under the Obama stimulus package, states that elect to expand their programs in certain ways receive federal funds to finance these changes for at least two to three years. States can make unemployment benefits more available in a number of ways:

• Changing the base period used to determine whether a worker qualifies for benefits and if so, the amount he or she will receive.

• Making unemployment insurance available to certain individuals who are seeking only part-time work and/or to those who lost or left their jobs due to certain compelling family reasons (for example, domestic violence or a spouse relocating).

• Providing an additional 26 weeks of compensation to workers who have exhausted regular unemployment benefits and are enrolled in and making satisfactory progress in certain training programs.

• Paying an additional dependents' allowance of at least $15 per dependent per week to eligible beneficiaries.

Another potential reform relates to the extension of benefits beyond the regular 13- to 26-week period. States are required to offer extended benefits during periods of especially high unemployment (with half the cost covered by the federal government) only if certain trigger requirements are met—and that does not happen often. The ARRA offers states the option of adopting a new, less stringent trigger requirement. As of mid-July, 29 of the 30 states adopting the new trigger requirements have had extended benefits go into effect, compared with only six of the 20 states that have kept earlier triggers. Last year Congress authorized a separate program, Emergency Unemployment Compensation, to provide federally funded benefits after regular benefits are exhausted. The National Employment Law Project estimated that about 1.2 million workers would exhaust their benefits under *this* program before July 2009 and so become eligible for extended benefits.

A permanent expansion of coverage to a larger share of the unemployed, with or without an increase in benefit levels, would cost more than the average $23 per month in unemployment insurance taxes currently paid per worker. This could be achieved by expanding the portion of wages on which the tax is levied. To reduce the negative impact on low-income workers, this could be accompanied by adjustments to the earned income tax credit.

Even if the reforms contained in the Obama administration's stimulus package were fully enacted, benefits and coverage would be low in the United States in comparison to Europe. Much remains to be done to ensure minimal income security here. As the unemployment rate approaches 10%, it is time to revamp our broken system.

Sources: U.S. Department of Labor, especially www.ows.doleta.gov/unemploy/finance.asp; U.S. Bureau of Labor Statistics; National Employment Law Project, www.nelp.org; William Conerly, "European Unemployment: Lessons for the United States," National Center for Policy Analysis, May 26, 2004; National Institutes of Health, www.pubmedcentral.nih.gov; Marcus Walker and Roger Thurow, "U.S., Europe Are an Ocean Apart on Human Toll of Joblessness," *Wall Street Journal,* May 7, 2009.

Article 6.6

WHAT CAN WE DO TO RAISE WAGES?

BY ARTHUR MacEWAN
May/June 2009

> Dear Dr. Dollar:
> *Since the big problem in our national economy seems to be low wages for so many,*
> *how can we, or why can't we, just raise wages?*
> —Ben Leet, San Leandro, Calif.

A large part of the low wage story is explained by political power—political actions that have weakened unions and social support programs. So political action—in the other direction!—is a large part of what we can do to raise wages.

The biggest decline in wages took place in the 1980s and early 1990s. In 1993, average hourly wages, adjusted for inflation, were 18% below their 1972 peak. The 1980s started off with Ronald Reagan's firing of the air traffic controllers when they went on strike in 1981. This act directly weakened unions and was a harbinger of things to come. The pro-business appointments by Reagan and Bush I to the National Labor Relations Board (NLRB) allowed firms to aggressively resist unions' organizing efforts.

A recent report from the Center for Economic and Policy Research shows that during the 1980s and on into the early 1990s, over 25% of union election campaigns were marred by illegal firings. While the rate of illegal firings then dropped off substantially in the later 1990s, it jumped up again to over 25% in the Bush II era. The report points out that in the conditions of the 1980s, early 1990s, and since 2000, "almost one-in-five union organizers or activists [could] expect to be fired as a result of their activities in a union election campaign." With the NLRB favoring the employers, workers had little recourse against these illegal firings.

Also in the 1980s, the minimum wage was continually eroded by inflation. It slid down (in terms of 2008 prices) from $7.93 in 1981 to $5.82 in 1989, as the nominal minimum wage remained unchanged at $3.35 in this period. More recently, with the nominal minimum wage of $5.15 unchanged between 1997 and 2006, these years saw a similar erosion of the real minimum wage. In the absence of upward pressure at the bottom, employers could more easily maintain lower wages over a wide range.

Good social support programs—childcare, health care, housing subsidies, and other such programs—tend to redistribute income directly, but they also create upward pressure on wages because they give the people at the bottom more options. Yet the same rightward political shift that weakened unions also undermined social support programs. A process that was well underway in the 1980s reached its apex in the late 1990s when Bill Clinton presided over the "ending of welfare as we know it."

With the bottom of the labor market kept down by the lack of social support programs and a declining minimum wage, the bargaining power of workers at every level has been weakened. In 2008 (before the impact of the current downturn), the average real hourly wage was still 10% below the 1972 peak, even after a slow rise since the early '90s.

Although the current crisis is dramatically raising the unemployment rate and thus weakening workers' bargaining power, these circumstances also create possibilities for new, progressive programs. The Obama administration seems open to at least some of these programs. The President has voiced support for the Employee Free Choice Act that would greatly facilitate union organizing, and Obama's appointments to the NLRB will probably be more sympathetic to unions. On social programs, at least the door is open (a crack) to some positive developments with health care. On all these fronts, however, we cannot expect good results without popular efforts.

There are, however, limits to what we can accomplish domestically. Unions have been weakened by political actions, but they have also been weakened by international competition. Of course the nature of our economic connections to the rest of the world are shaped by political power, but with virtually any set of international connections it is difficult to maintain the high wages of U.S. workers while workers elsewhere live in poverty. A long-run strategy for improving workers' wages has to take account of all workers, not just those in the United States.

Article 6.7

CREATING DECENT JOBS: THE ROLE OF UNIONS

BY JEANNETTE WICKS-LIM

January/February 2010

The turmoil of the current recession is deflecting attention from a longer-term challenge facing the U.S. economy: how to create decent jobs. Even before the recession, nearly two-thirds of U.S. jobs failed the "decent job" test—they paid too little to cover a small family's basic needs. Between now and 2016, the strongest job growth will be largely in low-pay occupations, according to Department of Labor projections. So barring any structural changes, the U.S. economy will be no better at producing jobs that can support a worker and his or her family at a very basic living standard in 2016 than it was in 2006.

Collective bargaining through labor unions could brighten this forecast, raising the quality of future jobs even if the economy continues to produce the same types of jobs. Bringing the unionized share of the U.S. workforce back up to around its level in the 1970s—admittedly no easy task—would lift an estimated 2.5 million additional jobs over the decent-job threshold in 2016.

A reasonable definition of a decent job is one with the minimum pay and benefits necessary to provide a healthy and safe standard of living for a small family. This benchmark is substantially above the U.S. Census Bureau's official poverty threshold, widely viewed as far too low. Based on very basic family budgets the Economic Policy Institute has developed, a decent job has to pay at least $17 an hour with health and retirement benefits, or $22 an hour without.

A recent Labor Department report examines trends through 2006 to predict the jobs picture in 2016. Here are the ten occupations slated to add the most jobs: orderlies and nursing/home-health aides; registered nurses; retail salespersons; customer service representatives; food preparation and serving workers; general office clerks; personal/home-care aides; postsecondary teachers; janitors; and accounting clerks. In only two—RNs and postsecondary teachers—do the majority of existing jobs meet the decent job standard. The other eight fall short.

It's no surprise, then, that an analysis of the complete 2016 jobs projection shows little change in the overall proportion of decent jobs. By my estimates, in 2016 some 35.2% of all jobs will meet this standard, barely changed from the 2006 figure of 34.8%. These projections pre-date the current recession, and so reveal a long-term problem likely to persist well after the economy revives.

If we cannot count on a raft of novel, more lucrative occupations in the next several years, then expanding the number of decent jobs will require improving the compensation of jobs in existing occupations. Unions enable workers to do exactly that. Suppose union representation rose by a meaningful amount, say 10 percentage points to about 24%, by 2016. The proportion of decent jobs in 2016 would rise by an estimated 1.5 percentage points to 36.7%, representing an additional 2.5 million decent jobs. This is four times the projected increase if union representation levels remain the same.

But what about globalization? Forget about more decent jobs—how can U.S. workers stop decent jobs from disappearing in an increasingly integrated world economy with a large supply of labor that is cheaper than any in the United States, whether unionized or not?

One answer is to focus on jobs that are not off-shore-able and on sectors in which U.S.-based firms have a competitive edge. Clean energy initiatives fit the bill: they involve activities that can only be done locally such as retrofitting buildings, plus, renewable energy is an area where U.S.-based firms' technological edge counts.

This strategy has another potential benefit for workers: greater international solidarity. By reducing the pressure they face from the global "race to the bottom," robust clean-energy job growth would better position U.S. workers to focus on cross-border organizing that can raise the floor of the global labor market.

What would it take to bring an additional 10% of U.S. workers into unions? That is the subject of another article. But the fact that the Employee Free Choice Act, which would make it easier for workers to join unions, is under serious consideration in Congress gives reason for hope. Any policies that expand opportunities for workers to join unions would help ensure that employment growth in the coming years produces decent jobs.

Sources: *Creating Decent Jobs in the United States: The Role of Labor Unions and Collective Bargaining*, peri.umass.edu; Constance F. Citro and Robert T. Michael, eds., *Measuring Poverty: A New Approach*, National Academy Press, 1995; Arlene Dohm and Lyn Shniper, "Employment outlook 2006-2016: Occupational employment projections to 2016," *Monthly Labor Review*, Nov. 2007; David Howell, Dean Baker, Andrew Glyn, and John Schmitt, "Are Protective Labor Market Institutions at the Root of Unemployment? A Critical Review of the Evidence," *Capitalism and Society* 2(1), 2007; James Heckman, "Comments on 'Are Protective Labor Market Institutions at the Root of Unemployment? A Critical Review of the Evidence'," *Capitalism and Society* (2)1, 2007; James Lin and Jared Bernstein, What We Need To Get By, Economic Policy Institute, 2008.

Article 6.8

THE RELATIONSHIP OF UNEMPLOYMENT AND INFLATION

BY RAMAA VASUDEVAN
September/October 2006

Dear Dr. Dollar:
Back in first-year economics we learned that there is a tradeoff between unemployment and inflation, so you can't really have both low inflation and low unemployment at the same time. Do economists still consider that to be true?
—Edith Bross, Cambridge, Mass.

The trade-off between inflation and unemployment was first reported by A. W. Phillips in 1958—and so has been christened the Phillips curve. The simple intuition behind this trade-off is that as unemployment falls, workers are empowered to push for higher wages. Firms try to pass these higher wage costs on to consumers, resulting in higher prices and an inflationary buildup in the economy. The trade-off suggested by the Phillips curve implies that policymakers can target low inflation rates or low unemployment, but not both. During the 1960s, monetarists emphasized price stability (low inflation), while Keynesians more often emphasized job creation.

The experience of so-called stagflation in the 1970s, with simultaneously high rates of both inflation and unemployment, began to discredit the idea of a stable trade-off between the two. In place of the Phillips curve, many economists began to posit a "natural rate of unemployment." If unemployment were to fall below this "natural" rate, however slightly, inflation would begin to accelerate. Under the "natural rate of unemployment" theory (also called the Non-Accelerating Inflation Rate of Unemployment, or NAIRU), instead of choosing between higher unemployment and higher inflation, policymakers were told to focus on ensuring that the economy remained at its "natural" rate: the challenge was to accurately estimate its level and to steer the economy toward growth rates that maintain price stability, no matter what the corresponding level of unemployment.

The NAIRU has been extremely difficult to pin down in practice. Not only are estimates of it notoriously imprecise, the rate itself evidently changes over time. In the United States, estimates of the NAIRU rose from about 4.4% in the 1960s, to 6.2% in the 1970s, and further to 7.2% in the 1980s. This trend reversed itself in the 1990s, as officially reported unemployment fell. In the latter half of the 1990s, U.S. inflation remained nearly dormant at around 3%, while unemployment fell to around 4.6%. In the later Clinton years many economists warned that if unemployment was brought any lower, inflationary pressures might spin out of control. But growth in these years did not spill over into accelerating inflation. The United States, apparently, had achieved the Goldilocks state—everything just right!

What sustained this combination of low inflation and low unemployment? Explanations abound: a productivity boom, the high rates of incarceration of those who would otherwise fall within the ranks of the unemployed, the openness of the U.S. economy to world trade and competition, among others.

The full story, however, has to do with class conflict and the relatively weak position of workers in the 1990s. Both the breakdown of the Phillips curve in the 1970s and the recent "disappearance" of the natural rate of unemployment are in essence a reflection of institutional and political changes that affect the bargaining strength of working people—in other words, their ability to organize effective unions and establish a decent living wage.

Following the Reagan offensive against trade unions, workers' power fell dramatically. Consequently, unionization rates and the real value of the minimum wage each fell precipitously between the late 1970s and the 1990s. The period of stagflation, in contrast, had been one of labor militancy and rising wages. (Although "stagflation" has a negative ring, by many measures nonsupervisory workers—i.e., the vast majority of the U.S. labor force—fared better in the economy of the early-to mid-1970s than they do today, even after the long 1990s economic expansion.) Labor's weaker position in the 1990s meant that despite low unemployment, workers were not able to win higher wages that would have spurred inflation.

The long period of stable prices and low interest rates in the United States now seems to be coming to a close. The cost of the Iraq War and rising oil prices, among other factors, have fueled expectations of a resurgence of inflation. At the same time, the near jobless recovery from the last recession might suggest that the "natural rate" of unemployment is on the rise again—and that we are witnessing yet another twist in the strange history of the Phillips curve!

With inflation rising (albeit slowly, and still relatively mild at around 4.2%), some business sectors will no doubt begin clamoring for tighter monetary policies that sacrifice job-creation and wage growth by slowing the economy growth. But these fears of inflation are probably misplaced. A moderate rate of inflation is conducive to the growth of real investment, and in the context of a decades-long squeeze on workers' wage share, there is room to expand employment without setting off a wage-price spiral. What workers need is not greater fiscal and monetary austerity, but rather a revival of a Keynesian program of "employment targeting" that would sustain full employment and empower workers to push for higher wages. It's not likely, however, that the owners of capital and their political allies would sit idly by were such a program to be enacted.

Article 6.9

HOT COMMODITIES, STUFFED MARKETS, AND EMPTY BELLIES

What's behind higher food prices?

BY BEN COLLINS
July/August 2008

Since 2003, prices of basic agricultural commodities such as corn, wheat, soybeans, and rice have skyrocketed worldwide, threatening to further impoverish hundreds of millions of the world's poor.

Shifts in fundamental supply and demand factors for food grains have undoubtedly contributed to higher food prices. Prominent among these shifts are the increasing diversion of food crops for biofuel production in the United States and Europe; sustained drought and water scarcity in Australia's wheat-growing regions; flooding in the U.S. grain belt; rising prices for oil and fertilizer worldwide; and the adoption of European and American meat-rich diets by the growing middle classes throughout Asia.

On top of these recent developments, long-term threats to worldwide agricultural output have eroded the world food system's resilience in the face of changing supply and demand. Although decades in the making, a loss of agricultural capacity worldwide caused by soil depletion, climate change, water scarcity, and urbanization has begun to take its toll on food production. Moreover, half a century of import restrictions and cheap agricultural exports by wealthy countries has devastated domestic food production capacity in poorer countries, forcing many countries that were once self-sufficient to rely on imported food from the world market.

At the same time, however, the growing presence of buy-and-hold investors in commodity markets has prompted heated debate among commodity traders, economists, and politicians over other possible causes of higher commodity prices apart from supply and demand shifts.

Since 2001, the declining value of the U.S. dollar, low U.S. interest rates, weak stock market returns, and accelerating inflation have drawn investment dollars away from stocks and into non-traditional investments such as commodities. This flight to perceived safety in commodity markets turned into a stampede in 2007 and early 2008, as a credit-induced financial crisis in the United States compounded these existing stresses on global financial markets.

Rising commodity prices and financial speculation on food are not new phenomena. The 1970s saw a similar rise in commodity prices in the United States, and in the 1920s, U.S. investors formed commodity pools to bet on commodity price movements. But the quantity and liquidity of money flowing through today's global markets is unprecedented in history. The current commodities boom could be a sign of looming agricultural scarcity, or it may prove to be a short-lived speculative bubble that will deflate over the next few months or years. But regardless of where agricultural commodity prices are headed, the boom has already begun to transform how food is financed, grown, and sold, and may dramatically change how people around the world eat (or don't).

Commodity Investment Goes Retail

Commodity exchanges exist as a mechanism for the producers and consumers of grains, energy, and livestock to transfer risk to financial institutions and other traders. For example, wheat farmers might seek to reduce the risk of price fluctuations by selling a contract for the future delivery of their wheat crop on a commodity exchange. This futures contract will guarantee a price for the farmer selling the contract, enabling them to pay for their planting costs, and avoid the risk that the price of wheat may decrease between the date they sell the contract and the date they agree to deliver the wheat. Food giants such as Kraft and Nabisco, as well as smaller bakers and grain consumers, typically purchase commodity futures contracts to avoid the opposite risk—that the price of their raw materials may increase in the future. (Commodity markets also trade "spot" contracts, which entitle the purchaser to the immediate delivery of a commodity.)

Because producers and consumers seek to reduce risk, they function as so-called hedgers in commodity markets. In contrast, commercial trading firms and other speculators bet on the price of a commodity rising or falling, buying and selling futures contracts frequently in order to profit from short-term changes in their prices.

Since 2001, commodity funds have gained in popularity as a mechanism for institutions and individuals to profit from increases in commodity prices. These funds purchase commodity futures contracts in order to simulate ownership of a commodity. By periodically rolling over commodity futures contracts prior to their maturity date and reinvesting the proceeds in new contracts, the funds allow investors to gain investment returns equivalent to the change in price of a single commodity, or an "index" of several commodities (hence the name "index investor").

Investors in these commodity index funds include public pension funds, university endowments, and even individual investors, through mutual funds, for example. Although these investors are similar to traditional commodity speculators in that both seek to profit from changes in price, traditional speculators zero in on short-term price shifts, while index investors are almost exclusively long-term buyers betting on higher commodity prices in the future.

Some observers have argued that index investors themselves may have pushed already-high prices of commodities even higher. Hedge fund manager Michael Masters testified to the U.S. Senate that the total holdings of commodity index investors on regulated U.S. exchanges have increased from $13 billion in 2003 to nearly $260 billion as of March 2008. And as of April 2008, index investors owned approximately 35% of all corn futures contracts on regulated exchanges in the United States, 42% of all soybean contracts, and 64% of all wheat contracts, compared to minimal holdings in 2001. As Masters emphasized, these are immense commodity holdings. The wheat contracts, for example, are good for the delivery of 1.3 billion bushels of wheat, equivalent to twice the United States' annual wheat consumption.

Index fund managers have defended against charges that commodity index investment contributes to higher prices, arguing that because index funds never take delivery on their futures contracts, they simulate commodity price shifts for their investors without affecting the price of the underlying commodity. Some economists have also expressed skepticism that investment demand has driven commodity prices higher. Paul Krugman of Princeton University has noted that there is no evidence of "the usual telltale signs of a speculative price boom" such as physical hoarding of commodities. Furthermore, Krugman and others have pointed to non-exchange traded commodities such as iron ore that have also experienced rapid price increases during recent years, arguing that fundamental supply and demand factors, not investors, are to blame for higher commodity prices.

Other economists and commodity market observers have argued that despite price increases in non-exchange traded commodities, and an absence of physical hoarding, the recent flood of money into commodity markets has altered the balance between speculators and hedgers, leading to higher prices and greater price volatility. Mack Frankfurter, a commodities trading advisor at Cervino Capital Management, suggests that the influx of commodity index investors has transformed commodity futures from tools for risk management to long-term investments, "causing a self-perpetuating feedback loop of ever higher prices."

One reason the precise impact of index investors on commodity prices is difficult to determine is that the U.S. commodity trading regulator, the Commodity Futures Trading Commission (CFTC), does not collect data on so-called "over-the-counter" commodity trading—that is, trading on unregulated markets—even though the agency estimated that 85% of commodity index investment takes place on these markets. Because Masters's data on the holdings of commodity index investors only include the 15% of index investor contracts that are held on CFTC-regulated exchanges, total commodity index investor holdings may be much higher than his estimates.

In testimony that warned of the influence of these unregulated markets on commodity prices, Michael Greenberger, the former head of the CFTC's Division of Trading and Markets, estimated that if unregulated trading of energy and agricultural commodities were eliminated, the price of oil would drop by 25% to 50% "overnight." If Greenberger is correct, the effect on food commodity prices would likely be similar. However, index investment is just one of many avenues through which money can enter commodity markets, making it difficult to assess the impact of index investors without taking into account the recent deregulation of U.S. commodity markets that has facilitated the current boom in food and energy investments.

Commodity Trading Regulation, Enron-Style

Commodity index investment is deeply intertwined with the growth of unregulated commodity trading authorized by the Commodity Futures Modernization Act of 2000. Before 2000, U.S. commodity futures contracts were traded exclusively on regulated exchanges under the oversight of the CFTC. Traders were required to disclose their holdings of each commodity and adhere to strict position limits, which set a maximum number of futures contracts that an individual institution could hold. These regulations were intended to prevent market manipulation by traders who might otherwise attempt to build up concentrated holdings of futures contracts in order to manipulate the price of a commodity.

The 2000 law effectively deregulated commodity trading in the United States by exempting over-the-counter commodity trading outside of regulated exchanges from CFTC oversight. Soon after the bill was passed, several unregulated commodity exchanges opened for trading, allowing investors, hedge funds, and investment banks to trade commodities futures contracts without any position limits, disclosure requirements, or regulatory oversight. Since then, unregulated over-the-counter commodity trading has grown exponentially. The total value of all over-the-counter commodity contracts was estimated to be $9 trillion at the end of 2007, or nearly twice the value of the $4.78 trillion in commodity contracts traded on regulated U.S. exchanges.

Once these unregulated commodity markets were created, energy traders and hedge funds began to use them to place massive bets on commodity prices. Enron famously exploited deregulated electricity markets in 2001, when the firm managed to generate unheard-of profits by using its trading operations to effectively withhold electricity and charge extortionate rates from power grids in California and other western states.

Although Enron went bankrupt later that year, the hedge fund Amaranth later exploited unregulated natural gas markets prior to its 2006 collapse. The fund had been heavily invested in complicated bets on the price of natural gas, borrowing eight times its assets to trade natural gas futures, and lost $6.5 billion when natural gas prices moved in the wrong direction. One month prior to Amaranth's collapse, the New York Mercantile Exchange (NYMEX), which is regulated by the CFTC, asked Amaranth to reduce its huge natural gas position. Amaranth reduced its position at NYMEX's request, but purchased identical positions on the unregulated InterContinental Exchange, where its transactions were invisible to regulators until the fund finally collapsed.

Amaranth's implosion demonstrated the ineffectiveness of regulating some commodity exchanges but not others. Thanks to the Commodity Futures Modernization Act, traders could flout position limits and disclosure rules with impunity, simply by re-routing trades to unregulated exchanges. Although index investment in commodities does not typically involve white-knuckle, leveraged bets on a single commodity's short-term performance, index investment was made possible by the same deregulated environment exploited by Amaranth and Enron. Like Amaranth, commodity index investors commonly purchase futures contracts on unregulated markets when they exceed CFTC position limits on futures contracts for a particular commodity. And other financial actors such as investment banks, hedge funds, or even the sovereign wealth funds of other countries may also be heavily invested in these over-the-counter commodity contracts, but since this trading is unregulated and unreported, the holders of these $9 trillion worth of contracts remain anonymous.

This year, the CFTC has faced intense scrutiny from investors, politicians, farmers, and agricultural traders over the unprecedented volatility and price increases of several agricultural and energy commodities traded on U.S. exchanges. A lively CFTC roundtable on commodity markets in April appeared to confirm arguments made by Frankfurter, Greenberger, Masters, and other critics of commodity index investment. Representatives for farmers, grain elevator operators, and commercial bankers at the hearing repeatedly stressed that commodity markets were "broken," while the only pleas for calm came from CFTC economists and representatives for index investors and the financial industry. Unlike index investors, farmers have not benefited greatly from higher commodity prices, because extremely high levels of market volatility have made it difficult for some farmers to finance crop planting. National Farmers Union president Tom Buis sounded a particularly dire warning about the consequences of tight commodity supplies and burgeoning index investment demand: "We've got a train wreck coming in agriculture that's bigger than anything else we've seen."

Following these warnings from farmers and food producers about the presence of index investors in commodity markets, the CFTC's acting chair publicly acknowledged the ongoing debate over "whether the massive amount of money coming into the markets is overwhelming the system." Despite this admission, Greenberger, the former CFTC official, remains skeptical of the agency's capacity and willingness to regulate commodity markets effectively. He urged Congress and the Federal Trade Commission to circumvent the CFTC's authority and eliminate unregulated over-the-counter commodity trading. Recently, faced with strong criticism from Congress, the CFTC retreated further from its claim that commodity markets are functioning normally. A CFTC commissioner admitted: "We didn't have the data that we needed to make the statements that we made, and the data we did have didn't support our declarative statements. If we were so right, why the heck are we doing a study now?"

The Consequences of Financializing Food

Facing political pressure by constituents over high oil and food prices, several members of Congress have sponsored legislation that would bar index investors from commodity markets. One bill proposed by Sen. Joseph Lieberman (Ind-Conn.) would prohibit public and private pension funds with more than $500 million in assets from trading in commodity futures, and other bills would limit the maximum number of futures contracts an index investor could hold. These bills may stem the flood of money from index investors into commodities, but comprehensive reform is needed to reverse the Commodity Futures Modernization Act's authorization of over-the-counter commodity trading. Absent an outright repeal of this so-called "Enron loophole," energy and agricultural commodities will continue to be traded outside the reach of government regulation, making future Enron- and Amaranth-style market disruptions inevitable.

Ultimately, eliminating unregulated commodity trading cannot address the fundamental causes of higher agricultural prices. Even if speculative buying is curtailed, supply and demand factors such as falling crop yields, destructive trade policies, and the growing use of biofuels have likely brought the age of cheap food to an end. However, if the critics of commodity index investment are correct, then these investors have amplified recent food price shocks and are needlessly contributing to the impoverishment of the world's poorest citizens. Even though commodity market transparency and regulatory oversight will not solve the global food crisis, eliminating unregulated commodity trading can help resolve the debate over the effects of index investors on commodity prices and restore the accountability of commodity markets to the social interests they were originally established to serve.

Sources: Michael Masters, testimony before the Committee on Homeland Security and Government Affairs, United States Senate, May 20, 2008; Daniel P. Collins, "CFTC to up spec limits," *Futures,* May 1, 2005; Paul Krugman, "Fuels on the Hill," *New York Times,* June 27, 2008; Michael Frankfurter, *The Mysterious Case of the Commodity Conundrum, Securitization of Commodities, and Systemic Concerns,* Parts 1-3, www.marketoracle.co.uk; Michael Frankfurter and Davide Accomazzo, "Is Managed Futures an Asset Class? The Search for the Beta of Commodity Futures," December 31, 2007, *Graziadio Business Report*; "Regulator Admits to Futures Tracking Volatility," Associated Press, June 4, 2008; Commodity Futures Trading Commission, *CFTC Announces Agricultural Market Initiatives.* June 3, 2008; Michael Greenberger, testimony before the Committee on Commerce, Science, and Transportation, United States Senate, June 3, 2008; Sinclair Stewart and Paul Waldie. "Who is responsible for the global food crisis?" *Globe and Mail,* May 30, 2008; Commodity Futures Trading Commission, *Agricultural Markets Roundtable,* April 22, 2008; Ann Davis, "Commodities Regulator Under Fire—CFTC Scrutinized As Congress Looks Into Oil-Price Jump," *Wall Street Journal,* July 7, 2008; Ed Wallace, "ICE, ICE, Baby," *Houston Chronicle,* May 19, 2008; Laura Mandaro, "Lieberman plans would bar funds from commodities," *Marketwatch,* June 18, 2008; "Our Confusing Economy, Explained," *Fresh Air,* April 3, 2008, www.npr.org.

Chapter 7

PERSPECTIVES ON MACROECONOMIC POLICY

INTRODUCTION

A few years back, political economist Bob Sutcliffe developed a sure-fire economic indicator that he called the Marx/Keynes ratio—the ratio of references to Karl Marx to references to John Maynard Keynes in Paul Samuelson's *Economics*, the best-selling introductory economics textbook during the decades following World War II. In a recession or a period of sluggish economic growth, the Marx/Keynes ratio would climb, as social commentators and even economists fretted over the future of capitalism. In economic booms, however, Marx's predictions of the collapse of capitalism disappeared from the pages of Samuelson's textbook, while the paeans to Keynesian demand-management policies multiplied.

Today Sutcliffe's ratio wouldn't work very well. Marx has been pushed off the pages of most introductory macroeconomics textbooks altogether, and even Keynes has been given only a minor role. Mainstream textbooks now favor the "New Classical" economics, which depicts the private economy as inherently stable and self-regulating, and dismiss Keynesian demand-management policies as ineffectual or counterproductive. Our authors disagree. In this chapter, they reintroduce schools of thought that have been removed from economics textbooks in recent decades and critically assess New Classical economics. And they offer a critical assessment of the forces that brought on the economic crisis of 2008 and 2009 and what to do about it.

John Miller and Gina Neff start with a down-to-earth account of New Classical "rational expectations" models, in which markets clear instantaneously and bungling government bureaucrats can only make a mess of things. Drawing on the writings of Keynesian and New Keynesian economists, Miller and Neff argue that rational expectations models are contradicted by the historical record, which shows that bigger government has brought milder, not more severe, business cycle fluctuations (Article 7.1).

Robert Pollin (Article 7.2) attacks the underpinnings of the neoliberal policy prescription for the global economy. As he sees it, the unfettered globalization of free markets will be unable to resolve three basic problems: an ever-larger reserve army of the unemployed that reduces the bargaining power of workers in all countries (the Marx problem); the inherent instability and volatility of investment and financial markets (the Keynes problem); and the erosion of the protections of the welfare state (the Polanyi problem).

Alejandro Reuss takes a close look at what Keynes actually had to say about the efficacy of fiscal policy in his most famous book, *The General Theory*. Keynes was a strong advocate of fiscal policy, especially government spending. Reuss explains how Keynes challenged the "Treasury view" that government spending could not get the economy going because it would "crowd out" private investment, the same argument today's conservatives have invoked against the Obama stimulus package (Article 7.3).

Reuss also contributes a primer on Marxist economics. Marx rejected the idea of a self-equilibrating economy, and argued that capitalism was inherently dynamic and unstable. Reuss describes some of Marx's key ideas, including the nature of capitalist exploitation, and what Marx saw as two ingredients of an eventual crisis of capitalism: overproduction and the falling rate of profit (Article 7.4).

Randy Albelda offers a feminist analysis of poverty and gender. Feminist economists have illuminated the ways in which having and caring for children alters the economic status of women—including those who are not mothers but are still relegated to poorly paid care-giving jobs. Feminist economists, argues Albelda, provide the best understanding of the obstacles low-income families face and the options that might improve their position in today's economy (Article 7.5).

The remaining articles in the chapter examine the recent financial and economic crisis through the wider lens offered by a political-economy perspective. Arthur MacEwan identifies three root causes of the crisis—growing economic and social power in the hands of the wealthy, free-market ideology, and rising inequality. He argues that addressing these factors through expanded social programs, stronger unions, and market regulation are all crucial steps to making the economy more egalitarian, and will go a long way toward resolving capitalism's current problems (Article 7.6). John Miller takes the measure of this disastrous downturn, the worst since the Great Depression. Miller argues that undoing the repressive and deregulatory policies that brought on the crisis is the key to getting the economy going again in a way that will improve the lot of most people, not just economic elites (Article 7.7).

Discussion Questions

1. (Article 7.1) How do classical economists argue that macroeconomies are inherently stable, and that government intervention is ineffective or counterproductive? Are their arguments convincing?

2. (Article 7.1) Why are Keynesians convinced that markets don't clear instantaneously, and that government intervention can and must stabilize market economies? Evaluate the evidence for their position.

3. (Article 7.2) Summarize the Marx, Keynes, and Polanyi problems. Why does Pollin think that neoliberal globalization policies will be unable to resolve them?

4. (Article 7.3) Why did Keynes think that the dollar-for-dollar crowding-out argument (the "Treasury view") is mistaken? And how might Keynes respond to the arguments today's conservatives have leveled against the Obama stimulus package?

5. (Article 7.4) In Marxist theory, how is a dynamic capitalist economy felled by instability? What roles do a "falling rate of profit," a "reserve army of the unemployed," and "overproduction" play in Marx's theory of how capitalism will fall into crisis? Do you think today's macroeconomy displays any of those tendencies?

6. (Article 7.5) How does feminist economics' focus on gender challenge other theories of poverty? How are feminist theories of poverty different from Keynesian, Marxist, Institutionalist, and neoclassical analyses?

7. (Article 7.6) In MacEwan's analysis, how did inequality, power, and ideology lead to the current crisis? In what ways would addressing these causes alleviate the crisis?

8. (Article 7.7) According to Miller, "The Repression" is the right name for the current economic crisis. Why does he choose that name? In your opinion, what is the right name for today's economic crisis? Why?

Article 7.1

THE REVENGE OF THE CLASSICS

BY JOHN MILLER AND GINA NEFF
May/June 1996, revised April 2002

Nineteen ninety-five was not a good year for the welfare state. A Gingrich-led Congress attempted to pull the plug on universal entitlements for the poor, from welfare to Medicaid. And the Royal Swedish Academy of Science awarded the Nobel Prize in economics to Robert Lucas, a 58-year-old University of Chicago economist, for his "insights into the difficulties of using economic policy to control the economy."

Using sophisticated mathematics and economic models, Lucas has persuaded much of the economics profession that the economic policies John Maynard Keynes developed to combat the Great Depression—the economic underpinnings of the welfare state and the mixed economy—are ineffective.

What would Lucas do instead? Forsake those policies, dismantle the welfare state, and embrace the market. That was a job that, back in the mid-1990s, Gingrich and his crowd seemed only too happy to take up. They were glad to join forces with a Federal Reserve Board (the "Fed") already under the influence of the conservative counterrevolution in macroeconomics, led initially by Milton Friedman, another University of Chicago monetary theorist, and then by Lucas.

The Fed has accepted the futility of using monetary policy to promote long-run employment, leaving inflation alone as the ultimate target of its policies. In addition, the Fed's practice of making early announcements of changes in monetary policy, which is probably a good thing, can be directly attributed to Lucas. He has argued that unannounced changes provoke instability in the private sector instead of muting it.

Lucas and his school of followers call themselves New Classical economists. Like the classical economists who predated Keynes, these modern conservatives believe the economy possesses powerful self-correcting forces that guarantee full employment. Their vision of a stable market economy rests on three building blocks: rational expectations, market clearing, and imperfect information.

Let's look first at rational expectations, a notion which does seem rational enough. After all, every one of our economic actions is directed toward the future. Using whatever economic information we can get our hands on about prices, growth, and other economic activity, we predict our economic future. And usually we are good at it. When fellow workers are getting laid off at the company we are employed in, for instance, chances are that buying an expensive house is not at the top of our to-do list.

When we do get things wrong, we reevaluate our predictions. And, says Lucas, we keep up this process of prediction and evaluation until there is no way to improve those predictions, ensuring that we won't consistently make the same forecasting mistakes. In that way we form what Lucas calls "rational expectations." As he sees it, people act much like experienced bettors at the track. They get good at picking horses, but are never able to pick the winning horse every time.

Lucas has made a career out of expressing these ideas in mathematical terms. He argues that predictions about the rates of interest, unemployment, and inflation shape how consumers, workers, and business people decide their economic future. From consumers buying a new home to workers looking for a new job to bosses hiring or laying off employees, rational expectations theory seeks to describe what motivates economic actors.

Adam Smith Returns

But Lucas does not stop there—with merely a theory of how people make economic decisions. New Classical economic theory also assumes that markets "clear" instantaneously. In the bat of an eye, prices adjust so that how much sellers bring to market just matches whatever buyers take away. For instance, in a labor market, wages (the price of labor) fall quickly enough to guarantee that every worker willing to work (or sell their labor) at the going wage finds a job with an employer (or buyer of labor). For New Classical economists that constitutes full employment. Only workers unwilling to work at the market clearing wage are out of a job. Those workers are voluntarily unemployed—they chose not to work and brought unemployment upon themselves.

The point here is simple: Market capitalism is stable. "Price flexibility" and "market clearing" guarantee a booming full-employment economy—one that does not need economic policymaking to stabilize it. In fact, in Lucas's framework, government attempts to fine tune the economy actually backfire.

Here's why. If people expect the government to change economic policy, they too change their economic actions. That is rational expectations at work. And when prices and wages adjust instantaneously as people scramble to match their economic actions to their new expectations, those adjustments nullify the government's actions.

For instance, suppose the Fed tries to reduce unemployment by increasing the money supply, in the hope of raising spending and putting people to work. Lucas's rational workers anticipate that more spending and hiring will bring not only higher wages but also instantaneously higher prices, leaving their purchasing power unchanged. In this world people are not forced to work to avoid starving, but rather choose to offer their services only when their inflation-adjusted wages are sufficiently high. So no rational worker is lured into the market. The Fed's actions fail to lower unemployment, and succeed only in driving up prices.

As far-fetched as this theory might seem, the stagflation (simultaneous stagnation and inflation) of the 1970s lent these ideas plausibility. New Classical economics gathered adherents as Keynesian policies seemed increasingly ineffectual.

In New Classical economics, meddlesome government is not only ineffective, it is the enemy. Why does Lucas's inherently stable capitalism suffer through the ups and downs of the business cycle? His answer: Washington types trying to fine tune the economy. This is where imperfect information, the third building block of Lucas' theory, enters the model. Even Lucas's rational actors in this market-clearing world possess only limited information and can be fooled by bungling bureaucrats and re-election minded politicians who launch surprise (unannounced) changes in government policy.

People know the economy around them—their own wages or profits, the prices of the products they sell and those that they buy—better than what is going on across the economy. So if the Federal Reserve, without announcing it, increases the money supply in order to beef up spending and lower unemployment, even people with rational expectations can be confounded. They see their prices or wages go up, but don't anticipate prices going up elsewhere in the economy.

And that causes a problem. Corporate managers, for instance, hike up production, thinking that a higher price must signal a soaring demand for their products. Output rises across the economy. But soon inventories pile up, because the price increases were due to general inflation rather than greater demand. Corporate managers realize that the higher production levels were unwarranted, and they order a cutback—below even the initial output. The economy contracts, causing a recession.

What can return stability to the economy? Forsaking government intervention into the economy. In Lucas's world, unannounced changes in government policy cause the ups and downs of the business cycle. And announced changes in government policies are fully anticipated and therefore ineffective. For Lucas, the only rational course of action is to turn our backs on active government attempts to soften the blows of the market economy.

Keynesian Critics

Not all economists are convinced by Lucas's arguments or support the draconian policy implications of New Classical economics. The proponents of Keynesian economic policy have been among the most vocal critics. While Keynesians may accept the idea of rationally formed expectations, they find the ideas of flexible prices and clearing markets preposterous. One Nobel laureate, James Tobin, called these ideas a "great myth"—powerful in its effect on how we see the economy, but nonetheless a myth.

Another Keynesian Nobel winner, Franco Modigliani, railed that it is as if "what happened in the United States in the 1930s was a severe attack of contagious laziness." For these dyed-in-the-wool Keynesians, the private economy will not necessarily be driven toward full employment even in the long run and Keynes's fundamental message still holds: "a modern monetized economy needs to be stabilized, can be stabilized, and should be stabilized" by government intervention.

More recently, "New Keynesian" economists have fashioned a different critique of New Classical economics. These modern Keynesians accept not only the idea that people form rational expectations about what will happen in the economy, but also the idea that in the long run the private economy tends toward full employment. Still, they argue that for good economic reasons, wages and prices are "sticky" and much slower to adjust than Lucas suggests. For instance, given the high cost of negotiating a wage settlement, most labor contracts are long term. In the United States, nearly 80% of union contracts are for three years and only about two-fifths of them contain cost-of-living adjustments. Corporations also often rely on long-term pricing agreements to afford them the price stability necessary to bid on contracts.

Thus, while the economy might eventually reach the full employment outcome Lucas' model predicts, the wait is likely to be intolerably long. What's needed is active government intervention designed for the workable policy time frame of three to five years, for as Keynes once wrote, "in the long run we are all dead."

More fundamentally, Lucas's way of thinking exaggerates the amount of power people really have over their economic lives. Economist E. Ray Canterbery writes mockingly that in the New Classical school, "The marginal blue collar worker on his way to the factory anticipates an increase in the money supply then fully anticipates the inflation within his monetarist model ... and a fall in the real interest rates and a fall in real wages. The worker does a U-turn, drives home, and voluntarily disemploys himself." In New Classical economics bosses raise their workers' wages when the economy is doing well rather than pocketing the extra profits. And workers have the power to choose whether or not to work, to ask for higher wages when they expect inflation to go up, or to move into a different industry when they fear the worst for their own job. This is indeed a great myth.

Perhaps the most mythical aspect of New Classical economics is its claim that capitalism is stable—that if only policy makers would cease their interventions, economic stability would be assured and full employment guaranteed. But the instability of capitalism has been with us since long before Keynesian economic policy, which after all was a response to the Great Depression of the 1930s.

And that instability will worsen if New Classical economics is able to undo what Keynesian policy makers have done to mitigate the instability of capitalism since World War II. Current economic anxiety will heighten as workers struggle with real-life adjustments like stagnant wages and rising layoffs. At the same time, Lucas and his New Classical followers will continue to construct mathematical paeans to the rationality of these adjustments and the inherent stability of capitalism, even if that stability is evident only in their seminar rooms and the the Royal Swedish Academy of Science.

Resources: Robert J. Gordon, *Macroeconomics*, 6th ed., 1994; Robert Lucas, *Studies in Business Cycle Theory*, 1989; N. Gregory Mankiw, "A Quick Refresher Course in Macroeconomics," *Journal of Economic Literature*, December 1990; James Tobin, *Asset Accumulation and Economic Activity*, 1980; *The End of Economic Man*, reviewed by E. Ray Canterbery in *Challenge*, Nov./Dec. 1995.

Article 7.2

WHAT'S WRONG WITH NEOLIBERALISM?
The Marx, Keynes, and Polanyi problems.

BY ROBERT POLLIN

During the years of the Clinton administration, the term "Washington Consensus" began circulating to designate the common policy positions of the U.S. administration along with the International Monetary Fund (IMF) and World Bank. These positions, implemented in the United States and abroad, included free trade, a smaller government share of the economy, and the deregulation of financial markets. This policy approach has also become widely known as *neoliberalism*, a term which draws upon the classical meaning of the word *liberalism*.

Classical liberalism is the political philosophy that embraces the virtues of free-market capitalism and the corresponding minimal role for government interventions, especially as regards measures to promote economic equality within capitalist societies. Thus, a classical liberal would favor minimal levels of government spending and taxation, and minimal levels of government regulation over the economy, including financial and labor markets. According to the classical liberal view, businesses should be free to operate as they wish, and to succeed or fail as such in a competitive marketplace. Meanwhile, consumers rather than government should be responsible for deciding which businesses produce goods and services that are of sufficient quality as well as reasonably priced. Businesses that provide overexpensive or low-quality products will then be out-competed in the marketplace regardless of the regulatory standards established by governments. Similarly, if businesses offer workers a wage below what the worker is worth, then a competitor firm will offer this worker a higher wage. The firm unwilling to offer fair wages would not survive over time in the competitive marketplace.

This same reasoning also carries over to the international level. Classical liberals favor free trade between countries rather than countries operating with tariffs or other barriers to the free flow of goods and services between countries. They argue that restrictions on the free movement of products and money between countries only protects uncompetitive firms from market competition, and thus holds back the economic development of countries that choose to erect such barriers.

Neoliberalism and the Washington Consensus are contemporary variants of this longstanding political and economic philosophy. The major difference between classical liberalism as a philosophy and contemporary neoliberalism as a set of policy measures is with implementation. Washington Consensus policy makers are committed to free-market policies when they support the interests of big business, as, for example, with lowering regulations at the workplace. But these same policy makers become far less insistent on free-market principles when invoking such principles might damage big business interests. Federal Reserve and IMF interventions to bail out wealthy asset holders during the frequent global financial crises in the 1990s are obvious violations of free-market precepts.

Broadly speaking, the effects of neoliberalism in the less developed countries over the 1990s reflected the experience of the Clinton years in the United States. A high proportion of less developed countries were successful, just in the manner of the United States under Clinton, in reducing inflation and government budget deficits, and creating a more welcoming climate for foreign trade, multinational corporations, and financial market investors. At the same time, most of Latin America, Africa, and Asia—with China being the one major exception—experienced deepening problems of poverty and inequality in the 1990s, along with slower growth and frequent financial market crises, which in turn produced still more poverty and inequality.

If free-market capitalism is a powerful mechanism for creating wealth, why does a neoliberal policy approach, whether pursued by Clinton, Bush, or the IMF, produce severe difficulties in terms of inequality and financial instability, which in turn diminish the market mechanism's ability to even promote economic growth? It will be helpful to consider this in terms of three fundamental problems that result from a free-market system, which I term "the Marx Problem," "the Keynes problem," and "the Polanyi problem." Let us take these up in turn.

The Marx Problem

Does someone in your family have a job and, if so, how much does it pay? For the majority of the world's population, how one answers these two questions determines, more than anything else, what one's standard of living will be. But how is it decided whether a person has a job and what their pay will be? Getting down to the most immediate level of decision-making, this occurs through various types of bargaining in labor markets between workers and employers. Karl Marx argued that, in a free-market economy generally, workers have less power than employers in this bargaining process because workers cannot fall back on other means of staying alive if they fail to get hired into a job. Capitalists gain higher profits through having this relatively stronger bargaining position. But Marx also stressed that workers' bargaining power diminishes further when unemployment and underemployment are high, since that means that employed workers can be more readily replaced by what Marx called "the reserve army" of the unemployed outside the office, mine, or factory gates.

Neoliberalism has brought increasing integration of the world's labor markets through reducing barriers to international trade and investment by multinationals. For workers in high-wage countries such as the United States, this effectively means that the reserve army of workers willing to accept jobs at lower pay than U.S. workers expands to include workers in less developed countries. It isn't the case that businesses will always move to less developed countries or that domestically produced goods will necessarily be supplanted by imports from low-wage countries. The point is that U.S. workers face an increased *credible* threat that they can be supplanted. If everything else were to remain the same in the U.S. labor market, this would then mean that global integration would erode the bargaining power of U.S. workers and thus tend to bring lower wages.

But even if this is true for workers in the United States and other rich countries, shouldn't it also mean that workers in poor countries have greater job opportunities and better bargaining positions? In fact, there are areas where workers in poor countries are gaining enhanced job opportunities through international trade and multinational investments. But these gains are generally quite limited. This is because a long-term transition out of agriculture in poor countries continues to expand the reserve army of unemployed and underemployed workers in these countries as well. Moreover, when neoliberal governments in poor countries reduce their support for agriculture—through cuts in both tariffs on imported food products and subsidies for domestic farmers—this makes it more difficult for poor farmers to compete with multinational agribusiness firms. This is especially so when the rich countries maintain or increase their own agricultural supports, as has been done in the United States under Bush. In addition, much of the growth in the recently developed export-oriented manufacturing sectors of poor countries has failed to significantly increase jobs even in this sector. This is because the new export-oriented production sites frequently do not represent net additions to the country's total supply of manufacturing firms. They rather replace older firms that were focused on supplying goods to domestic markets. The net result is that the number of people looking for jobs in the developing countries grows faster than the employers seeking new workers. Here again, workers' bargaining power diminishes.

This does not mean that global integration of labor markets must necessarily bring weakened bargaining power and lower wages for workers. But it does mean that unless some non-market forces in the economy, such as government regulations or effective labor unions, are able to counteract these market processes, workers will indeed continue to experience weakened bargaining strength and eroding living standards.

The Keynes Problem

In a free-market economy, investment spending by businesses is the main driving force that produces economic growth, innovation, and jobs. But as John Maynard Keynes stressed, private investment decisions are also unavoidably risky ventures. Businesses have to put up money without knowing whether they will produce any profits in the future. As such, investment spending by business is likely to fluctuate far more than, say, decisions by households as to how much they will spend per week on groceries.

But investment fluctuations will also affect overall spending in the economy, including that of households. When investment spending declines, this means that businesses will hire fewer workers. Unemployment rises as a result, and this in turn will lead to cuts in household spending. Declines in business investment spending can therefore set off a vicious cycle: the investment decline leads to employment declines, then to cuts in household spending and corresponding increases in household financial problems, which then brings still more cuts in business investment and financial difficulties for the business sector. This is how capitalist economies produce mass unemployment, financial crises, and recessions.

Keynes also described a second major source of instability associated with private investment activity. Precisely because private investments are highly risky propositions, financial markets have evolved to make this risk more manageable for any given investor. Through financial markets, investors can sell off their investments if they need or want to, converting their office buildings, factories, and stock of machinery into cash much more readily than they could if they always had to find buyers on their own. But Keynes warned that when financial markets convert long-term assets into short-term commitments for investors, this also fosters a speculative mentality in the markets. What becomes central for investors is not whether a company's products will produce profits over a long term, but rather whether the short-term financial market investors *think* a company's fortunes will be strong enough in the present and immediate future to drive the stock price up. Or, to be more precise, what really matters for a speculative investor is not what they think about a given company's prospects per se, but rather what they think *other investors are thinking*, since that will be what determines where the stock price goes in the short term.

Because of this, the financial markets are highly susceptible to rumors, fads, and all sorts of deceptive accounting practices, since all of these can help drive the stock price up in the present, regardless of what they accomplish in the longer term. Thus, if U.S. stock traders are convinced that Alan Greenspan is a *maestro*, and if there is news that he is about to intervene with some kind of policy shift, then the rumor of Greenspan's policy shift can itself drive prices up, as the more nimble speculators try to keep one step ahead of the herd of Greenspan-philes.

Still, as with the Marx problem, it does not follow that the inherent instability of private investment and speculation in financial markets are uncontrollable, leading inevitably to persistent problems of mass unemployment and recession. But these social pathologies will become increasingly common through a neoliberal policy approach committed to minimizing government interventions to stabilize investment.

The Polanyi Problem

Karl Polanyi wrote his classic book *The Great Transformation* in the context of the 1930s depression, World War II, and the developing worldwide competition with Communist governments. He was also reflecting on the 1920s, dominated, as with our current epoch, by a free-market ethos. Polanyi wrote of the 1920s that "economic liberalism made a supreme bid to restore the self-regulation of the system by eliminating all interventionist policies which interfered with the freedom of markets."

Considering all of these experiences, Polanyi argued that for market economies to function with some modicum of fairness, they must be embedded in social norms and institutions that effectively promote broadly accepted notions of the common good. Otherwise, acquisitiveness and competition—the two driving forces of market economies—achieve overwhelming dominance as cultural forces, rendering life under capitalism a Hobbesian "war of all against all." This same idea is also central for Adam Smith. Smith showed how the invisible hand of self-interest and competition will yield higher levels of individual effort that increases the wealth of nations, but that it will also produce the corruption of our moral sentiments unless the market is itself governed at a fundamental level by norms of solidarity.

In the post-World War II period, various social democratic movements within the advanced capitalist economies adapted the Polanyi perspective. They argued in favor of government interventions to achieve three basic ends: stabilizing overall demand in the economy at a level that will provide for full employment; creating a financial market environment that is stable and conducive to the effective allocation of investment funds; and distributing equitably the rewards from high employment and a stable investment process. There were two basic means of achieving equitable distribution: relatively rapid wage growth, promoted by labor laws that were supportive of unions, minimum wage standards, and similar interventions in labor markets; and welfare state policies, including progressive taxation and redistributive programs such as Social Security. The political ascendancy of these ideas was the basis for a dramatic increase in the role of government in the post-World War II capitalist economies. As one indicator of this, total government expenditures in the United States rose from 8% of GDP in 1913, to 21% in 1950, then to 38% by 1992. The International Monetary Fund and World Bank were also formed in the mid-1940s to advance such policy ideas throughout the world—that is, to implement policies virtually the opposite of those they presently favor. John Maynard Keynes himself was a leading intellectual force contributing to the initial design of the International Monetary Fund and World Bank.

From Social Democracy to Neoliberalism

But the implementation of a social democratic capitalism, guided by a commitment to full employment and the welfare state, did also face serious and persistent difficulties, and we need to recognize them as part of a consideration of the Marx, Keynes, and Polanyi problems. In particular, many sectors of business opposed efforts to sustain full employment because, following the logic of the Marx problem, full employment provides greater bargaining power for workers in labor markets, even if it also increases the economy's total production of goods and services. Greater worker bargaining power can also create inflationary pressures because businesses will try to absorb their higher wage costs by raising prices. In addition, market-inhibiting financial regulations limit the capacity of financial market players to diversify their risk and speculate.

Corporations in the United States and Western Europe were experiencing some combination of these problems associated with social democratic capitalism. In particular, they were faced with rising labor costs associated with low unemployment rates, which then led to either inflation, when corporations had the ability to pass on their higher labor costs to consumers, or to a squeeze on profits, when competitive pressures prevented corporations from raising their prices in response to the rising labor costs. These pressures were compounded by the two oil price "shocks" initiated by the Oil Producing Exporting Countries (OPEC)—an initial fourfold increase in the world price of oil in 1973, then a second four-fold price spike in 1979.

These were the conditions that by the end of the 1970s led to the decline of social democratic approaches to policymaking and the ascendancy of neoliberalism. The two leading signposts of this historic transition were the election in 1979 of Margaret Thatcher as Prime Minister of the United Kingdom and in 1980 of Ronald Reagan as the President of the United States. Indeed, it was at this point that Mrs. Thatcher made her famous pronouncement that "there is no alternative" to neoliberalism.

This brings us to the contemporary era of smaller government, fiscal stringency and deregulation, i.e., to neoliberalism under Clinton, Bush, and throughout the less-developed world. The issue is not a simple juxtaposition between either regulating or deregulating markets. Rather it is that markets have become deregulated to support the interests of business and financial markets, even as these same groups still benefit greatly from many forms of government support, including investment subsidies, tax concessions, and rescue operations when financial crises get out of hand. At the same time, the deregulation of markets that favors business and finance is correspondingly the most powerful regulatory mechanism limiting the demands of workers, in that deregulation has been congruent with the worldwide expansion of the reserve army of labor and the declining capacity of national governments to implement full-employment and macroeconomic policies. In other words, deregulation has exacerbated both the Marx and Keynes problems.

Given the ways in which neoliberalism worsens the Marx, Keynes, and Polanyi problems, we should not be surprised by the wreckage that it has wrought since the late 1970s, when it became the ascendant policy model. Over the past generation, with neoliberals in the saddle almost everywhere in the world, the results have been straightforward: worsening inequality and poverty, along with slower economic growth and far more unstable financial markets. While Margaret Thatcher famously declared that "there is no alternative" to neoliberalism, there are in fact alternatives. The experience over the past generation demonstrates how important it is to develop them in the most workable and coherent ways possible.

Article 7.3

FISCAL POLICY AND "CROWDING OUT"

BY ALEJANDRO REUSS
May/June 2009

In response to the deepest recession in the United States since the Great Depression, the Obama administration proposed a large fiscal "stimulus" plan. (Fiscal policies involve government spending and taxation. A fiscal stimulus involves increases in government spending or tax cuts, or both.) The current stimulus plan, after some compromises between the Obama administration and Republicans in Congress, included both substantial tax cuts and increases in government spending. Together, they would increase the federal government deficit by over $700 billion.

A fiscal stimulus is a standard "Keynesian" response to a recession. The logic behind these policies is that recessions can be caused by insufficient total demand for goods and services. If saving (a "leakage" from demand) exceeds investment (an "injection" of demand), there will not be enough demand to buy all the goods and services that the economy is capable of producing at the "full employment" level. Some goods will go unsold, and firms will reduce output. They will cut jobs, cancel supply orders, and even close production facilities. The economy will spiral into a recession.

In standard Keynesian models, either tax cuts or increased government spending can increase total demand, and therefore total output and employment. An initial increase in spending (by either the government or the recipients of the tax cuts) results in new income for other individuals, who then go on to spend part (not all) of this income, which results in new income for still other individuals, and so on. Ultimately, this series of additions to income results in a total increase in GDP greater than the original increase in government spending or reduction in taxes. The increase in real GDP divided by the initial spending increase is called the "multiplier." The standard Keynesian view implies a multiplier greater than one.

The Conservative Critique

Conservative economists, whose intellectual heritage includes decades-old attempts to refute Keynesian theory, disagree with this view. They argue that government spending cannot possibly increase overall economic activity, and that the stimulus plan is therefore doomed to fail. This position is sometimes known as the "Treasury view" (because it mirrors the arguments of the British Treasury Department during the Great Depression) or the theory of "crowding out." The new government spending, these economists argue, "has to come from somewhere," either from higher taxes or increased government borrowing. Either way, the increase in government spending will come at the expense of private spending.

If the spending is financed by tax increases, conservative economists argue, this will reduce individuals' after-tax incomes and therefore reduce their spending. If it is financed through borrowing, the increased government demand for loans will drive up interest rates, and this will "crowd out" private investment. (Some private investment projects that would have been profitable at lower interest rates would not be profitable at the higher rates, and therefore would not be undertaken.) Extreme versions of this theory, known as "dollar-for-dollar" crowding out, argue that the decrease in private investment will exactly offset the increase in government spending, and there will be no change in the overall output of goods and services.

Government intervention is not only incapable of pulling the economy out of a recession, conservative economists argue, it is also unnecessary. If there is more saving than investment, the quantity of funds people are willing to loan out will exceed the quantity that people are willing to borrow at the current interest rate. The surplus of loanable funds will drive down the interest rate. People will save less (since the reward to saving is lower) and borrow more and invest more (since the cost of borrowing is lower), until the injection of investment and the leakage of saving are equal. In short, if insufficient demand ever caused a recession, the economy would quickly pull itself back to full employment without any need for government intervention.

Keynes' Rejoinder

Keynes agreed with the idea that saving equals investment. In his view, however, this is true not only when the economy is producing at its full-employment capacity, but also when it is producing at far less than its capacity. Keynes argued that the "classical" economists (as he called the conservative orthodoxy of his time) had an incorrect view of the relationship between interest rates and savings, and that this was at the heart of their errors about the possibility of prolonged recessions.

The classicals believed that as interest rates increased, savings would increase, and that as interest rates declined, savings would decline. Keynes agreed that this was true at "a given income," but that a change in the interest rate would also affect the amount investment and therefore the level of income. A higher interest rate, he argued, was associated with lower investment, lower incomes, and therefore lower saving; a lower interest rate, with higher investment, higher incomes, and therefore higher saving. (As people's incomes increase, they spend more *and* save more; as their incomes decline, they spend less *and* save less.) In Keynes' view, saving will equal investment whether investment and saving are both high (at or near the full employment level of output) or if investment and saving are both low (in a low-output, high-unemployment economy). In the latter case, Keynes believed, there was no guarantee that the economy would pull itself back to full employment.

Keynes was also well aware, long before his critics, that government borrowing could crowd out some private investment. In *The General Theory* itself, he noted that the effects of the government directly increasing employment on public works may include "increasing the rate of interest and so retarding investment in other directions." This does not imply, however, dollar-for-dollar crowding out. Keynes still believed, and the empirical evidence confirms, that under depression conditions an increase in government spending can result in an increase in total output larger than the initial spending increase (a multiplier greater than one).

Of Spending and Multipliers

In a recent article in the *Wall Street Journal*, conservative economist Robert Barro declares, as a "plausible starting point," that the multiplier actually equals zero. That's what the dollar-for-dollar crowding-out theory means—an increase in government spending will be matched by equal decreases in private spending, and so will have zero effect on real GDP. When it comes to estimating the multiplier, based on historical data from 1943-1944, however, Barro finds that it is not zero, but 0.8.

First, contrary to Barro's intent, this is actually a disproof of dollar-for-dollar crowding out. It means that increased government spending brought about increased real GDP, though not by as much as the spending increase. It increased the production of public-sector goods by (much) more than it reduced the production of private-sector goods. Unless one views private-sector goods as intrinsically more valuable than public-sector goods, this is not an argument against government spending.

Second, Barro chose to base his study on two years at the height of the U.S. mobilization for World War II. When the economy is at or near full employment, the multiplier is bound to be small. If all resources are already being used, the only way to produce more of some kinds of goods (say, tanks and war planes) is to produce less of some others (say, civilian cars). Keynesian economists certainly understand this. Their point, however, is that government spending creates a large multiplier effect when the economy is languishing in a recession, not when it is already at full employment.

Economist Mark Zandi of Moody's Economy.com reports much higher multipliers for government spending. Zandi estimates multipliers between 1.3 and 1.6 for federal aid to states and for government infrastructure expenditures. The multipliers are even larger for government transfers (such as food stamps or unemployment compensation) to the hardest-hit, who are likely to spend all or almost all of their increase in income. Zandi estimates these multipliers at between 1.6 and 1.8. Tax cuts for high income individuals and corporations, who are less likely to spend their additional disposable income, have the lowest multipliers—between 0.3 and 0.4.

Why the General Theory?

The conservative case against standard Keynesian fiscal stimulus policy rests on the assumption that all of the economy's resources are already being used to the fullest. Keynes titled his most important work *The General Theory* because he thought that the orthodox economics of his time confined itself to this special case, the case of an economy at full employment. He did not believe that this was generally the case in capitalist economies, and he sought to develop a theory that explained this.

The argument conservatives make against government spending—"it has to come from somewhere"—is actually no less true for private investment. If dollar-for-dollar crowding out were true, therefore, it would be just as impossible for private investment to pull the economy out of a recession. This, of course, would be nonsense unless the economy was already at full employment (and an increase in one kind of production would have to come at the expense of some other kind of production).

If the economy were already operating at full capacity—imagine a situation in which all workers are employed, factories are humming with activity 24/7, and no unused resources would be available to expand production if demand increased—the argument that increased government spending could not increase overall economic output might be plausible. But that is manifestly not the current economic situation.

Real GDP declined at an annual rate of 6.3% in the fourth quarter of 2008. The official unemployment rate surged to 8.5%, the highest rate in 30 years, in March 2009. Over 15% of workers are unemployed, have given up looking for work, or can only find part-time work. Employment is plummeting by more than half a million workers each month. A theory that assumes the economy is already at full employment can neither help us understand how we got into this hole—or how we can get out.

Sources: John Maynard Keynes, *The General Theory of Employment, Interest, and Money*, 1964; Associated Press, "Obama: Stimulus lets Americans claim destiny," February 17, 2009; Paul Krugman, "A Dark Age of macroeconomics (wonkish)," January 27, 2009; J. Bradford DeLong, "More 'Treasury View' Blogging," February 5,2009; J. Bradford DeLong, "The Modern Revival of the 'Treasury View,'" January 18, 2009; Robert J. Barro,"Government Spending is No Free Lunch," *Wall Street Journal*, January 22, 2009; Paul Krugman, "War and non-remembrance," January 22, 2009; Paul Krugman, "Spending in wartime," January 23, 2009; Mark Zandi, "The Economic Impact of a $750 Billion Fiscal Stimulus Package," Moody'sEconomy.com, March 26, 2009; Bureau of Labor Statistics, Alternative measures of labor underutilization; Bureau of Labor Statistics Payroll Employment.

Article 7.4

OPENING PANDORA'S BOX
The basics of Marxist economics.

BY ALEJANDRO REUSS
February 2000

In most universities, what is taught as "economics" is a particular brand of orthodox economic theory. The hallmark of this school is a belief in the optimal efficiency (and, it goes without saying, the equity) of "free markets."

The orthodox macroeconomists—who had denied the possibility of general economic slumps—were thrown for a loop by the Great Depression of the 1930s, and by the challenge to their system of thought by John Maynard Keynes and others. Even so, the orthodox system retains at its heart a view of capitalist society in which individuals, each equal to all others, undertake mutually beneficial transactions tending to a socially optimal equilibrium. There is no power and no conflict. The model is a perfectly bloodless abstraction, without all the clash and clamor of real life.

Karl Marx and the Critique of Capitalist Society

One way to pry open and criticize the orthodox model of economics is by returning to the idiosyncracies of the real world. That's the approach of most of the articles in this book, which describe real-world phenomena that the orthodox model ignores or excludes. These efforts may explain particular facts better than the orthodoxy, while not necessarily offering an alternative general system of analysis. They punch holes in the orthodox lines but, ultimately, leave the orthodox model in possession of the field.

This suggests the need for a different conceptual system that can supplant orthodox economics as a whole. Starting in the 1850s and continuing until his death in 1883, the German philosopher and revolutionary Karl Marx dedicated himself to developing a conceptual system for explaining the workings of capitalism. The system which Marx developed and which bears his name emerged from his criticism of the classical political economy developed by Adam Smith and David Ricardo. While Marx admired Smith and Ricardo, and borrowed many of their concepts, he approached economics (or "political economy") from a very different standpoint. He had developed a powerful criticism of capitalist society before undertaking his study of the economy. This criticism was inspired by French socialist ideas and focused on the oppression of the working class. Marx argued that wage workers—those working for a paycheck—were "free" only in the sense that they were not beholden to a single lord or master, as serfs had been under feudalism. But they did not own property, nor were they craftspeople working for themselves, so they were compelled to sell themselves for a wage to one capitalist or another. Having surrendered their freedom to the employer's authority, they were forced to work in the way the employer told them while the latter pocketed the profit produced by their labor.

Marx believed, however, that by creating this oppressed and exploited class of workers, capitalism was creating the seeds of its own destruction. Conflict between the workers and the owners was an essential part of capitalism. But in Marx's view of history, the workers could eventually overthrow the capitalist class, just as the capitalist class, or "bourgeoisie," had grown strong under feudalism, only to supplant the feudal aristocracy. The workers, however, would not simply substitute a new form of private property and class exploitation, as the bourgeoisie had done. Rather, they would bring about the organization of production on a cooperative basis, and an end to the domination of one class over another.

This line of thinking was strongly influenced by the ideas of the day in German philosophy, which held that any new order grows in the womb of the old, and eventually bursts forth to replace it. Marx believed that the creation of the working class, or proletariat, in the heart of capitalism was one of the system's main contradictions. Marx studied capitalist economics in order to explain the conditions under which it would be possible for the proletariat to overthrow capitalism and create a classless society. The orthodox view depicts capitalism as tending towards equilibrium (without dynamism or crises), serving everyone's best interests, and lasting forever. Marx saw capitalism as crisis-ridden, full of conflict, operating to the advantage of some but not others, and far from eternal.

Class and Exploitation

Marx studied history closely. Looked at historically, he saw capitalism as only the latest in a succession of societies based on exploitation. When people are only able to produce the bare minimum needed to live, he wrote, there is no room for a class of people to take a portion of society's production without contributing to it. But as soon as productivity exceeds this subsistence level, it becomes possible for a class of people who do not contribute to production to live by appropriating the surplus for themselves. These are the masters in slave societies, the lords in feudal societies, and the property owners in capitalist society.

Marx believed that the owners of businesses and property—the capitalists—take part of the wealth produced by the workers, but that this appropriation is hidden by the appearance of an equal exchange, or "a fair day's work for a fair day's pay."

Those who live from the ownership of property—businesses, stocks, land, etc—were then a small minority and now are less than 5% of the population in countries like the United States (Marx wrote before the rise of massive corporations and bureaucracies, and did not classify managers and administrators who don't own their own businesses as part of the bourgeoisie.) The exploited class, meanwhile, is the vast majority who lived by earning a wage or salary—not just the "blue collar" or industrial workers but other workers as well.

Marx's view of how exploitation happened in capitalist society depended on an idea, which he borrowed from Smith and Ricardo, called the Labor Theory of Value. The premise of this theory, which is neither easily proved nor easily rejected, is that labor alone creates the value which is embodied in commodities and which creates profit for owners who sell the goods. The workers do not receive the full value created by their labor and so they are exploited.

Students are likely to hear in economics classes that profits are a reward for the "abstinence" or "risk" of a businessperson—implying that profits are their just desserts. Marx would argue that profits are a reward obtained through the exercise of power—the power owners have over those who own little but their ability to work and so must sell this ability for a wage. That power, and the tribute it allows owners of capital to extract from workers, is no more legitimate in Marx's analysis than the power of a slaveowner over a slave. A slaveowner may exhibit thrift and take risks, after all, but is the wealth of the slaveowner the just reward for these virtues, or a pure and simple theft from the slave?

As Joan Robinson, an important 20th-century critic and admirer of Marx, argues, "What is important is that owning capital is not a productive activity. The academic economists, by treating capital as productive, used to insinuate the suggestion that capitalists deserve well by society and are fully justified in drawing income from their property."

The Falling Rate of Profit

Marx believed that his theory had major implications for the crises that engulf capitalist economies. In Marx's system, the value of the raw materials and machinery used in the manufacture of a product does not create the extra value that allows the businessman to profit from its production. That additional value is created by labor alone.

Marx recognized that owners could directly extract more value out of workers in three ways: cutting their wages, lengthening their working day, or increasing the intensity of their labor. This need not be done by a direct assault on the workers. Capitalists can achieve the same goal by employing more easily exploited groups or by moving their operations where labor is not as powerful. Both of these trends can be seen in capitalism today, and can be understood as part of capital's intrinsic thirst for more value and increased exploitation.

With the mechanization of large-scale production under capitalism, machines and other inanimate elements of production form a larger and larger share of the inputs to production. Marx believed this would result in a long-term trend of the rate of profit to fall as less of production depended on the enriching contribution of human labor. This, he believed, would make capitalism increasingly vulnerable to economic crises.

This chain of reasoning, of course, depends on the Labor Theory of Value (seeing workers as the source of the surplus value created in the production process) and can be avoided by rejecting this theory outright. Orthodox economics has not only rejected the Labor Theory of Value, but abandoned the issue of "value" altogether. After lying fallow for many years, value analysis was revived during the 1960s by a number of unorthodox economists including the Italian economist Piero Sraffa. Marx was not the last word on the subject.

Unemployment, Part I: The "Reserve Army of the Unemployed"

Marx is often raked over the coals for arguing that workers, under capitalism, were destined to be ground into ever more desperate poverty. That living standards improved in rich capitalist countries is offered as proof that his system is fatally flawed. While Marx was not optimistic about the prospect of workers raising their standard of living very far under capitalism, he was critical of proponents of the "iron law of wages," such as Malthus, who held that any increase in wages above the minimum necessary for survival would simply provoke population growth and a decline in wages back to subsistence level.

Marx emphasized that political and historical factors influencing the relative power of the major social classes, rather than simple demographics, determined the distribution of income.

One economic factor to which Marx attributed great importance in the class struggle was the size of the "reserve army of the unemployed." Marx identified unemployment as the major factor pushing wages down—the larger the "reserve" of unemployed workers clamoring for jobs, the greater the downward pressure on wages. This was an influence, Marx believed, that the workers would never be able to fully escape under capitalism. If the workers' bargaining power rose enough to raise wages and eat into profits, he argued, capitalists would merely substitute labor-saving technology for living labor, recreating the "reserve army" and reasserting the downward pressure on wages.

Though this has not, perhaps, retarded long-term wage growth to the degree that Marx expected, his basic analysis was visionary at a time when the Malthusian (population) theory of wages was the prevailing view. Anyone reading the business press these days—which is constantly worrying that workers might gain some bargaining power in a "tight" (low unemployment) labor market, and that their wage demands will provoke inflation—will recognize its basic insight.

Unemployment, Part II: The Crisis of Overproduction

Marx never developed one definitive version of his theory of economic crises (recessions) under capitalism. Nonetheless, his thinking on this issue is some of his most visionary. Marx was the first major economic thinker to break with the orthodoxy of "Say's Law." Named after the French philosopher Jean-Baptiste Say, this theory held that each industry generated income equal to the output it created. In other words, "supply creates its own demand." Say's conclusion, in which he was followed by Smith, Ricardo, and orthodox economists up through the Great Depression, was that while a particular industry such as the car industry could overproduce, no generalized overproduction was possible. In this respect, orthodox economics flew in the face of all the evidence. In his analysis of overproduction, Marx focused on what he considered the basic contradiction of capitalism—and, in microcosm, of the commodity itself—the contradiction between "use value" and "exchange value." The idea is that a commodity both satisfies a specific need (it has "use value") and can be exchanged for other articles (it has "exchange value"). This distinction was not invented by Marx; it can be found in the work of Smith. Unlike Smith, however, Marx emphasized the way exchange value—what something is worth in the market—overwhelms the use value of a commodity. Unless a commodity can be sold, the portion of society's useful labor embodied in it is wasted (and the product is useless to those in need). Vast real needs remain unsatisfied for the majority of people, doubly so when—during crises of overproduction—vast quantities of goods remain unsold because there is not enough "effective demand."

It is during these crises that capitalism's unlimited drive to develop society's productive capacity clashes most sharply with the constraints it places on the real incomes of the majority to buy the goods they need. Marx developed this notion of a demand crisis over 75 years before the so-called "Keynesian revolution" in economic thought (whose key insights were actually developed before Keynes by the Polish economist Michal Kalecki on the foundations of Marx's analysis).

Marx expected that these crises of overproduction and demand would worsen as capitalism developed, and that the crises would slow down more and more the development of society's productive capacities (what Marx called the "forces of production"). Ultimately, he believed, these crises would be capitalism's undoing. He also pointed to them as evidence of the basic depravity of capitalism. "In these crises," Marx writes in the *Communist Manifesto*,

> there breaks out an epidemic that, in all earlier epochs would have seemed an absurdity, the epidemic of overproduction. Society suddenly finds itself put back into a state of momentary barbarism; it appears as if a famine, a universal war of devastation had cut off the supply of every means of subsistence; industry and commerce seem to be destroyed; and why? Because there is too much civilization, too much means of subsistence, too much industry, too much commerce ...

And how does the bourgeoisie get over these crises? On the one hand by enforced destruction of productive force; on the other hand, by the conquest of new markets, and by the more thorough exploitation of old ones.

This kind of crisis came so close to bringing down capitalism during the Great Depression that preventing them became a central aim of government policy. While government intervention has managed to smooth out the business cycle, especially in the wealthiest countries, capitalism has hardly become crisis-free.

While the reigning complacency about a new, crisis-free capitalism is much easier to sustain here than in, say, East Asia, capitalism clearly has not yet run up against any absolute barrier to its development. In fact, Marx's discussions (in the *Communist Manifesto* and elsewhere) of capitalism's irresistible expansive impulse— capital breaking down all barriers, expanding into every crevice, always "thirsting for surplus value" and new fields of exploitation—seem as apt today as they did 150 years ago.

Marx as Prophet

Marx got a great deal about capitalism just right—its incessant, shark-like forward movement; its internal chaos, bursting forth periodically in crisis; its concentration of economic power in ever fewer hands. Judged on these core insights, the Marxist system can easily stand toe-to-toe with the orthodox model. Which comes closer to reality? The capitalism that incessantly bursts forth over new horizons, or the one that constantly gravitates towards comfortable equilibrium? The one where crisis is impossible, or the one that lurches from boom to bust to boom again? The one where perfect competition reigns, or the one where a handful of giants towers over every industry?

In all these respects, Marx's system captures the thundering dynamics of capitalism much better than the orthodox system does. As aesthetically appealing as the clockwork harmony of the orthodox model may be, this is precisely its failing. Capitalism is anything but harmonious.

There was also a lot that Marx, like any other complex thinker, predicted incorrectly, or did not foresee. In this respect, he was not a prophet. His work should be read critically, and not, as it has been by some, as divine revelation. Marx, rather, was the prophet of a radical approach to reality. In an age when the "free market" rides high, and its apologists claim smugly that "there is no alternative," Joan Robinson's praise of Marx is apt: "[T]he nightmare quality of Marx's thought gives it ... an air of greater reality than the gentle complacency of the orthodox academics. Yet he, at the same time, is more encouraging than they, for he releases hope as well as terror from Pandora's box, while they preach only the gloomy doctrine that all is for the best in the best of all *possible* worlds."

Resources: Joan Robinson, *An Essay on Marxian Economics* (Macmillan, 1952); "Manifesto of the Community Party," and "Crisis Theory (from Theories of Surplus Value)," in Robert C. Tucker, ed., *The Marx-Engels Reader* (W.W. Norton, 1978); Roman Rosdolsky, *The Making of Marx's 'Capital'* (Pluto Press, 1989); Ernest Mandel, "Karl Heinrich Marx"; Luigi L. Pasinetti, "Joan Violet Robinson"; and John Eatwell and Carlo Panico, "Piero Sraffa"; in John Eatwell, Murray Milgate, and Peter Newman, eds., *The New Palgrave: A Dictionary of Economics* (Macmillan, 1987).

Article 7.5

UNDER THE MARGINS
Feminist economists look at gender and poverty

BY RANDY ALBELDA
September/October 2002

For all the hype about welfare-to-work, most former welfare recipients are still living in poverty. It is true that, since the advent of 1990s-style "welfare reform," families no longer on welfare are earning more, on average, than those still on welfare. But more often than not, the jobs that former welfare mothers find don't provide employer-sponsored health insurance, vacation time, sick leave, or wages sufficient to support their families. In fact, the percentage of families who are "desperately" poor (with incomes at or below 50% of the official poverty line) has gone up since the mid-1990s, and so has the percentage of former welfare recipients who report hardships such as difficulty feeding their families or paying bills. And remember: All of this occurred during a so-called economic boom.

So why does the emphasis on work (and now marriage) continue to dominate the welfare debate? In large part, this is because the poverty "story" of the last 20 years—created and perpetuated by conservative ideologues and politicians—blames poor people for their own poverty. Women supposedly have too many children without husbands, poor black urban dwellers exhibit pathological behaviors, and liberal welfare policies—by expanding government spending and providing an attractive alternative to jobs and marriage—have made matters worse.

At least one group of theorists—feminist economists—says it isn't so. It is women's particular economic role in capitalism—as caregiver—that shapes their relationship to the labor market, men, and the state. Feminist economists have shown how having and caring for children affects the economic status of women—including women who are not mothers but are still relegated to poorly paid care-giving jobs. While their voices are largely ignored in research and policy circles, feminist economists' analyses provide the best understanding of the obstacles low-income families face and the range of policy options that might work.

Women and Poverty

Almost everywhere, women are the majority of poor adults. Recently, a group of sociologists from several U.S. universities looked at poverty in eight industrialized nations. Using a relative poverty measure (half of median family income), they found that, in the 1990s, women's poverty rates exceeded men's in all countries but Sweden. Further, they found that single-mother poverty rates—even in countries with deep social welfare systems—are exceptionally high. (See Figure 1.)

In the United States in 2000, women comprised just over half of the adult population but constituted 61% of all poor adults. (The U.S. poverty income threshold is based on an absolute dollar figure determined in the 1960s and since indexed for inflation.) Toss in children, and the data are even grimmer; 16.2% of all children were poor, while over one-third of all single-mother families were poor. Together, women and children comprised 76% of the poor in the United States, far surpassing their 62% representation in the population as a whole.

Since the late 1950s (when the data were first collected), single-mother families in the United States have never constituted more than 13% of all families; however, they form just under half of all poor families. Figure 2 depicts the proportion of all families—and all poor families—that are single-mother families. The steepest increase occurred in the late 1960s on the heels of the War on Poverty, as poverty rates for everyone were falling.

Economic Theory and Poverty

From Adam Smith onward, most economists have understood poverty by looking at labor markets, labor-market inequality, and economic growth. According to this approach, it is underemployment or the lack of employment—and the resulting lack of income—that causes poverty. A brief summary of the dominant economic theories in the last half of the 20th century illustrates the point.

Keynesian economic theory argues that the lack of demand in the economy as a whole leads to unemployment. When investors and consumers can't jumpstart the economy, we need fiscal or monetary economic stimuli to induce demand. It was this wisdom that has guided economists to promote economic growth as a way to

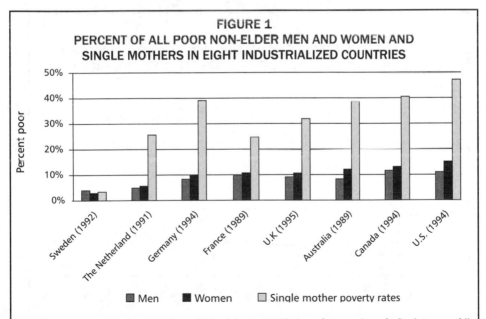

FIGURE 1
PERCENT OF ALL POOR NON-ELDER MEN AND WOMEN AND SINGLE MOTHERS IN EIGHT INDUSTRIALIZED COUNTRIES

■ Men ■ Women ☐ Single mother poverty rates

Note: Poverty rates are the proportion of non-elderly adults ages 25-54 whose after-tax and transfer family incomes fall below 50% of the median family income.

Source: Table 1, in Karen Christopher et al., "Gender Inequality in Poverty in Affluent Nations: The Role of Single Motherhood and the State," in Karen Vleminckx and Timothy Smeeding, eds., *Child Well-Being, Child Poverty and Child Policy in Modern Nations* (London: Policy Press, 2001).

reduce poverty, arguing that "a rising tide lifts all boats"—as, for example, during the Kennedy and Johnson administrations.

Marxian theorists say that, under capitalism, unemployment cannot be totally eliminated because it is a necessary component of capitalist production that serves to "discipline" workers. Unless we make radical changes to the economic system, there will always be families that are without employment and therefore poor.

Like Marxian economists, *institutional* economists also believe that economic outcomes aren't simply the result of pure market forces; cultural, social, and political forces also come into play. In the 1970s, economists Peter Doeringer and Michael Piore identified distinct labor-market segments. Younger workers, workers of color, and women tend to end up in what they call the "secondary labor market"—characterized by low wages, few promotional opportunities, and easy-to-acquire skills—more than other workers. These workers are particularly vulnerable to unemployment and hence more likely to be poor. The way to relieve poverty is to help these workers move into better jobs, or to create policies that make their jobs better.

These understandings of poverty offer little or no gender analysis—presumably what ails men is equally applicable to women. Analyses of insufficient (aggregate) demand, unemployment, and labor-market inequality rarely mention women or discuss how and why gender matters—unless feminist scholars provide them.

Neoclassical (mainstream) economists also argue that poverty is caused by lack of employment and low wages—but they consider workers responsible for their own

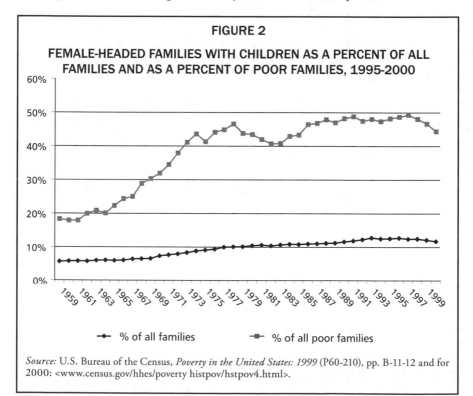

FIGURE 2

FEMALE-HEADED FAMILIES WITH CHILDREN AS A PERCENT OF ALL FAMILIES AND AS A PERCENT OF POOR FAMILIES, 1995-2000

◆ % of all families   ■ % of all poor families

Source: U.S. Bureau of the Census, *Poverty in the United States: 1999* (P60-210), pp. B-11-12 and for 2000: <www.census.gov/hhes/poverty histpov/hstpov4.html>.

wage levels. Workers who choose not to pursue education, training, or on-the-job experience will participate in the labor force less often than more highly trained and skilled workers, be less productive, and receive lower wages. Unlike the political economy theorists just discussed, many non-feminist economists—the most well known being Nobel Prize winner Gary Becker—have tackled the topic of women's lower wages. But they consistently conclude that women's lack of employment, or employment at low wages, results from rational individual choice. Only policies that boost incentives for individuals to invest in themselves (like tax credits for education) will alleviate poverty.

Gender Matters

It is true that one reason women are poor is that they are not in the labor force or are underemployed. But while employment is an important underpinning to understanding poverty, it is not the same for women as for men.

Most economists who study labor markets assume that workers in capitalist economies are "unencumbered"—that they don't have significant constraints on their time outside of paid work. Encumbered workers are treated as a "special case" worthy of examination, but understood and analyzed as an exception rather than the rule.

Since the beginnings of capitalism, however, female workers have almost always been "encumbered." And women's role as caregivers—their main encumbrance—has shaped their participation in the economy, as feminist historians and economic historians have shown. Historically, women's economic opportunities have been severely constricted, with race, age, and marital status sending important market "signals" about where women could or should be employed. For example, until the 1960s, many professional and some clerical jobs had "marriage bars," i.e., employers refused to hire married women on the assumption that they did not need the salaries these jobs paid, and would not stick around once they had children. Similarly, before anti-discrimination laws were enacted, many workers of color could not get jobs as managers in many professions, or even as sales clerks if the business catered to a white clientele.

For more than a century, this labor market "ordering" has given rise to employment, income, and wage policies that reinforce and reproduce women's political and economic dependence on men (and non-whites' inferior status in relation to whites). These policies assume that the standard family is a heterosexual married couple with a lone male breadwinner employed in industrial production. For example, in order to collect unemployment insurance benefits, workers must work a minimum number of hours and receive a minimum amount of earnings. Because many women work part-time and earn low wages, they are much less likely to qualify for benefits than men. Similarly, Social Security benefits are based on previous earnings over a sustained period of employment. Women who have spent most of their adult lives as caregivers are thus ineligible for benefits on their own, and must rely on their husbands' contributions instead.

Men's and women's employment patterns are very different. Women's labor force participation rates are lower than men's, and women's employment experiences in economic downturns often differ from men's. Women's job options and choices are also highly influenced by care-giving responsibilities; mothers are more likely than fathers to trade higher-paying jobs for jobs that are closer to childcare, have more flexible schedules, or require fewer hours.

In addition to shaping women's paid labor-market activities, care work has been economically, socially, and politically undervalued, as feminist economists point out. This is true both when that work is done in the home for free and when others do it for low pay. Among the few jobs immigrant women and women of color can almost always find are low-paying care-work jobs, and they are disproportionately represented in those jobs. For example, in 2001, women were 47% of all workers but 97% of child care workers, 93% of registered nurses, 90% of health aides, and 72% of social workers. Black workers comprised 11% of the workforce but were 33% of health aides, 23% of licensed practical nurses, and 20% of cleaning service workers. This type of occupational "stereotyping" reinforces the care-giving roles that women and people of color fill, and the low pay (relative to jobs with similar skill requirements) reinforces women's dependence on men and racial inequality. Economist Nancy Folbre, in her 2001 book *The Invisible Heart: Economics and Family Values*, calls this the "care penalty."

It is because of their low-paid and unpaid care work, then, that women are particularly economically vulnerable and much more likely to be poor than are men. The role of care giving—as distinct from other factors like employment, economic growth, and labor-market inequality—helps to explain not only women's employment patterns but also women's poverty. So theories of poverty that rely on analyses of employment that assume all people are men—or that women are a special case of men—are not only incomplete, they are wrong.

Feminist Analyses of Poverty

It is no coincidence that, when there has been a viable women's movement—in the early part of the 20th century and in the late 1960s—feminists and women researchers have paid particular attention to poor women.

Documenting poor families: early efforts

In the early 20th century, there was a good deal of concern about how women fit into the capitalist economy. Social scientists living in or near poor communities—often in settlement houses established by women reformers—conducted surveys of women workers, mostly through government-sponsored research. Many of the surveys found that the biggest problems faced by two-parent families were a lack of employment and insufficient wages. Researchers readily recognized that families headed by women were constrained by women's role as caregiver and women's low wages. Instead of advocating more employment for women, they promoted relatively meager levels of public assistance.

In the 1910s and 1920s, women reformers were key players not only in doing research but also in creating policies directed toward poor women and children. These women imposed white middle-class values about child-rearing, hygiene, and education; their construction of "deservingness" replicated and reinforced the ways in which women and men, immigrants and non-immigrants, were supposed to act. At the same time, they successfully implemented income supplement programs for single-mother families at the state level, and they were instrumental in incorporating AFDC (Aid to Families with Dependent Children) into the Social Security Act of 1935. Feminist poverty researchers and reformers did not emerge again until the late 1960s.

Sisterhood may be powerful, but motherhood is not: recent efforts

The women's movement of the late 1960s and 1970s laid some important foundations for understanding women's poverty, even though its main economic strategies were aimed at improving the wages of women who were employed. Feminists fought for affirmative action, which was most successful in creating opportunities for college-educated women. Today, women hold 46% of executive and professional jobs—exactly their representation in all jobs—and comprise just under 30% of all doctors and lawyers. Feminists also organized for comparable worth, which was intended to lift wages for low-income women by recognizing and rewarding the skill level and effort needed to perform low-paying women's jobs (including care-giving ones).

At the same time, feminist scholars called attention to women's "double day" (now called "work/family conflict") and theorized about the role of care work and reproduction in capitalist economies. From the outset, feminist analysts understood that "housework" was work and a vital component of capitalist production. This intellectual work paralleled "wages for housework" campaigns that were launched in Italy, Canada, Great Britain, and the United States.

Using these tools to reinterpret poverty was not hard. Among the first to apply a feminist analysis to women's poverty was sociologist Diana Pearce, in an 1978 article entitled "The Feminization of Poverty: Women, Work, and Welfare." Pearce called attention to the fact that women were disproportionately represented among the poor. Her phrase—"the feminization of poverty"—became very popular in feminist circles as well as in the mainstream press.

Economist Nancy Folbre followed up with a theoretical framework directly linking women's care work as mothers to their poverty. In her 1985 article, "The Pauperization of Motherhood: Patriarchy and Social Policy in the U.S.," she argued that, when the costs of raising children are shifted onto women, women (and children) become dependent on men. Then, when fathers abandon their families, women and children are consigned to poverty. Folbre also argues that public policies around divorce, child support, unemployment insurance, and welfare reinforce this relationship. For example, welfare policies—even before the 1990s reforms—never provided enough income for women to support their families without working "under the table" or getting unreported income, paying a big price for not being married.

Single mothers especially bear the burden of these policies in the form of incredibly high poverty rates. But, Folbre points out, the benefits of care labor—healthy, productive children who become tax-paying adults—are enjoyed by all of society, not merely the mothers who provided the care. If society recognized the value of women's care work and compensated them for it, then fewer women would be poor.

Current trends

Currently, some feminist scholars are addressing the ways that gender influences government allocation of income supports (like pensions, unemployment insurance, and welfare) and non-cash assistance (e.g., education and child care). Sociologist Ann Orloff and political scientists Diane Sainsbury and Jane Lewis argue that state welfare policies (construed broadly) embody deeply gendered notions of citizenship and need. Much of this work is theoretical and does not explicitly address poverty. However, it helps to explain the lack of policies that would correct women's poverty.

Other researchers are focusing on how people's capacity—access to health and education, living conditions, how they are treated in a society—affects their potential to generate income and causes poverty. Building on the work of economist Amartya Sen, feminist economists in the United States have shown that it is unreasonable and unlikely to expect single mothers to "work" their way out of poverty—because women earn lower wages than men, because they have care-giving responsibilities, and because the additional costs associated with caring for children restrict their capacity to be employed even while family needs remain high. For example, Barbara Bergmann and Trudi Renwick developed budgets for low-income families in the 1990s. Chris Tilly and I have demonstrated that the income needs of single-mother families far exceed their earnings possibilities—even with full-time employment. This work refutes the claims of liberals who supported welfare reform in the naïve belief that welfare recipients could easily substitute earnings for public assistance.

Finally, feminist economists are documenting how low-income women—especially single-mother families in which the same adult is both caregiver and breadwinner—relate to the labor market, fathers, and the state. Using longitudinal data, feminist social scientists Roberta Spalter-Roth and Heidi Hartmann found that many poor single-mother families either combine government assistance with wages (under or above the table) or cycle between the two. This research is confirmed and extended by feminist sociologists like Kathryn Edin and Laura Lein, who, through extensive interviews with poor single mothers, documented the particular ways and times that poorly paying jobs as well as men and their incomes drift in and out of women's lives. These studies make it clear that women's employment is not family-sustaining, and that, to survive, single-mother families need a sane combination of earnings, child support, *and* government assistance. In contrast to the narrowly focused, incentive-based literature that characterizes poor women's behavior as pathological, these approaches demonstrate that poor women's lives are dynamic yet fragile, and that the decisions they make are creative, adaptive, and almost always child-centered.

Who Cares?

Despite their efforts, feminist scholars have not had much impact on the poverty literature—at least not in economics—nor have they influenced policies intended to alleviate poverty. Much (though not all) poverty research is grant-funded, and it tends to focus narrowly on evaluating the individual impact of welfare reform, mostly by looking at welfare "leavers." These factors discourage the use of feminist analysis, since most funding goes either to conservative think tanks with a specific ideological aversion to feminism or to "liberal" think tanks that have made their fortunes in mainstream analysis fitted to their main consumer—the federal government.

Further, these conventional studies often preclude the larger political economy approach taken by feminists. Welfare reform is a mechanism of social control over poor single women—especially women of color—that is part of a larger conservative agenda to justify if not exacerbate economic inequality, assure a large pool of low-wage labor, and silence important political movements. Feminist analysis suggests the need for policies that would not only reduce poverty but also change women's (and people of color's) relationship to the labor market, (white) men, and the state, thus loosening the grip of economic dependence. This isn't in line with the right-wing agenda at all.

However, feminist economic analysis has been very useful to activists who are trying to help poor women. For example, in the mid-1990s, Wider Opportunity for Women (WOW), a feminist group based in Washington, D.C., started conducting family economic self-sufficiency standard projects. Currently, WOW operates projects in 40 states and D.C. The studies demonstrate how much income a single mother family needs to survive, and are being used as organizing tools in the states.

During the mid-1990s welfare reform debates and now in discussions about reauthorization of Temporary Assistance for Needy Families (TANF), feminist scholars—connected informally through the "Women's Committee of 100"—have argued that raising children is work and that responsible legislation should recognize unpaid work as work. The Committee has called for a caregiver's allowances (see "Wages for Housework," article 1.5, and <www. welfare2002.org>). And while Congress has not embraced these ideas, a TANF reauthorization bill sponsored by Representative Patsy Mink (D-Hawaii) in the spring of 2002 garnered support from close to 90 members of the House.

Feminist economists argue that the role of economists is to understand how societies do or do not provide for people's needs. Through their research and skills, they provide the tools for activists to argue that women's employment status and care-giving responsibilities place many at the bottom of the economic pecking order. At the same time, feminist economists are connecting their work directly to social movements, lending their expertise—and their own voices—to living wage campaigns, efforts to improve compensation for child care workers and home health aides, and efforts to eliminate poverty, not welfare.

Resources: Kathryn Edin and Laura Lein, *Making Ends Meet: How Single Mothers Survive Welfare and Low Wage Work* (Russell Sage Foundation, 1997); Nancy Folbre, "The Pauperization of Motherhood: Patriarchy and Social Policy in the U.S.," *Review of Radical Political Economics*, vol. 16, no. 4 (1984): 72-88; Nancy Folbre, *The Invisible Heart: Economics and Family Values* (New York: The New Press, 2001); Jane Lewis, "Gender and the Development of Welfare Regimes," *Journal of European Social Policy* 3 (1992): 159-73; Alice O'Connor, *Poverty Knowledge: Social Science, Social Policy, and the Poor in Twentieth Century U.S. History* (Princeton, N.J.: Princeton

University Press, 2001); Ann Orloff, "Gender and the Social Rights of Citizenship: The Comparative Analysis of Gender Relations and Welfare States," *American Sociological Review* 58 (1993): 303-28; Diana Pearce, "The Feminization of Poverty: Women, Work, and Welfare," *Urban and Social Change Review* (February 1978); Trudi Renwick and Barbara Bergmann, "A Budget-based Definition of Poverty with an Application to Single-parent Families," *Journal of Human Resources* 28, no. 1 (1993): 1-24; Diane Sainsbury, *Gender, Equality, and Welfare States* (Cambridge: Cambridge University Press, 1996); Amartya K. Sen, *Development as Freedom* (New York: Alfred A. Knopf, 1999); Roberta SpalterRoth et al., *Welfare That Works: The Working Lives of AFDC Recipients* (Washington, D.C.: Institute for Women's Policy Research, 1995); Chris Tilly and Randy Albelda, "Family Structure and Family Earnings: The Determinants of Earnings Differences among Family Types," *Industrial Relations* 33, no. 2 (1994): 151-167; U.S. Census, *Current Population Surveys* <www.census. gov/hhes/income/histinc/histpovtb.html>; Bureau of Labor Statistics, *Employment and Earnings*, Table 11 <*www.bls.gov/cps/home.htm#charemp.§§*>

Article 7.6

INEQUALITY, POWER, AND IDEOLOGY

Getting it right about the causes of the current economic crisis.

BY ARTHUR MacEWAN
March/April 2009

It is hard to solve a problem without an understanding of what caused it. For example, in medicine, until we gained an understanding of the way bacteria and
viruses cause various infectious diseases, it was virtually impossible to develop effective cures. Of course, dealing with many diseases is complicated by the fact that
germs, genes, diet, and the environment establish a nexus of causes.

The same is true in economics. Without an understanding of the causes of the
current crisis, we are unlikely to develop a solution; certainly we are not going to
get a solution that has a lasting impact. And determining the causes is complicated
because several intertwined factors have been involved.

The current economic crisis was brought about by a nexus of factors that involved: a growing concentration of political and social power in the hands of the
wealthy; the ascendance of a perverse leave-it-to-the-market ideology which was an
instrument of that power; and rising income inequality, which both resulted from
and enhanced that power. These various factors formed a vicious circle, reinforcing
one another and together shaping the economic conditions that led us to the present
situation. Several other factors were also involved—the growing role of credit, the
puffing up of the housing bubble, and the increasing deregulation of financial markets have been very important. However, these are best understood as transmitters
of our economic problems, arising from the nexus that formed the vicious circle.

What does this tell us about a solution? Economic stimulus, repair of the housing market, and new regulation are all well and good, but they do not deal with the
underlying causes of the crisis. Instead, progressive groups need to work to shift each
of the factors I have noted—power, ideology, and income distribution—in the other
direction. In doing so, we can create a *virtuous* circle, with each change reinforcing
the other changes. If successful, we not only establish a more stable economy, but we
lay the foundation for a more democratic, equitable, and sustainable economic order.

A crisis by its very nature creates opportunities for change. One good place to
begin change and intervene in this "circle"—and transform it from vicious to virtuous—is through pushing for the expansion and reform of social programs, programs that directly serve social needs of the great majority of the population (for
example: single-payer health care, education programs, and environmental protection and repair). By establishing changes in social programs, we will have impacts on
income distribution and ideology, and, perhaps most important, we set in motion *a
power shift* that improves our position for preserving the changes. While I emphasize
social programs as a means to initiate social and economic change, there are other
ways to intervene in the circle. Efforts to re-strengthen unions would be especially
important; and there are other options as well.

Causes of the Crisis: A Long Time Coming

Sometime around the early 1970s, there were some dramatic changes in the U.S. economy. The twenty-five years following World War II had been an era of relatively stable economic growth; the benefits of growth had been widely shared, with wages rising along with productivity gains, and income distribution became slightly less unequal (a good deal less unequal as compared to the pre-Great Depression era). There were severe economic problems in the United States, not the least of which were the continued exclusion of African Americans, large gender inequalities, and the woeful inadequacy of social welfare programs. Nonetheless, relatively stable growth, rising wages, and then the advent of the civil rights movement and the War on Poverty gave some important, positive social and economic character to the era—especially in hindsight!

In part, this comparatively favorable experience for the United States had depended on the very dominant position that U.S. firms held in the world economy, a position in which they were relatively unchallenged by international competition. The firms and their owners were not the only beneficiaries of this situation. With less competitive pressure on them from foreign companies, many U.S. firms accepted unionization and did not find it worthwhile to focus on keeping wages down and obstructing the implementation of social supports for the low-income population. Also, having had the recent experience of the Great Depression, many wealthy people and business executives were probably not so averse to a substantial role for government in regulating the economy.

A Power Grab

By about 1970, the situation was changing. Firms in Europe and Japan had long recovered from World War II, OPEC was taking shape, and weaknesses were emerging in the U.S. economy. The weaknesses were in part a consequence of heavy spending for the Vietnam War combined with the government's reluctance to tax for the war because of its unpopularity. The pressures on U.S. firms arising from these changes had two sets of consequences: slower growth and greater instability; and concerted efforts—a power grab, if you will—by firms and the wealthy to shift the costs of economic deterioration onto U.S. workers and the low-income population.

These "concerted efforts" took many forms: greater resistance to unions and unionization, battles to reduce taxes, stronger opposition to social welfare programs, and, above all, a push to reduce or eliminate government regulation of economic activity through a powerful political campaign to gain control of the various branches and levels of government. The 1980s, with Reagan and Bush One in the White House, were the years in which all these efforts were solidified. Unions were greatly weakened, a phenomenon both demonstrated and exacerbated by Reagan's firing of the air traffic controllers in response to their strike in 1981. The tax cuts of the period were also important markers of the change. But the change had begun earlier; the 1978 passage of the tax-cutting Proposition 13 in California was perhaps the first major success of the movement. And the changes continued well after the 1980s, with welfare reform and deregulation of finance during the Clinton era, to say nothing of the tax cuts and other actions during Bush Two.

Ideology Shift

The changes that began in the 1970s, however, were not simply these sorts of concrete alterations in the structure of power affecting the economy and, especially, government's role in the economy. There was a major shift in ideology, the dominant set of ideas that organize an understanding of our social relations and both guide and rationalize policy decisions.

Following the Great Depression and World War II, there was a wide acceptance of the idea that government had a major role to play in economic life. Less than in many other countries but nonetheless to a substantial degree, at all levels of society, it was generally believed that there should be a substantial government safety net and that government should both regulate the economy in various ways and, through fiscal as well as monetary policy, should maintain aggregate demand. This large economic role for government came to be called Keynesianism, after the British economist John Maynard Keynes, who had set out the arguments for an active fiscal policy in time of economic weakness. In the early 1970s, as economic troubles developed, even Richard Nixon declared: "We are all Keynesians now."

The election of Ronald Reagan, however, marked a sharp change in ideology, at least at the top. Actions of the government were blamed for all economic ills: government spending, Keynesianism, was alleged to be the cause of the inflation of the 1970s; government regulation was supposedly crippling industry; high taxes were, it was argued, undermining incentives for workers to work and for businesses to invest; social welfare spending was blamed for making people dependent on the government and was charged with fraud and corruption (the "welfare queens"); and so on and so on.

Alan Greenspan, Symbol of an Era

One significant symbol of the full rise of the conservative ideology that became so dominant in the latter part of the 20th century was Alan Greenspan, who served from 1974 through 1976 as chairman of the President's Council of Economic Advisers under Gerald Ford and in 1987 became chairman of the Federal Reserve Board, a position he held until 2006. While his predecessors had hardly been critics of U.S. capitalism, Greenspan was a close associate of the philosopher Ayn Rand and an adherent of her extreme ideas supporting individualism and *laissez-faire* (keep-the-government-out) capitalism.

When chairman of the Fed, Greenspan was widely credited with maintaining an era of stable economic growth. As things fell apart in 2008, however, Greenspan was seen as having a large share of responsibility for the non-regulation and excessively easy credit (see article) that led into the crisis.

Called before Congress in October of 2008, Greenspan was chastised by Rep. Henry Waxman (D-Calif.), who asked him: "Do you feel that your ideology pushed you to make decisions that you wish you had not made?" To which Greenspan replied: "Yes, I've found a flaw. I don't know how significant or permanent it is. But I've been very distressed by that fact."

And Greenspan told Congress: "Those of us who have looked to the self-interest of lending institutions to protect shareholders' equity, myself included, are in a state of shocked disbelief."

Greenspan's "shock" was reminiscent of the scene in the film *Casablanca* in which Captain Renault (played by Claude Rains) declares: "I'm shocked, shocked to find that gambling is going on in here!" At which point, a croupier hands Renault a pile of money and says, "Your winnings, sir." Renault replies, *sotto voce*, "Thank you very much."

On economic matters, Reagan championed supply-side economics, the principal idea of which was that tax cuts yield an increase in government revenue because the cuts lead to more rapid economic growth through encouraging more work and more investment. Thus, so the argument went, tax cuts would reduce the government deficit. Reagan, with the cooperation of Democrats, got the tax cuts—and, as the loss of revenue combined with a large increase in military spending, the federal budget deficit grew by leaps and bounds, almost doubling as a share of GDP over the course of the 1980s. It was all summed up in the idea of keeping the government out of the economy; let the free market work its magic.

Growing Inequality

The shifts of power and ideology were very much bound up with a major redistribution upwards of income and wealth. The weakening of unions, the increasing access of firms to low-wage foreign (and immigrant) labor, the refusal of government to maintain the buying power of the minimum wage, favorable tax treatment of the wealthy and their corporations, deregulation in a wide range of industries, and lack of enforcement of existing regulation (e.g., the authorities turning a blind eye to offshore tax shelters) all contributed to these shifts.

Many economists, however, explain the rising income inequality as a result of technological change that favored more highly skilled workers; and changing technology has probably been a factor. Yet the most dramatic aspect of the rising inequality has been the rapidly rising share of income obtained by those at the very top (see figures), who get their incomes from the ownership and control of business, not from their skilled labor. For these people the role of new technologies was most important through its impact on providing more options (e.g., international options) for the managers of firms, more thorough means to control labor, and more effective ways—in the absence of regulation—to manipulate fi-

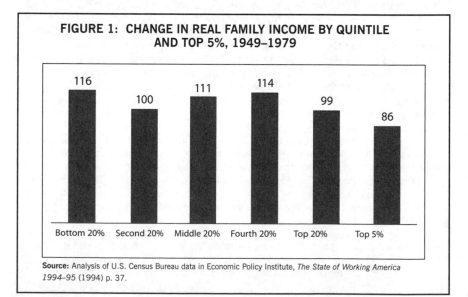

FIGURE 1: CHANGE IN REAL FAMILY INCOME BY QUINTILE AND TOP 5%, 1949–1979

Bottom 20%	Second 20%	Middle 20%	Fourth 20%	Top 20%	Top 5%
116	100	111	114	99	86

Source: Analysis of U.S. Census Bureau data in Economic Policy Institute, *The State of Working America 1994–95* (1994) p. 37.

nance. All of these gains that might be associated with new technology were also gains brought by the way the government handled, or didn't handle (failed to regulate), economic affairs.

Several sets of data demonstrate the sharp changes in the distribution of income that have taken place in the last several decades. Most striking is the changing position of the very highest income segment of the population. In the mid-1920s, the share of all pre-tax income going to the top 1% of households peaked at 23.9%. This elite group's share of income fell dramatically during the Great Depression and World War II to about 12% at the end of the war and then slowly fell further during the next thirty years, reaching a low of 8.9% in the mid-1970s. Since then, the top 1% has regained its exalted position of the earlier era, with 21.8% of income in 2005. Since 1993, more than one-half of all income gains have accrued to this highest 1% of the population.

Figures 1 and 2 show the gains (or losses) of various groups in the 1947 to 1979 period and in the 1979 to 2005 period. The difference is dramatic. For example, in the earlier era, the bottom 20% saw its income in real (inflation-adjusted) terms rise by 116%, and real income of the top 5% grew by only 86%. But in the latter era, the bottom 20% saw a 1% decline in its income, while the top 5% obtained a 81% increase.

The Emergence of Crisis

These changes, especially the dramatic shifts in the distribution of income, set the stage for the increasingly large reliance on credit, especially consumer and mortgage credit, that played a major role in the emergence of the current economic crisis. Other factors were involved, but rising inequality was especially important in effecting the increase in both the demand and supply of credit.

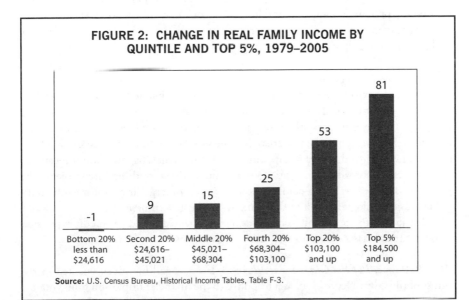

FIGURE 2: CHANGE IN REAL FAMILY INCOME BY QUINTILE AND TOP 5%, 1979–2005

Bottom 20% less than $24,616	Second 20% $24,616– $45,021	Middle 20% $45,021– $68,304	Fourth 20% $68,304– $103,100	Top 20% $103,100 and up	Top 5% $184,500 and up
-1	9	15	25	53	81

Source: U.S. Census Bureau, Historical Income Tables, Table F-3.

Credit Expansion

On the demand side, rising inequality translated into a growing gap between the incomes of most members of society and their needs. For the 2000 to 2007 period, average weekly earnings in the private sector were 12% below their average for the 1970s (in inflation-adjusted terms). From 1980 to 2005 the share of income going to the bottom 60% of families fell from 35% to 29%. Under these circumstances, more and more people relied more and more heavily on credit to meet their needs—everything from food to fuel, from education to entertainment, and especially housing.

While the increasing reliance of consumers on credit has been going on for a long time, it has been especially marked in recent decades. Consumer debt as a share of after-tax personal income averaged 20% in the 1990s, and then jumped up to an average of 25% in the first seven years of the new millennium. But the debt expansion was most marked in housing, where mortgage debt as a percent of after-tax personal income rose from 89% to 94% over the 1990s, and then ballooned to 140% by 2006 as housing prices skyrocketed.

On the supply side, especially in the last few years, the government seems to have relied on making credit readily available as a means to bolster aggregate demand and maintain at least a modicum of economic growth. During the 1990s, the federal funds interest rate averaged 5.1%, but fell to an average of 3.4% in the 2000 to 2007 period—and averaged only 1.4% in 2002 to 2004 period. (The federal funds interest rate is the rate that banks charge one another for overnight loans and is a rate directly affected by the Federal Reserve.) Corresponding to the low interest rates, the money supply grew twice as fast in the new millennium as it had in the 1990s. (And see the box on the connection of the Fed's actions to the Iraq War.)

The increasing reliance of U.S. consumers on credit has often been presented as a moral weakness, as an infatuation with consumerism, and as a failure to look beyond the present. Whatever moral judgments one may make, however, the expansion of the credit economy has been a response to real economic forces—inequality and government policies, in particular.

The Failure to Regulate

The credit expansion by itself, however, did not precipitate the current crisis. Deregulation—or, more generally, the failure to regulate—is also an important part of the story. The government's role in regulation of financial markets has been a central feature in the development of this crisis, but the situation in financial markets has been part of a more general process—affecting airlines and trucking, telecommunications, food processing, broadcasting, and of course international trade and investment. The process has been driven by a combination of power (of large firms and wealthy individuals) and ideology (leave it to the market, get the government out).

The failure to regulate financial markets that transformed the credit expansion into a financial crisis shows up well in three examples:

The 1999 repeal of the Glass-Steagall Act. Glass-Steagall had been enacted in the midst of the Great Depression, as a response to the financial implosion following the

---

Joseph Stiglitz on the War and the Economy

On October 2, 2008, on the Pacifica radio program *Democracy Now!*, Amy Goodman and Juan Gonzalez interviewed Joseph Stiglitz about the economic situation. Stiglitz was the 2001 winner of the Nobel Prize in Economics, former chief economist at the World Bank, and former chair of President Clinton's Council of Economic Advisers. He is a professor at Columbia University. Following is an excerpt from that interview:

AMY GOODMAN: Joseph Stiglitz, you're co-author of *The Three Trillion Dollar War: The True Cost of the Iraq Conflict*. How does the bailout [of the financial sector] connect to war?

JOSEPH STIGLITZ: Very much. Let me first explain a little bit how the current crisis connects with the war. One of the reasons that we have this crisis is that the Fed flooded the economy with liquidity and had lax regulations. Part of that was this ideology of "regulations are bad," but part of the reason was that the economy was weak. And one of the reasons the economy was weak was oil prices were soaring, and part of the reason oil prices were soaring is the Iraq war. When we went to war in 2003, before we went, prices were $23 a barrel. Futures markets thought they would remain at that level. They anticipated the increase in demand, but they thought there would be a concomitant increase in supply from the low-cost providers, mainly in the Middle East. The war changed that equation, and we know what happened to the oil prices.

Well, why is that important? Well, we were spending—Americans were spending hundreds of millions—billions of dollars to buy—more, to buy imported oil. Normally, that would have had a very negative effect on our economy; we would have had a slowdown. Some people have said, you know, it's a mystery why we aren't having that slowdown; we repealed the laws of economics. Whenever anybody says that, you ought to be suspect.

It was actually very simple. The Fed engineered a bubble, a housing bubble to replace the tech bubble that it had engineered in the '90s. The housing bubble facilitated people taking money out of their . . . houses; in one year, there were more than $900 billion of mortgage equity withdrawals. And so, we had a consumption boom that was so strong that even though we were spending so much money abroad, we could keep the economy going. But it was so shortsighted. And it was so clear that we were living on borrowed money and borrowed time. And it was just a matter of time before, you know, the whole thing would start to unravel.

---

stock market crash of 1929. Among other things, it required that different kinds of financial firms—commercial banks, investment banks, insurance companies—be separate. This separation both limited the spread of financial problems and reduced conflicts of interest that could arise were the different functions of these firms combined into a single firm. As perhaps the most important legislation regulating the financial sector, the repeal of Glass-Steagall was not only a substantive change but was an important symbol of the whole process of deregulation.

The failure to regulate mortgage lending. Existing laws and regulations require lending institutions to follow prudent practices in making loans, assuring that borrowers have the capacity to be able to pay back the loans. And of course fraud—lying about the provisions of loans—is prohibited. Yet in an atmosphere where regulation was "out," regulators were simply not doing their jobs. The consequences are illustrated in a December 28, 2008, *New York Times* story on the failed Washington Mutual Bank. The article describes a supervisor at a mortgage processing center as having been "accustomed to seeing babysitters claiming salaries worthy of college presidents, and schoolteachers with incomes rivaling stockbrokers'. He rarely questioned them. A real estate frenzy was under way and WaMu, as his bank was known, was all about saying yes."

One may wonder why banks—or other lending institutions, mortgage firms, in particular—would make loans to people who were unlikely to be able to pay them back. The reason is that the lending institutions quickly combined such loans into packages (i.e., a security made up of several borrowers' obligations to pay) and sold them to other investors in a practice called "securitization."

Credit-default swaps. Perhaps the most egregious failure to regulate in recent years has been the emergence of credit-default swaps, which are connected to securitization. Because they were made up of obligations by a diverse set of borrowers, the packages of loans were supposedly low-risk investments. Yet those who purchased them still sought insurance against default. Insurance sellers, however, are regulated—required, for example, to keep a certain amount of capital on hand to cover possible claims. So the sellers of these insurance policies on packages of loans called the policies "credit-default swaps" and thus were allowed to avoid regulation. Further, these credit-default swaps, these insurance policies, themselves were bought and sold again and again in unregulated markets in a continuing process of speculation.

The credit-default swaps are a form of derivative, a financial asset the value of which is derived from some other asset—in this case the value of packages of mortgages for which they were the insurance policies. When the housing bubble began to collapse and people started to default on their mortgages, the value of credit-default swaps plummeted and their future value was impossible to determine. No one would buy them, and several banks that had speculated in these derivatives were left holding huge amounts of these "toxic assets."

Bubble and Bust

The combination of easy credit and the failure to regulate together fueled the housing bubble. People could buy expensive houses but make relatively low monthly payments. Without effective regulation of mortgage lending, they could get the loans even when they were unlikely to be able to make payments over the long run. Moreover, as these pressures pushed up housing prices, many people bought houses simply to resell them quickly at a higher price, in a process called "flipping." And such speculation pushed the prices up further. Between 2000 and 2006, housing prices rose by 90% (as consumer prices generally rose by only 17%).

While the housing boom was in full swing, both successful housing speculators and lots of people involved in the shenanigans of credit markets made a lot of money. However, as the housing bubble burst—as all bubbles do—things fell apart. The packages of loans lost value, and the insurance policies on them, the credit-default swaps, lost value. These then became "toxic" assets for those who held them, assets not only with reduced value but with unknown value. Not only did large financial firms—for example, Lehman Brothers and AIG—have billions of dollars in losses, but no one knew the worth of their remaining assets. The assets were called "toxic" because they poisoned the operations of the financial system. Under these circumstances, financial institutions stopped lending to one another—that is, the credit markets "froze up." The financial crisis was here.

The financial crisis, not surprisingly, very quickly shifted to a general economic crisis. Firms in the "real" economy rely heavily on a well-functioning financial system to supply them with the funds they need for their regular operations—loans to car buyers, loans to finance inventory, loans for construction of new facilities, loans for new equipment, and, of course, mortgage loans. Without those loans (or with the loans much more difficult to obtain), there has been a general cut-back in economic activity, what is becoming a serious and probably prolonged recession.

What Is to Be Done?

So here we are. The shifts in power, ideology, and income distribution have placed us in a rather nasty situation. There are some steps that will be taken that have a reasonable probability of yielding short-run improvement. In particular, a large increase in government spending—deficit spending—will probably reduce the depth and shorten the length of the recession. And the actions of the Federal Reserve and Treasury to inject funds into the financial system are likely, along with the deficit spending, to "un-freeze" credit markets (the mismanagement and, it seems, outright corruption of the bailout notwithstanding). Also, there is likely to be some re-regulation of the financial industry. These steps, however, at best will restore things to where they were before the crisis. They do not treat the underlying causes of the crisis—the vicious circle of power, ideology, and inequality.

Opportunity for Change

Fortunately, the crisis itself has weakened some aspects of this circle. The cry of "leave it to the market" is still heard, but is now more a basis for derision than a guide to policy. The ideology and, to a degree, the power behind the ideology, have been severely weakened as the role of "keeping the government out" has shown to be a major cause of the financial mess and our current hardships. There is now widespread support among the general populace and some support in Washington for greater regulation of the financial industry.

Whether or not the coming period will see this support translated into effective policy is of course an open question. Also an open question is how much the turn away from "leaving it to the market" can be extended to other sectors of the economy. With regard to the environment, there is already general acceptance of the principle that the government (indeed, many governments) must take an active role in regulating economic activity. Similar principles need to be recognized with regard to health care, education, housing, child care, and other support programs for low-income families.

The discrediting of "keep the government out" ideology provides an opening to develop new programs in these areas and to expand old programs. Furthermore, as the federal government revs up its "stimulus" program in the coming months, opportunities will exist for expanding support for these sorts of programs. This support is important, first of all, because these programs serve real, pressing needs—needs that have long existed and are becoming acute and more extensive in the current crisis.

Breaking the Circle

Support for these social programs, however, may also serve to break into the vicious power-ideology-inequality circle and begin transforming it into a virtuous circle. Social programs are inherently equalizing in two ways: they provide their benefits to low-income people and they provide some options for those people in their efforts to demand better work and higher pay. Also, the further these programs develop, the more they establish the legitimacy of a larger role for public control of—government involvement in—the economy; they tend to bring about an ideological shift. By affecting a positive distributional shift and by shifting ideology, the emergence of stronger social programs can have a wider impact on power. In other words, efforts to promote social programs are one place to start, an entry point to shift the vicious circle to a virtuous circle.

There are other entry points. Perhaps the most obvious ones are actions to strengthen the role of unions. The Employee Free Choice Act may be a useful first step, and it will be helpful to establish a more union-friendly Department of Labor and National Labor Relations Board. Raising the minimum wage—ideally indexing it to inflation—would also be highly desirable. While conditions have changed since the heyday of unions in the middle of the 20th century, and we cannot expect to restore the conditions of that era, a greater role for unions would seem essential in righting the structural conditions at the foundation of the current crisis.

Shifting Class Power

None of this is assured, of course. Simply starting social programs will not necessarily mean that they have the wider impacts that I am suggesting are possible. No one should think that by setting up some new programs and strengthening some existing ones we will be on a smooth road to economic and social change. Likewise, rebuilding the strength of unions will involve extensive struggle and will not be accomplished by a few legislative or executive actions.

Also, all efforts to involve the government in economic activity—whether in finance or environmental affairs, in health care or education, in work support or job training programs—will be met with the worn-out claims that government involvement generates bureaucracy, stifles initiative, and places an excessive burden on private firms and individuals. We are already hearing warnings that in dealing with the financial crisis the government must avoid "over-regulation." Likewise, efforts to strengthen unions will suffer the traditional attacks, as unions are portrayed as corrupt and their members privileged. The unfolding situation with regard to the auto firms' troubles has demonstrated the attack, as conservatives have blamed the United Auto Workers for the industry's woes and have demanded extensive concessions by the union.

Certainly not all regulation is good regulation. Aside from excessive bureaucratic controls, there is the phenomenon by which regulating agencies are often captives of the industries that they are supposed to regulate. And there are corrupt unions. These are real issues, but they should not be allowed to derail change.

The current economic crisis emerged in large part as a shift in the balance of class power in the United States, a shift that began in the early 1970s and continued into the new millennium. Perhaps the present moment offers an opportunity to shift things back in the other direction. Recognition of the complex nexus of causes of the current economic crisis provides some guidance where people might start. Rebuilding and extending social programs, strengthening unions, and other actions that contribute to a more egalitarian power shift will not solve all the problems of U.S. capitalism. They can, however, begin to move us in the right direction.

Article 7.7

RECESSION, DEPRESSION, REPRESSION: WHAT'S IN A NAME?

BY JOHN MILLER
July/August 2009

A frightening financial panic, a virulent housing bust, and plummeting economic output have left global capitalism facing its worst crisis since the Great Depression.

Economies across the globe are in trouble. The European and Japanese economies shrank at double-digit rates in the first three months of this year; even China's growth rate is slowing precipitously. U.S. autoworkers, European and U.S. finance workers, Japanese electronics workers, Chinese garment workers, and Indian software workers are losing their jobs as their economies slow and world export markets dry up.

In the United States, where the crisis hit first, the downturn that began in December 2007 is now the longest since World War II, with the greatest job losses and, by some measures, the highest unemployment of the postwar period.

Housing prices, the fountainhead of the crisis, have now fallen more than they did during the housing bust of the Great Depression. Record levels of mortgage defaults and foreclosures have spread panic through a rickety global financial system. In a six-month span, three of the five largest U.S. investment banks disappeared. Leading U.S. mortgage company Countrywide bit the dust. Washington Mutual collapsed, the largest commercial bank failure in U.S. history.

The stock market has crashed as well. Stock prices fell to below one-half of their peak value in most indices, matching the initial declines in 1929.

In brief, the current contraction is no run-of-the-mill recession. But neither, at least at this point, is it comparable to the decade-long Great Depression, in which output fell by one-quarter and more than one-quarter of the U.S. workforce went without work.

So what is it? A recession or a depression? Truth is, economists make no precise distinction between the two other than that recessions are mild and depressions are more severe.

Even with their imprecision, neither term properly fits our current economic decline at this point, although it may yet become inarguably a depression. What term would fit? "The Great Recession," the name favored by former Fed chair Paul Volcker among others, is one candidate. "The Panic of 2008-2009" is another.

But better yet is "The Repression," a name suggested by University of Massachusetts economist Arthur MacEwan. Part recession, part depression, today's economic meltdown is very much a product of the large dose of economic repression that preceded it. Deregulatory, pro-rich, anti-labor public policy guaranteed that the benefits of economic growth, at least what we had of it this decade, went almost exclusively to the most well-to-do among us, leaving many vulnerable. The latest business cycle, both its expansion beginning in 2001 and its catastrophic downturn now underway, make those consequences clear for all to see. In a very real way, the Repression of 2008 and 2009 has now pushed many people out of the frying pan and into the fire. And not only does the term "repression" describe the causes of the current crisis; it also points us toward its consequences, and toward prospective cures for today's economic woes.

The Frying Pan: The Expansion of 2001–07

Economic expansions are supposed to improve our life chances, not just swell the economy. For some time now, however, economic upswings have done less to improve the lot of most people than they used to.

During the first two decades after World War II, the U.S. economy grew rapidly, lifted incomes and wages, reduced inequality, and alleviated poverty. With its global dominance, the U.S. economy grew an average of 5.0% a year during the expansions between 1950 and 1969. Strong trade unions and expanding government programs helped to protect workers, fight poverty, and spread the benefits of economic growth widely, at least by today's standards.

No subsequent expansion has met those standards. But in this decade the capacity of economic growth to make most people better off all but evaporated. First off, the U.S. economy has grown more slowly in this decade than in any of the earlier postwar decades, even before accounting for the current crisis. Beginning in November 2001, the economy grew for 73 months or just over six years, reaching a peak in December 2007. That is longer than the 57-month average duration of postwar expansions. But GDP grew at an anemic annual rate of 2.5% in the 2001–07 expansion, far below the 4.3% average for postwar expansions. (See Table 1.)

Along with slower growth that failed to engage the productive capacity of the U.S. economy, successive economic expansions have created fewer and fewer jobs. In the last three business cycles, the economy has continued to lose jobs even after an economic recovery was underway. On top of that, recoveries have taken longer and longer to replace the jobs lost in the downturn. (See Table 2.)

TABLE 1: SIZING UP THE 2001–07 EXPANSION

	2001–07 Expansion	Average Postwar Expansion
Length of Expansion	73 Months	57 Months
GDP Growth	2.5%	4.3%
Employment Gains	0.9%	2.5%
Wage and Salary Growth	1.8%	3.8%
Corporate Profits	10.8%	7.4%

Notes: GDP, employment, wages and salaries, and corporate profits are all measured as annual rates of change and corrected for inflation. The average for postwar expansions is calculated for the six expansions from 1961 to 2001.

Sources: Bureau of Economic Analysis, Bureau of Labor Statistics, and Federal Reserve Board.

TABLE 2: JOB MARKET DECLINE AND RECOVERY
IN SIX POSTWAR RECESSIONS (NUMBERS IN MONTHS)

Recession	Length of Recession	Months of Job Losses	Months until Jobs Recovery
Nov. 1969 – Nov. 1970	12	14	19
Dec. 1973 – March 1975	16	16	25
Jan. 1980 – July 1980	6	6	11
July 1981 – Nov. 1982	16	19	29
July 1990 – March 1991	8	11	30
March 2001 – Nov. 2001	8	32	48

Source: Bureau of Labor Statistics.

In this decade, "the great American jobs machine" truly met its maker. Shockingly, the economy continued to lose jobs *for the first two and half years* of this last expansion. A full four years passed before the economy had added back the jobs lost during the 2001 recession, more than twice as long as in the average expansion since 1970.

The economic expansion from 2001 to the end of 2007 added jobs more slowly than any other expansion since World War II. The number of jobs in the economy increased by just 0.9% a year, about one-third of the 2.5% rate posted by the average postwar expansion.

Sluggish economic growth left employers with little need for new hires. Another drain on U.S. job creation was the increasing number of jobs lost to global outsourcing. Not only manufacturing jobs went abroad, but so did white collar work from backroom office operations (bookkeeping, customer service, and marketing) to engineering and computer software design.

All told, during the eight years of the Bush administration, job growth averaged a meager 0.28% annually. That's just 378,000 new jobs a year, a total we would expect a growing economy to add in a single month.

Expansion and Repression

The sluggish economic growth of the first six years of this decade not only created fewer jobs than earlier postwar expansions, it also, not surprisingly, did less to lift incomes, alleviate poverty, or improve the economic well-being of all but the best-off. Those lopsided results are easily documented:

• For the first time in the postwar period, median household income (corrected for inflation) at the peak of this expansion was still below its level at the previous peak in 2000.

- By 2007, 5.9 million more people were without health insurance than when the expansion began in 2001.

- For the first time in a postwar expansion, the poverty rate failed to decline. In 2007 at the peak of this expansion, the U.S. poverty rate stood at 12.5%, well above the 11.7% rate when the expansion began.

- After correcting for inflation, wages and salaries grew just 1.8% a year during this expansion, less half the 3.8% rate during the average postwar expansion.

- At the same time, real corporate profits skyrocketed, increasing 10.8% a year, after adjusting for inflation, compared to the 8.3% average growth rate in other postwar growth periods.

Not surprisingly, inequality, which by 2001 was already unprecedented by postwar standards, continued to worsen during the decade. But just how much of the population missed out on the benefits of economic growth was astonishing. The average real income of the poorest 20% of households declined, but so did that of the best-off 20% of households. The incomes of the three quintiles in between stagnated; none grew by more than 1.1% over the entire period. Even the average income of the richest 5% declined during this expansion.

The top one percent of households, on the other hand, continued to make out like bandits. Their real income grew by 10.9% each year from 2002 to 2006, reports economist Emmanuel Saez using the most recent data available. That small sliver of the population monopolized 73% of the income growth during those years. In contrast, the bottom 99% of households saw their real incomes grow just 1.0% in each of those years.

As these figures make clear, the combination of sluggish economic growth, few new jobs, stagnant wages and incomes, and extreme inequality left many people behind long before the economy collapsed in 2008.

Bubbles Bursting

The economic collapse, however, began before 2008 with the bursting of the housing bubble. Despite spanning the 2001 recession, that ten-year bubble, from 1996 to 2006, drove up housing prices further and for longer than in any period since 1890. According to Yale economist Robert Shiller's long-term U.S. home price index, real (i.e., inflation-adjusted) housing prices increased an unprecedented 84.5% in that period.

Skyrocketing housing prices allowed homeowners to use their homes as ATMs, as economics journalist Doug Henwood first put it, taking out loans on the rising value of their houses. The volume of these so-called mortgage equity withdrawals more than doubled from 2000 to the peak of the housing bubble in 2005-6 and financed about one-third of the growth in consumption over those years.

U.S. housing prices are now down by more than one-quarter from their peak in late 2005. That is not only the sharpest decline of the postwar period, it is the biggest drop in housing prices since the 32.3% drop from 1914 to 1921—including the housing bust during the Great Depression. The collapse of housing prices put the kibosh on consumer spending, precipitated a crisis of mortgage defaults and foreclosures, and punched a hole in the financial system.

The crash of the stock market is unprecedented by postwar standards as well. By March 2, 2009, the Dow Jones Industrial Average of 30 blue-chip stocks had fallen 53.2% from its October 2007 peak. Broader stock indices, such as the Standard & Poor's 500, had registered even sharper declines. In comparison, the high-tech stock market crash earlier this decade had knocked 35.2% off the price of blue-chip stocks at its low point; the bear market of 1973, 42.2%. Only the Great Depression took more out of stock prices. At their low point in June 1932, stocks had lost a stunning 88.8% of their October 1929 value. While the stock market lately has shown some life, the turnaround in stock prices is unlikely to be rapid even if the stock market has already seen its bottom. It took 6 years, 9 years, and 25 years respectively for the stock market to replace the value lost in the 2001, 1973, and 1929 crashes.

The Fire: Increased Repression in 2007–09

Dismal labor market conditions were the cutting edge of the economic downturn proper. The economy began shedding jobs long before economic growth plummeted. Even the National Bureau of Economic Research (NBER), which determines the turning points of U.S. business cycles, took notice. In 2008 the economy lost jobs every month of the year for the first time since the Great Depression. The mounting monthly job losses convinced the NBER to declare the recession's start-date December 2007, even though at that point the economy had not yet suffered two consecutive quarters of negative economic growth—the standard definition of a recession.

In other words, in this downturn job losses are no lagging indicator. But don't expect employment to be a leading indicator of the recovery either. Job losses will almost certainly continue even after economic growth returns. Before things are over,

TABLE 3: THE DEPTH OF THE CURRENT DOWNTURN

	2007-09 Recession to Date	Average Postwar Recession
Length of Downturn	17 Months	10 Months
Economic Output Loss	-2.4 (1st five quarters)	-2.05%
Industrial Production	-13.6%	-4.0%**
Retail Sales	-11.8%	-3.5%**
Employment Losses	-4.1%	-2.1%**

Notes: Economic output loss is the cumulative loss of output over a recession measured as the decline of GDP corrected for inflation. The industrial production index is again the cumulative decline in the index over the recession. Retails sales are measured as the total decline in retail sales corrected for inflation. Employment losses are measured as the drop in total employment over the recession. The averages for industrial production, retail sales, and employment losses are for the six recessions from 1969 to 2001. The GDP average is for 10 recessions from 1948 to 2001.

Sources: Bureau of Economic Analysis, Bureau of Labor Statistics, and Federal Reserve Board.

the labor market downturn and the suffering endured by all those looking for work will have persisted far longer than the contraction of economic output.

The U.S. economy is losing jobs as never before in the postwar period. Seventeen months into the downturn, the economy has lost more jobs than in any previous downturn and has lost nearly twice the share of its employment base as in the typical postwar recession. (See Table 3.) Construction, manufacturing of all sorts, and the financial industry, all male-dominated employments, have been especially hard hit. But even software giant Microsoft and major law firms are now laying off workers.

The fact that the 2001–2007 economic expansion created so few jobs heightens the effects of this extreme job loss. With few new jobs, especially full-time ones, workers' connection to the labor force is ever more tenuous. By the first quarter of 2009, marginally attached workers (those who want a job and have looked for work in the last year but not in the last month, hence are not counted as unemployed) formed a larger share of the labor force than in the 2001 recession. (Data are available only from 1994 on.) Also, the proportion of the labor force forced to work part-time because they could not find full-time jobs was higher than in any recession since 1970, including the severe 1974–75 and 1982 recessions. (Data are available from 1968 on.) By April 2009, forced part-time workers made up twice the share of the labor force as in the 2001 recession.

The failure of the 2001 expansion to lift incomes is also intensifying the suffering in this crisis. In the nearly decade-long expansion of the 1960s, the income of the median household, corrected for inflation, rose nearly 4% a year. But the 2001 to 2007 expansion added a measly 0.2% a year to real median incomes.

As income stagnated with increasingly repressive economic growth, households went deeper into debt. In the 1982 recession, 10.7% of U.S. households' disposable income went to service debt payments. In December 2007, at the onset of this downturn, that figure had reached 14.3%. It dipped slightly in 2008 as worried households began to cut back on their borrowing, but it is no longer dropping as mounting unemployment has pushed down households' disposable income.

This downturn has already gone on longer than even the two longest postwar downturns, in 1973–75 and 1981–1982, both of which lasted 16 months. Even if the economy begins to recover in the last quarter of 2009, the downturn would have lasted 22 months, more than twice as long as the 10-month average length of postwar recessions.

To date, the loss of output has not matched that in the worst postwar recessions. Through its first five quarters, inflation-adjusted GDP in the current downturn has fallen 2.4%—more than the average loss of output during all postwar recessions of 2.05% but less than the steeper declines in output during the 1974–75 and 1982 recessions. In the first half of 2008 the economy continued to grow slowly even as it shed jobs. Then the contraction began; output fell at annual rates of over 6% in the last quarter of 2008 and the first quarter of 2009. Even the most optimistic forecasts do not see a return to economic growth until the last quarter of 2009. By that time the loss of output over the last two years will surely have outdistanced that of any postwar downturn.

In specific sectors the current loss of output has already outdistanced all postwar recessions. Industrial production, which includes hard-hit manufacturers of automobiles, home electronics, and construction supplies, has fallen off at double-digit rates—more than three times its decline in the average postwar recession. Today's loss of industrial output has already matched the shredding of industry in the 1982 recession, the worst previous case (see Table 3).

Retail sales have been decimated as well. In the typical postwar recession, retail sales dropped off by about 3.5%, stabilizing within half a year after the onset of the downturn. But this time, retail sales have dropped 12.9% and are still falling. Circuit City, the electronics giant, closed its doors; Filene's Basement, the venerable department store, laid off workers; and even eBay, the internet retailer, issued pink slips.

Fighting Repression

The cure to the Repression is to fight repressive policies. Public policy must make the fight by promoting genuine full employment, legalizing card check union drives by passing the Employee Free Choice Act, enforcing labor laws already on the books by expanding the workplace inspection staff of the Department of Labor, and extending health insurance to all. Reducing payroll taxes, the bulk of most people's federal tax bill, will help, along with letting the Bush tax cuts targeted at the wealthy expire in 2010. Those policies would do much to enhance workers' bargaining power, lessen labor abuse, and arrest today's worsening inequality—or if you will, to undo repression.

Realizing those goals would take active and progressive government intervention into the labor markets and substantial funding for government programs that will put people to work repairing our decaying infrastructure and making it greener, restoring the social services cut out of state budgets in the crisis, and providing relief to those who have lost their homes or their jobs. And that spending would also get the economy going and counteract the Repression.

None of that will happen without massive public pressure. The Obama administration must not succumb to the calls of deficit hawks to slash government spending. Their do-nothing strategy, or worse yet more tax cuts for the wealthy, would saddle the federal government with even larger deficits as the economy and tax revenues fell through the floor. And unlike a program of progressive government spending, which holds the potential to spark a period of economic growth that could pay the public debt, a do-nothing strategy would likely lead us into a depression that would impose costs far more serious than a rise in government debt.

In addition, the Obama administration will need to impose strict controls on a financial industry to which it has close ties: one of its most senior economic advisors played a key role in deregulation. It will also have to convert its stress tests of troubled banks into a lever to take over any distressed bank, mortgage house, or insurer that is too big to fail and then run them as mutual savings banks for the benefit of the public.

Those steps will help to end the Repression by getting the economy going and to disable the drivers that have shaped economic growth so lopsidedly in favor of so few while repressing so many. Without them we will see either a return of the kind of economic growth that creates few jobs and does little to alleviate economic repression, or worst yet a decade-long period of economic stagnation and worsening economic suffering.

Sources: Kelly Evans and Robert Guy Matthews, "Manufacturing Tumbles Globally," *Wall Street Journal*, Jan. 3, 2009; *Left Business Observer* #118, Dec. 22, 2008; Josh L. Bivens and John Irons, "A Feeble Recovery: The Fundamental Economic Weaknesses of the 2001-2007 Expansion," Economic Policy Institute Briefing Paper #214, May 1, 2008; Jon Hilsenrath and Kelly Evans, "Mixed Economic Data Show a Changing Business Cycle," *Wall Street Journal*, September 8, 2008; National Bureau of Economic Research, "Determination of the 2007 Peak in Economic Activity," December 11, 2008; John Schmitt and Dean Baker, "What We're In For: Projected Economic Impact of the Next Recession," Center for Economic and Policy Research, January 2008; Marcus Walker et al., "Global Slump Seen Deepening," *Wall Street Journal*, Jan. 1, 2009; Tom Lauricella and Annelena Lobb, "Stocks Hit '97 Level, Signaling Long Slump," *Wall Street Journal*, March 3, 2009; Sudeep Reedy, "Jobless Rate Hits 8.5%," *Wall Street Journal*, April 4, 2009; Charles Gascon, "The Current Recession: How Bad Is It?" Economic Synopsis No. 4, St. Louis Federal Reserve Bank, 2009; Kevin Klieson, "Recession or Depression," *Economic Synopsis* No. 15, St. Louis Federal Reserve Bank, 2009; Robert Shiller, "Online Data," at www.econ.yale.edu/~shiller/data. htm.

Chapter 8

INTERNATIONAL TRADE AND FINANCE

INTRODUCTION

When it comes to the global economy, most textbooks line up behind the "Washington Consensus"—a package of free trade and financial liberalization policies that the U.S. Treasury Department, the International Monetary Fund (IMF), and the World Bank have spun into the prevailing prescriptions for the world's developing economies. Mainstream textbook discussions of exchange rates, international trade, and economic development policies almost always promote a market-dictated integration into the world economy. Outside the classroom, however, popular discontent with the Washington Consensus has spawned a worldwide movement calling into question the myth of self-regulating markets on which these policies rest.

While the doctrines of free trade and financial liberalization are seldom questioned in mainstream economics textbooks, both are scrutinized here. Arthur Mac-Ewan gives an overview of the process of globalization today, what is new and what continues long-established patterns, and the difficulties opposition groups face coming to grips with the power and the complexity of these forces (Article 8.1). Mac-Ewan's second article shows how industrialized economies developed by protecting their own manufacturing sectors—never preaching the "gospel of free trade" until they were highly developed. Today, he argues, these countries prescribe free trade not because it's the best way for others to develop, but because it gives U.S. corporations free access to the world's markets and resources, which in turn strengthens the power of businesses against workers (Article 8.2).

Ramaa Vasudevan takes a critical look at the doctrine of comparative advantage, the backbone of free trade theory, and shows that it comes up short as a guide for economic development (Article 8.3). John Miller debunks the Economic Freedom Index that the Heritage Foundation and other backers of neoliberal globalization use to argue that economic freedom and prosperity go hand-in-hand. Miller argues that the Index measures neither prosperity nor freedom, but rather corporate freedom from accountability (Article 8.4). Smriti Rao assesses the impact of the recent global economic crisis and traces how the crisis, which largely began in the United States, was transmitted to the developing world (Article 8.7). And Dariush

Sokolov reports on the efforts of some South American countries to establish a regional development fund that would allow them to escape the clutches of the world creditors' cartel controlled by the IMF and the World Bank (Article 8.8).

Economist Marie Duggan lays bare the financial flows and policies that lie behind the United States' unprecedented current account deficit and its increased reliance of the U.S. economy on foreign capital, especially from China. She traces the flight of foreign capital from the United States with the onset of current crisis and why that capital flight ceased when other economies across the globe fell into crisis (Article 8.5). Economist Katherine Sciacchitano also examines these flows, tracing the evolution of the regimes that have governed global trade since World War II. She asks whether the large U.S. trade deficit threatens the dollar's status as global reserve currency (Article 8.6).

Two important factors in the huge U.S. current account deficit come from U.S. dependence on foreign oil and the sizable remittances from workers in the United States to their families in the developing world. Alissa Thuotte looks at the large and growing flow of remittances that have improved the standard of living of families in the developing world but left them vulnerable to far-off economic disturbances, as the current crisis illustrates (Article 8.11). Higher remittances are associated with a modest reduction in global poverty. But just what is the proper way to measure global poverty? MacEwan assesses the different measures of poverty in the developing world (Article 8.9).

Labor standards are another casualty of neoliberal globalization. In his last article, Arthur MacEwan argues that using trade agreements to pressure governments to allow unhindered union organizing is always a good thing. But when it comes to including other labor standards in trade agreements, from child labor restrictions to health and safety standards, MacEwan counsels first-world activists to take their lead from the workers in the developing world affected by those agreements (Article 8.12). John Miller replies to *New York Times* columnist Nicholas Kristof, who steadfastly maintains that more sweatshops, not fewer, are the key to lifting young men and women in sub-Saharan Africa out of poverty. Miller then offers an alternative set of policies to bring development to the region (Article 8.13). Martha Ojeda, executive director of the Coalition for Justice in the Maquiladoras, paints a devastating picture of the effects of the North American Free Trade Agreement (NAFTA) on workers in *maquiladoras*, or border factories, over the last twenty years. In her article, she recounts how women played a central role in the struggle to establish a democratic union at a Sony plant in the Mexican border city of Nuevo Laredo (Article 8.10).

Discussion Questions

1. (Article 8.1) According to MacEwan, what aspects of today's globalization are new and what continues earlier trends? How might opposition forces best push for a more democratic and equitable globalization process?

2. (Article 8.2) MacEwan claims that the "infant industry" argument for trade protection is much more widely applicable than standard theory suggests. To what countries

and industries might it apply in today's world economy? Explain your answer.

3. (Article 8.2) Free trade, MacEwan argues, gives business greater power relative to labor. Why is this so? Is it a good reason to oppose free trade?

4. (Article 8.3) What is the doctrine of comparative advantage? And why, according to Vasudevan, is it not a good guide to successful economic development?

5. (Article 8.4) According to Miller, how is the Economic Freedom Index misleading about the relationship between "free market policies," economic growth, and vulnerability to economic crises?

6. (Article 8.5) What is a current account deficit and what causes it? What problems does the present U.S. current account deficit create for the U.S. economy and people?

7. (Article 8.5) Why did foreign capital leave the United States with the onset of the current crisis in 2007 and why did it return a year later?

8. (Article 8.6) How does the denomination of oil prices in dollars affect the U.S. trade deficit and sustain the value of the dollar?

9. (Article 8.7) How was the economic crisis that originated in the developed world transmitted to the developing world? How might its devastating effects be remedied?

10. (Article 8.8) What advantages might a regional development fund offer South American countries over IMF funding? And how are these and other countries trying to change the way the IMF operates?

11. (Article 8.9) What are the standard measures of global poverty? What is a more effective way to measure global poverty?

12. (Article 8.10) What was the role of women workers in organizing the Sony *maquiladora* factory? How has NAFTA affected the rights of Mexican workers in the *maquiladora* plants?

13. (Article (8.11) How big are remittances? Where do they come from and where do they go? Finally, what sort of effect are they having on families in the developing world?

14. (Article 8.12) What are the pros and cons of including labor standards in trade agreements? Why does MacEwan consider the right to organize unions a special case? Do you agree with MacEwan that first-world activists pressing for more stringent labor standards across the global economy should take their cues from workers in the developing world?

15. (Article 8.13) What is the basis of journalist Nicholas Kristof's claim that young men on the streets of Namibia's capital city need the opportunity to work in

sweatshops? Why does Miller find Kristof's claim unconvincing? Who do you think is right? Why?

———————————————————

Article 8.1

WHAT IS GLOBALIZATION?

BY ARTHUR MacEWAN

Reprinted with permission from Radical Teacher, *Issue 61, 2001*

Ever since Adam and Eve left the garden, people have been expanding the geographic realm of their economic, political, social and cultural contacts. In this sense of extending connections to other peoples around the world, globalization is nothing new. Also, as a process of change that can embody both great opportunities for wealth and progress and great trauma and suffering, globalization at the beginning of the 21st century is following a well established historical path. Yet the current period of change in the international system does have its own distinctive features, not the least important of which is the particular sort of political conflict it is generating.

"Greatest Events" and "Dreadful Misfortunes"

We are fond of viewing our own period as one in which great transformations are taking place, and it is easy to recite a list of technological and social changes that have dramatically altered the way we live and the way we connect to peoples elsewhere in the world. Yet, other surges of globalization in the modern era have been similarly disruptive to established practices. The first surge by which we might mark the beginning of modern globalization came with the invasion of the Western Hemisphere by European powers and with their extension of ocean trade around Africa to Asia. Adam Smith, writing *The Wealth of Nations* in 1776, did not miss the significance of these developments:

The discovery of America, and that of a passage to the East Indies by the Cape of Good Hope, are the two greatest and most important events recorded in the history of mankind... By uniting, in some measure, the most distant parts of the world, by enabling them to relieve one another's wants, to increase one another's enjoyments, and to encourage one another's industry, their general tendency would seem to be beneficial.

Alongside of what Adam Smith saw as the great gains of globalization (not his term!), were the slaughter, by battle and disease, of millions of Native Americans, the enslavement and associated deaths of millions of Africans, and the subjugation of peoples in Asia. Smith did recognize the "dreadful misfortunes" that fell upon the peoples of the East and West Indies as a result of these "greatest events" (though he does not mention Africans in this expression of concern). He saw these misfortunes, however, as arising "rather from accident than from any thing in the nature of the events themselves."

The first stage of modern globalization illustrates not only the combined great gains and "dreadful misfortunes" that have characterized globalization but also the vast scope of the process. The political and economic changes that followed from the European conquest of the Americas and forays into Asia are relatively well known.

Equally momentous were the huge cultural transformations that were tied to the great expansion of economic contacts among the continents. Peoples moved, or they were moved by force. As they came to new locations and in contact with other peoples, almost every aspect of their lives was altered—from what people eat ("Italian" spaghetti with tomato sauce comes from Asia, the spaghetti, and America, the tomatoes) to their music (jazz is now the best known example, blending the backgrounds of different continents to emerge in America) to religion (the cross accompanied the sword in the era of colonial conquest).

The second great surge of modern globalization came in the 19th century, both as product and cause of the Industrial Revolution. On the one hand, the expansion of industry generated large reductions in transport costs that brought huge increases in international commerce. On the other hand, for the emerging commercial centers of Europe and North America, the opening of foreign markets and access to foreign sources of raw materials fueled (sometimes literally) the expansion of industry. Great Britain, as the "workshop of the world," was at the center of these changes and over the course of the century saw its foreign trade increase three times as rapidly as national income.

Britain during the 19th century provided a foreshadowing of current-day globalization as it officially touted "free trade" as the proper mode of organization for commerce—not just for itself, but for the entire world. The gospel of "free trade" was then carried around the globe by the British navy, and heroic ideological gymnastics allowed a growing colonial empire to be included under this same rubric. As the British historian E. J. Hobsbawm has commented, "British industry could grow up, by and large, in a protected home market until strong enough to demand free entry into other people's markets, that is 'Free Trade'." In today's globalization it is the United States, a country that also attained its economic power on the foundation of protectionism, that preaches the gospel of "free trade" to the rest of the world.

Current day globalization is, by and large, a continuation of the process that began in the 19th century (which in turn had its roots in the great transformation that began along with the 16th century). Two world wars and the Great Depression disrupted the progress of globalization for some sixty years and shifted its center from Britain to the United States, but it is now back on track. By the 1980s, the extent of economic connections that had been established among the world's national economies by 1913 had been reattained, and in subsequent years international trade and investment have continued to expand their roles in the economies of most nations.

Homogenization and Competition

Change in the world economy today, however, is not simply an extension of what went on in earlier periods, not simply a quantitative extension of well established trends. What distinguishes the current era from earlier phases of globalization is that now capitalism is ubiquitous. Virtually everywhere, production takes place for profit and is based on wage labor. In the 19th century, capitalism may have provided the leading dynamic of the international economy, but in many parts of the world—most everywhere outside of Europe and North America—a great deal of economic activity was organized through families (peasant farms or shops), under semi-feudal conditions, or through slavery. These activities were all connected to markets and to a world capitalist system, but they were not capitalist in themselves. Certainly there are important aspects of life and work today which take place outside of markets and are not directly capitalist—for example, work in the home, interactions within governments, volunteer activity, and some other forms of production. Yet capitalism holds sway, dominating and defining economic relationships in almost all parts of the world.

The ubiquity of capitalism gives a new character to the economic connections among peoples in distant parts of the world. There has, in particular, been a grand homogenization, both of consumer markets and of production activity. Wal-Mart and McDonald's establish themselves in Mexico to sell the same sorts of products in the same way as in the United States. At the same time, Mexican workers at the Ford plant in Hermosillo produce the same cars that are produced in US factories and they do so with equipment and procedures that are among the most "modern" in the world. Also on the production side, plants in Mexico and the United States are sometimes integrated with one another in a "global assembly line," with Mexican workers engaged in the labor intensive aspects of the operation and US workers engaged in the more highly skilled activities; for example, in clothing production, design and cutting is done in the United States while the pieces are stitched together on the Mexican side of the border.

Mexico, because of its proximity to the United States and the reduction of trade restrictions between the two countries, presents an extreme example of the cross-border integration of production. Yet in broad terms, we are presented today with a new international organization of production, as people on different corners of the globe produce the same sorts of products with the same technologies and often for the same employers—though the ultimate employers often operate through local subcontractors.

The homogenization of the world economy creates a new set of relationships, a direct competition, among workers in different parts of the world. Although such competition always existed, it is much more extensive and intense than in the past and, most important, it takes place between workers whose wages are dramatically different from each other. It is one thing when US and Canadian workers, who have very similar wages and standards of living, are in competition with each other. It is quite another thing when the US and Canadian workers are in competition with Mexican workers.

This new relationship among workers in different countries presents obvious problems for the workers in the rich countries: they simply cannot compete with workers who, using the same equipment and methods of production (i.e., the same technology), are paid far, far lower wages. Yet similar, though perhaps less obvious, problems exist for the low-wage workers as well. With wage labor markets existing throughout most of the world, virtually all workers are placed in competition with one another. While workers in Bangladesh may be willing to accept very low wages to assemble clothing for the European market, they are always faced with the prospect that Vietnamese workers may accept even lower wages. Or Indonesian workers, who assemble sports shoes for the US market, may face the prospect of production innovations that will substitute machinery and skilled workers for unskilled work-ers on an assembly line, making it profitable for the firms to move their production back to the United States.

In a capitalist world, where many different sites around the world provide firms with the labor markets they need, those firms can have a great advantage over work-ers. That advantage, however, depends upon "free trade," the elimination of govern-ment barriers to the movement of goods and funds across national boundaries. Free trade has given firms the option of either moving themselves or moving their sources of supply in response to cost differences (wage differences, but also other cost dif-ferences). Free trade, however, does not include the reduction—let alone the elimi-nation—of barriers to the movement of workers. So labor does not enjoy the same freedom in the globalized economy as does capital. Since "freedom" means having alternatives, and having alternatives means having power, a system that enhances the freedom of firms relative to the freedom of labor means giving businesses more power relative to labor. (Even were barriers to migration to be reduced, there are still substantial costs to labor movement compared to capital movement; and capital's advantage, while reduced, would not be eliminated.)

The drive for free trade existed, as pointed out above, in the British-led global-ization of the 19th century, but the United States has been able to push the concept to a whole new level. In part, free trade is important for the power it confers on business, but it is also important as ideology. The ideology of free trade has provided the defining rationale for the North American Free Trade Agreement (NAFTA), the Free Trade Agreement of the Americas (FTAA), the World Trade Organization (WTO), and the programs pushed on low income countries by the International Monetary Fund (IMF) and the World Bank. The opening of markets, the opening of sources of supply, the spread of private economic activity—all of this is supposed to provide a new era of rapid economic growth for the world and serve the needs of the poor as well as the rich.

Not So Fast

The concept of free trade has a certain intuitive appeal. After all, if the firms and people of a nation are free to buy their supplies from the lowest-cost source of sup-ply, then they will be able to buy more and satisfy their needs more thoroughly than if their government limits the sources from which they can buy those supplies (bans imports) or imposes extra costs (tariffs) on supplies from abroad. For low income countries, desperate for economic growth, it would seem absurd for their govern-ments to place restrictions on imports, forcing firms and people to waste resources on expensive domestic goods. Moreover, it only takes a moment's reflection to note the huge gains we attain from international commerce: not only the banana I eat for breakfast and a good portion of the oil that fuels my car and heats my home, but also the ideas and culture from elsewhere in the world—to say nothing of the competi-tive pressures from abroad that help drive economic advances in my own country. For a small country, the gains from foreign commerce are a virtual necessity.

Another moment's reflection, however, reveals that things are not so simple. Free trade is not the only way to engage extensively in international commerce. In fact, none of the countries we now denote as "developed" attained their development through free trade, though all engaged extensively in international commerce. There are, it seems, some substantial advantages to having the production of certain kinds of goods take place within a country, as compared to obtaining those same goods from abroad. The US textile industry in the 19th century, the US auto industry through most of the 20th century, the Japanese computer industry in the mid-20th century, the South Korean steel and ship building industries later in the 20th century—all generated broad economic gains in terms of the transformation of technology and the formation of a skilled work force that far surpassed the costs that arose from the government protection they received in their early stages of expansion. None of this provides a justification for protectionism in general; continuing protection of sugar and steel production in the United States imposes costs with no off-setting benefits (except to those directly engaged in the industries). Yet the experience of two centuries of capitalist development does demonstrate the fallacy of the free trade argument. Efforts by the US government to push free trade on low income countries today may make sense from the perspective of the interests of US firms, but it is hardly a prescription for economic advancement in low income countries.

But there is more. Globalization as it is being organized under the banner of free trade is doing nothing to reduce the "development gap," the huge difference in material well-being between the peoples of the rich nations and the peoples of most of the rest of the world. In fact, there is some evidence that under the regime of increasingly open world markets, the "development gap" is increasing. Worse yet: there is a good deal of evidence that free trade globalization is contributing to increasing inequality within nations, not only within the low income countries of the "South" but also within the United States and the other high income countries of the "North."

As the international economy is increasingly organized in a way that enhances the power of firms and tends to undermine the power of labor, it is certainly likely that greater inequality would be the outcome. Unfortunately, available data do not allow us to draw strong conclusions about what has been happening to world income inequality in recent decades. What we do know is that income distribution in today's world is already grossly unequal, with hundreds of millions of people living at the edge of subsistence, while the elites in all countries live in obscene luxury. We also know that, although some low income countries have made substantial gains (South Korea and some other countries of East Asia), the current surge of globalization has provided no general relief for the world's poor. Furthermore, we know that globalization—new patterns of international trade and investment—has disrupted people's lives, pushed people out of their traditional lines of work, shifted the location of economic activity, and forced people to adopt new patterns of consumption. All of this makes many people's lives very unpleasant, regardless of what can be uncovered with the aggregate statistics regarding income distribution and economic growth.

What Else Is New?

One might well absorb this summary of change in the world economy and respond with the comment: So, what else is new? It does seem that periods of great change in the world economy, whatever immediate benefits they may generate for the elite and whatever their long run benefits for society in general, are accompanied by severe disruptions, hardships and inequalities. Current day experience seems to fit well with the pattern established in the 16th and 19th centuries, to say nothing of earlier eras of imperial expansion. (Many commentators quite reasonably reject the term "globalization" in favor of "imperialism" precisely because the latter term underscores the great inequalities of power and income that are always so important in international affairs.)

Yet perhaps there is something new in the current era in the particular type of political response to globalization that has been generated in recent years. The "dreadful misfortunes" of earlier eras have also generated political responses—sometimes in the form of spontaneous rebellion, sometimes as more organized resistance and revolution, and sometimes as waves of new oppositional organizations and alliances. The political response to globalization at the beginning of the 21st century, however, has some distinguishing characteristics that are worth emphasizing.

Most important, parts of the response to globalization are themselves global. The coming out "party" for the anti-globalization movement in Seattle in the fall of 1999 involved people and organizations from all over the world. As a coordinated effort by groups from many rich countries and many poor countries, the action in Seattle—and the ones that have followed in Washington, Quebec, Prague, Puerto Allegre, and elsewhere—suggest something is different about the nature of political action. Many times, opposition movements based on national identities have, at least implicitly, been in conflict with one another; at other times, organizations in rich countries have opted to "support" groups in poor countries, but not as a joint and coordinated effort. While progressive movements have always talked about their internationalism, this time around the talk may translate more effectively into practice.

Also, the globalization of political opposition to globalization has included steps by labor unions, which have long adhered to highly nationalist positions. So far, more of the new internationalism of the US labor movement has been in the realm of rhetoric rather than practice, but US unions have made some important efforts at cross border organizing—in the form, for example, of supporting efforts of Mexican workers to organize firms in their country that supply the US market. (NAFTA, while allowing corporations, the organizations of capital, to operate in both the United States and Mexico, as well as Canada, makes no parallel provision for unions, the organizations of labor.) The rhetoric of internationalism, too, is important, especially because it marks such a departure from the past practices of the US labor movement. Some critics complain that the new-found interest of the US labor movement in conditions abroad arises from its own immediate concerns, the competition from low-cost imports, instead from a concern for workers elsewhere in the world. But that is just the point. If globalization forces US unions to secure the interests of their own members by pursuing a new internationalism, then that is certainly a change of significance.

The organized opposition to globalization goes far beyond the labor movement, however, involving a wide spectrum of social movements. Environmental and women's organizations, peasant groupings, student-based action committees, and others have all been a part of the actions. In addition, well established non-governmental organizations such as Oxfam, while not engaged in the protest actions in Seattle and elsewhere, have been a part of the general opposition to globalization. Not only is this opposition based on a wide range of social movements, but these different movements have at least begun to work in alliance with one another. Some aspects of this alliance, particularly that between environmental groups and labor unions, suggest a major shift from past conflicts.

Opposition actions have taken place in a wide spectrum of countries. On the one hand, there have been the much publicized actions led by young, often middle-class activists in the United States, focused on meetings of the principal international economic agencies such as the IMF, World Bank, and WTO. On the other hand, there have been actions in India, where peasant organizations have demonstrated against the international pharmaceutical and seed companies that are trying to use the internationalization of patent regulations to secure their control of world markets. While these geographically disparate actions are not coordinated through any cohesive international organization, they are part of an interconnected movement.

The opposition that has developed to globalization is not a cohesive movement, and it is not so well developed that we can have confidence in its lasting impact. Furthermore, it has many problems. Opposition to globalization sometimes is expressed as an opposition to connections with other peoples rather than as an opposition to the way those connections are exacerbating inequalities of power and income. Thus xenophobic protectionism is sometimes just below the surface of protest actions. By and large, however, the opposition to globalization appears to be based on an internationalism that may provide a basis for a progressive, and perhaps lasting, movement.

The more serious problems of this opposition arise from the difficulties in coming to grips with the power and complexity of the globalization process itself. A small example is provided by efforts in the rich countries to respond to the proliferation of imports of goods produced in "sweat shop" conditions in low income countries. Protests against the companies that utilize these shops—firms such as Nike and Gap—are met with the response that workers in these "sweat shops" are eager to obtain their jobs because these jobs are significantly better in terms of pay and working conditions than other available jobs. What's more, the response is often true. A sophisticated movement can come to terms with this reality by emphasizing the need to alter the context that impoverishes workers in low income countries and by stressing that such a context is most effectively transformed through political struggle. Also, by focusing on workers' right to political freedom—in particular, the right to organize unions—rather than on particular aspects of workers' conditions, anti-sweat shop activists can have a positive impact.

The "sweat shop" example helps clarify that globalization is not simply a collection of practices, not simply a peculiar set of connections among peoples around the globe. It is part of the long historical development and spread of capitalism. Within the framework of capitalism, it is difficult to solve problems that are based on the inequality of income and power, because those problems are generated by the system itself. Nonetheless, capitalism is not an immutable system, and it is probably not a permanent system. The oppositional struggles are not only responses to globalization, but they are part of the process of globalization itself. They will play a role in shaping events and in shaping the entire nature of the process. And they will contribute to answering the question: What is globalization?

———————————————————

Article 8.2

THE GOSPEL OF FREE TRADE: THE NEW EVANGELISTS

BY ARTHUR MacEWAN
November 1991, updated July 2009

Free trade! With the zeal of Christian missionaries, for decades the U.S. government has been preaching, advocating, pushing, and coercing around the globe for "free trade."

As the economic crisis emerged in 2007 and 2008 and rapidly became a global crisis, it was apparent that something was very wrong with the way the world economy was organized. Not surprisingly, as unemployment rose sharply in the United States, there were calls for protecting jobs by limiting imports and for the government to "buy American" in its economic stimulus program. Similarly, in many other countries, as unemployment jumped upwards, pressure emerged for protection—and some actual steps were taken. Yet, free trade missionaries did not retreat; they continued to preach the same gospel.

The free-traders were probably correct in claiming that protectionist policies would do more harm than good as a means to stem the rising unemployment generated by the economic crisis. Significant acts of protectionism in one country would lead to retaliation—or at least copying—by other countries, reducing world trade. The resulting loss of jobs from reduced trade would most likely outweigh any gains from protection.

Yet the argument over international economic policies should not be confined simply to what should be done in a crisis. Nor should it simply deal with trade in goods and services. The free-traders have advocated their program as one for long-run economic growth and development, yet the evidence suggests that free trade is not a good economic development strategy. Furthermore, the free-traders preach the virtue of unrestricted global movement of finance as well as of goods and services. As it turns out, the free flow of finance has been a major factor in bringing about and spreading the economic crisis that began to appear in 2007—as well as earlier crises.

The Push

While the U.S. push for free trade goes back several decades, it has become more intense in recent years. In the 1990s, the U.S. government signed on to the North American Free Trade Agreement (NAFTA) and in 2005 established the Central American Free Trade Agreement (CAFTA). Both Republican and Democratic presidents, however, have pushed hard for a *global* free trade agenda. After the demise of the Soviet Union, U.S. advisers prescribed unfettered capitalism for Eastern and Central Europe, and ridiculed as unworkable any move toward a "third way." In low-income countries from Mexico to Malaysia, the prescription has been the same: open markets, deregulate business, don't restrict international investment, and let the free market flourish.

In the push for worldwide free trade, the World Trade Organization (WTO) has been the principal vehicle of change, establishing rules for commerce that assure markets are open and resources are available to those who can pay. And the International Monetary Fund (IMF) and World Bank, which provide loans to many governments, use their financial power to pressure countries around the world to accept the gospel and open their markets. In each of these international organizations, the United States—generally through the U.S. Treasury—plays a dominant role.

Of course, as with any gospel, the preachers often ignore their own sermons. While telling other countries to open their markets, the U.S. government continued, for instance, to limit imports of steel, cotton, sugar, textiles, and many other goods. But publicly at least, free-trade boosters insist that the path to true salvation—or economic expansion, which, in this day and age, seems to be the same thing—lies in opening our market to foreign goods. Get rid of trade barriers at home and abroad, allow business to go where it wants and do what it wants. We will all get rich.

Yet the history of the United States and other rich countries does not fit well with the free-trade gospel. Virtually all advanced capitalist countries found economic success through heavy government regulation of their international commerce, not in free trade. Likewise, a large role for government intervention has characterized those cases of rapid and sustained economic growth in recent decades—for example, Japan after World War II, South Korea in the 1970s through the 1990s, and China most recently.

Free trade does, however, have its uses. Highly developed nations can use free trade to extend their power and control of the world's wealth, and business can use it as a weapon against labor. Most important, free trade can limit efforts to redistribute income more equally, undermine social programs, and keep people from democratically controlling their economic lives.

A Day in the Park

At the beginning of the 19th century, Lowell, Massachusetts, became the premier site of the U.S. textile industry. Today, thanks to the Lowell National Historical Park, you can tour the huge mills, ride through the canals that redirected the Merrimack River's power to those mills, and learn the story of the textile workers, from the Yankee "mill girls" of the 1820s through the various waves of immigrant laborers who poured into the city over the next century.

During a day in the park, visitors get a graphic picture of the importance of 19th-century industry to the economic growth and prosperity of the United States. Lowell and the other mill towns of the era were centers of growth. They not only created a demand for Southern cotton, they also created a demand for new machinery, maintenance of old machinery, parts, dyes, *skills*, construction materials, construction machinery, *more skills*, equipment to move the raw materials and products, parts maintenance for that equipment, *and still more skills*. The mill towns also created markets—concentrated groups of wage earners who needed to buy products to sustain themselves. As centers of economic activity, Lowell and similar mill towns contributed to U.S. economic growth far beyond the value of the textiles they produced.

The U.S. textile industry emerged decades after the industrial revolution had spawned Britain's powerful textile industry. Nonetheless, it survived and prospered. British linens inundated markets throughout the world in the early 19th century, as the British navy nurtured free trade and kept ports open for commerce. In the United States, however, hostilities leading up to the War of 1812 and then a substantial tariff made British textiles relatively expensive. These limitations on trade allowed the Lowell mills to prosper, acting as a catalyst for other industries and helping to create the skilled work force at the center of U.S. economic expansion.

Beyond textiles, however, tariffs did not play a great role in the United States during the early 19th century. Southern planters had considerable power, and while they were willing to make some compromises, they opposed protecting manufacturing in general because that protection forced up the prices of the goods they purchased with their cotton revenues. The Civil War wiped out the planters' power to oppose protectionism, and from the 1860s through World War I, U.S. industry prospered behind considerable tariff barriers.

Different Countries, Similar Experiences

The story of the importance of protectionism in bringing economic growth has been repeated, with local variations, in other advanced capitalist countries. During the late 19th century, Germany entered the major league of international economic powers with substantial protection and government support for its industries. Likewise, in 19th-century France and Italy, national consolidation behind protectionist barriers was a key to economic development.

Britain—which entered the industrial era first—is often touted as the prime example of successful development without tariff protection. Yet, Britain embraced free trade only after its industrial base was well established; as in the U.S., the early and important textile industry was erected on a foundation of protectionism. In addition, Britain built its industry through the British navy and the expansion of empire, hardly prime ingredients in any recipe for free trade.

Japan provides an especially important case of successful government protection and support for industrial development. In the post-World War II era, when the Japanese established the foundations for their economic "miracle," the government rejected free trade and extensive foreign investment and instead promoted its national firms.

In the 1950s, for example, the government protected the country's fledgling auto firms from foreign competition. At first, quotas limited imports to $500,000 (in current dollars) each year; in the 1960s, prohibitively high tariffs replaced the quotas. Furthermore, the Japanese allowed foreign investment only insofar as it contributed to developing domestic industry. The government encouraged Japanese companies to import foreign technology, but required them to produce 90% of parts domestically within five years.

The Japanese also protected their computer industry. In the early 1970s, as the industry was developing, companies and individuals could only purchase a foreign machine if a suitable Japanese model was not available. IBM was allowed to produce within the country, but only when it licensed basic patents to Japanese firms. And IBM computers produced in Japan were treated as foreign-made machines.

In the 20th century, no other country matched Japan's economic success, as it moved in a few decades from a relative low-income country, through the devastation of war, to emerge as one of the world's economic leaders. Yet one looks back in vain to find a role for free trade in this success. The Japanese government provided an effective framework, support, and protection for the country's capitalist development.

Likewise, in many countries that have been late-comers to economic development, capitalism has generated high rates of economic growth where government involvement, and not free trade, played the central role. South Korea is a striking case. "Korea is an example of a country that grew very fast and yet violated the canons of conventional economic wisdom," writes Alice Amsden in *Asia's Next Giant: South Korea and Late Industrialization*, widely acclaimed as perhaps the most important analysis of the South Korean economic success. "In Korea, instead of the market mechanism allocating resources and guiding private entrepreneurship, the government made most of the pivotal investment decisions. Instead of firms operating in a competitive market structure, they each operated with an extraordinary degree of market control, protected from foreign competition."

Free trade, however, has had its impact in South Korea. In the 1990s, South Korea and other East Asian governments came under pressure from the U.S. government and the IMF to open their markets, including their financial markets. When they did so, the results were a veritable disaster. The East Asian financial crisis that began in 1997 was a major setback for the whole region, a major disruption of economic growth. After extremely rapid economic growth for three decades, with output expanding at 7% to 10% a year, South Korea's economy plummeted by 6.3% between 1997 and 1998.

Mexico and Its NAFTA Experience

While free trade in goods and services has its problems, which can be very serious, it is the free movement of capital, the opening of financial markets that has sharp, sudden impacts, sometimes wrecking havoc on national economies. Thus, virtually as soon as Mexico, the United States and Canada formed NAFTA at the beginning of 1994, Mexico was hit with a severe financial crisis. As the economy turned downward at the beginning of that year, capital rapidly left the country, greatly reducing the value of the Mexican peso. With this diminished value of the peso, the cost of servicing international debts and the costs of imports skyrocketed—and the downturn worsened.

Still, during the 1990s, before and after the financial crisis, free-traders extolled short periods of moderate economic growth in Mexico —3% to 4% per year—as evidence of success. Yet, compared to earlier years, Mexico's growth under free trade has been poor. From 1940 to 1990 (including the no-growth decade of the 1980s), when Mexico's market was highly protected and the state actively regulated economic affairs, output grew at an average annual rate of 5%.

Most important, Mexico's experience discredits the notion that free-market policies will improve living conditions for the masses of people in low-income countries. The Mexican government paved the way for free trade policies by reducing or eliminating social welfare programs, and for many Mexican workers wages declined sharply during the free trade era. The number of households living in poverty rose dramatically, with some 75% of Mexico's population below the poverty line at the beginning of the 21st century.

China and Its Impact

Part of Mexico's problem and its economy's relatively weak performance from the 1990s onward has been the full-scale entrance of China into the international economy. While the Mexican authorities thought they saw great possibilities in NAFTA, with the full opening of the U.S. market to goods produced with low-wage Mexican labor, China (and other Asian countries) had even cheaper labor. As China also gained access to the U.S. market, Mexican expectations were dashed.

The Chinese economy has surely gained in terms of economic growth as it has engaged more and more with the world market, and the absolute levels of incomes of millions of people have risen a great deal. However, China's rapid economic growth has come with a high degree of income inequality. Before its era of rapid growth, China was viewed as a country with a relatively equal distribution of income. By the beginning of the new millennium, however, it was much more unequal than any of the other most populace Asian countries (India, Indonesia, Bangladesh, Pakistan), and more in line with the high-inequality countries of Latin America. Furthermore, with the inequality has come a great deal of social conflict. Tens of thousands of "incidents" of conflict involving violence are reported each year, and most recently there have been the major conflicts involving Tibetans and Ouigers.

In any case, the Chinese trade and growth success should not be confused with "free trade." Foundations for China's surge of economic growth were established through state-sponsored infrastructure development and the vast expansion of the country's educational system. Even today, while private business, including foreign business, appears to have been given free rein in China, the government still plays a controlling role—including a central role in affecting foreign economic relations.

A central aspect of the government's role in the county's foreign commerce has been in the realm of finance. As Chinese-produced goods have virtually flooded international markets, the government has controlled the uses of the earnings from these exports. Instead of simply allowing those earnings to be used by Chinese firms and citizens to buy imports, the government has to a large extent held those earnings as reserves. Using those reserves, China's central bank has been the largest purchaser of U.S. government bonds, in effect becoming a major financer of the U.S. government's budget deficit of recent years.

China's reserves have been one large element in creating a giant pool of financial assets in the world economy. This "pool" has also been built up as the doubling of oil prices following the U.S. invasion of Iraq put huge amounts of funds in the pockets of oil-exporting countries and firms and individuals connected to the oil industry. Yet slow growth of the U.S. economy and extremely low interest rates, resulting from the Federal Reserve Bank's efforts to encourage more growth, limited the returns that could be obtained on these funds. One of the consequences—through a complex set of connections—was the development of the U.S. housing bubble, as financial firms, searching for higher returns, pushed funds into more and more risky mortgage loans.

It was not simply free trade and the unrestricted flow of international finance that generated the housing bubble and subsequent crisis in the U.S. economy. However, the generally unstable global economy—both in terms of trade and finance—that has emerged in the free trade era was certainly a factor bringing about the crisis. More-over, as is widely recognized, it was not only the U.S. economy and U.S. financial institutions that were affected. The free international flow of finance has meant that banking has become more and more a global industry. So as the U.S. banks got in trouble in 2007 and 2008, their maladies spread to many other parts of the world.

The Uses of Free Trade

While free trade is not the best economic growth or development policy and, es-pecially through the free flow of finance, can precipitate financial crises, the larg-est and most powerful firms in many countries find it highly profitable. As Britain preached the loudest sermons for free trade in the early 19th century, when its own industry was already firmly established, so the United States—or at least many firms based in the United States—find it a profitable policy at the beginning of the 21st century. The Mexican experience provides an instructive illustration.

For U.S. firms, access to foreign markets is a high priority. Mexico may be rela-tively poor, but with a population of 105 million it provides a substantial market. Furthermore, Mexican labor is cheap relative to U.S. labor; and using modern pro-duction techniques, Mexican workers can be as productive as workers in the United States. For U.S. firms to obtain full access to the Mexican market, the United States has to open its borders to Mexican goods. Also, if U.S. firms are to take full advan-tage of cheap foreign labor and sell the goods produced abroad to U.S. consumers, the United States has to be open to imports.

On the other side of the border, wealthy Mexicans face a choice between ad-vancing their interests through national development or advancing their interests through ties to U.S. firms and access to U.S. markets. For many years, they chose the former route. This led to some development of the Mexican economy but al-so—due to corruption and the massive power of the ruling party, the PRI—huge concentrations of wealth in the hands of a few small groups of firms and individu-als. Eventually, these groups came into conflict with their own government over regulation and taxation. Having benefited from government largesse, they came to see their fortunes in greater freedom from government control and, particularly, in greater access to foreign markets and partnerships with large foreign companies. National development was a secondary concern when more involvement with inter-national commerce would produce greater riches more quickly.

In addition, the old program of state-led development in Mexico ran into severe problems. These problems came to the surface in the 1980s with the international debt crisis. Owing huge amounts of money to foreign banks, the Mexican govern-ment was forced to respond to pressure from the IMF, the U.S. government, and large international banks which sought to deregulate Mexico's trade and investment. That pressure meshed with the pressure from Mexico's own richest elites, and the result was the move toward free trade and a greater opening of the Mexican economy to foreign investment.

Since the early 1990s, these changes for Mexico and the United States (as well as Canada) have been institutionalized in NAFTA. The U.S. government's agenda since then has been to spread free trade policies to all of the Americas through more regional agreements like CAFTA and ultimately through a Free Trade Area of the Americas. On a broader scale, the U.S. government works through the WTO, the IMF, and the World Bank to open markets and gain access to resources beyond the Western Hemisphere. In fact, while markets remain important everywhere, low-wage manufacturing is increasingly concentrated in Asia—especially China—instead of Mexico or Latin America.

The Chinese experience involves many of the same advantages for U.S. business as does the Mexican—a vast market, low wages, and an increasingly productive labor force. However, the Chinese government, although it has liberalized the economy a great deal compared to the pre-1985 era, has not abdicated its major role in the economy. For better (growth) and for worse (inequality and repression), the Chinese government has not embraced free trade.

Who Gains, Who Loses?

Of course, in the United States, Mexico, China and elsewhere, advocates of free trade claim that their policies are in everyone's interest. Free trade, they point out, will mean cheaper products for all. Consumers in the United States, who are mostly workers, will be richer because their wages will buy more. In Mexico and China, on the one hand, and in the United States, on the other hand, they argue that rising trade will create more jobs. If some workers lose their jobs because cheaper imported goods are available, export industries will produce new jobs.

In recent years this argument has taken on a new dimension with the larger entrance of India into the world economy and with the burgeoning there of jobs based in information technology —programming and call centers, for example. This "outsourcing" of service jobs has received a great deal of attention and concern in the United States. Yet free-traders have defended this development as good for the U.S. economy as well as for the Indian economy.

Such arguments obscure many of the most important issues in the free trade debate. Stated, as they usually are, as universal truths, these arguments are just plain silly. No one, for example, touring the Lowell National Historical Park could seriously argue that people in the United States would have been better off had there been no tariff on textiles. Yes, in 1820, they could have purchased textile goods more cheaply, but in the long run the result would have been less industrial advancement and a less wealthy nation. One could make the same point with the Japanese auto and computer industries, or indeed with numerous other examples from the last two centuries of capitalist development.

In the modern era, even though the United States already has a relatively developed economy with highly skilled workers, a freely open international economy does not serve the interests of most U.S. workers, though it will benefit large firms.

U.S. workers today are in competition with workers around the globe. Many different workers in many different places can produce the same goods and services. Thus, an international economy governed by the free trade agenda will tend to bring down wages for many U.S. workers. This phenomenon has certainly been one of the factors leading to the substantial rise of income inequality in the United States during recent decades.

The problem is not simply that of workers in a few industries—such as auto and steel, or call-centers and computer programming—where import competition is an obvious and immediate issue. A country's openness to the international economy affects the entire structure of earnings in that country. Free trade forces down the general level of wages across the board, even of those workers not directly affected by imports. The simple fact is that when companies can produce the same products in several different places, it is owners who gain because they can move their factories and funds around much more easily than workers can move themselves around. Capital is mobile; labor is much less mobile. Businesses, more than workers, gain from having a larger territory in which to roam.

Control Over Our Economic Lives

But the difficulties with free trade do not end with wages. In both low-income and high-income parts of the world, free trade is a weapon in the hands of business when it opposes any progressive social programs. Efforts to place environmental restrictions on firms are met with the threat of moving production abroad. Higher taxes to improve the schools? Business threatens to go elsewhere. Better health and safety regulations? The same response.

Some might argue that the losses from free trade for people in the United States will be balanced by gains for most people in poor countries—lower wages in the United States, but higher wages in Mexico and China. Free trade, then, would bring about international equality. Not likely. In fact, as pointed out above, free trade reforms in Mexico have helped force down wages and reduce social welfare programs, processes rationalized by efforts to make Mexican goods competitive on international markets. China, while not embracing free trade, has seen its full-scale entrance into global commerce accompanied by increasing inequality.

Gains for Mexican or Chinese workers, like those for U.S. workers, depend on their power in relation to business. Free trade or simply the imperative of international "competitiveness" are just as much weapons in the hands of firms operating in Mexico and China as they are for firms operating in the United States. The great mobility of capital is business's best trump card in dealing with labor and popular demands for social change—in the United States, Mexico, China and elsewhere.

None of this means that people should demand that their economies operate as fortresses, protected from all foreign economic incursions. There are great gains that can be obtained from international economic relations—when a nation manages those relations in the interests of the great majority of the people. Protectionism often simply supports narrow vested interests, corrupt officials, and wealthy industrialists. In rejecting free trade, we should move beyond traditional protectionism.

Yet, at this time, rejecting free trade is an essential first step. Free trade places the cards in the hands of business. More than ever, free trade would subject us to the "bottom line," or at least the bottom line as calculated by those who own and run large companies.

Article 8.3

COMPARATIVE ADVANTAGE

BY RAMAA VASUDEVAN
July/August 2007

> Dear Dr. Dollar:
> *When economists argue that the outsourcing of jobs might be a plus for the U.S. economy, they often mention the idea of comparative advantage. So free trade would allow the United States to specialize in higher-end service-sector business- es, creating higher-paying jobs than the ones that would be outsourced. But is it really true that free trade leads to universal benefits?*
> —David Goodman, Boston, Mass.

You're right: The purveyors of the free trade gospel do invoke the doctrine of comparative advantage to dismiss widespread concerns about the export of jobs. Attributed to 19th-century British political-economist David Ricardo, the doctrine says that a nation always stands to gain if it exports the goods it produces *relatively* more cheaply in exchange for goods that it can get *comparatively* more cheaply from abroad. Free trade would lead to each country specializing in the products it can produce at *relatively* lower costs. Such specialization allows both trading partners to gain from trade, the theory goes, even if in one of the countries production of *both* goods costs more in absolute terms.

For instance, suppose that in the United States the cost to produce one car equals the cost to produce 10 bags of cotton, while in the Philippines the cost to produce one car equals the cost to produce 100 bags of cotton. The Philippines would then have a comparative advantage in the production of cotton, producing one bag at a cost equal to the production cost of 1/100 of a car, versus 1/10 of a car in the United States; likewise, the United States would hold a comparative advantage in the produc- tion of cars. Whatever the prices of cars and cotton in the global market, the theory goes, the Philippines would be better off producing only cotton and importing all its cars from the United States, and the United States would be better off producing only cars and importing all of its cotton from the Philippines. If the international terms of trade—the relative price—is one car for 50 bags, then the United States will take in 50 bags of cotton for each car it exports, 40 more than the 10 bags it forgoes by putting its productive resources into making the car rather than growing cotton. The Philippines is also better off: it can import a car in exchange for the ex- port of 50 bags of cotton, whereas it would have had to forgo the production of 100 bags of cotton in order to produce that car domestically. If the price of cars goes up in the global marketplace, the Philippines will lose out in relative terms—but will still be better off than if it tried to produce its own cars.

The real world, unfortunately, does not always conform to the assumptions un- derlying comparative-advantage theory. One assumption is that trade is balanced. But many countries are running persistent deficits, notably the United States, whose trade deficit is now at nearly 7% of its GDP. A second premise, that there is full employment within the trading nations, is also patently unrealistic. As global trade intensifies, jobs created in the export sector do not necessarily compensate for the jobs lost in the sectors wiped out by foreign competition.

The comparative advantage story faces more direct empirical challenges as well. Nearly 70% of U.S. trade is trade in similar goods, known as *intra-industry trade*: for example, exporting Fords and importing BMWs. And about one third of U.S. trade as of the late 1990s was trade between branches of a single corporation located in different countries (*intra-firm trade*). Comparative advantage cannot explain these patterns.

Comparative advantage is a static concept that identifies immediate gains from trade but is a poor guide to economic development, a process of structural change over time which is by definition dynamic. Thus the comparative advantage tale is particularly pernicious when preached to developing countries, consigning many to "specialize" in agricultural goods or be forced into a race to the bottom where cheap sweatshop labor is their sole source of competitiveness.

The irony, of course, is that none of the rich countries got that way by following the maxim that they now preach. These countries historically relied on tariff walls and other forms of protectionism to build their industrial base. And even now, they continue to protect sectors like agriculture with subsidies. The countries now touted as new models of the benefits of free trade—South Korea and the other "Asian tigers," for instance—actually flouted this economic wisdom, nurturing their technological capabilities in specific manufacturing sectors and taking advantage of their lower wage costs to *gradually* become effective competitors of the United States and Europe in manufacturing.

The fundamental point is this: contrary to the comparative-advantage claim that trade is universally beneficial, nations as a whole do not prosper from free trade. Free trade creates winners and losers, both within and between countries. In today's context it is the global corporate giants that are propelling and profiting from "free trade": not only outsourcing white-collar jobs, but creating global commodity chains linking sweatshop labor in the developing countries of Latin America and Asia (Africa being largely left out of the game aside from the export of natural resources such as oil) with ever-more insecure consumers in the developed world. Promoting "free trade" as a political cause enables this process to continue.

It is a process with real human costs in terms of both wages and work. People in developing countries across the globe continue to face these costs as trade liberalization measures are enforced; and the working class in the United States is also being forced to bear the brunt of the relentless logic of competition.

Sources: Arthur MacEwan, "The Gospel of Free Trade: The New Evangelists," *Dollars & Sense*, July/August 2002; Ha-Joon Chang, *Kicking away the Ladder: The Real History of Fair Trade*, Foreign Policy in Focus, 2003; Anwar Shaikh, "Globalization and the Myths of Free Trade," in *Globalization and the Myths of Free Trade: History, Theory, and Empirical Evidence*, ed. Anwar Shaikh, Routledge 2007.

Article 8.4

(ECONOMIC) FREEDOM'S JUST ANOTHER WORD FOR...CRISIS-PRONE

BY JOHN MILLER
September/October 2009

In "Capitalism in Crisis," his May op-ed in the *Wall Street Journal*, U.S. Court of Appeals judge and archconservative legal scholar Richard Posner argued that "a capitalist economy, while immensely dynamic and productive, is not inherently stable." Posner, the long-time cheerleader for deregulation added, quite sensibly, "we may need more regulation of banking to reduce its inherent riskiness."

That may seem like a no-brainer to you and me, right there in the middle of the road with yellow-lines and dead armadillos, as Jim Hightower is fond of saying. But *Journal* readers were having none of it. They wrote in to set Judge Posner straight. "It is not free markets that fail, but government-controlled ones," protested one reader.

And why wouldn't they protest? The *Journal* has repeatedly told readers that "economic freedom" is "the real key to development." And each January for 15 years now the *Journal* tries to elevate that claim to a scientific truth by publishing a summary of the Heritage Foundation Index of Economic Freedom, which they assure readers proves the veracity of the claim. But in the hands of the editors of the *Wall Street Journal* and the researchers from the Heritage Foundation, Washington's foremost right-wing think tank, the Index of Economic Freedom is a barometer of corporate and entrepreneurial freedom from accountability rather than a guide to which countries are giving people more control over their economic lives and over the institutions that govern them.

This January was no different. "The 2009 Index provides strong evidence that the countries that maintain the freest economies do the best job promoting prosperity for all citizens," proclaimed this year's editorial, "Freedom is Still the Winning Formula." But with economies across the globe in recession, the virtues of free markets are a harder sell this year. That is not lost on *Wall Street Journal* editor Paul Gigot, who wrote the foreword to this year's report. Gigot allows that, "ostensibly free-market policymakers in the U.S. lost their monetary policy discipline, and we are now paying a terrible price." Still Gigot maintains that, "the *Index of Economic Freedom* exists to chronicle how steep that price will be and to point the way back to policy wisdom."

What the Heritage report fails to mention is this: while the global economy is in recession, many of the star performers in the Economic Freedom Index are tanking. Fully one half of the ten hardest-hit economies in the world are among the 30 "free" and "mostly free" economies at the top of the Economic Freedom Index rankings of 179 countries.

Here's the damage, according to the IMF. Singapore, the Southeast Asian trading center and perennial number two in the Index, will suffer a 10.0% drop in output this year. Slotting in at number four, Ireland, the so-called Celtic tiger, has seen its rapid export-led growth give way to an 8.0% drop in output. Number 13 and

number 30, the foreign-direct-investment-favored Baltic states, Estonia and Lithu-
ania, will each endure a 10.0% loss of output this year. Finally, the economy of Ice-
land, the loosely regulated European banking center that sits at number 14 on the
Index, will contract 10.6% in 2009.

As a group, the Index's 30 most "free" economies will contract 4.1% in 2009.
All of the other groups in the Index ("moderately free," "mostly unfree," and "re-
pressed" economies) will muddle through 2009 with a much smaller loss of output
or with moderate growth. The 67 "mostly unfree" countries in the Index will post
the fastest growth rate for the year, 2.3%.

So it seems that if the Index of Economic Freedom can be trusted, then Judge
Posner was not so far off the mark when he described capitalism as dynamic but "not
inherently stable." That wouldn't be so bad, one *Journal* reader pointed out in a letter:
"Economic recessions are the cost we pay for our economic freedom and economic
prosperity is the benefit. We've had many more years of the latter than the former."

Not to be Trusted

But the Index of Economic Freedom cannot and should not be trusted. How free
or unfree an economy is according to the Index seems to have little do with how
quickly it grows. For instance, economist Jeffrey Sachs found "no correlation" between a country's ranking in the Index and its per capita growth rates from 1995
to 2003. Also, in this year's report North America is the "freest" of its six regions
of the world, but logged the slowest average rate over the last five years, 2.7% per
annum. The Asia-Pacific region, which is "less free" than every other region except
Sub-Saharan Africa according to the Index, posted the fastest average growth over
the last five years, 7.8% per annum. That region includes several of the fastest growing of the world's economies, India, China, and Vietnam, which ranked 123, 132,
and 145 respectively in the Index and were classified as "mostly unfree." And there
are plenty of relatively slow growers among the countries high up in the Index, including Switzerland (which ranks ninth).

The Heritage Foundation folks who edited the Index objected to Sachs' criticisms, pointing out that they claimed "a close relationship" between *changes* in eco-

ECONOMIC FREEDOM AND ECONOMIC GROWTH IN 2009	
Degree of Economic Freedom	IMF Projected Growth Rate for 2009
"Free" (7 Countries)	-4.54%
"Mostly Free" (23 Counties)	-3.99%
"Moderately Free" (53 Countries)	-0.92%
"Mostly Unfree" (67 Countries)	+2.31%
"Repressed" (69 Counties)	+1.65%
Sources: International Monetary Fund, *World Economic Outlook,: Crisis and Recovery*, April 2009, Tables A1, A2, A3; Terry Miller and Kim R. Holmes, eds., *2009 Index of Economic Freedom*, heritage.org/Index/, Executive Summary.	

nomic freedom, not the *level* of economic freedom, and growth. But even that claim is fraught with problems. Statistically it doesn't hold up. Economic journalist Doug Henwood found that improvements in the index and GDP growth from 1997 to 2003 could explain no more than 10% of GDP growth. In addition, even a tight correlation would not resolve the problem that many of the fastest growing economies are "mostly unfree" according to the Index.

But even more fundamental flaws with the Index render any claim about the relationship between prosperity and economic freedom, as measured by the Heritage Foundation, questionable. Consider just two of the ten components the Economic Freedom Index uses to rank countries: fiscal freedom and government size.

Fiscal freedom (what we might call the "hell-if-I'm-going-to-pay-for-government" index) relies on the top income tax and corporate income tax brackets as two of its three measures of the tax burden. These are decidedly flawed measures even if all that concerned you was the tax burden of the rich and owners of corporations (or the super-rich). Besides ignoring the burden of other taxes, singling out these two top tax rates doesn't get at effective corporate and income tax rates, or how much of a taxpayer's total income goes to paying these taxes. For example, on paper U.S. corporate tax rates are higher than those in Europe. But nearly one half of U.S. corporate profits go untaxed. The effective rate of taxation on U.S. corporate profits currently stands at 15%, far below the top corporate tax rate of 35%. And relative to GDP, U.S. corporate income taxes are no more than half those of other OECD countries.

Even their third measure of fiscal freedom, government tax revenues relative to GDP, bears little relationship to economic growth. After an exhaustive review, economist Joel Selmrod, former member of the Reagan Treasury Department, concludes that the literature reveals "no consensus" about the relationship between the level of taxation and economic growth.

The Index's treatment of government size, which relies exclusively on the level of government spending relative to GDP, is just as flawed as the fiscal freedom index. First, "richer countries do not tax and spend less" than poorer countries, reports economist Peter Lindhert. Beyond that, this measure does not take into account how the government uses its money. Social spending programs—public education, child-care and parental support, and public health programs—can make people more productive and promote economic growth. That lesson is not lost on Hong Kong and Singapore, number one and number two in the index. They both provide universal access to health care, despite the small size of their governments.

The size-of-government index also misses the mark because it fails to account for industrial policy. This is a serious mistake, because it overestimates the degree to which some of the fastest growing economies of the last few decades, such as Taiwan and South Korea, relied on the market and underestimates the positive role that government played in directing economic development in those countries by guiding investment and protecting infant industries.

This flaw is thrown into sharp relief by the recent report of the World Bank's Commission on Growth and Development. That group studied 13 economies that grew at least 7% a year for at least 25 years since 1950. Three of the Index's "free" and "mostly free" countries made the list (Singapore, Hong Kong, and Japan) but so did three of the index's "mostly unfree" countries (China, Brazil, and Indonesia). While these rapid growers were all export-oriented, their governments "were not free-market purists," according the Commission's report. "They tried a variety of policies to help diversify exports or sustain competitiveness. These included industrial policies to promote new investments."

Still More

Beyond all that, the Index says nothing about political freedom. Consider once again the two city-states, Hong Kong and Singapore, which top their list of free countries. Both are only "partially free" according to Freedom House, which the editors have called "the Michelin Guide to democracy's development." Hong Kong is still without direct elections for it legislatures or its chief executive and a proposed internal security laws threaten press and academic freedom as well as political dissent. In Singapore, freedom of the press and rights to demonstrate are limited, films, TV, and the like are censored, and preventive detention is legal.

So it seems that the Index of Economic Freedom in practice tells us little about the cost of abandoning free market policies and offers little proof that government intervention into the economy would either retard economic growth or contract political freedom. In actuality, this rather objective-looking index is a slip-shod measure that would seem to have no other purpose than to sell the neoliberal policies that brought on the current crisis, and to stand in the way of policies that might correct the crisis.

Sources: "Capitalism in Crisis," by Richard A Posner, *Wall Street Journal,* 5/0//09; "Letters: Recessions are the Price We Pay for Economic Freedom," *Wall Street Journal,* 5/19/09/; "Freedom is Still the Winning Formula," by Terry Miller, *Wall Street Journal,* 1/13/09 ; "The Real Key to Development," by Mary Anastasia O'Grady, *Wall Street Journal,* 1/15/08; Terry Miller and Kim R. Holmes, eds., *2009 Index of Economic Freedom,* heritage.org/Index/; Freedom House, "Freedom in the World 2009 Survey," freedomhouse.org; Joel Selmrod and Jon Bakija, *Taxing Ourselves: A Citizen's Guide to the Debate over Taxes,* MIT Press, 2008; International Monetary Fund, *World Economic Outlook,: Crisis and Recovery,* April 2009; Peter H. Lindert, *Growing Public,* Cambridge University Press, 2004; Doug Henwood, "*Laissez-faire* Olympics: An LBO Special Report," leftbusinessobserver.com, March 26, 2005; Jeffrey Sachs, *The End of Poverty: Economic Possibilities for Our Time,* Penguin, 2005.

Article 8.5

THE SPECTER OF CAPITAL FLIGHT

How long will the power of the dollar protect the United States?

BY MARIE DUGGAN
January/February 2009

The depth and scope of the unfolding financial crisis have taken most observers by surprise. Yet there were definite warning signs. One was the United States' growing dependence on foreign capital, an issue that came to my attention in 2005 when I was preparing a lecture on Mexico's mid-1990s financial crisis. This was the so-called Tequila Crisis: foreign investors and wealthy Mexicans abruptly fled dollar-denominated Mexican bonds called Tesebonos as well as Mexican stocks, moving their money into safer U.S. assets. In hindsight, many observers point to Mexico's increased borrowing from abroad in the early 1990s, reflected in its worsening current account deficit, as a sign of impending trouble. (See box, "Current Account Explained," p. 332)

Curious about where the United States stood, I was shocked to discover that the U.S. current account deficit in 2005, measured as a percent of GDP, was approaching the same level as Mexico's had been in 1993—and getting worse (see Figure 1). In other words, in the early 2000s the United States became as dependent on foreign financing as Mexico was just prior to its crisis.

Mexico was only the first of many emerging markets to undergo spectacular financial crises in the late 1990s and early 2000s. The list includes Thailand, Indonesia, South Korea, Malaysia, Russia, and Argentina, among others.

The typical financial crisis story in an emerging market begins with capital flight—the sudden withdrawal of money by foreign investors from an economy's stocks, bonds, and banking system. Often locals decide to move their wealth abroad as well. Stock markets crash, banks fail, the local currency drops in value, and governments face default. Interest rates rise as governments try to woo foreign investors and their own citizens back into the home currency with the promise of high returns, but then the high interest rates push domestic borrowers, whether firms or households, toward bankruptcy. Unemployment shoots up and GDP falls. In some emerging markets, the magnitude of these difficulties mirrored those the United States experienced in the Great Depression of the 1930s.

At the time, the United States and the other developed countries were widely viewed as immune from such financial crises.

Now it is clear that the United States is not immune. The current crisis began in the financial sector in the summer of 2007 and hit the real side of the economy in fall 2008, with the unemployment rate rising by more than 26% in just five months, from 5.7% in July to 7.2% in December. Since 1979, the real side of the U.S. economy has suffered (think deindustrialization) while the financial side has thrived. With stagnant or falling real wages coinciding with a lengthy period of low interest rates, many working people went into debt in order to purchase homes and stocks so that they would be able to participate in some modest way in the rise of finance. The collapse of finance, then, is pulling working Americans down with it.

But the United States' crisis is departing from the typical pattern. For one thing, far from dropping in value, the dollar has risen against other currencies in recent months. The factors which were supposed to make the United States immune to financial crisis did not do so, but they are causing the crisis to play out in new and unpredictable ways.

Swimming Pool of Savings

The United States' dependence on foreign financing is one reason the collapse of housing prices has sparked an economy-wide financial crisis.

Imagine the pool of savings in an economy as a giant swimming pool; the water in the pool represents money available to borrowers. Everyone who saves money in a bank account, in the stock market, or in government bonds—whether a U.S. resident or a foreign investor—adds water to the pool.

In recent years an increasingly large share of the water in the United States' pool has been coming from abroad. And when foreign capital is a substantial part of the water in the pool, the sheer volume of capital that can fly in and out of a country's assets is much larger, making its stock market and other asset markets more volatile. Here we are not talking about foreign investment in factories or other economic activity on U.S. soil, termed foreign direct investment, which would take months or years to liquidate. Rather, this is portfolio investment—investment in paper assets such as stocks and bonds—and this money can fly out of a country at the touch of a computer key.

You can see in Figure 1 the moment when foreign investors suddenly stopped putting money into Mexico, forcing the nation to live within its means. Mexico's current account deficit went from 7% of GDP in 1994 to 1% of GDP in 1995. So

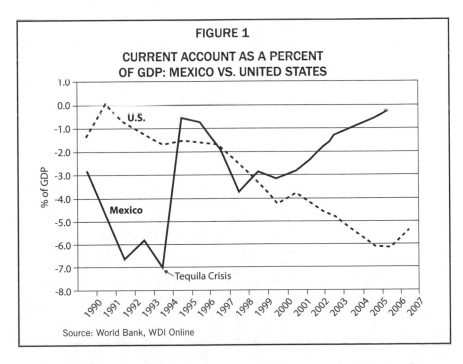

FIGURE 1

CURRENT ACCOUNT AS A PERCENT OF GDP: MEXICO VS. UNITED STATES

Source: World Bank, WDI Online

one might think that foreign investors pulling out of the United States would be a good thing—Americans would finally be forced to live within our means.

But it's not quite that simple. Most Americans with debts—whether student loans, a mortgage, a car loan, or credit card balances—do not think of themselves as borrowing from foreigners. But part of the reason banks were willing to provide all this credit to U.S. consumers at fairly low interest rates was that foreign investors were filling the pool with plenty of water by buying U.S. stocks or bonds or putting their savings into U.S. deposit accounts. It is not only our government that borrows from foreign investors, but U.S. households and firms as well.

As a result, as large numbers of both foreign and domestic investors have pulled out of U.S. stocks and banks over the past 18 months, it has become harder for my students, for small businesses, and even for General Motors to get loans. Without access to student loans, the poorest students are dropping out of college; some colleges may close their doors. Fewer people now qualify for mortgage loans, so houses sell more slowly and at cut prices. Car loans are drying up, so dealerships are laying people off. If the credit crunch pushes credit-card interest rates up, then even consumers who stop making new purchases will be stuck with high interest rates on existing balances. In Mexico in 1995, credit card interest rates of 65% were considered on the low side.

Until 2007, this kind of capital flight and ensuing financial crisis were widely viewed as impossible in the United States. Three factors were supposed to account for U.S. immunity:

- The dollar is the world's reserve currency, so foreign investors will always hold it.

- U.S. debt is denominated in dollars, so the exchange rate depreciation that would result from capital flight would not increase the debt burden on domestic borrowers.

Current Account Explained

For over 15 years, the United States has been spending more foreign currency annually on imports than the country has earned through its exports—and borrowing from foreign investors every year to cover the difference. The amount a nation's spending on imports differs from its income from exports is called the current account. If imports exceed exports, the current account is negative; in other words, the country has a current account deficit.

Specifically, in 2007 U.S. imports exceeded exports to the tune of $731 billion. That current account deficit was covered by a $774 billion "net financial inflow," i.e., the amount U.S. borrowing from abroad exceeded U.S. lending to foreigners. (The $41 billion difference between the current account deficit and the country's net borrowing is mostly a statistical discrepancy.) Note that the United States' total foreign debt is going to be much higher, the pile of net financial inflows accumulated year after year.

• U.S. political and financial institutions are far more functional and less corrupt than those in emerging markets.

Let's look at how each of these factors has played out in the current crisis.

Dollars Are Special

Many countries around the world hold onto U.S. Treasury bonds as a so-called reserve asset.

To explore what reserves are, consider a professor suddenly faced with $30,000 in urgent home repairs she cannot cover out of her current income. This is not a problem as long as relatively cheap credit is available; for instance, she may plan to take out a home equity loan to pay for the repairs. But suppose that loan suddenly becomes unavailable. What will she do?

Many people do have other sources of financing, and in a sense, these are their reserves. They resort to liquidating the savings account and the IRA or selling off the wedding ring.

Countries, too, have reserves. Typically, they hoard gold and U.S. Treasury bonds for rainy days. The dollar has been the world's reserve currency since the close of World War II. This means that U.S. Treasury bonds (which are issued by the U.S. government to finance its debt) are the safest, most stable place for countries to park their reserves because the U.S. government has the power to print the reserve currency.

In fact, one reason the United States has been able to run so large a current account deficit has been other countries' desire to hold more reserves.

In 1997, suddenly unable to borrow from abroad, many Asian countries used up their reserves. Then they turned to the International Monetary Fund (IMF) for emergency loans. This is analogous to the professor turning to her parents for an emergency loan. Her parents may well agree to finance the repairs—but only on the condition that she never buy another caffè latte at Starbucks. Likewise, the IMF agreed to these loans, but only if the Asian nations acquiesced to certain conditions, generally much more onerous ones than giving up lattes. For example, then-Treasury Secretary Robert Rubin basically withheld South Korea's IMF rescue package until the country agreed to sell shares of its profitable companies, like Samsung, to U.S. investors. The Asian nations agreed to the IMF's conditions, but they swore "never again," and have since hoarded vast amounts of dollars. Today, about 20% of the United States' total borrowing comes from foreign governments that are buying up dollar assets as reserves.

But it is starting to seem possible that other countries might not want to use the dollar as their reserve currency forever.

By July 2008, China, which alone holds about $1.8 trillion in U.S. assets, admitted that "it has been looking to strike deals with private equity firms in Europe as part of a strategy to reduce its dollar holdings," and "a big sovereign fund in the [Persian] Gulf has cut its dollar denominated holdings from more than 80% a year ago to less than 60% today," the *Financial Times* reported.

The euro is emerging as an alternative, as is gold. Between August 2007, when it became clear that the subprime debacle would cause widespread losses for investors, and March 2008, when fear of a U.S. financial meltdown reached fever pitch, the price of gold jumped by over 45%, breaking the $1,000/ounce mark. Investors in large numbers were evidently selling U.S. assets and buying gold as an alternative safe haven.

Debt Stable; Net Worth Down

So maybe the dollar's role as reserve currency cannot prevent capital flight from the United States. But even if it did occur, capital flight was not supposed to hurt the U.S. economy the way it damaged so many emerging markets in the late 1990s and early 2000s.

When other nations borrow in a foreign currency—which is common in many emerging markets—then any devaluation of their home currency automatically swells the size of the debts owed by their citizens, governments, and businesses. Here's an example: In 1995 my landlady in Mexico City owed $1,000 on a dollar-denominated credit card. She earned her income in pesos, so this meant 3,000 pesos of debt prior to January 1995. But that turned into 12,000 pesos of debt a few weeks later, when capital flight from the peso had caused it to devalue from three pesos to the dollar to twelve pesos to the dollar. (Her income, of course, did not quadruple!) In 2001, many Argentineans had taken out mortgage loans in dollars, so that when the Argentine peso devaluated from one to three pesos per dollar, their monthly mortgage payments effectively tripled.

With the debts of U.S. households and businesses denominated in our own currency, a devaluation of the dollar does not affect the size of those debts. But capital flight can damage net worth anyway—by causing asset values to fall.

The current fall in home prices, for instance, is directly tied to the United States' dependence on foreign lending. International buyers were swelling the U.S. housing bubble by buying up the now-infamous mortgage-backed securities comprised of bundles of individual mortgage loans. So long as there was international (as well as domestic) demand for these securities, U.S. lenders could not issue new mortgages fast enough. But once foreign investors realized that these securities were not the safe investment they'd been marketed as and dumped them, U.S. banks were much less interested in making mortgages since they could no longer sell them off. With fewer buyers able to get home loans, houses are harder to sell and their prices are falling.

It's a parallel story in the stock market, which has lost close to half its value just since last summer as both foreign and U.S. investors have pulled their money out.

Although data on household wealth trends are not immediately available, this one-two punch almost certainly means that the net worth of U.S. households has taken a big hit. In my case, until recently home equity and pension funds performed the miracle of giving me positive net worth despite my typical debt load. They are not pulling this miracle off today.

The loss of wealth that occurs when assets lose value can in itself cause problems in the real economy. Even though net worth is somewhat intangible, it is disconcerting to watch it fall. Vacations get cancelled, new car purchases delayed, and home improvements put off. This is happening on a massive scale today, resulting in significant layoffs by airlines, car dealerships, and construction firms, with spin-off effects throughout the economy. The pain on the real side of the economy has only just begun.

Are U.S. Institutions More Sound?

In the mid-1990s, one of the major clues that Argentina was heading for crisis was the country's high level of government debt, nearly 40% of GDP. At the time, the IMF opposed new loans to Argentina until the country got its government debt down to 34% of GDP.

By these IMF guidelines, the United States has been in the danger zone since 2003. U.S. central government debt as a percent of GDP jumped from the 30% range in 2002 to the 47% range just a year later—presumably due to the combination of Bush's 2001 tax cut and the wars in Iraq and Afghanistan. It is unusual for a nation to cut taxes while it is entering two wars.

Economist Paul Blustein's description of the Menem regime in Argentina so resonates with George W. Bush's time in office that it bears repeating here:

> Former Argentine policymakers acknowledge that foreign money made the
> government less concerned than it should have been about its debt burden and
> more inclined to treat admonitions with indifference. [One Argentine advisor
> stated,] "You can say to the politicians 'We need fiscal balance.' But if you get
> the money so easily, as we did, it's very tough to tell the politicians, 'Don't spend
> more, be more prudent,' because the money was there, and they knew it."

George Bush is a consummate politician. Like Menem, he used money (including big tax cuts for his well-to-do patrons) to build up debts and loyalty. Throwing money around helped keep Menem (and Bush) in power, but it built up debt which hamstrings economic policy in a crunch. Had Bush maintained the surpluses of the Clinton years, the U.S. economy might be in a different place today.

Of course, as recent events have underscored, the government has no monopoly on dysfunction. At first glance, it may seem ludicrous to suggest that U.S. banks could be fragile in a way similar to the banks in, say, Indonesia. In the years leading up to the Asian financial crises, Indonesia's banks held many non-performing loans, often loans made to President Suharto's cronies that no one ever expected would be repaid. Thus, the banking system's net worth on paper was an overstatement, inflated by what were essentially political donations by the banks.

But it turns out that U.S. banks have also been claiming worthless paper as assets. As of March 2008, when U.S. banks had reported only $160 billion in losses, independent analysts argued that their losses were in fact at least $300 billion and possibly as high as $1.2 trillion, according to the *Financial Times*. Clearly, many banks had lost more than they were willing to admit.

U.S. regulatory institutions were slow to force banks to reveal the real magnitude of their losses. However, investors do not rely solely on regulators to verify the value of the financial instruments they buy or hold. They also rely on private credit rating agencies. Here too, though, a kind of institutionalized corruption has crept in. One reason international holders of mortgage-backed securities and other similarly complex investments (broadly known as collateralized debt obligations, or CDOs) began dropping them like hot potatoes in August 2007 was that they realized the AAA credit rating these investments bore was false. A triple-A credit rating was supposed to mean that these securities were a very safe investment. But credit ratings are not what they used to be. Traditionally, it was the buyers of securities who paid agencies such as Moody's to rate them, but today it is the sellers of securities who pay for the ratings. So ratings agencies now have an incentive to please the issuers of CDOs by calling them safe.

Once the credibility of the rating system was put into question, the collapse in the value of CDOs had the potential to spark capital flight from many U.S. assets. International faith in Wall Street as a place of transparent and reasonably honest institutions was shaken—and with it, at least potentially, the dollar's role as key global currency.

A Peculiar Crisis

All in all, the factors that were supposed to inoculate the United States against any threat of capital flight turned out to work not quite in the way economists and financial analysts had expected. In the summer of 2007, capital flight struck. The dramatic announcement came two months after the fact, when the data were released:

> Foreign investors slashed their holdings of US securities by a record amount ... The Treasury said net sales of US market assets—including bonds, notes, and equities, were $69.3 billion in August ... The August outflow exceeded the previous record decline of $21.2 billion in March 1990. [*Financial Times*, October 17, 2007]

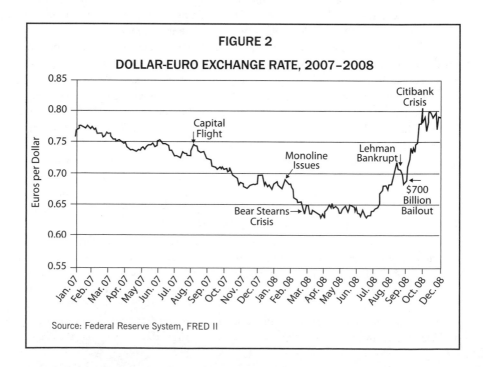

FIGURE 2

DOLLAR-EURO EXCHANGE RATE, 2007–2008

Source: Federal Reserve System, FRED II

As in the standard capital-flight scenario, the dollar's value did fall (see Figure 2). Then, in February 2008, the dollar fell further when it turned out that U.S. firms with only $46 billion in assets had sold so-called credit default swaps—a kind of quasi-insurance against financial losses—on $2 trillion worth of securities.

The dollar depreciation that occurred between August 2007 and April 2008 had a silver lining. With foreign investors selling more U.S. assets than they were buying, U.S. borrowing from abroad declined. Plus, a devalued dollar made U.S. products cheaper abroad, so exports rose. Both factors contributed to an improvement in the U.S. current account deficit. At the time, this was hailed as an "orderly" change in trajectory. Many observers breathed a sigh of relief, believing the U.S. current account deficit would shrink gradually, allowing the United States to avoid a severe contraction such as Mexico had experienced.

But then a strange thing happened. Shortly after major investment bank Bear Stearns collapsed, and while the larger financial crisis was far from over, the dollar exchange rate bottomed out and began to rise.

This was probably not on account of foreign investors suddenly renewing their faith in the securities Wall Street was selling. Rather, global investors had fled dollar-denominated assets when they got nervous in the summer of 2007, but when they got a full-blown case of panic around March 2008, they flocked to the safest haven in the financial world: U.S. Treasury bonds. (See Figure 3.) Between January and July 2007, the monthly net inflow of foreign capital into the stocks and bonds of U.S. corporations averaged over $65 trillion, more than four times the net foreign capital flowing into U.S. Treasuries. But from August 2007 to October 2008, the

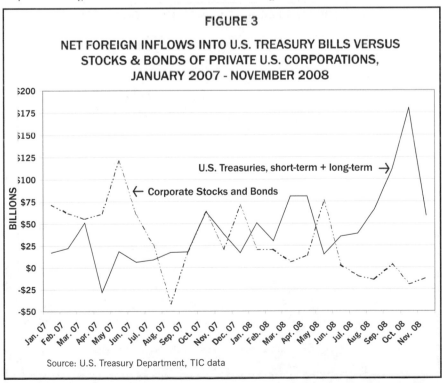

FIGURE 3

NET FOREIGN INFLOWS INTO U.S. TREASURY BILLS VERSUS STOCKS & BONDS OF PRIVATE U.S. CORPORATIONS, JANUARY 2007 - NOVEMBER 2008

Source: U.S. Treasury Department, TIC data

average monthly net inflow from abroad to U.S. stocks and bonds fell by over 75% compared to the earlier period, while the inflow to U.S. Treasuries quadrupled. At this point, almost twice as much foreign capital is flowing into Treasuries per month as into stocks and corporate bonds.

On balance, money was now coming into the United States, so the dollar appreciated. Unfortunately, that makes U.S. exports more expensive and imports a bargain, and as a result the current account worsens. By April 2008, the current account was already beginning to dive back down (see Figure 4). Hopes for an orderly escape from dependence on foreign capital evaporated.

Capital flight has played out in the United States in an unusual, even perverse way. Capital has been fleeing from U.S. stocks and private banks for over a year now. But as the saying goes, when the United States sneezes, other parts of the world get pneumonia. The U.S. financial crisis has shaken stock markets around the world. As a result, rather than continuing to leave U.S. shores, investment capital from abroad started to be re-routed to U.S. Treasury bonds. And panicky U.S. investors are augmenting the sums flowing into U.S. Treasuries as they repatriate their money from foreign stock markets.

The stampede into Treasury bonds means that money is available to the federal government at extremely low interest rates, close to 0%. The effect is to push

FIGURE 4

U.S. CURRENT ACCOUNT, QUARTERLY, 1960–2008

Source: U.S. Dept. of Commerce, Bureau of Economic Analysis, "International Economic Accounts."

the U.S. government to the forefront of all financing, putting it in the driver's seat of the economy whether or not the political leadership believes in laissez-faire. No surprise then that the private sector is seeking financing from the government on a massive scale.

The key to any kind of recovery for working people is going to be persuading the government to use that money to rebuild the real side of the economy, not just the financial sector. Of course, families want to see the value of their houses and 401(k)s go back up. What they really need, though, are jobs that pay enough so they don't have to count on asset bubbles and ballooning debt to meet their expenses. Talk of rebuilding infrastructure is welcome: both the labor market and a lot of bridges need to be strengthened. Stimulus dollars would be welcome in the economy's care sector too—in child care, in education, in elder care.

And yes, the United States needs a functioning financial sector so that small businesses, students, and even GM have access to credit. But not one as large as it was before the crisis. In recent years finance has acted as a weight on the real economy. Foreign investment in U.S. assets was causing the dollar to appreciate to such levels that U.S. products were less and less affordable overseas. So yes, fix the financial sector, but don't let it get awash with cash to the extent that the dollar appreciates U.S. manufacturers out of business, and that Wall Street CEOs pay themselves tens of millions of dollars a year with which to buy political influence. Don't let the financiers use the money that the government is borrowing today to rebuild finance as the primary engine of the U.S. economy.

Sources: Gerard Dumenil & Dominique Levy, *Capital Resurgent*, 2004; Nora Lustig, *Mexico: The Remaking of an Economy*, 1998; Paul Blustein, *And the Money Kept Rolling In (and Out)*, 2005

Article 8.6

W(H)ITHER THE DOLLAR?

The U.S. trade deficit, the global economic crisis, and the dollar's status as the world's reserve currency.

BY KATHERINE SCIACCHITANO

For more than half a century, the dollar was both a symbol and an instrument of U.S. economic and military power. At the height of the financial crisis in the fall of 2008, the dollar served as a safe haven for investors, and demand for U.S. Treasury bonds ("Treasuries") spiked. More recently, the United States has faced a vacillating dollar, calls to replace the greenback as the global reserve currency, and an international consensus that it should save more and spend less.

At first glance, circumstances seem to give reason for concern. The U.S. budget deficit is over 10% of GDP. China has begun a long-anticipated move away from Treasuries, threatening to make U.S. government borrowing more expensive. And the adoption of austerity measures in Greece—with a budget deficit barely 3% higher than the United States—hovers as a reminder that the bond market can enforce wage cuts and pension freezes on developed as well as developing countries.

These pressures on the dollar and for fiscal cut-backs and austerity come at an awkward time given the level of public outlays required to deal with the crisis and the need to attract international capital to pay for them. But the pressures also highlight the central role of the dollar in the crisis. Understanding that role is critical to grasping the link between the financial recklessness we've been told is to blame for the crisis and the deeper causes of the crisis in the real economy: that link is the outsize U.S. trade deficit.

Trade deficits are a form of debt. For mainstream economists, the cure for the U.S. deficit is thus increased "savings": spend less and the bottom line will improve. But the U.S. trade deficit didn't balloon because U.S. households or the government went on a spending spree. It ballooned because, from the 1980s on, successive U.S. administrations pursued a high-dollar policy that sacrificed U.S. manufacturing for finance, and that combined low-wage, export-led growth in the Global South with low-wage, debt-driven consumption at home. From the late nineties, U.S. dollars that went out to pay for imports increasingly came back not as demand for U.S. goods, but as demand for investments that fueled U.S. housing and stock market bubbles. Understanding the history of how the dollar helped create these imbalances, and how these imbalances in turn led to the housing bubble and sub-prime crash, sheds important light on how labor and the left should respond to pressures for austerity and "saving" as the solution to the crisis.

Gold, Deficits, and Austerity

A good place to start is with the charge that the Federal Reserve triggered the housing bubble by lowering interest rates after the dot-com bubble burst and plunged the country into recession in 2001.

In 2001, manufacturing was too weak to lead a recovery, and the Bush administration was ideologically opposed to fiscal stimulus other than tax cuts for the wealthy. So the real question isn't why the Fed lowered rates; it's why it was able to. In 2000, the U.S. trade deficit stood at 3.7% of GDP. Any other country with this size deficit would have had to tighten its belt and jump-start exports, not embark on stimulating domestic demand that could deepen the deficit even more.

The Fed's ability to lower interest rates despite the U.S. trade deficit stemmed from the dollar's role as the world's currency, which was established during the Bretton Woods negotiations for a new international monetary system at the end of World War II.

A key purpose of an international monetary system—Bretton Woods or any other—is to keep international trade and debt in balance. Trade has to be mutual. One country can't do all the selling while other does all the buying; both must be able to buy and sell. If one or more countries develop trade deficits that persist, they won't be able to continue to import without borrowing and going into debt. At the same time, some other country or countries will have corresponding trade surpluses. The result is a global trade imbalance. To get back "in balance," the deficit country has to import less, export more, or both. The surplus country has to do the reverse.

In practice, economic pressure is stronger on deficit countries to adjust their trade balances by importing less, since it's deficit countries that could run out of money to pay for imports. Importing less can be accomplished with import quotas (which block imports over a set level) or tariffs (which decrease demand for imports by imposing a tax on them). It can also be accomplished with "austerity"—squeezing demand by lowering wages.

Under the gold standard, this squeezing took place automatically. Gold was shipped out of a country to pay for a trade deficit. Since money had to be backed by gold, having less gold meant less money in domestic circulation. So prices and wages fell. Falling wages in turn lowered demand for imports and boosted exports. The deficit was corrected, but at the cost of recession, austerity, and hardship for workers. In other words, the gold standard was deflationary.

Bretton Woods

The gold standard lasted until the Great Depression, and in fact helped to cause it. Beyond the high levels of unemployment, one of the most vivid lessons from the global catastrophe that ensued was the collapse of world trade, as country after country tried to deal with falling exports by limiting imports. After World War II, the industrialized countries wanted an international monetary system that could correct trade imbalances without imposing austerity and risking another depression. This was particularly important given the post-war levels of global debt and deficits, which could have suppressed demand and blocked trade again. Countries pursued these aims at the Bretton Woods negotiations in 1944, in Bretton Woods, New Hampshire.

John Maynard Keynes headed the British delegation. Keynes was already famous for his advocacy of government spending to bolster demand and maintain employment during recessions and depressions. England also owed large war debts to the United States and had suffered from high unemployment for over two decades. Keynes therefore had a keen interest in creating a system that prevented the build-up of global debt and avoided placing the full pressure of correcting trade imbalances on debtor countries.

His proposed solution was an international clearing union—a system of accounts kept in a fictitious unit called the "bancor." Accounts would be tallied each year to see which countries were in deficit and which were in surplus. Countries with trade deficits would have to work to import less and export more. In the meantime, they would have the unconditional right—for a period—to an "overdraft" of bancors, the size of the overdraft to be based on the size of previous surpluses. These overdrafts would both support continued imports of necessities and guarantee uninterrupted global trade. At the same time, countries running trade surpluses would be expected to get back in balance too by importing more, and would be fined if their surpluses persisted.

Keynes was also adamant that capital controls be part of the new system. Capital controls are restrictions on the movement of capital across borders. Keynes wanted countries to be able to resort to macroeconomic tools such as deficit spending, lowering interest rates, and expanding money supplies to bolster employment and wages when needed. He worried that without capital controls, capital flight—investors taking their money and running—could veto economic policies and force countries to raise interest rates, cut spending, and lower wages instead, putting downward pressure on global demand as the gold standard had.

Keynes's system wouldn't have solved the problems of capitalism—in his terms, the problem of insufficient demand, and in Marx's terms the problems of overproduction and under-consumption. But by creating incentives for surplus countries to import more, it would have supported global demand and job growth and made the kind of trade imbalances that exist today—including the U.S. trade deficit—much less likely. It would also have taken the pressure off deficit countries to adopt austerity measures. And it would have prevented surplus countries from using the power of debt to dictate economic policy to deficit countries.

At the end of World War II, the United States was, however, the largest surplus country in the world, and it intended to remain so for the foreseeable future. The New Deal had lowered unemployment during the Depression. But political opposition to deficit spending had prevented full recovery until arms production for the war restored manufacturing. Many feared that without continued large U.S. trade surpluses and expanded export markets, unemployment would return to Depression-era levels.

The United States therefore blocked Keynes' proposal. Capital controls were permitted for the time being, largely because of the danger that capital would flee war-torn Europe. But penalties for surplus countries were abandoned; pressures remained primarily on deficit countries to correct. Instead of an international clearing union with automatic rights to overdrafts, the International Monetary Fund (IMF) was established to make short-term loans to deficit countries. And instead of the neutral bancor, the dollar—backed by the U.S. pledge to redeem dollars with gold at $35 an ounce—would be the world currency.

Limits of the System

The system worked for just over twenty-five years, not because trade was balanced, but because the United States was able and willing to recycle its huge trade surpluses. U.S. military spending stayed high because of the U.S. cold-war role as "global cop." And massive aid was given to Europe to rebuild. Dollars went out as foreign aid and military spending (both closely coordinated). They came back as demand for U.S. goods.

At the same time, memory of the Depression created a kind of Keynesian consensus in the advanced industrial democracies to use fiscal and monetary policy to maintain full employment. Labor movements, strengthened by both the war and the post-war boom, pushed wage settlements and welfare spending higher. Global demand was high.

Two problems doomed the system. First, the IMF retained the power to impose conditions on debtor countries, and the United States retained the power to control the IMF.

Second, the United States stood outside the rules of the game: The larger the world economy grew, the more dollars would be needed in circulation; U.S. trade deficits would eventually have to provide them. Other countries would have to correct their trade deficits by tightening their belts to import less, exporting more by devaluing their currencies to push down prices, or relying on savings from trade surpluses denominated in dollars (known as "reserves") to pay for their excess of imports over exports. But precisely because countries needed dollar reserves to pay for international transactions and to provide cushions against periods of deficits, other countries would need to hold the U.S. dollars they earned by investing them in U.S. assets. This meant that U.S. dollars that went out for imports would come back and be reinvested in the United States. Once there, these dollars could be used to finance continued spending on imports—and a larger U.S. trade deficit. At that point, sustaining world trade would depend not on recycling U.S. surpluses, but on recycling U.S. deficits. The ultimate result would be large, destabilizing global capital flows.

The Crisis of the 'Seventies

The turning point came in the early 'seventies. Europe and Japan had rebuilt from the war and were now export powers in their own right. The U.S. trade surplus was turning into a deficit. And the global rate of profit in manufacturing was falling. The United States had also embarked on its "War on Poverty" just as it increased spending on its real war in Vietnam, and this "guns and butter" strategy—an attempt to quell domestic opposition from the civil right and anti-war movements while maintaining global military dominance—led to high inflation.

The result was global economic crisis: the purchasing power of the dollar fell, just as more and more dollars were flowing out of the United States and being held by foreigners.

What had kept the United States from overspending up to this point was its Bretton Woods commitment to exchange dollars for gold at the rate of $35 an ounce. Now countries and investors that didn't want to stand by and watch as the purchasing power of their dollar holdings fell—as well as countries that objected to the Vietnam War—held the United States to its pledge.

There wasn't enough gold in Ft. Knox. The United States would have to retrench its global military role, reign in domestic spending, or change the rules of the game. It changed the rules of the game. In August 1971, Nixon closed the gold window; the United States would no longer redeem dollars for gold. Countries and individuals would have to hold dollars, or dump them and find another currency that was more certain to hold its value. There was none.

The result was that the dollar remained the global reserve currency. But the world moved from a system where the United States could spend only if could back its spending by gold, to a system where its spending was limited only by the quantity of dollars the rest of the world was willing to hold. The value of the dollar would fluctuate with the level of global demand for U.S. products and investment. The value of other currencies would fluctuate with the dollar.

Trading Manufacturing for Finance

The result of this newfound freedom to spend was a decade of global inflation and crises of the dollar. As inflation grew, each dollar purchased less. As each dollar purchased less, the global demand to hold dollars dropped—and with it the dollar's exchange rate. As the exchange rate fell, imports became even more expensive, and inflation ratcheted up again. The cycle intensified when OPEC—which priced its oil in dollars—raised its prices to compensate for the falling dollar.

Owners of finance capital were unhappy because inflation was eroding the value of dollar assets. Owners of manufacturing capital were unhappy because the global rate of profit in manufacturing was dropping. And both U.S. politicians and elites were unhappy because the falling dollar was eroding U.S. military power by making it more expensive.

The response of the Reagan administration was to unleash neoliberalism on both the national and global levels—the so-called Reagan revolution. On the domestic front, inflation was quelled, and the labor movement was put in its place, with high interest rates and the worst recession since the Depression. Corporate profits were boosted directly through deregulation, privatization, and tax cuts, and indirectly by attacks on unions, unemployment insurance, and social spending.

When it was over, profits were up, inflation and wages were down, and the dollar had changed direction. High interest rates attracted a stream of investment capital into the United States, pushing up demand for the currency, and with it the exchange rate. The inflows paid for the growing trade and budget deficits—Reagan had cut domestic spending, but increased military spending. And they provided abundant capital for finance and overseas investment. But the high dollar also made U.S. exports more expensive for the rest of the world. The United States had effectively traded manufacturing for finance and debt.

Simultaneously, debt was used as a hammer to impose neoliberalism on the Third World. As the price of oil rose in the seventies, OPEC countries deposited their growing trade surpluses—so-called petro-dollars—in U.S. banks, which in turn loaned them to poor countries to pay for the soaring price of oil. Initially set at very low interest rates, loan payments skyrocketed when the United States jacked up its rates to deal with inflation. Third World countries began defaulting, starting with Mexico in 1981. In response, and in exchange for more loans, the U.S.-controlled IMF imposed austerity programs, also known as "structural adjustment programs."

The programs were similar to the policies in the United States, but much more severe, and they operated in reverse. Instead of pushing up exchange rates to attract finance capital as the United States had done, Third World countries were told to devalue their currencies to attract foreign direct investment and export their way out of debt. Capital controls were dismantled to enable transnational corporations to enter and exit at will. Governments were forced to slash spending on social programs and infrastructure to push down wages and demand for imports. Services were privatized to create opportunities for private capital, and finance was deregulated.

Policies dovetailed perfectly. As the high dollar hollowed out U.S. manufacturing, countries in the Global South were turned into low-wage export platforms. As U.S. wages stagnated or fell, imports became cheaper, masking the pain. Meanwhile, the high dollar lowered the cost of overseas production. Interest payments on third world debt—which continued to grow—swelled the already large capital flows into the United States and provided even more funds for overseas investment.

The view from the heights of finance looked promising. But Latin America was entering what became known as "the lost decade." And the United State was shifting from exporting goods to exporting demand, and from recycling its trade surplus to recycling its deficit. The world was becoming dependent on the United States as the "consumer of last resort." The United States was becoming dependent on finance and debt.

Consolidating Neoliberalism

The growth of finance in the eighties magnified its political clout in the nineties. With the bond market threatening to charge higher rates for government debt, Clinton abandoned campaign pledges to invest in U.S. infrastructure, education, and industry. Instead, he balanced the budget; he adopted his own high-dollar policy, based on the theory that global competition would keep imports cheap, inflation low, and the living standard high regardless of sluggish wage growth; and he continued deregulation of the finance industry—repealing Glass-Steagall and refusing to regulate derivatives. By the end of Clinton's second term, the U.S. trade deficit had hit a record 3.7% of GDP; household debt had soared to nearly 69% of GDP and financial profits had risen to 30% of GDP, almost twice as high as they had been at any time up to the mid 1980s.

Internationally, Clinton consolidated IMF-style structural adjustment policies under the rubric of "the Washington Consensus," initiated a new era of trade agreements modeled on the North American Free Trade Agreement, and led the charge to consolidate the elimination of capital controls.

The elimination of capital controls deepened global economic instability in several ways.

First, eliminating restrictions on capital mobility made it easier for capital to go in search of the lowest wages. This expanded the globalization of production, intensifying downward pressure on wages and global demand.

Second, removing capital controls increased the political power of capital by enabling it to "vote with its feet." This accelerated the deregulation of global finance and—as Keynes predicted—limited countries' abilities to run full-employment policies. Regulation of business was punished, as was deficit spending, regardless of its purpose. Low inflation and deregulation of labor markets—weakening unions and making wages more "flexible"—were rewarded.

Finally, capital mobility fed asset bubbles and increased financial speculation and exchange rate volatility. As speculative capital rushed into countries, exchange rates rose; as it fled, they fell. Speculators began betting more and more on currencies themselves, further magnifying rate swings. Rising exchange rates made exports uncompetitive, hurting employment and wages. Falling exchange rates increased the competitiveness of exports, but made imports and foreign borrowing more expensive, except for the United States, which borrows in its own currency. Countries could try to prevent capital flight by raising interest rates, but only at the cost of dampening growth and lost of jobs. Lacking capital controls, there was little countries could do to prevent excessive inflows and bubbles.

Prelude to a Crash

This increased capital mobility, deregulation, and speculation weakened the real economy, further depressed global demand, and greatly magnified economic instability. From the eighties onward, international financial crises broke out approximately every five years, in countries ranging from Mexico to the former Soviet Union.

By far the largest crisis prior to the sub-prime meltdown took place in East Asia in the mid-nineties. Speculative capital began flowing into East Asia in the mid nineties. In 1997, the bubble burst. By the summer of 1998, stock markets around the world were crashing from the ripple effects. The IMF stepped in with $40 billion in loans, bailing out investors but imposing harsh conditions on workers and governments. Millions were left unemployed as Asia plunged into depression.

When the dust settled, Asian countries said "never again." Their solution was to build up large dollar reserves—savings cushions—so they would never have to turn to the IMF for another loan. To build up reserves, countries had to run large trade surpluses. This meant selling even more to the United States, the only market in the world able and willing to run ever-larger trade deficits to absorb their exports.

In addition to further weakening U.S. manufacturing, the Asia crisis set the stage for the sub-prime crisis in several ways.

First, as capital initially fled Asia, it sought out the United States as a "safe haven," igniting the U.S. stock market and nascent housing bubbles.

Second, the longer-term recycling of burgeoning Asian surpluses ensured an abundant and ongoing source of capital to finance not only the mounting trade deficit, but also the billowing U.S. consumer debt more generally.

Third, preventing their exchange rates from rising with their trade surpluses and making their exports uncompetitive required Asian central banks to print money, swelling global capital flows even more.

Between 1998 and 2007, when the U.S. housing bubble burst, many policy makers and mainstream economists came to believe this inflow of dollars and debt would never stop. It simply seemed too mutually beneficial to end. By financing the U.S. trade deficit, Asian countries guaranteed U.S. consumers would continue to purchase their goods. The United States in turn got cheap imports, cheap money for consumer finance, and inflated stock and real estate markets that appeared to be self-financing and to compensate for stagnating wages. At the same time, foreign holders of dollars bought increasing quantities of U.S. Treasuries, saving the U.S. government from having to raise interest rates to attract purchasers, and giving the United States cheap financing for its budget deficit as well.

It was this ability to keep interest rates low—in particular, the Fed's ability to lower rates after the stock market bubble collapsed in 2000—that set off the last and most destructive stage of the housing bubble. Lower interest rates simultaneously increased the demand for housing (since lower interest rates made mortgages cheaper) and decreased the returns to foreign holders of U.S. Treasuries. These lower returns forced investors to look for other "safe" investments with higher yields. Investors believed they found what they needed in U.S. mortgage securities.

As Wall Street realized what a lucrative international market they had, the big banks purposefully set out to increase the number of mortgages that could be repackaged and sold to investors by lowering lending standards. They also entered into complicated systems of private bets, known as credit default swaps, to insure against the risk of defaults. These credit default swaps created a chain of debt that exponentially magnified risk. When the bubble finally burst, only massive stimulus spending and infusions of capital by the industrialized countries into their banking systems kept the world from falling into another depression.

Deficit Politics

The political establishment—right and center—is now licking its chops, attacking fiscal deficits as if ending them were a solution to the crisis. The underlying theory harks back to the deflationary operation of the gold standard and the conditions imposed by the IMF: Government spending causes trade deficits and inflation by increasing demand. Cutting spending will cut deficits by diminishing demand.

Like Clinton before him, Obama is now caving in to the bond market, fearful that international lenders will raise interest rates on U.S. borrowing. He has created a bi-partisan debt commission to focus on long-term fiscal balance—read: cutting Social Security and Medicare—and revived "PAYGO," which requires either cuts or increases in revenue to pay for all new outlays, even as unemployment hovers just under 10%.

By acquiescing, the U.S. public is implicitly blaming itself for the crisis and offering to pay for it twice: first with the millions of jobs lost to the recession, and again by weakening the safety net. But the recent growth of the U.S. budget deficit principally reflects the cost of cleaning up the crisis and of the wars in Iraq and Afghanistan. Assumptions of future deficits are rooted in projected health-care costs in the absence of meaningful reform. And the U.S. trade deficit is driven mainly by the continued high dollar.

The economic crisis won't be resolved by increasing personal savings or enforcing fiscal discipline, because its origins aren't greedy consumers or profligate governments. The real origins of the crisis are the neoliberal response to the crisis of the

1970s—the shift from manufacturing to finance in the United States, and the transformation of the Global South into a low-wage export platform for transnational capital to bolster sagging profit rate. The U.S. trade and budget deficits may symbolize this transformation. But the systemic problem is a global economic model that separates consumption from production and that has balanced world demand—not just the U.S. economy—on debt and speculation.

Forging an alternative will be the work of generations. As for the present, premature tightening of fiscal policy as countries try to "exit" from the crisis will simply drain global demand and endanger recovery. Demonizing government spending will erode the social wage and undermine democratic debate about the public investment needed for a transition to an environmentally sustainable global economy.

In the United States, where labor market and financial deregulation have garnered the most attention in popular critiques of neoliberalism, painting a bulls-eye on government spending also obscures the role of the dollar and U.S. policy in the crisis. For several decades after World War II, U.S. workers benefited materially as the special status of the dollar helped expand export markets for U.S. goods. But as other labor movements throughout the world know from bitter experience, it's the dollar as the world's currency, together with U.S. control of the IMF, that ultimately provided leverage for the United States to create the low-wage export model of growth and financial deregulation that has so unbalanced the global economy and hurt "first" and "third" world workers alike.

Looking Ahead

At the end of World War II, John Maynard Keynes proposed an international monetary system with the bancor at its core; the system would have helped balance trade and avoid the debt and deflation in inherent in the gold standard that preceded the Great Depression. Instead, Bretton Woods was negotiated, with the dollar as the world's currency. What's left of that system has now come full circle and created the very problems it was intended to avoid: large trade imbalances and deflationary economic conditions.

For the past two and a half decades, the dollar enabled the United States to run increasing trade deficits while systematically draining capital from some of the poorest countries in the world. This money could have been used for development in the Global South, to replace aging infrastructure in the United States, or to prepare for and prevent climate change. Instead, it paid for U.S. military interventions, outsourcing, tax cuts for the wealthy, and massive stock market and housing bubbles.

This mismanagement of the dollar hasn't served the long-term interests of workers the United States any more than it has those in of the developing world. In domestic terms, it has been particularly damaging over the last three decades to U.S. manufacturing, and state budgets and workers are being hit hard by the crisis. Yet even manufacturing workers in the United States cling to the high dollar as if it were a life raft. Many public sector workers advocate cutting back on government spending. And most people in the United States would blame bankers' compensation packages for the subprime mess before pointing to the dismantling of capital controls.

After suffering through the worst unemployment since the Depression and paying for the bailout of finance, U.S. unions and the left are right to be angry. On the global scale, there is increased space for activism. Since the summer of 2007, at least 17 countries have imposed or tightened capital controls. Greek workers have been in the streets protesting pension cuts and pay freezes for months now. And a global campaign has been launched for a financial transactions tax that would slow down speculation and provide needed revenue for governments. Together, global labor and the left are actively rethinking and advocating reform of the global financial system, the neoliberal trade agreements, and the role and governance of the International Monetary Fund. And there is increasing discussion of a replacement for the dollar that won't breed deficits, suck capital out of the developing world, impose austerity on deficit countries—or blow bubbles.

All these reforms are critical. All will require more grassroots education. None will come without a struggle.

Sources: C. Fred Bergsten, "The Dollar and the Deficits: How Washington Can Prevent the Next Crisis," Peterson Institute for International Economics, *Foreign Affairs*, Volume 88 No. 6, November 2009; Dean Baker, "The Budget, the Deficit, and the Dollar," Center for Economic Policy and Research, www.cepr.net; Martin Wolf, "Give us fiscal austerity, but not quite yet," *Financial Times* blogs, November 24, 2009; Tom Palley, "Domestic Demand-led Growth: A New Paradigm for Development," paper presented at the Alterantives to Neoliberalism Conference sponsored by the New Rules for Global Finance Coalition, May 21-24, 2002, www.economicswebinstitute.org; Sarah Anderson, "Policy Handcuffs in the Financial Crisis: How U.S. Government And Trade Policy Limit Government Power To Control Capital Flows, " Institute for Policy Studies, February 2009; Susan George, "The World Trade Organisation We Could Have Had," *Le Monde Diplomatique*, January 2007.

Article 8.7

PUTTING THE "GLOBAL" IN THE GLOBAL ECONOMIC CRISIS

BY SMRITI RAO
November/December 2009

There is no question that the current economic crisis originated in the developed world, and primarily in the United States. Much of the analysis of the crisis has thus focused on institutional failures within the United States and there is, rightly, tremendous concern here about high rates of domestic unemployment and under-employment. But after three decades of globalization, what happens in the United States does not stay in the United States; the actions of traders in New York City will mean hunger for children in Nairobi. We now know what crisis looks like in the age of globalization and it is not pretty.

This crisis is uniquely a child of the neoliberal global order. For developing countries the key elements of neoliberalism have consisted of trade liberalization and an emphasis on exports; reductions in government social welfare spending; a greater reliance on the market for determining the price of everything from the cur-rency exchange rate to water from the tap; and, last but not least, economy-wide privatization and deregulation. In each case, the aim was also to promote cross-border flows of goods, services, and capital—and, to a far lesser degree, of people.

Despite Thomas Friedman's assertions of a "flat" world, this age of globalization did not in fact eliminate global inequality. Indeed if we exclude China and India, in-equality between countries actually increased during this period. The globalization of the last 30 years was predicated upon the extraction by the developed world of the natural resources, cheap labor, and, in particular, capital of the developing world, the latter via financial markets that siphoned the world's savings to pay for U.S. middle-class consumption. What could be more ironic than the billions of dollars in capital flowing every year from developing countries with unfunded domestic needs to developed countries, which then failed to meet even their minimum obligations with respect to foreign aid? Africa, for example, has actually been a net creditor to the United States for some time, suggesting that the underlying dynamic of the world economy today is not that different from the colonialism of past centuries.

These "reverse flows" are partly the result of attempts by developing countries to ward off balance-of-payment crises by holding large foreign exchange reserves. With-in the United States, this capital helped sustain massive borrowing by households, corporations, and governments, exacerbating the debt bubble of the last eight years. Meanwhile, the global "race to the bottom" among developing-county exporters en-sured that the prices of most manufactured goods and services remained low, taking the threat of inflation off the table and enabling the U.S. Federal Reserve to keep in-terest rates low and facilitate the housing bubble.

Now that this debt bubble has finally burst, it is no surprise that the crisis has been transmitted back to the global South at record speed.

Measuring the Impact

A country-by-country comparison of the growth in real (i.e., inflation-adjusted) GDP from 2007 to 2008 against the average annual growth of the preceding three years (2005-2007) gives us a picture of the differential impact of the economic crisis—at least in its early stages—on various countries. Consistent data are available for 178 developed and developing countries.

Overall, GDP growth for these 178 countries was down by 1.3 percentage points in 2008 compared to the average for 2005-2007. Of course, the financial crisis only hit in full force in September 2008, so the 2009 data will give us a more complete picture of the impact of the crisis. The International Monetary Fund (IMF) estimates that global GDP will decline in 2009 for the first time since World War II. Currently, the IMF is expecting a 1.4% contraction this year. According to the International Labor Organization, global unemployment increased by 10.7 million in 2008, with a further increase of 19 million expected in 2009 by relatively conservative estimates. As a result, the number of people living in poverty will increase by an estimated 46 million this year according to the World Bank.

The initial impact in 2008 was greatest in Eastern Europe and Central Asia: six of the ten countries with the steepest declines in real GDP growth were from the Eastern Europe/Central Asia region (see Table 1). Joined by Ireland, this is a list of global high-fliers—countries with very high rates of growth (before 2008, that is) that had globalized rapidly and enthusiastically in the last decade and a half. Singapore of course was an early adopter of globalization, touted by the IMF as a model for other small countries, while Seychelles has depended heavily on international tourism. Myanmar would seem to be the exception to this pattern of intensive globalization, given its political isolation. From an economic perspective, however, this was a country whose economic growth depended heavily on the rising prices of its commodity exports (natural gas and gems).

Indeed, if we rank these 178 countries by the share of their GDP represented by exports before the crisis, we find a correlation between dependence on exports and steeper declines in GDP growth. The 50 most export-dependent countries actually saw larger declines in GDP in 2008 than those less dependent on exports (see Table 2). Likewise with certain other key markers of neoliberal globalization.

That globalizers appear to be most affected by the crisis is no accident. It turns out that each of the three primary channels through which the crisis has been transmitted from the United States to other countries is a direct outcome of the policy choices that developing countries were urged and sometimes coerced into making—with assurances that this particular form of globalization was the best way to build a healthy and prosperous economy.

Transmission Channels of the Crisis

Lowered exports and remittances. The recession in the United States and Europe has hit exports from the developing world hard. Globally, trade in goods and services did rise by 3% in 2008, but that was compared to 10% and 7% in the previous two years. Trade is expected to decline by a sharp 12% in 2009. The United States, the world's most important importer, has seen imports drop by an unprecedented 30% since July 2008. For countries ranging from Pakistan to Cameroon, this has meant lower foreign exchange earnings, slower economic growth, and higher unemployment.

Meanwhile, for many developing countries, the emphasis on export promotion meant the increasing export not of goods and services but of people, who sought work in richer countries and sent part of their earnings back home. Remittance flows from temporary and permanent migrants accounted for 25% of net inflows of private capital to the global South in 2007. These flows are also affected by the crisis, although they have proved more resilient than other sources of private capital.

Migrant workers in construction, in particular, find that they are no longer able to find work and send money back home, and countries in Latin America have seen sharp declines in remittance inflows. However, as Indian economist Jayati Ghosh points out, women migrants working as maids, nurses, and nannies in the West have not been as hard hit by the recession. This has meant that remittance flows to countries with primarily female migrants, such as Sri Lanka and the Philippines, are not as badly affected. The Middle Eastern countries that are important host countries for many Asian migrants have also been relatively shielded from the crisis. As a result, for the developing world as a whole, remittances actually rose in 2008. Because other private capital flows declined sharply post-crisis, remittances accounted for 46% of net private capital inflows to the developing world in 2008.

Outflows of portfolio capital. In the boom years up to 2007, developing countries were encouraged to liberalize their financial sectors. This meant removing regulatory barriers to the inflow (and outflow) of foreign investors and their

TABLE 1: STEEPEST DECLINES IN ECONOMIC GROWTH

TOP TEN COUNTRIES BY DECLINE IN 2008 REAL GDP GROWTH VS. 2005-07 ANNUAL AVERAGE.		
	Country	Change in 2008 real GDP growth compared to 2005-07 average(in percentage points)
1	Latvia	−15.56
2	Azerbaijan	−14.44
3	Estonia	−12.26
4	Georgia	−8.42
5	Myanmar	−8.32
6	Ireland	−8.30
7	Seychelles	−7.62
8	Armenia	−6.85
9	Singapore	−6.66
10	Kazakhstan	−6.57

Source: Author's calculations based on data from World Development Indicators online, World Bank, June 2009.

money. While some foreign investors did buy factories and other actual physical assets in the developing world, a substantial portion of foreign capital came in the form of portfolio capital—short-term investments in stock and real estate markets. Portfolio capital is called "hot money" for a reason: it tends to be incredibly mobile, and its mobility has been enhanced by the systematic dismantling of various government restrictions ("capital controls") that formerly prevented this money from entering or leaving countries at the volume and speed it can today.

Around the time of the collapse of Bear Stearns in the United States in early 2008, various global financial powerhouses began pulling their money out of developing-country markets. The pace of the pullout only accelerated after the crash that September. One consequence for developing countries was a fall in their stock market indices, which in turn depressed growth. Another was that as foreign investors converted their krona, rupees, or rubles into dollars in order to leave, the value of the local currency got pushed down.

The IMF has long touted the virtues of allowing freely floating exchange rates, where market forces determine the value of each currency. In the aftermath of the

TABLE 2: EXPORTS AND FOREIGN INVESTMENT

CHANGE IN 2008 REAL GDP GROWTH COMPARED TO 2005-07 AVERAGE (IN PERCENTAGE POINTS) FOR COUNTRIES RANKED BY:		
	Export share of GDP	FDI share of GDP
Average for top 50 countries	−2.25	−1.85
Average for countries ranked 51-100	−1.50	−1.70
Average for the remaining countries	−0.88	−1.07
Total number of countries	167	171

TABLE 3: EXCHANGE RATE AND FISCAL POLICY

AVERAGE CHANGE IN 2008 REAL GDP GROWTH COMPARED TO 2005-07 AVERAGE (IN PERCENTAGE POINTS) FOR COUNTRY GROUPINGS:			
Exchange Rate Policy		Fiscal Policy	
Countries with fixed exchange rate	−1.19	Countries with no inflation targeting	−1.18
Countries with managed float or other mixed policy	−1.19	Countries with inflation targeting	−2.35
Countries with freely floating exchange rate	−2.04		
Total number of countries	178		171

Sources: Author's calculations based on data from World Development Indicators online, World Bank, June 2009 and De Facto Classification of Exchange Rate Regimes and Monetary Policy Frameworks as of April 31, 2008, IMF.

financial crisis, this meant a sharp depreciation in the value of many local currencies relative to the dollar. This in turn meant that every gallon of oil priced in dollars would cost that many more, say, rupees. Similarly, any dollar-denominated debt a country held became harder to repay. The dollar cost of imports and debt servicing went up, just as exports and remittances—the ability to earn those dollars—were falling. Predictably, countries with floating (i.e., market-determined) exchange rates were harder hit in 2008 (see Table 3).

Falling flows of FDI and development aid. Meanwhile, one other source of foreign exchange, foreign investment in actual physical assets such as factories (known as foreign direct investment, or FDI), is stagnant and likely to fall as companies across the world shelve expansion plans. The signs of vulnerability are evident in the fact that countries most dependent upon FDI inflows (as a percentage of GDP) between 2005 and 2007 suffered greater relative GDP declines in 2008 (see Table 2).

Developed countries are also cutting back on foreign aid budgets, citing the cost of domestic stimulus programs and reduced tax revenues. Such cuts particularly affect the poorest countries. With the economic slowdown their governments are losing domestic tax and other revenues, so falling aid flows are likely to hurt even more. The importance of continued aid flows can be seen in the fact that higher levels of aid per capita from 2005 to 2007 were actually associated with more mild drops in GDP growth in 2008 (see Table 2). This may be partly due to the fact that these countries already had low or negative rates of GDP growth so that 2008 declines appear smaller relative to that baseline. Nevertheless, aid flows appear to have protected the most vulnerable countries from even greater economic disaster. In fact the so-called HIPC group (highly indebted poor countries) actually saw an increase of one percentage point in GDP growth rates when compared to the 2005-2007 average.

Both FDI and aid work their way into and out of economies more slowly, so we may have to wait for 2009 data to estimate the full impact of the crisis via this channel.

The simultaneous transmission of the crisis through these three channels has left developing countries reeling. What makes the situation even worse is that unlike developed countries, developing countries are unlikely to be able to afford generous stimulus packages (China is an important exception). Meanwhile, the IMF and its allies, rather than supporting developing-country governments in their quest to stimulate domestic demand and investment, are hindering the process by insisting on the same old policy mix of deficit reductions and interest rate hikes. In an illustration of how ruinous this policy mix can be, countries that had followed IMF advice and adopted "inflation targeting" before the crisis suffered greater relative GDP declines once the crisis hit (see Table 3).

The tragedy of course is that while the remnants of the welfare state still protect citizens of the developed world from the very worst effects of the crisis, developing countries have been urged for two decades to abandon the food and fuel subsidies and public sector provision of essential services that are the only things that come close to resembling a floor for living standards. They were told they didn't need that safety net, that it only got in the way; now, of course, they are free to fall.

For those unwilling to let this tragedy unfold, this is the time to apply pressure on developed-country governments to maintain aid flows. Even more importantly, this is the time to apply pressure on the IMF and the other multilateral development banks, and on their supporters in the halls of power, so that they offer developing countries a genuine chance to survive this crisis and begin to rebuild for the future.

It is worth recalling that the end of the previous "age of globalization," signaled by the Great Depression, led to a renewed role for the public sector the world over and an attempt to achieve growth alongside self-reliance. In the years after World War II, led by Latin America, newly independent developing countries attempted to prioritize building a domestic producer and consumer base. In the long run, perhaps this crisis will result in a similar rethinking of the currently dominant model of development. In the short run, however, the world seems ready to stand by and watch while the poor and vulnerable in developing countries, truly innocent bystanders, suffer.

Sources: Dilip Ratha, Sanket Mohapatra, and Ani Silwal, "Migration and Development Brief 10," Migration and Remittances Team, Development Prospects Group, World Bank, July 13, 2009; Atish R. Ghosh et al. 2009, "Coping with the Crisis: Policy Options for Emerging Market Countries," IMF Staff Position Note, SPN/09/08, April 23, 2009; World Bank, "Swimming Against the Tide: How Developing Countries Are Coping with the Global Crisis," Background Paper prepared by World Bank Staff for the G20 Finance Ministers and Central Bank Governors Meeting, Horsham, United Kingdom on March 13-14, 2009; Jayati Ghosh, "Current Global Financial Crisis: Curse or Blessing in Disguise for Developing Countries?" Presentation prepared for the IWG-GEM Workshop, Levy Economics Institute, New York, June 29-July 10, 2009.

Article 8.8

BEYOND THE WORLD CREDITORS' CARTEL

In Latin America and elsewhere, the IMF may be re-emerging—but in a changed landscape.

BY DARIUSH SOKOLOV
September/October 2009

O ne group of financiers seems to be doing nicely out of the global recession: the International Monetary Fund and other international financial institutions (IFIs) are enjoying a return to relevance and lining up for increased funding.

The London G20 Summit in April was the IMF's big comeback gig. In 2007 the fund's loan book was down to just $20 billion; now its capital is set to triple to $750 billion, plus permission to issue $250 billion in "special drawing rights" (the fund's quasi-currency which allows member countries to borrow from each others' reserves). Since September 2008 a range of East European and ex-Soviet states have taken out new loans. So too have Pakistan, El Salvador, and Iceland—the fund's first Western European client since Britain in 1976.

The World Bank and regional development banks are also getting in on the party. In Latin America, the World Bank's regional vice president Pamela Cox says she expects lending to triple in 2009 to $14 billion. The Inter-American Development ment Bank (IDB), the most active IFI in the region, expects to lend $18 billion—its typical loan portfolio is under $8 billion. And the development banks are queuing up behind the IMF with their caps out for capital increases: the Asian Development Bank wants to triple its capital to $165 billion; the IDB is asking for an extra $50 to $80 billion on top of its current $101 billion.

Why now? The IFIs, says Vince McElhinny of the Bank Information Center, a group that monitors them, are opportunists at heart. Just like any private bank or corporation they fight for market share, and as the world economy and global capital markets grow they need to increase their lending apace or lose relevance. The freezing of world capital markets, particularly severe in emerging markets, has created a need which they can seize as opportunity. The Institute of International Finance predicts private net capital flows to emerging markets of $141 billion in 2009, down from $392 billion in 2008, after a record $890 billion in 2007. The IFIs see themselves helping to fill this gap.

But the issues at stake here go beyond the IFIs' own agendas. On the one hand, their revival implies a reassertion of U.S. and global North dominance. They aren't called "Washington-based" just as a matter of real estate: the United States has a 17% voting share on the IMF and World Bank, enough to give it a veto on some major changes; Europe and the United States control the top management positions.

On the other hand, the story underscores how parts of the global South are gaining in economic power. In the crises of the 1990s, or so the neoliberal story went, the IMF stepped in to clean up the messes made when fragile Third World economies exploded. This time around things are very different: the mess is in the North, and the likelihood is that the emerging economies of Asia and Latin America will emerge from it stronger and more independent. (It's important to note, though, that large areas in the South, notably Africa, are not part of this story—nor is Eastern Europe.) The so-called BRIC nations in particular (Brazil, Russia, India, China) are getting the bargaining power to back up their claims on the global financial system. Will these claims be met within the existing institutions, or by creating a new financial architecture that bypasses Washington altogether? The future of the IFIs is a key arena in which global rebalancing of economic power is playing out.

New Financial Architecture?

In May 2007 finance ministers from Brazil, Argentina, Venezuela, Bolivia, and Ecuador signed the "Quito declaration" in the Ecuadorian capital. The plan includes a regional monetary fund and moves toward a South American single currency, but the first step is the creation of the Banco del Sur, a new regional development bank. While the bank's launch is behind schedule, this March its constitution was agreed to, with an initial capitalization of $7 billion. Besides the original five, Paraguay and Uruguay are also members. (Even Colombia had announced its support before its late-2007 row with Venezuela over hostages.)

The aim of Banco del Sur is to replace the Washington-based lenders altogether with institutions run by and for South America. Maria Jose Romero, who researches the IFIs at the Third World Institute in Montevideo, encapsulates this spirit. "In responding to the crisis Latin American countries have two options," she says. "We can return to the old institutions and the failed recipes of the 1990s, or we can move forward with alternatives."

For many Latin American countries a return to the IMF is politically out of the question. According to Mark Weisbrot, co-director of the Center for Economic and Policy Research in Washington, the decline of the IMF started with the Asian financial crisis over a decade ago. After the fund's failure to act as emergency lender of last resort to Asian banking systems in 1997, those states moved to build up sizeable currency reserves, determined not to be dependent on the fund again; others followed suit.

This turning away has been more dramatic in Latin America, where IMF policies are blamed for precipitating the 1998 crisis in Argentina which led to the collapse of its banking system and eventually to its 2002 default. Argentina and Bolivia both paid off the last of their debts to the fund in 2006; in April 2007 Ecuador announced it had paid off its IMF loans and requested the fund withdraw its country manager; the same month Venezuela announced itself debt-free, and a few weeks later said it would withdraw from fund membership altogether. When Daniel Ortega won the Nicaraguan presidential election in May 2007 he promised the country would be "free from the fund" within five years.

How has this freedom-from-Washington line held in the current crisis? U.S.-friendly Mexico was the first to sign up for the new Flexible Credit Lines the IMF is granting without conditions to "pre-approved" governments, followed by Colombia—though neither has yet drawn on them. So far only El Salvador and Costa Rica have taken out new loans. In sharp contrast to Eastern Europe, most Latin American states had healthy reserve cushions coming into the crunch. And with commodity prices now rising again, it may be that the region's anti-IMF resolve is not going to face the test many had anticipated.

As for Banco del Sur, the arrival of crisis no doubt slowed the process: domestic firefighting comes before regional cooperation. But, according to Romero, in the medium term it will help push change:

"The crisis has focused attention to the failings of the existing financial system," she says. "It is helping build the impetus for Banco del Sur, as well as for moves to settle bilateral trade in local currencies [rather than dollars], which is the first step towards monetary union, and for broader South-South cooperation initiatives."

To be fair, Banco del Sur may not live up to proponents' hopes. With just $7 billion in capital, the bank won't be in the same league as the Washington-based IFIs. Nor is there any immediate plan to create an emergency monetary fund—an Ecuadorian proposal to that effect has been dropped. And the principle of one country one vote, perhaps the biggest rallying point of all, has been modified: equal votes will apply only on loans under $70m, above which approval is required from members with two-thirds of the capital contributions.

Finally, there is still no clarity on the focus of lending. Campaigners hope for a true emphasis on poverty reduction and projects to build regional cooperation, and have scored the provision of a socially focused "audit board." But some fear that more conservative members (read: Brazil) could push Banco del Sur toward being just one more development bank.

Across Asia, there are parallel developments. A proposal by Japan to set up an Asian Monetary Fund met the same fate as an earlier Malaysian-backed scheme called the East Asian Economic Caucus—both were dropped after expressions of disapproval from the IMF and U.S. officials. But now the Chiang Mai Initiative, a longstanding plan for a system of swap arrangements between the central banks of the southeast Asian countries plus China, Japan, and South Korea is expected to come on line this year, and the proposed size of the scheme was upped to $120 billion in February. Chiang Mai is linked to the IMF (members need IMF agreements in place to withdraw more than 20% of the total), but some see it leading towards an eventual independent regional fund. For now, though, at least officially, the talk is usually of "complementing," not supplanting, the IMF.

Rise of the BRICs

If the Quito project is the idealistic side of the regionalization movement, the BRIC bloc is global power shift as realpolitik. The BRICs together now account for 22% of world production (by purchasing power parity), up from 16% ten years ago and rising.

Even as they move ahead with building regional institutions independent of the IFIs, the BRICs are pushing for more power within the Washington-based institutions. Increased say at the IMF is one of the four governments' main demands. In March 2008 China's vote share was raised all the way up to 3.7%—putting the world's most populous country on a par with Belgium plus the Netherlands, combined population 27 million. The BRICs jointly muster a 9.82% quota.

According to Vince McElhinny, the BRICs' contributions to the fund's current capital boost are aimed at bolstering their demands for more say in IFI governance.

When, a week before the BRIC summit, Brazil's President Lula announced a $10 billion contribution, he talked of thereby gaining "moral authority to keep pushing for changes needed at the IMF."

The IMF's desire to placate emerging powers such as the BRICs may explain the makeover it has displayed in its current comeback—dubbed "IMF 2.0" by *Time* magazine. Managing director Dominique Strauss-Kahn has called for the fund to spend against recession: less structural adjustment, more counter-cyclical stimulus. But the changes may be largely cosmetic. According to a study by the Third World Network, the actual conditions of recent IMF loans to Pakistan, Hungary, Ukraine, and other countries are familiar: the borrowers must reduce their fiscal deficits through public spending cuts, wage freezes, higher fuel tariffs, and interest rate hikes.

What real changes are the BRICs really likely to get? There's plenty of gossip flying around: some are touting Lula as the next World Bank president; perhaps China will get to pick Strauss-Kahn's successor.

Mark Weisbrot, however, does not see the U.S. government giving any ground on voting shares. "The U.S. would rather walk away from the IMF than give up control," he says.

Beyond the Cartel

Weisbrot describes the IMF as "the most important instrument of influence the U.S. government has in developing countries—beyond the military, beyond the CIA. Or, at least, that's the role it's played for most of the last 30 years. A good part of that influence has been lost recently; now they're trying to get it back."

The IMF's power has never really been about its own lending, however. Its influence over countries' economic policies is far greater than would be suggested by its share in overall capital flows. The real issue is the fund's role as "gatekeeper" of a global "creditors' cartel."

Multilateral loans from the World Bank and regional development banks and bilateral loans from the wealthy countries typically come with some form of "cross-conditionality" clause. You only get your loan if you first have an IMF agreement in place, installments only keep flowing so long as you stick to it. Similar conditions can also apply in private capital transactions. For instance, Venezuela's 2007 threat to give up its IMF membership triggered a market sell-off because under covenants written into its sovereign bonds, a break with the fund would count as a "technical default."

Now, though, recent shifts in Latin America have dealt what Weisbrot says could be "a final blow to the IMF creditors' cartel in middle-income countries."

This is a continental tale, but Argentina is a good place to begin. The country cut itself off from international capital markets with its 2002 default, and is still being chased by "hold-out" bond investors in the New York courts. Yet Argentina grew at almost 9% a year from 2003 through 2007—the country's most rapid growth in 50 years, and some of the fastest growth rates on the continent. This expansion has been funded largely by selling bonds to another emerging regional power, Venezuela. These bond transfers are no subsidies—Argentina pays commercial interest rates—but they do come free of Washington conditions. For Weisbrot,

"Venezuela's offers of credit, without policy conditions, to Argentina, Bolivia, Ecuador, Nicaragua, and other countries has changed the equation."

It's true that easy Venezuelan credit dried up early on in the crisis as oil prices plummeted. It's also true that Argentina is now allowing IMF staff in to monitor its economy and taking out new loans from the World Bank and the IDB. But it's telling that Argentina got these loans without any IMF agreement in place: the cartel, at least in its old form, appears to be broken. And then there's the other plank in Argentina's current crisis management strategy: a $10.2 billion swap line direct with China.

In short, the IMF and allied institutions have regained some lost ground in the crisis, but forms of "South-South cooperation" that stand to weaken the Washington-based creditors' cartel have kept on building too.

According to one very plausible interpretation, this crisis has been about the consequences of the rich countries' capital piling into the financial services sphere to compensate for the loss of manufacturing production to the Third World. Control of the world's financial capital flows was one last highly profitable channel where Northern capital still ruled unopposed. Increasingly, though, global-South states and corporations are cutting out the middle man to trade directly with each other. It's against the background of these new possibilities that the next chapter in the story of the IFIs will play out.

Article 8.9

MEASURES OF GLOBAL POVERTY

BY ARTHUR MacEWAN
January/February 2008

Dear Dr. Dollar:
I hear all kinds of views about poverty in the developing world from different corners of the media. One minute you can get the impression that a huge swell is lifting everyone up and that millions of people in Asia are no longer in poverty. Then from a different source you get the impression that poverty is deepening and getting worse—the pictures of the kids with swollen bellies, etc. What's the reality?

—William Chin, Randolph, Mass.

The reality of poverty, like many other "realities," is elusive! There are disputes over how to define poverty, and, even when we can agree on a definition, there are disputes over how to measure poverty. However, one aspect of the poverty reality is fairly clear: there are still a great many very poor people in the world.

One widely used standard used to measure poverty is $2 per day—that is, people whose income is less than $2 per day are considered "in poverty." And people are viewed as in "extreme poverty" if their income is less than $1 per day. By these standards, in 2004 about 2.5 billion people, 39% of the world's 6.4 billion people, were in poverty, and 969 million were in extreme poverty.

This standard, however, requires a bit of explanation. The $2/day and the $1/day are based on what people could buy in 1990. Translated into today's prices, these figures would be about $3.20/day and $1.60/day. Also, these amounts are defined in terms of real purchasing power, not in terms of actual exchange rates. Thus $1.60 per day represents what a person could buy with that amount in the United States, not what could be bought in a low-income country if the $1.60 were exchanged for the local currency. Generally the latter would be substantially more than the former.

The World Bank makes annual attempts to update the figures on how many people are in poverty and how many are in extreme poverty by these standards. According to the Bank, there has been some substantial progress in the last fifteen years. By the Bank's count, the number of people in extreme poverty dropped from 1.25 billion in 1990 to below a billion in 2004—or from 24% of the world's people to its 2004 figure of 15%. The absolute number below $2/day fell only slightly in this period, from 2.6 billion to 2.5 billion, but this was a drop from 49% to 39% of the population (because the population increased).

The World Bank's appraisal of the situation, however, is open to dispute. To begin with, there are always problems in measuring what happens to people's incomes over time, because prices change. While the Bank adjusts for price changes, it does not do so adequately. To measure what happens in a country, the bank uses price changes for that country as a whole. It seems, however, that the prices of the goods that the poor buy have generally risen more rapidly than prices for the society as a whole. Thus the Bank's estimates of poverty reduction are probably overstated.

Furthermore, as the Bank recognizes, its picture of overall progress for the world obscures some very great differences between countries. By the $2/day and $1/day standard, the last fifteen years have seen great progress in China and India, two countries that together account for more than one-third of the world's population and which have grown quite rapidly. Other parts of the world, especially much of sub-Saharan Africa and parts of Latin America, have not done so well.

But there is a bigger difficulty. The $2/day and $1/day definitions of extreme poverty and poverty are, at best, a questionable way to frame the problem. It is misleading to define the poverty line simply in absolute terms, as the value of a certain quantity of goods and services that people must purchase to meet their basic needs (as represented by the $2/day and $1/day cutoffs). Raising people's absolute incomes is important and leads to improvements in nutrition, shelter, longevity, and general well-being. But there is more to poverty than an absolute level of income.

Poverty is a social status, a relation among people, and our standard of what it means to be in poverty varies across societies and over time. As a society's economy grows, its standard of "need" changes, and thus the meaning of poverty changes. For example, as an economy grows, more work takes place away from the home, and thus people's need for transportation increases. Also, as incomes rise, people's standards of what they need in terms of food, clothing, shelter, and everything else change.

Roughly speaking, we can think of a society's standard of needs as determined by what the people in the middle have. If so, people are in poverty when their level of income is far below what the people in the middle have. This means that poverty is greatly affected by the distribution of income. In two societies where the absolute income of the bottom segment (say the bottom 20%) is the same, poverty will be greater in the society where income distribution is more unequal because in that society the bottom segment will be further from the norm and thus more lacking in that society's socially determined needs.

In China and India, in particular, the countries responsible for large reductions in poverty by the $2/day measure, income inequality has increased dramatically in recent decades. Thus, if we define poverty as a certain distance (in income terms) form the middle, it is possible that there are more people in poverty in China and India than there were twenty years ago, in spite of rapid economic expansion. And China and India are not unusual. Over the last few decades, many countries have seen rising inequality.

Even if one accepts the absolute poverty definition—the $2/day and $1/day standards—rising inequality makes the reduction of poverty with economic growth much less than it would be if, along with growth, income distribution were improving. The problem is that the World Bank and much of the U.N. effort to "make poverty history" largely ignore the issue of income distribution. For example, land redistribution is not on the table in World Bank and U.N. programs, yet unequal land holdings are at the foundation of the lack of income and political power experienced by the poor in many parts of the world. Or another example: the Bank and the United Nations tout education as a cure-all for poverty, but they give no consideration to the ways inequalities of income and political power restrict the emergence of effective school programs.

Whether one emphasizes the absolute or relative concept of poverty—or takes both into account—it is doubtful that much progress can be attained while ignoring the underlying issues of power and social structure that create and maintain poverty.

Article 8.10

WOMEN OF NAFTA

BY MARTHA OJEDA, FELICITAS CONTRERAS, AND YOLANDA TREVIÑO
September/October 2007

The outstanding collection *NAFTA From Below: Maquiladora Workers, Farmers, and Indigenous Communities Speak Out on the Impact of Free Trade in Mexico*, combines worker testimony with analytical and historical essays to provide a devastating picture of the effects of neoliberal international trade policies—culminating in the North American Free Trade Agreement (NAFTA)—on workers throughout Mexico. The book, available in both English and Spanish, also offers inspiring accounts of resistance to those policies.

The book's early chapters focus on *maquiladora* workers in the north of the country, addressing key labor issues such as health and safety, environmental concerns, and freedom of association. Later chapters take up organizing by agricultural workers in the south, especially in the state of Chiapas, in response to neoliberal "reforms." That the Zapatista uprising in Chiapas began on January 1, 1994, the very day that NAFTA went into effect, was no accident.

One of the book's achievements is to show how the struggles of industrial workers in the north of Mexico are related to those of agricultural workers in the south. Knitting these struggles together is one of the central aims of the Coalition for Justice in the Maquiladoras, which produced *NAFTA From Below*. The coalition has helped bring *maquila* workers and organizers from the north together with members of grassroots *campesino* and indigenous groups in the south to help strengthen cooperative projects in both regions and to share information about the history of organized struggle in the workplace. Women's strong leadership roles in workplace struggles in the north have been of particular interest to organizers in the south, especially as former agricultural workers from the south migrate to work in *maquiladoras* near the northern border.

Women played a central role in the struggle of workers at a Sony plant in Nuevo Laredo for a democratic union, described in the selections that follow. The events at Sony vividly illustrate the frequent conflicts between Mexico's corrupt official unions and rival independent unions that Chris Tilly and Marie Kennedy describe (pp. 26-30). The Sony workers' struggle was also a key early test of NAFTA's labor side-agreement, the North American Agreement on Labor Cooperation, and the bodies it established, known as National Administrative Offices (NAOs), to investigate violations.

These excerpts include testimony from Martha Ojeda (co-editor of *NAFTA From Below*, with Rosemary Hennessy), a *maquila* worker from 1973 to 1994 who is now executive director of the Coalition for Justice in the Maquiladoras; from Felicitas (Fela) Contreras, an activist with CETRAC (Center for Workers and Communities) in Nuevo Laredo who worked at the Sony plant from 1985 through 1998; and from Yolanda Treviño, a former Sony worker who testified before the NAO as part of the Sony workers' NAFTA complaint.

MARTHA A. OJEDA: Official history is always written so that the reality people were living is hidden. If everyone told the part they lived or knew, the truth would be in their collective word.

In 1979 Sony arrived in my town [Nuevo Laredo].... Sony manually assembled audiocassettes and Beta videocassettes. In 1982, after the first devaluation of the peso, there were more than 1,000 workers working three shifts in five plants, and by then the workers were also producing the VHS videocassette and the 3.5 inch diskette.

They began to bring machines for semiautomatic and automatic assembly of the cassettes. The plastic molding injection plant was providing the plastic cases and the components for the audio and video plants. It was the boom of assembly line production.

In this era children with birth defects began to be born, but the company doctor said that this happened because the parents were alcoholics or because they had genetic problems. By 1993 there were 2,000 employees in seven plants in three shifts. There was a lot of overtime, but still it wasn't enough to meet production quotas.

The molding ingestion plants never stopped working; they were going three shifts seven days a week. For the first time the company proposed 12 hour shifts for four and three days a week. This implied that Sony got their production, because the machines were running around the clock, but they avoided paying overtime. This twelve-hour shift was unknown to workers because it didn't exist in the Federal Labor Law.

It was in this labor and political context that in October 1993 we visited Fidel Velázquez, the CTM national leader, in Mexico City and solicited union elections within the framework of the CTM. All of the *maquilas* were affiliated with this union because it was the only one; if you didn't belong to them there was no other alternative for workers anywhere. But the leaders negotiated the contract with the company even before it was established in the locality.

Fidel told us that he agreed with the elections (but he never said when they would be). We trusted his word and began the process that the Federal Labor Law sets down for forming the union sections.

On January 1, 1994, we were informed of the Zapatista uprising, but equally surprising to us was to find out in the newspaper on January 4 that Chema Morales had declared that on the order of Fidel Velázquez he would be the new Secretary General of the *maquilas*—without sectionals—and, worst of all, he was already named to the Labor Board at the state level because of his position as Secretary General, not only of the Maquila Union but also of the Workers Federation of Nuevo Laredo.

Shocked, we tried to communicate with Fidel Velázquez, but our efforts were in vain. Then we learned that he was coming to Ciudad Victoria, the capital of Tamaulipas, on January 12. We traveled all night. But when we arrived it was obvious that they would not let us enter. We guessed that Fidel would come in by the side door and we waited there until he arrived with the media.

I demanded publicly that he retract his authorization of Chema Morales as Secretary General. Then I asked for a public debate with him and with Chema. I don't know if I was the only woman from the provinces who had publicly challenged him, but what I do know is that so much corruption repulsed me and gave me the courage to make sure that the two of them, both Chema and Fidel, would be exposed even to the President of the Labor Board of the state who was present. He had authorized naming Chema to be Secretary General even though he had never worked in the *maquilas*, and according to the union by-laws that was one of the requirements.

In the face of the media and all of the evidence, Fidel looked ridiculous and he had no alternative but to accept that there would be union elections. So he declared that he would send a national representative to hold them. When I went to say good-bye to him at the podium he told me, "You are going to eat fire." And I told him, "I'm ready." But I never imagined what he was referring to.

FELICITAS ("FELA") CONTRERAS: In 1993 they began to change the delegates in all of the *maquiladoras* who were not agreed with the CTM. I heard that there were going to be elections in all the *maquilas*, not only in Sony, and we were asking when Sony's turn would be. But before the elections they were changing the delegates. They fired the ones we wanted and after work we had meetings to change the delegates so that they would really be for us. We met in one house and another with Martha because we wanted to change the delegates who were im-posed by the CTM. I would get home at 4:00 or 5:00 in the morning. We always were hiding here and there, and that is how we put together a slate, even though they fired our candidates.

Those union delegates who were with Chema Morales (of the CTM) developed their slates with the old delegates from Sony… They preferred Chema instead of our democratic union. In April of 1994 the day arrived for the elections, and Chema's representative from the union and a representative of Fidel Velázquez were set up in the parking lot of Plant #7. We had our slate, but they didn't give us a chance to let our other co-workers know that the voting was taking place.

Representatives of Fidel Velázquez and of the company were there. They told the people to go to the parking lot and they arranged to meet the other shift and take them out to vote. They said on this side go all those in favor of the blue slate, on the other side those in favor of the CTM slate. Our slate won because everyone came to our side. But Fidel's representative said that the other delegates from the CTM won. And so we said, "How is that possible if we are all here, voting for our slate? We were the majority. What are we going to do?" We were really mad! Those who were working came out and we took to the streets to protest that they were doing this fraudulent election, and we made signs that said, "We want democratic elections!!"

YOLANDA TREVIÑO: On Saturday April 16, which was my day off, I went to plant #3 to see what resolution Mayor Horacio Garza had been able to make as to when we would have new elections. The *compañeras* who had spoken with him told us that he wasn't going to help us. That's when we started to hold our protest on the side-walk in front of the plants, showing our frustration, but in a peaceful manner. We didn't stop anyone who wanted to from going into work and we didn't commit any act of violence.

We continued protesting in this way until Horacio Garza and Maricela López arrived. We had a meeting there with Horacio and he told us to stop the protest and that afterwards he would help us. We answered that the only thing we wanted was

Señor Avila's word that they would hold new elections. But he said no. So Horacio Garza left and soon afterward the police and the firemen arrived. The girls were afraid when they saw the police and some of them asked if the were going to take us away, but we told them if we didn't act violently then they shouldn't either.

But that wasn't the case. Francisco Xavier Rios [Vice President of Human Resources at Sony] signaled to the police with a motion of his hand to enter through a side door, and they positioned themselves on the inside lot of the company. Then without any warning the police began to push us with their Plexiglas shields and their billy clubs. They beat us badly; they knocked a *compañera* unconscious, a woman named Alicia Soto, and they pushed the rest of us down with their shields, insulting us all the while, calling us names like "goddamn bitches."

I have been told that the company claims that the police didn't commit any acts of violence and that they only person who acted violently was Alicia who attacked the police with a magazine. I ask you: how is it possible that a 24 year old woman can harm a group of 35 well-armed police agents carrying Plexiglas shields and billy clubs? How is it possible to say they didn't commit acts of violence when my friend Alicia was knocked out by a blow to the head and has had problems ever since? I have here the newspaper *El Mañana*, dated 17 April, which shows very clearly a picture of Alicia unconscious. If they don't want to read the newspapers they should just look at their own videos because they were filming the entire attack.

FELICITAS ("FELA") CONTRERAS: They had pressed charges against us—Martha Ojeda and various others—because Sony had lost millions with the work stoppage. They issued a summons for us to appear at the police department and told us that our lives were not even worth enough to pay for the company's losses.

They wanted us to say that Martha was responsible, and they pitted us against each other. They told Lupe that I had confessed that Martha was doing it all, and they told me that Lupe confessed that Martha told us to stop working. But of the 40 they called to testify all of us said, "We are all responsible, and so you will have to arrest all of us not just Martha." All of our *compañeras* were outside the police department yelling that they would have to arrest everyone. But since there were more than a thousand and we didn't all fit in the cells, after hours of interrogations and threats they let us go.

On the fifth day, in the early morning, around 5:00 am the governor –Manuel Cavazos Lerma- ordered that they state police from Reynosa, Matamoros and Cd. Victoria be brought in. The police arrived and the soldiers with machine guns and rifles. And they said to you, "Get out of here or I'll kill you." According to them they came to restore order, and with blows and kicks. They awakened us and ran after those who were sleeping on the sidewalk. You were waking up with a gun pointing in your face and they were yelling, "Get out or we will kill you."

We withdrew, and we were like this for five days and nights. In those days the trucks tried to mow us down because they wanted to take out the production, but we were all sleeping in the main gate so they couldn't cross and take it out.

Unfortunately, we didn't get it. We didn't get our union, and they fired a lot of people without giving them any severance payment because they said that they were leaders of the movement. We stayed there because we wanted an independent union.

In 1994 NAFTA was signed, and they said that the rights of workers would not be violated. But they beat us up and violated our rights. With the help of CJM and the lawyers from ANAD a demand was presented to the NAO. In 1995 we had a hearing and we all went to San Antonio to testify. Sony brought lawyers from New York and they said that our testimony was a lie, but we took the newspapers and the evidence, the videos. We won this trial, but we didn't really win anything because they didn't punish or fine Sony and we never had the elections or anything. They just put in these offices [the NAO] just to prop us NAFTA.

For me NAFTA was no good. The workers are still just as poor. The only difference is that now there are many settlements, *colonias*, many squatters, a lot of insecurity and a contaminated river. Before I used to drink water from the river and now you cant, and you cant go into it either. Our air is contaminated. There is a lot of sickness. There is a lot of illiteracy. The only one NAFTA helped were the businessmen because they are the ones that have gotten rich. And now they say, "I am going to China; I screwed the Mexicans so now I'm going to screw the Chinese." That is what says with me about NAFTA. We are poor and screwed.

MARTHA A. OJEDA: Each one of my *compañeras* risked her life, her children, and her family. They kidnapped Yolanda and threatened her. They persecuted the others, calling them on the phone and intimidating them. Wherever any of them are, because there were many and I will never forget one, to each of them I render homage and a special tribute to their "*coraje*"—their courage and bravery—for trying to reclaim workers' right to freedom of association. For resisting and never giving up.

That is what NAFTA left me after 20 years in the *maquilas*: it gave me the opportunity to denounce at a global level the failure of this agreement and of the side agreements and to share the rebellion and resistance of my *compañeras*. It taught me that there is a world of solidarity. It clarified the horizon we are looking for, and above all the hope to reach it with a team like this team of women, united until the end.

To order NAFTA From Below *or for more information, visit www.coalitionforjustice.net write to The Coalition for Justice in the Maquiladoras, 4207 Willowbrook Dr., San Antonio, TX 78228, or call 210-732-8324.*

Article 8.11

REMITTANCES TO THE RESCUE?

BY ALISSA THUOTTE
May/June 2008

Remittances—the money sent home to families by migrants living in foreign countries—have been gaining attention in the last few years from international institutions such as the World Bank, the Inter-American Development Bank (IDB), and the International Monetary Fund. These organizations and others have begun to study remittances with an eye to their potential for reducing poverty in the poor and near-poor countries to which most of these funds flow. It turns out that remittances are a mixed blessing. They offer a relatively stable source of incoming funds. At the same time, however, they can create an alarming dependence on behalf of their recipients, heightening their vulnerability to shifting political and economic winds in the host countries over which they have no control.

Remittances have been, until very recently, very much on the rise, with about 10% of the world's population now receiving some remittance income. In 2006, 150 million migrants across the globe sent $300 billion in 1.5 billion transactions. Remittances now represent nearly one-third of total financial flows to the developing world—more than official development assistance and, depending on the country, more even than foreign direct investment. Fifty-nine countries receive more than $1 billion annually in remittances, and 45 receive more than 10% of their GDP. Moreover, remittance flows have tended to be much more stable than foreign direct investment or portfolio (stocks and bonds) investment (see graph, "Remittances versus Other External Financing").

One third of the money sent originates in the United States; most of the rest is sent from Europe and the Middle East. A significant volume of remittance money circulates within the developing world as well, however: so-called "South-South" flows account for 30% to 45% of total remittances, according to the World Bank.

Latin America and the Caribbean is the region receiving the highest level of remittances per capita, averaging $102 annually, and the region's remittance flows have risen tenfold in real terms over the last 20 years. In 2006 the region received $62.3 billion from migrants abroad—five times the amount of "official development assistance" it received—with remittances to Mexico ($24.2 billion) accounting for over a third. After climbing at double-digit rates in the last decade, the flow now appears to be leveling off: a recent survey by an IDB fund estimated 2007 remittances to the region at $66.5 billion, only a 7% increase over the previous year.

Most of the money received in this region is used for everyday living expenses, everything from food and home repairs to school tuition. What interests economists most, though, is the potential for remittances to contribute to economic development—when, for example, recipients put the money toward new small business ventures that may over time provide employment to others and expand local economies. According to a 2007 World Bank report, the data suggest that remittances do tend to increase bank deposits, reflecting at least some potential for such investment.

Research has generally found that higher remittance flows are, to a modest degree, associated with lower poverty, better health, and higher levels of education in the developing world. In ten out of eleven Latin American and Caribbean countries examined in a 2006 World Bank study, children from families receiving remittances were more likely to remain in school than those whose parents were not supported by such funds.

Yet the increasing remittance flows have a downside: families and national economies that come to rely on the extra income become vulnerable to far-distant events and trends. Take the case of Mexico. One consequence of the current bust in the U.S. housing market is that construction, which employs many Mexican workers, has slowed—and along with it, the flow of money back home. Remittances to Mexico grew only 1% in 2007, and in January of this year *fell* 6% compared to the same period last year, according to the IDB.

And the falloff in construction work is not the only factor depressing Mexican migrants' ability to send money home. Thanks to increasingly visible anti-immigrant sentiment in the United States, stricter border enforcement—including the threat of incarceration, as opposed to just deportation, for undocumented migrants caught crossing the border—and penalties for employers who hire undocumented

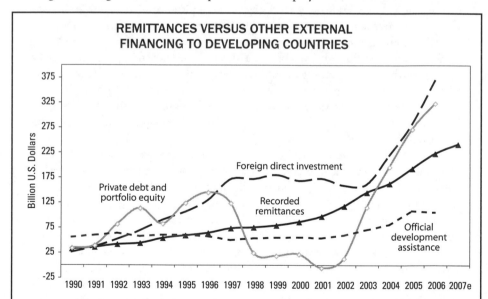

REMITTANCES VERSUS OTHER EXTERNAL FINANCING TO DEVELOPING COUNTRIES

Note: **Private debt and portfolio equity** refers to the net flow of stock and bond purchases by foreign investors plus commercial bank loans from foreign banks. **Foreign direct investment** refers to the net flow of funds invested directly by companies to establish or control business enterprises abroad. **Official development assistance** refers to loans, grants, and other aid given by the governments of developed countries. Remittance figure for 2007 is estimated.

Sources: World Bank: "Global Economic Prospects 2006: Economic Implications of Remittances and Migration," "World Development Indicators 2008," and "Global Development Finance 2008."

workers, it has become harder for immigrants to enter the country and find decent jobs. As the dollar falls in value against foreign currencies, those who have been in the United States for some time may have to work longer hours and cut their expenses just to be able to send home the same amounts.

Migration and remittances have certainly transformed many Latin American towns, but not always for the better. So-called "migra-villages" have seen their working-age adult population shrink. Remittance money can help build new homes, but they often remain empty in their owners' absence; new schools get built, but enrollment does not necessarily increase. Family members left behind may stop working and wait month-to-month for money from overseas, weakening local economies—not a sustainable set-up in the long run.

And surprisingly, remittances do not necessarily flow most heavily toward the poorest families that need them the most. In fact, the World Bank's 2006 study found that in the 11 Latin American and Caribbean countries for which data were available, remittance income was actually distributed slightly more unequally than total household income: the top 20% took in 51% of total income, but 54% of remittances. Who receives remittances varies sharply from country to country. Contrast Mexico, for instance, where 61% of the households receiving remittances in 2004 were in the bottom 20% by (non-remittance) income, with Peru, where fewer than 6% were, while 40% were in the top income quintile.

Today, remittance checks are helping millions of households across the global

WESTERN UNION CALLING

While it has undeniably become easier and more convenient to send money across the border in the last decade, activists charge transfer services, especially Western Union, with taking advantage of their most loyal customers. Remittances represent a nearly $1 billion a year industry for Western Union; global migration is so central to the company's profits that "forecasts of border movements drive the company's stock," according to the *New York Times*. Western Union's huge slice of the industry pie allows the company to charge fees from 4% to as high as 20% of the amount remitted.

The Oakland, Calif.-based Boycott Western Union campaign asserts that the company fails to invest an adequate portion of its earnings in the communities of the customers from which it profits. Its campaign aims to convince Western Union to sign a Transnational Community Benefits Agreement—like the Community Reinvestment Act for banks—that would "ensure community reinvestment of $1 per every transaction while also forcing the company to reduce its fees and establish fairer exchange rates."

In the meantime, experts at the IDB and elsewhere insist that this is a perfect opportunity for banks to get more involved, and are trying to encourage partnerships between U.S. and Latin American banks and to extend networks into Latin America's more rural areas, where access to banking is notoriously scarce. More competition, they argue, would help push transfer fees down and improve customer service.

South to keep food on the table and a roof overhead. Although the evidence hardly hails them as a long-term solution to global poverty, as long as remittance flows continue, they should be both facilitated *and* rigorously regulated.

Sources: Jason DeParle, "Migrant Money Flow: A $300 Billion Current," *New York Times*, 11/18/07; Pablo Fajnzylber and J. Humberto Lopez, "Close to Home: The DevelopmentaImpact of Remittances in Latin America," (World Bank, 2007); "Sending Money Home: Worldwide Remittance Flows to Developing Countries," (IFAD/IDB, 2007); Manuel Orozco, "The Remittance Marketplace: Prices, Policy, and Financial Institutions," (Pew Hispanic Center, 6/7/04); Elisabeth Malkin, "Mexicans Barely Increased Remittances in '07," *New York Times*, 2/26/08; Jason DeParle, "World Banker and His Cash Return Home," *New York Times*, 3/17/08; Donald Greenlees, "As the Dollar Slides, Two Continents Feel the Side Effects in Divergent Ways," *New York Times*, 3/27/08; Jason DeParle, "Western Union Empire Moves Migrant Cash Home," *New York Times*, 11/22/07; Eduardo Porter, "Struggling to Draw Workers Sending Money Back Home," *New York Times*, 6/7/04; Devesh Kapur, "Remittances: the New Development Mantra?" (U.N. Conf. on Trade and Dev't, April 2004); Kevin Plumberg, "Weak Dollar Makes Immigrant Life Tougher," Reuters, 2/11/08; Ami Bonilla, "Mexicans Send Less Cash Home, Bad News for All," New America Media, 8/9/07; Maria Sacchetti, "Beating the Bank," *Boston Globe*, 4/15/08.

Article 8.12

INTERNATIONAL LABOR STANDARDS

BY ARTHUR MacEWAN
September/October 2008

> Dear Dr. Dollar:
> *U.S. activists have pushed to get foreign trade agreements to include higher labor standards. But then you hear that developing countries don't want that because cheaper labor without a lot of rules and regulations is what's helping them to bring industries in and build their economies. Is there a way to reconcile these views? Or are the activists just blind to the real needs of the countries they supposedly want to help?*
> —Philip Bereaud, Swampscott, Mass.

In 1971, General Emilio Medici, the then-military dictator of Brazil, commented on economic conditions in his country with the infamous line: "The economy is doing fine, but the people aren't."

Like General Medici, the government officials of many low-income countries today see the well-being of their economies in terms of overall output and the profits of firms—those profits that keep bringing in new investment, new industries that "build their economies." It is these officials who typically get to speak for their countries. When someone says that these countries "want" this or that—or "don't want" this or that—it is usually because the countries' officials have expressed this position.

Do we know what the people in these countries want? The people who work in the new, rapidly growing industries, in the mines and fields, and in the small shops and market stalls of low-income countries? Certainly they want better conditions—more to eat, better housing, security for their children, improved health and safety. The officials claim that to obtain these better conditions, they must "build their economies." But just because "the economy is doing fine" does not mean that the people are doing fine.

In fact, in many low-income countries, economic expansion comes along with severe inequality. The people who do the work are not getting a reasonable share of the rising national income (and are sometimes worse off even in absolute terms). Brazil in the early 1970s was a prime example and, in spite of major political change, remains a highly unequal country. Today, in both India and China, as in several other countries, economic growth is coming with increasingly severe inequality.

Workers in these countries struggle to improve their positions. They form—or try to form—independent unions. They demand higher wages and better working conditions. They struggle for political rights. It seems obvious that we should support those struggles, just as we support parallel struggles of workers in our own country. The first principle in supporting workers' struggles, here or anywhere else, is supporting their right to struggle—the right, in particular, to form independent unions without fear of reprisal. Indeed, in the ongoing controversy over the U.S.-Colombia Free Trade Agreement, the assassination of trade union leaders has rightly been a major issue.

Just how we offer our support—in particular, how we incorporate that support into trade agreements—is a complicated question. Pressure from abroad can help, but applying it is a complex process. A ban on goods produced with child labor, for example, could harm the most impoverished families that depend on children's earnings, or could force some children into worse forms of work (e.g., prostitution). On the other hand, using trade agreements to pressure governments to allow unhindered union organizing efforts by workers seems perfectly legitimate. When workers are denied the right to organize, their work is just one step up from slavery. Trade agreements can also be used to support a set of basic health and safety rights for workers. (Indeed, it might be useful if a few countries refused to enter into trade agreements with the United States until we improve workers' basic organizing rights and health and safety conditions in our own country!)

There is no doubt that the pressures that come through trade sanctions (restricting or banning commerce with another country) or simply from denying free access to the U.S. market can do immediate harm to workers and the general populace of low-income countries. Any struggle for change can generate short-run costs, but the long-run gains—even the hope of those gains—can make those costs acceptable. Consider, for example, the Apartheid-era trade sanctions against South Africa. To the extent that those sanctions were effective, some South African workers were deprived of employment. Nonetheless, the sanctions were widely supported by mass organizations in South Africa. Or note that when workers in this country strike or advocate a boycott of their company in an effort to obtain better conditions, they both lose income and run the risk that their employer will close up shop.

Efforts by people in this country to use trade agreements to raise labor standards in other countries should, whenever possible, take their lead from workers in those countries. It is up to them to decide what costs are acceptable. There are times, however, when popular forces are denied even basic rights to struggle. The best thing we can do, then, is to push for those rights—particularly the right to organize independent unions—that help create the opportunity for workers in poor countries to choose what to fight for.

Article 8.13

NIKE TO THE RESCUE?

Africa needs better jobs, not sweatshops.

BY JOHN MILLER
September/October 2006

"In Praise of the Maligned Sweatshop"

WINDHOEK, Namibia—Africa desperately needs Western help in the form of schools, clinics and sweatshops.

On a street here in the capital of Namibia, in the southwestern corner of Africa, I spoke to a group of young men who were trying to get hired as day laborers on construction sites.

"I come here every day," said Naftal Shaanika, a 20-year-old. "I actually find work only about once a week."

Mr. Shaanika and the other young men noted that the construction jobs were dangerous and arduous, and that they would vastly prefer steady jobs in, yes, sweatshops. Sure, sweatshop work is tedious, grueling and sometimes dangerous. But over all, sewing clothes is considerably less dangerous or arduous—or sweaty—than most alternatives in poor countries.

Well-meaning American university students regularly campaign against sweatshops. But instead, anyone who cares about fighting poverty should campaign in favor of sweatshops, demanding that companies set up factories in Africa.

The problem is that it's still costly to manufacture in Africa. The headaches across much of the continent include red tape, corruption, political instability, unreliable electricity and ports, and an inexperienced labor force that leads to low productivity and quality. The anti-sweatshop movement isn't a prime obstacle, but it's one more reason not to manufacture in Africa.

Imagine that a Nike vice president proposed manufacturing cheap T-shirts in Ethiopia. The boss would reply: "You're crazy! We'd be boycotted on every campus in the country."

Some of those who campaign against sweatshops respond to my arguments by noting that they aren't against factories in Africa, but only demand a "living wage" in them. After all, if labor costs amount to only $1 per shirt, then doubling wages would barely make a difference in the final cost.

One problem ... is that it already isn't profitable to pay respectable salaries, and so any pressure to raise them becomes one more reason to avoid Africa altogether.

One of the best U.S. initiatives in Africa has been the African Growth and Opportunity Act, which allows duty-free imports from Africa—and thus has stimulated manufacturing there.

—Op-ed by Nicholas Kristof, *New York Times*, June 6, 2006

Nicholas Kristof has been beating the pro-sweatshop drum for quite a while. Shortly after the East Asian financial crisis of the late 1990s, Kristof, the Pulitzer Prize-winning journalist and now columnist for the *New York Times*, reported the story of an Indonesian recycler who, picking through the metal scraps of a garbage dump, dreamed that her son would grow up to be a sweatshop worker. Then, in 2000, Kristof and his wife, *Times* reporter Sheryl WuDunn, published "Two Cheers for Sweatshops" in the *Times Magazine*. In 2002, Kristof's column advised G-8 leaders to "start an international campaign to promote imports from sweatshops, perhaps with bold labels depicting an unrecognizable flag and the words 'Proudly Made in a Third World Sweatshop.'"

Now Kristof laments that too few poor, young African men have the opportunity to enter the satanic mill of sweatshop employment. Like his earlier efforts, Kristof's latest pro-sweatshop ditty synthesizes plenty of half-truths. Let's take a closer look and see why there is still no reason to give it up for sweatshops.

A Better Alternative?

It is hardly surprising that young men on the streets of Namibia's capital might find sweatshop jobs more appealing than irregular work as day laborers on construction sites.

The alternative jobs available to sweatshop workers are often worse and, as Kristof loves to point out, usually involve more sweating than those in world export factories. Most poor people in the developing world eke out their livelihoods from subsistence agriculture or by plying petty trades. Others on the edge of urban centers work as street-hawkers or hold other jobs in the informal sector. As economist Arthur MacEwan wrote a few years back in *Dollars & Sense*, in a poor country like Indonesia, where women working in manufacturing earn five times as much as those in agriculture, sweatshops have no trouble finding workers.

But let's be clear about a few things. First, export factory jobs, especially in labor-intensive industries, often are just "a ticket to slightly less impoverishment," as even economist and sweatshop defender Jagdish Bhagwati allows.

Beyond that, these jobs seldom go to those without work or to the poorest of the poor. One study by sociologist Kurt Ver Beek showed that 60% of first-time Honduran maquila workers were previously employed. Typically they were not destitute, and they were better educated than most Hondurans.

Sweatshops don't just fail to rescue people from poverty. Setting up export factories where workers have few job alternatives has actually been a recipe for serious worker abuse. In *Beyond Sweatshops*, a book arguing for the benefits of direct foreign investment in the developing world, Brookings Institution economist Theodore Moran recounts the disastrous decision of the Philippine government to build the Bataan Export Processing Zone in an isolated mountainous area to lure foreign investors with the prospect of cheap labor. With few alternatives, Filipinos took jobs in the garment factories that sprung up in the zone. The manufacturers typically paid less than the minimum wage and forced employees to work overtime in factories filled with dust and fumes. Fed up, the workers eventually mounted a series of crippling strikes. Many factories shut down and occupancy rates in the zone plummeted, as did the value of exports, which declined by more than half between 1980 and 1986.

Kristof's argument is no excuse for sweatshop abuse: that conditions are worse elsewhere does nothing to alleviate the suffering of workers in export factories. They are often denied the right to organize, subjected to unsafe working conditions and to verbal, physical, and sexual abuse, forced to work overtime, coerced into pregnancy tests and even abortions, and paid less than a living wage. It remains useful and important to combat these conditions even if alternative jobs are worse yet.

The fact that young men in Namibia find sweatshop jobs appealing testifies to how harsh conditions are for workers in Africa, not the desirability of export factory employment.

Oddly, Kristof's desire to introduce new sweatshops to sub-Saharan Africa finds no support in the African Growth and Opportunity Act (AGOA) that he praises. The Act grants sub-Saharan apparel manufacturers preferential access to U.S. markets. But shortly after its passage, U.S. Trade Representative Robert Zoellick assured the press that the AGOA would not create sweatshops in Africa because it requires protective standards for workers consistent with those set by the International Labor Organization.

Anti-sweatshop Activism and Jobs

Kristof is convinced that the anti-sweatshop movement hurts the very workers it intends to help. His position has a certain seductive logic to it. As anyone who has suffered through introductory economics will tell you, holding everything else the same, a labor standard that forces multinational corporations and their subcontractors to boost wages should result in their hiring fewer workers.

But in practice does it? The only evidence Kristof produces is an imaginary conversation in which a boss incredulously refuses a Nike vice president's proposal to open a factory in Ethiopia paying wages of 25 cents a hour: "You're crazy! We'd be boycotted on every campus in the country."

While Kristof has an active imagination, there are some things wrong with this conversation.

First off, the anti-sweatshop movement seldom initiates boycotts. An organizer with United Students Against Sweatshops (USAS) responded on Kristof's blog: "We never call for apparel boycotts unless we are explicitly asked to by workers at a particular factory. This is, of course, exceedingly rare, because, as you so persuasively argued, people generally want to be employed." The National Labor Committee, the largest anti-sweatshop organization in the United States, takes the same position.

Moreover, when economists Ann Harrison and Jason Scorse conducted a systematic study of the effects of the anti-sweatshop movement on factory employment, they found no negative employment effect. Harrison and Scorse looked at Indonesia, where Nike was one of the targets of an energetic campaign calling for better wages and working conditions among the country's subcontractors. Their statistical analysis found that the anti-sweatshop campaign was responsible for 20% of the increase in the real wages of unskilled workers in factories exporting textiles, footwear, and apparel from 1991 to 1996. Harrison and Scorse also found that "anti-sweatshop activism did not have significant adverse effects on employment" in these sectors.

Campaigns for higher wages are unlikely to destroy jobs because, for multinationals and their subcontractors, wages make up a small portion of their overall costs. Even Kristof accepts this point, well documented by economists opposed to sweatshop labor. In Mexico's apparel industry, for instance, economists Robert Pollin, James Heintz, and Justine Burns from the Political Economy Research Institute found that doubling the pay of nonsupervisory workers would add just $1.80 to the production cost of a $100 men's sports jacket. A recent survey by the National Bureau of Economic Research found that U.S. consumers would be willing to pay $115 for the same jacket if they knew that it had not been made under sweatshop conditions.

Globalization in Sub-Saharan Africa

Kristof is right that Africa, especially sub-Saharan Africa, has lost out in the globalization process. Sub-Saharan Africa suffers from slower growth, less direct foreign investment, lower education levels, and higher poverty rates than most every other part of the world. A stunning 37 of the region's 47 countries are classified as "low-income" by the World Bank, each with a gross national income less than $825 per person. Many countries in the region bear the burdens of high external debt and a crippling HIV crisis that Kristof has made heroic efforts to bring to the world's attention.

But have multinational corporations avoided investing in sub-Saharan Africa because labor costs are too high? While labor costs in South Africa and Mauritius are high, those in the other countries of the region are modest by international standards, and quite low in some cases. Take Lesotho, the largest exporter of apparel from sub-Saharan Africa to the United States. In the country's factories that subcontract with Wal-Mart, the predominantly female workforce earns an average of just $54 a month. That's below the United Nations poverty line of $2 per day, and it includes regular forced overtime. In Madagascar, the region's third largest exporter of clothes to the United States, wages in the apparel industry are just 33 cents per hour, lower than those in China and among the lowest in the world. And at Ramatex Textile, the large Malaysian-owned textile factory in Namibia, workers only earn about $100 per month according to the Labour Resource and Research Institute in Windhoek. Most workers share their limited incomes with extended families and children, and they walk long distances to work because they can't afford better transportation.

On the other hand, recent experience shows that sub-Saharan countries with decent labor standards *can* develop strong manufacturing export sectors. In the late 1990s, Francis Teal of Oxford's Centre for the Study of African Economies compared Mauritius's successful export industries with Ghana's unsuccessful ones. Teal found that workers in Mauritius earned ten times as much as those in Ghana— $384 a month in Mauritius as opposed to $36 in Ghana. Mauritius's textile and garment industry remained competitive because its workforce was better educated and far more productive than Ghana's. Despite paying poverty wages, the Ghanaian factories floundered.

Kristof knows full well the real reason garment factories in the region are shutting down: the expiration of the Multifiber Agreement last January. The agreement, which set national export quotas for clothing and textiles, protected the garment industries in smaller countries around the world from direct competition with China. Now China and, to a lesser degree, India, are increasingly displacing other garment producers. In this new context, lower wages alone are unlikely to sustain the sub-Saharan garment industry. Industry sources report that sub-Saharan Africa suffers from several other drawbacks as an apparel producer, including relatively high utility and transportation costs and long shipping times to the United States. The region also has lower productivity and less skilled labor than Asia, and it has fewer sources of cotton yarn and higher-priced fabrics than China and India.

If Kristof is hell-bent on expanding the sub-Saharan apparel industry, he would do better to call for sub-Saharan economies to gain unrestricted access to the Quad markets—the United States, Canada, Japan, and Europe. Economists Stephen N. Karingi, Romain Perez, and Hakim Ben Hammouda estimate that the welfare gains associated with unrestricted market access could amount to $1.2 billion in sub-Saharan Africa, favoring primarily unskilled workers.

But why insist on apparel production in the first place? Namibia has sources of wealth besides a cheap labor pool for Nike's sewing machines. The *Economist* reports that Namibia is a world-class producer of two mineral products: diamonds (the country ranks seventh by value) and uranium (it ranks fifth by volume). The mining industry is the heart of Namibia's export economy and accounts for about 20% of the country's GDP. But turning the mining sector into a vehicle for national economic development would mean confronting the foreign corporations that control the diamond industry, such as the South African De Beers Corporation. That is a tougher assignment than scapegoating anti-sweatshop activists.

More and Better African Jobs

So why have multinational corporations avoided investing in sub-Saharan Africa? The answer, according to international trade economist Dani Rodrik, is "entirely due to the slow growth" of the sub-Saharan economies. Rodrik estimates that the region participates in international trade as much as can be expected given its economies' income levels, country size, and geography.

Rodrik's analysis suggests that the best thing to do for poor workers in Africa would be to lift the debt burdens on their governments and support their efforts to build functional economies. That means investing in human resources and physical infrastructure, and implementing credible macroeconomic policies that put job creation first. But these investments, as Rodrik points out, take time.

In the meantime, international policies establishing a floor for wages and safeguards for workers across the globe would do more for the young men on Windhoek's street corners than subjecting them to sweatshop abuse, because grinding poverty leaves people willing to enter into any number of desperate exchanges. And if Namibia is closing its garment factories because Chinese imports are cheaper, isn't that an argument for trying to improve labor standards in China, not lower them in sub-Saharan Africa? Abusive labor practices are rife in China's export factories, as the National Labor Committee and *BusinessWeek* have documented. Workers put in 13- to 16-hour days, seven days a week. They enjoy little to no health and safety enforcement, and their take-home pay falls below the minimum wage after the fines and deductions their employers sometimes withhold.

Spreading these abuses in sub-Saharan Africa will not empower workers there. Instead it will take advantage of the fact that they are among the most marginalized workers in the world. Debt relief, international labor standards, and public investments in education and infrastructure are surely better ways to fight African poverty than Kristof's sweatshop proposal.

Sources: Arthur MacEwan, "Ask Dr. Dollar," *Dollars & Sense*, Sept–Oct 1998; John Miller, "Why Economists Are Wrong About Sweatshops and the Antisweatshop Movement," *Challenge*, Jan–Feb 2003; R. Pollin, J. Burns, and J. Heintz, "Global Apparel Production and Sweatshop Labor: Can Raising Retail Prices Finance Living Wages?" Political Economy Research Institute, Working Paper 19, 2004; N. Kristof, "In Praise of the Maligned Sweatshop,"*New York Times*, June 6, 2006; N. Kristof, "Let Them Sweat," *New York Times*, June 25, 2002; N. Kristof, "Two Cheers for Sweatshops," *New York Times*, Sept 24, 2000; N. Kristof, "Asia's Crisis Upsets Rising Effort to Confront Blight of Sweatshops," *New York Times*, June 15, 1998; A. Harrison and J. Scorse, "Improving the Conditions of Workers? Minimum Wage Legislation and Anti-Sweatshop Activism," *Calif. Management Review*, Oct 2005; Herbert Jauch, "Africa's Clothing and Textile Industry: The Case of Ramatex in Namibia," in *The Future of the Textile and Clothing Industry in Sub-Saharan Africa*, ed. H. Jauch and R. Traub-Merz (Friedrich-Ebert-Stiftung, 2006); Kurt Alan Ver Beek, "Maquiladoras: Exploitation or Emancipation? An Overview of the Situation of Maquiladora Workers in Honduras," *World Development*, 29(9), 2001; Theodore Moran, *Beyond Sweatshops: Foreign Direct Investment and Globalization in Developing Countries* (Brookings Institution Press, 2002); "Comparative Assessment of the Competitiveness of the Textile and Apparel Sector in Selected Countries," in *Textiles and Apparel: Assessment of the Competitiveness of Certain Foreign Suppliers to the United States Market*, Vol. 1, U.S. International Trade Commission, Jan 2004; S. N. Karingi, R. Perez, and H. Ben Hammouda, "Could Extended Preferences Reward Sub-Saharan Africa's Participation in the Doha Round Negotiations?," *World Economy*, 2006; Francis Teal, "Why Can Mauritius Export Manufactures and Ghana Can Not?," *The World Economy*, 22 (7), 1999; Dani Rodrik, "Trade Policy and Economic Performance in Sub-Saharan Africa," Paper prepared for the Swedish Ministry for Foreign Affairs, Nov 1997.

CONTRIBUTORS

Randy Albelda, a *Dollars & Sense* Associate, teaches economics at the University of Massachusetts-Boston.

Sylvia Allegretto is an economist at the Institute for Research on Labor and Employment at the University of California, Berkeley.

William K. Black is an associate professor of economics and law at the University of Missouri-Kansas City.

Heather Boushey is a senior economist at the Center for American Progress.

Ben Collins is a member of the *Dollars & Sense* collective and a research analyst at a socially responsible investment research firm.

James M. Cypher is professor of economics at California State University, Fresno and in the Programa de Doctorado en Estudios del Desarrollo, Universidad Autónoma de Zacatecas, Mexico. He is a *Dollars & Sense* Associate.

Ryan Dodd is a Ph.D. student in economics and a research associate at the Center for Full Employment and Price Stability, both at the University of Missouri-Kansas City.

Marie Duggan is an associate professor of economics at Keene State College in New Hampshire.

Katherine Faherty is a former *Dollars & Sense* intern.

Ellen Frank teaches economics at the University of Massachusetts-Boston and is a *Dollars & Sense* Associate.

Gerald Friedman is a professor of economics at the University of Massachusetts-Amherst.

Heidi Garrett-Peltier is a research fellow at the Political Economy Research Institute at the University of Massachusetts-Amherst.

Amy Gluckman is co-editor of *Dollars & Sense.*

Elise Gould is a staff economist at the Economic Policy Institute.

Lena Graber is a former *Dollars & Sense* intern.

William Greider is the author of many books, including Secrets of the Temple: How the Federal Reserve Runs the Country. A political journalist for 40 years, he is currently the national affairs correspondent for *The Nation* magazine.

Joel Harrison, PhD, MPH, is a consultant in epidemiology and research design. He has worked in the areas of preventive medicine, infectious diseases, medical outcomes research, and evidence-based clinical practice guidelines.

Marianne Hill, PhD, is a frequent contributor to economics journals. She also writes for the American Forum and the Mississippi Forum.

Joshua Holland is a senior writer and editor with AlterNet.org.

Paul Krugman, 2008 Nobel Prize winner, teaches economics at Princeton and is a columnist for the *New York Times.*

Arthur MacEwan, a *Dollars & Sense* Associate, is professor emeritus of economics at the University of Massachusetts-Boston.

Gretchen McClain, a former member of the *Dollars & Sense* collective, is an economic consultant.

John Miller, a *Dollars & Sense* collective member, teaches economics at Wheaton College.

Fred Moseley is a professor of economics at Mt. Holyoke College.

Gina Neff is the associate director of Economists Allied for Arms Reduction.

Martha A. Ojeda is the executive director of the Texas-based Coalition for Justice in the Maquiladoras.

Doug Orr teaches economics at Eastern Washington University.

Robert Pollin teaches economics and is co-director of the Political Economy Research Institute at the University of Massachusetts-Amherst. He is also a *Dollars & Sense* Associate.

Smriti Rao teaches economics at Assumption College in Worcester, Mass., and is a *Dollars & Sense* collective member.

Alejandro Reuss is an economist and historian, and a member of the *Dollars & Sense* collective.

Jonathan Rowe is a fellow at the Tomales Bay Institute and a former contributing editor at the *Washington Monthly*.

Katherine Sciacchitano is a former labor lawyer and organizer. She teaches political economy at the National Labor College.

Orlando Segura, Jr. has worked for an Atlanta-based global management consulting company that consults for private equity firms, and for a private equity firm based in Boston.

Bryan Snyder is a senior lecturer in economics at Bentley University.

Dariush Sokolov is an activist and independent journalist based in Argentina.

Bob Sutcliffe is an economist at the University of the Basque Country in Bilbao, Spain.

Alissa Thuotte is a former *Dollars & Sense* intern.

Chris Tilly, a *Dollars & Sense* Associate, is director of the Institute for Research on Labor and Employment and professor of urban planning, both at UCLA.

Ramaa Vasudevan is assistant professor of economics at Colorado State University and a member of the *Dollars & Sense* collective.

Jeannette Wicks-Lim is an assistant research professor at the Political Economy Research Institute at the University of Massachusetts-Amherst.

Marty Wolfson teaches economics at the University of Notre Dame and is a former economist with the Federal Reserve Board in Washington, D.C.